# God and Difference

MW00785079

*God and Difference* interlaces Christian systematic theology with queer and feminist theory for both critical and constructive ends. Linn Marie Tonstad uses queer theory to show certain failures of Christian thinking about God, gender, and sexuality. She employs queer theory to dissect trinitarian discourse and the resonances found in contemporary Christian thought between sexual difference and difference within the trinity. Tonstad critiques a broad swath of prominent Christian theologians who either use queer theory in their work or affirm the validity of same-sex relationships, arguing that their work inadvertently promotes gendered hierarchy. This volume contributes to central debates in Christianity over divine and human personhood, gendered relationality, and the trinity and provides original accounts of God, sexual difference, and Christian community that are both theologically rich and thoroughly queer.

**Linn Marie Tonstad** is assistant professor of systematic theology at Yale Divinity School and affiliate faculty in WGSS and LGBT studies at Yale University. Her articles have appeared in *Modern Theology*, *International Journal of Systematic Theology*, and *Theology & Sexuality*.

# Gender, Theology and Spirituality

Edited by Lisa Isherwood, University of Winchester, UK

# God and Difference

The Trinity, Sexuality, and the
Transformation of Finitude

**Linn Marie Tonstad**

Routledge
Taylor & Francis Group
New York London

First published 2016
by Routledge
711 Third Avenue, New York, NY 10017

and by Routledge
2 Park Square, Milton Park, Abingdon, Oxon OX14 4RN

First issued in paperback 2017

*Routledge is an imprint of the Taylor & Francis Group,
an informa business*

© 2016 Taylor & Francis

The right of Linn Marie Tonstad to be identified as author of this work
has been asserted by her in accordance with sections 77 and 78 of the
Copyright, Designs and Patents Act 1988.

All rights reserved. No part of this book may be reprinted or reproduced or
utilised in any form or by any electronic, mechanical, or other means, now
known or hereafter invented, including photocopying and recording, or in any
information storage or retrieval system, without permission in writing from
the publishers.

**Trademark notice:** Product or corporate names may be trademarks or
registered trademarks, and are used only for identification and explanation
without intent to infringe.

*Library of Congress Cataloging-in-Publication Data*
Tonstad, Linn Marie, 1978–
    God and difference : the Trinity, sexuality, and the transformation of
finitude / by Linn Marie Tonstad. — 1 [edition].
        pages cm. — (Gender, theology, and spirituality ; 17)
    Includes bibliographical references and index.
    1. Trinity.   2. Sex—Religious aspects—Christianity.   I. Title.
    BT111.3.T65 2015
    231'.044—dc23        2015019864

ISBN 13: 978-1-138-55454-2  (pbk)
ISBN 13: 978-1-138-93803-8  (hbk)

Typeset in Sabon
by Apex CoVantage, LLC

# Contents

# Acknowledgments

The writing of this book extended across three institutions, four US states, and four countries. The debts incurred in the course of its writing extend more widely yet.

Thanks to the participants in the doctoral and master's level seminars I taught at Yale in the fall of 2013, all of whom read and commented on the draft manuscript. Thanks especially to my colleagues Teresa Berger, John Hare, David Kelsey, John Pittard, Devin Singh, Kathryn Tanner, and Miroslav Volf for their thoughtful responses. Marilyn McCord Adams read and commented on several chapters; I am very grateful for her support of this project throughout. The first draft of chapter 5 was written for Mark Jordan's Religion and Sexuality seminar at Emory in 2010; I am grateful to him and to seminar participants for their feedback. Thanks also to Patrick Cheng, Siobhan Garrigan, Larisa Reznik, and the theology PhD colloquium at the University of Chicago, who read and commented on chapter 5. Patrick Cheng also arranged for me to present chapter 7 to the Boston Queer Theology Forum. Kent Brintnall, Luke Moorhead and Larisa Reznik were especially valuable conversation partners as the book took form. As I moved through the difficult final stages towards publication, Ellen Armour, Amy Hollywood, Catherine Keller, Katie Lofton, Laurel Schneider, and Graham Ward provided much-needed encouragement and valuable advice.

Thanks also to Dorothy Bass, Shannon Craigo-Snell, Justin Crisp, Noreen Khawaja, David Lott, Wendy Mallette, Bruce Marshall, and the academic dean's office at Perkins School of Theology.

An earlier version of chapter 1 was published as "Sexual Difference and Trinitarian Death: Cross, Kenosis, and Hierarchy in the *Theo-Drama*," *Modern Theology* 26, no. 4 (October 2010): 603–31. An earlier version of part of chapter 5 was published as "The Logic of Origin and the Paradoxes of Language: A Theological Experiment," *Modern Theology* 30, no. 3 (July 2014): 50–73. An earlier version of part of chapter 4 was published as " 'The ultimate consequence of his self-distinction from the Father . . .': Difference and Hierarchy in Pannenberg's Trinity," *Neue Zeitscrhift für Systematische Theologie und Religionsphilosophie* 51 (2009): 383–99; thanks to Walter de Gruyter for permission to reprint.

This project was supported in part by an award from the Yale Fund for Lesbian and Gay Studies (FLAGS).

Thanks to Margo Irvin and Nancy Chen at Routledge, to Lisa Isherwood, and to the anonymous readers for the press.

My parents, Sigve and Serena, raised me to care for what matters and disregard what does not. I am forever grateful to them and to my wonderful (not-so-)little sister, Kristel Manal.

Without Daniel Schultz, this book would never have begun, much less made it to completion.

Kathryn Tanner patiently read, and often disagreed with, every chapter of this book more than once. Without her incisive and critical eye, it would be a very different work.

# Prelude

Trinitarian theology has lost its way. It has become—as I demonstrate in this book—a way to enjoin practices of sacrifice and submission under the banner of countering the rapaciousness of modern subjectivity. The accompanying articulations of trinitarian personhood reflect deeply gendered and I argue, misguided assumptions about human and divine personhood. Yet the trinity's susceptibility to being used in such a way reflects a challenge as old as the debates through which the doctrine took form: How should one speak of the relations of the Father, Son, and Spirit without ascribing a lesser divine status to the latter two?

More than a decade ago, I found myself drawn to trinitarian reflection because of its possibilities for valuing difference, but I became increasingly skeptical of this potential for two reasons that shape this book's argument. The trinitarian value of difference has in recent years been worked out in terms of sexual difference, yet even queer-friendly and feminist theologians who attempt this often repeat and sometimes heighten the historical proclivity of Christianity to encode masculinism and (symbolic) heterosexuality within a trinitarian logic. I also became concerned about their seeming failure to avoid the importation into God of what trinitarian predication commonly rules out: for instance, the lesser status of a son in relation to a father. I came to believe that faithfulness to trinitarian aims—the affirmation of the full presence of God in Christ—requires revision of a founding assumption about the nature of divine difference: that relations of origin can distinguish the trinitarian persons without inequality and subordination of the Son and Spirit to the Father. Beyond critique of contemporary trinitarian theology, this book constructively reconfigures the doctrine, with implications for closely related theological topics such as eucharistic theology, ecclesiology, and anthropology, particularly with respect to their (often-implicit) visions of gender, sex, body, and sexuality.

As a queer and feminist theologian with an interest in dogmatics, I weave together queer and feminist theory with systematic theology. Trinitarian theology is often a masculinist discourse of mastery over the mystery of God in the voice of feminine submission, a highly technical engagement with centuries of debates over linguistic details, and a deeply conservative enterprise.

Kathryn Tanner lays out why one might nonetheless engage with it. Sometimes "[o]ne simply finds oneself believing as one does, despite the horrible history of actions perpetrated in the name of those beliefs, and one is pushed thereby to hope that such a history is not their necessary effect."[1] Although a feminist and queer project, it is also motivated by commitments often considered traditional: real distinction between trinitarian persons, the one divinity and full "equality" of each of the persons,[2] classical assumptions about divine transcendence,[3] the truth of the resurrection, theology's dependence on divine self-revelation, and anticipation of the return of Christ. My hope is that the sometimes-unexpected shape these commitments take here will not preclude engagement from the plural directions that motivate it. Despite the frequent and ongoing hostilities among many of these discourses and the sometime incompatibility of commitments to them, this book seeks to advance communities of discourse that move beyond hostility into conversations in which none of these commitments is excluded *ex ante*.

I think of this book as an experiment in trinitarian theology. Of all theological loci, trinitarian theology may seem the least experimental. Unlike trinitarian theology, liturgical theologies, pastoral theologies, and theological accounts of the economy or of gift-giving all appear testable in churches, life, and societies. Trinitarian theology apparently offers little room for experimentation: It is either "applied" as a trinitarian theology of this or that or invoked to safeguard the priority of revelation and the derived authority of those who participate in revelation's absoluteness by deferring to it. But trinitarian theology is only apparently removed from the present, from bodies, and from human persons, and it can be tested experimentally in multiple ways: in use, for internal and external consistency, and through mimetic readings that map the imagistic landscape through which trinitarian theologies accomplish their effects.

The use and function of trinitarian discourse are difficult to test as long as theological texts are read with a first naïveté, which assumes the innocence and transparency of theological argument. For instance, if the theologian stipulates that the persons of the trinity are coequal, later discussions of the eternal functional subordination or obedience of the Son should not be read to conflict with such a stipulation, one might insist. Such naïve reading is often justified by the need for Christian charity or by the transcendent referent of theological language—after all, God is not subject to the same antinomies as humankind. Even if "eternal functional subordination" suggests inequality in ordinary language use, the already stipulated equality of trinitarian persons must mean that no inequality is entailed, since language works differently for God.

Much as in arguments regarding gendered role differentiation, little useful argument can be had between those who assert that subordination without inequality is possible and those who consider such a statement nonsensical. Strategies are needed to *show* how and where the actual inequality appears. Feminist and queer thinkers have developed such strategies, using mimetic, over-literalizing, and imagistic interpretive methods, to make visible what stipulation naturalizes. Some of the ways theologians qualify their assertions serve to conceal the way their language *works*: the effects it engenders beyond intention or control. Making these effects visible requires interpretive strategies that are not frequently deployed in standard systematic-theological rhetoric.

In using such strategies, this book intervenes in debates over theological method. The book moves between genres, some of which will be especially shocking to theologians accustomed to the sedate genre conventions of most dogmatic theology. Queer-theoretical language can be especially challenging, since queer-theoretical genre conventions require careful intercalation of form and content. The argument of the book, taken as a whole, shows the potential of such genre play for dogmatics. The structure of the book is an argument for thinking differently about theological method—that structure performs (rather than describes or justifies) an interplay of different methods. It would have been easier to write one book in typical systematic form and another engaging queer-theoretical and -theological materials, which would have generated more easily recognizable products. But that would have done nothing to effect rapprochement between systematics and its others. Juxtaposing different argumentative and interpretive strategies permits an argument couched in very different terms to be recognized as—in significant ways—the *same* argument.

Although this book engages queer theory, it is not a book about whether queer persons should be included in the church. I do not call for inclusion, whether of women or of queers. Both sides in Christian debates over sexuality often take similarly bankrupt forms. Opponents of the full participation of queer persons commonly resort to proof-texting—tearing texts out of place, space, context, and history to deploy them as weapons, shutting down debate. Proponents of the full participation of queer persons tend to respond by an anemic assertion of historical difference between sexuality now and then, followed by self-congratulatory statements about God's love for everyone. These debates produce exhaustion and boredom and have done little to advance thinking about sexuality or to deepen theological reflection.[4]

The argument of this book is informed by anti-inclusive, antinormative, and antiequality queer critiques[5] and radical (rather than equality or difference) feminism. The discourses of inclusion and equality, when extended to the marginalized, help shore up the social reproduction of the body of the church and refuse what I'll call the apocalyptic logic of nonreproductive trinitarian temporality. Instead, this book asks two different sets of questions. First, where in the theological imaginary are heterosexism and heteronormativity grounded and maintained? Can resources internal to the Christian theological imaginary be found to render those grounds unstable? The gendering of the God–world relation turns out to be a quilting point here. Nuptial imagery for the God–world relation, when sexed (rather than used as a metaphor for intimate union), has deeply worrisome consequences, I will argue, even when opened up—as several theologians discussed in the following chapters do—to allow both men and women to move around different positions in the symbolic field. The God–world relation is a relation between unequal *relata*. God and creation cannot be measured by a single standard of value, and the relation between them is unilaterally established and determined by God. If the fundamental difference between male and female analogically encodes the God–world relation, then the difference between male and female is necessarily a difference of unequals. Not so, many theologians respond, for the God–world relation analogically encodes a different relation, that between coequal trinitarian persons. *Since* Father, Son, and Spirit are different yet equal, male and female, too, are different yet equal. But—as I shall argue with respect to Hans Urs von Balthasar—the theological *Anknupfungspunkt* provided by the God–world relation and encoded in the primary heterosexism of the marital relation between Christ and His bride, the church, has discomfiting consequences, both human and divine. The nuptial relation between Christ and the church refers "upward" to the difference between Father and Son and "downward" to the difference between male and female. These references go both ways. Grounding sexual difference in the trinity does not rescue sexual difference from hierarchical inequality; it can just as easily demonstrate the inequality of Father and Son, or so I shall seek to prove.

Second, what—if anything—can be learned for Christian theological purposes from conversation with queer theory? Christians do not need queer thought to discover that God loves everyone, that Jesus does not condemn sexual sinners, or that Christianity has always been riven by debates over insider and outsider and hierarchies of value (Jew/Gentile, slave/free, male/female). Where queer theory may help is as a reading strategy, a diagnostic for cultural and theological imaginaries, associative relationships, hidden creations and naturalizations, and so on. Theology always borrows hermeneutical strategies from elsewhere: queer theory becomes another in a long line of disciplines whose tools have been turned to theological purposes.

Another prefatory confessional note is needed. As I describe below, systematic theology—particularly in trinitarian forms—often proceeds by way of disagreement over the boundaries of communities of discourse. The church must be rid of its heretics. Perhaps the most marked development in contemporary world Christianity has been the number of churches and denominations that have made one or another stance on sexuality (and often gender) *the* stance by which the gospel stands or falls. Few denominational or national ecclesial bodies have not made a stance on sexuality determinative of Christian identity. This development is driven by efforts at ecclesial purification and self-nomination that contradict the nature of the reign of God in anticipation and realization, I contend.

In Matthew 7, we find that those who cry, "Lord, Lord," cast out demons, and even prophesy in the name of Christ may find themselves unrecognized by him. The text reminds those of us who are professing Christians of our own deepest temptation: to point out the faults of the other while ignoring our own; indeed, to establish our own righteousness *by* condemning the other, thus calling down fire upon our own heads. Matthew 7 makes clear the perversion of attempting to rid the church of sinners. One finds something similar in a much less famous story in Matthew 13. Servants one day discover weeds throughout a field otherwise sowed with good wheat and come to the householder offering to rid the field of them. Instead of approving, the householder tells the servants that if they get rid of the tares, they will also get rid of the wheat. Distinction belongs to the householder on the day of ingathering, not to the servants themselves.

Jesus does not—as it were—fall victim to a first naïveté. In Matthew 6:1–5, he warns: "Beware of practicing your piety before others in order to be seen by them; for then you have no reward from your Father in heaven. . . . And whenever you pray, do not be like the hypocrites; for they love to stand and pray in the synagogues and at the street corners, so that they may be seen by others. Truly I tell you, they have received their reward."[6] Using our own piety as a cudgel against others, whether in the local church, in the decision-making bodies of our denominations, or in theological debates—such as insisting that our particular construal of trinitarian doctrine distinguishes believers from idolaters or theologians worth engaging from those who may safely be ignored—risks more for us than it does for those we condemn. The search for idolaters who refuse to call God Father forgets that the verses in which Jesus instructs us to pray to "Our Father" reflect the conditioning of our relationship to God by our relation to others, not the problem of calling God by some other name. Do not make a visible demonstration of your piety, Jesus instructs: Pray in secret, fast in secret, and forgive as you hope to be forgiven.

This book is therefore also a critique of how getting the trinity right (e.g., speaking and praying Father rightly) becomes a pious cudgel protecting the wielder from seriously engaging the questions and concerns raised by those relegated to the pile of tares left to rot outside the church door. What Marcella Althaus-Reid terms "the economy of God's exchange-rate mechanism"[7] involves many exchanges: In a professional theological sense, speaking Father rightly becomes a shibboleth protecting the theologian from marginalization in the theological academy. On a divine level, the exchange rate is difference equals death, gratitude equals sacrificial thanksgiving, and sonship equals eternal crucifixion—or so I shall argue.

More conservative forms of feminism and antifeminist forms of Christian theology often charge that feminism and feminist theologies entail (or threaten) the replacement of a masculine idolatry with a feminine idolatry, a charge that must be countered at the outset. Although it may be tempting to retort that perhaps we should give feminine idolatries the same two thousand years that masculine idolatries had before we cut them off, doing so would miss the ways in which critique of all idolatries—that is, the (often-implicit)

assignation of ultimate value to selected persons or social roles—is fundamental to feminist theological method.[8] Critique of one's own idolatries,
a foundational task for all Christian theology, may require—if idolatries
proliferate, as history suggests they do—a variety of strategies beyond the
stipulative language often employed in theology and analytic philosophy
of religion. While theologians and philosophers strictly delineate the linguistic reach and semantic reference of their assertions (e.g., God is only
Father inner-trinitarianly, so God's paternity is utterly dissimilar to human
paternity though analogically related), feminist and queer theologians are
compelled to recognize idolatrous slippage between one form of fatherhood
and another. Feminist theologians identify different purgative strategies for
such idolatry.

One purgative strategy, with theological roots in Mary Daly yet closely
connected to the mimetic rereadings endemic to queer theory and theology, may be characterized as *over-literalization*. Over-literalization picks up
the interplay between cataphasis and apophasis to produce complex forms
of assertion and destabilization. Such over-literalizing theological language
and imagery, in its very impropriety, serves as a cataphatic theological apophasis. Martin Luther describes such cataphatic apophaticism beautifully
in his *Lectures on Genesis*: Those who say that God has eyes and ears, and
who use literal language for God's hands, are rightly taking hold of God
using the "wrapper" in which God appears. They are to be distinguished
from those whose concern for the correctness of theological language leads
them to serve as guardians of the God/not-God difference and tricks them
into thinking they have conceptual control over the difference between God
and what is other than God.[9] In what follows, I examine many strategies for
limiting the reach of language about God—especially its sexed and gendered
implications, but also the ways in which language about God means *beyond*
its limitations, often to the detriment of the intentions of the theological
proposals themselves. As in all cases of masquerade under transcendent signifiers, counterhegemonic criticism is most needed and most welcome—and
in some ways, most easily mobilized—where repudiation of fragmentation
and failure is most vehemently asserted, for the very intensity of the repudiation suggests a fundamental uncertainty. Yet counterhegemonic criticism
must offer more than unmasking, for exposing the soft underbelly of trinitarian constructions to attack would do nothing to shift the fundamental
tension in trinitarian thinking, which I believe to be necessary. Alternative
accounts must be developed and motivated.

## BEYOND GENEALOGY

Recent trinitarian theologies often take one of two approaches to the Christian past. Theologians examine the legitimacy of the development of trinitarian theology in the early centuries of Christian reflection with the intent

of either establishing or destabilizing genealogies of authority and revelation. One sort of theologian may wish to demonstrate the inner necessity of the developments that led up to the formulae of orthodox trinitarian theology in the fourth century. The near-inevitability of orthodoxy requires a correlative demonstration of the inadequacies of the heretical threats that generated it. Since orthodoxy was a necessary development, right trinitarian speech can be used as a shibboleth for determining which theologians ought to be engaged and which ignored. The selected hero of such investment is drawn from a small stable, with the occasional venture on an underdog: Athanasius, Augustine, either Cappadocian Gregory, and Aquinas are heavy favorites, while Hilary of Poitiers and Maximus the Confessor are dark-horse choices gaining quickly in the outer lanes. Another sort of theologian destabilizes the road to Nicaea by demonstrating the many political and economic considerations entwined with the development of orthodoxy, perhaps by retracing the entanglement of Nicaea and its theologians with empire. The presumed result is the deconstruction of doctrinal and ecclesiological orthodoxy.

These competing genealogical investigations mirror each other's approaches to the history of doctrine and its complicated itineraries. The first type needs to show the inner necessity of the theological innovations of trinitarian doctrine in order to establish the legitimacy, and by implication, requirement of belief in a triune God according to established canons of Christian interpretation. (But the most firmly established canon of Christian interpretation is that *Christians do not agree on it.*) In this form of genealogical investigation, the legitimacy of the origin-story of triune faith moves from revelation to a complicated intercalation of authorized interpretation, right liturgical practice, and submissive, obedient belief. The legitimacy of the birth of the "sons" of the church renders the patriarchal lines of inheritance themselves legitimate.

The other kind of genealogical investigation, in service of destabilization, tends either to assume or to demonstrate the ways in which assertion of revelational authority for any doctrinal object is intertwined with other distortive, political, or secular interests. Demonstrating the illegitimate birth of the "sons" of the church renders the patriarchal lines of inheritance illegitimate. The latter kind of investigation is often associated with materialist accounts of religion or projectionist accounts of belief, although there are alternatives that either do not have well-worked-out accounts of these relationships or that assume that ecclesiastical and secular histories almost inevitably move forward toward ever-greater inclusion and equality due to the seeds of both within the dry husks of orthodoxy.

By depending on genealogical investigation, both options imply the priority of origin, either as legitimate or illegitimate birth. But trinitarian theology does not need to be ruled by either of these imaginaries. Instead, trinitarian theologians may simply practice polyfidelity—faithfulness to multiple discourses, without seeking legitimation from total adherence to

the canons of any one.[10] Beyond the limits of patriarchal inheritance, the
dissolute borders of God sound their own call to pilgrimage. A theology of
the trinity that interrupts the production of normalizing discourse about the
trinity in order to queer it in fidelity to a God who "stick[s] to God's own
marginal identity" must fear neither failure nor lack in relation to authoriz-
ing narratives.[11] But as any reader of Althaus-Reid will recognize, there are
multiple moments in the following text that are disloyal to her. It may be
that engaging trinitarian theology on its own terms, even inside a differentiated and polyvalent study like the following, is a reidentification with a
colonial master discourse that cannot be loved without id(ea)olatry.

## TECHNICAL TRINITARIAN THEOLOGY AND ITS PROBLEMS

A brief description of the technical aspects of trinitarian theology is necessary to set up the problems that motivate this book. In Western ways of
distinguishing the persons of the trinity through relations of origin, the Son
proceeds from the Father and the Spirit proceeds from the Father and, of, or
through the Son. In, by, or through these relations of origin the three "persons" are constituted. "Person," when used of the trinity, does not mean an
independent center of self-consciousness and action in the way it (purportedly) does in the human case. Rather, person equals relation: each person is
individuated or constituted as such by the relations in which it stands to the
other persons.[12]

These relations extend beyond the Godhead in God's self-revelation. (The
processions are extended into the missions.) Thus, the incarnation of the
Son extends the Son's relation to the Father in the Godhead. The sending of
the Spirit reflects the Spirit's relation to the Father and the Son in some way,
depending on the particular theologian's construal of the Spirit's constitution but often involving the Spirit as the bond of love between Father and
Son. The trinity *ad extra* acts as the trinity is *ad intra*. The correspondence
of God's self-revelation to God's eternal being is thus secured. God really is
who God reveals Godself to be in Jesus the Christ.

Karl Rahner's famous axiom of the identity of economic and immanent trinity may be understood, as Catherine Mowry LaCugna argues, as
a "methodological" axiom connecting knowledge of God to the pattern of
the missions[13] and providing a minimum standard for a trinitarian theology.
The turn to the history of salvation, particularly the history of Jesus, as a
source for trinitarian theology is undoubtedly appropriate. The desire to
make the history of the trinity count for God, both to avoid a kind of as-if-
ness in the history of Jesus (is anything really at stake?) and to ensure that
what is encountered historically is *vere deo* and not some mere appearing or
semblance (a bad form of *deus absconditus*), is legitimate.

The relation between God and God's self-revelation in history is not one
of total identity; the revelation of God in a temporal, historical, finite, and

sinful medium makes some difference, so something must be said about the distinction between the immanent and the economic trinity. This need to distinguish the two remains even if (and this move is increasingly common) relating the immanent to the economic trinity misconstrues the issue by offering two separate starting points for theological reflection, one revelational and the other speculative. At stake in distinguishing the two is protecting the freedom of God and absolute dependence of creation on God. If God's self-revelation to creation is *exactly* and *wholly* identical with the fullness of God's being, then the world is necessary for God's self-revelation and self-realization. This threatens the gratuitousness of creation and makes the God–world relation one of reciprocal dependence rather than preserving the latter's absolute dependence on the former.[14] Yet, if immanent and economic trinity cannot be fully collapsed, their identity must nonetheless be asserted in order to respect the fact that only God can reveal Godself and that God reveals Godself as God truly is.[15]

For almost a century, academic theology has been done in the crater left by Karl Barth's *Römerbrief*, which arguably replaced limitations on knowledge of God that Immanuel Kant introduced with limitations derived from sin and finitude. The image of a crater—one of Barth's illustrations of the disjunction between God and creation—suggests the unavailability of God to human control; the church's task is to remain in the void left where the bomb of God went off. Some theologians have wished to play in the crater and dig it deeper or widen it—hence the turn to death-of-God theology and to (sometimes unfortunately simplistic) forms of apophatic theology. Others, perhaps including the later Barth himself, have tried to fill in or cover up the crater, and their primary building material has been trinitarian theology.

Much systematic theology chafes against modernity's restrictions on its pretensions to knowledge. Trinitarian theology counters those restrictions by identifying God's presence in history with God as God is. God's triune self-revelation seems to provide a secure point of departure for theology, rendering it impervious to epistemic challenge while proving a heavy bludgeon against antihierarchical and liberationist forms of theology. In response to the epistemological and metaphysical uncertainties introduced in the Enlightenment, the recovery of God's self-revelation provides a new Archimedean point of departure for theological knowledge.[16] This *theologoumenon*—valid in a minimal form, I will argue—has assumed a maximal form in which the history of Jesus provides detailed knowledge of the intra-trinitarian relations.[17] The being of God is revealed in the history of the Son, since the Son is the image of the Father in the mode of reception. The being of God must be read off the history of Christ through the metaphysical and epistemological connection provided by the correspondence of the sending of the Son with his procession from the Father, and by the correspondence of the sending of the Spirit with the Spirit's having-been-breathed.

As I will show, the basic theological axiom of God's self-revelation has been misused and mistakenly interpreted in recent trinitarian theology. Far too much of the history of Jesus has been read into the immanent trinity, without sufficient consideration of the difference between the economic and immanent trinity and between the immanent life of God and God's work in transforming the world. As a result, intra-trinitarian relations are read in speculative, mythopoetic ways that introduce aspects of sinful and finite human existence into the immanent trinity in order to overcome them there, rather than through the trinity's transformative work in history.

Trinitarian theology, like all theology, is political. It provides fertile ground for debates over socio-political order. Trinitarian theologians envision different forms of human life in relation to the (holy) ghosts of Christian negotiations over difference, equality, desire, ethics, and identity. Fundamental debates in Christian thought over the relationship between God and creation, the implications of Jesus' divine and (male) human personhood, and the relationship between sexual difference and God all pose political questions as they shape imaginaries of difference. For example, as Tanner points out, in trinitarian theology it may always be the case that "[o]rder among the divine persons is . . . ripe for justification of hierarchy." This problem is not ameliorated but intensified by focus on the history of Jesus because Jesus' relation to the Father is "subordinationist in flavor."[18] The problem of subordination—the first trinitarian problem that motivates this book—often appears as the object of a specific refusal: *even though* Jesus is subordinate or obedient to the Father in certain ways, *even though* the Son comes forth from the Father, *even though* the Son sends the Spirit, this is not true subordination.

Friedrich Schleiermacher clearly describes the problem of the "even though." He argues that creedal stipulation of the equality of the trinitarian persons is immediately undermined by the inequality entailed by the distinction of persons by means of origin and begetting. "Whichever way we take it, then, the Father is superior to the other two Persons, and the only subject of controversy is whether these two are equal to each other, or one of them subordinate to the other."[19] These *even thoughs* are hopelessly inadequate as well as unnecessary, I will argue. The first two parts of the book demonstrate the failure in multiple theologians of these *even thoughs* to achieve their ends. In chapter 5, I expand this argument to cover the constitutive *even thoughs* of trinitarian theology as such.

A second problem follows from the same use of the concrete history of Jesus for understanding the trinity. Jürgen Moltmann says "we can perceive the differences, the relationships and the unity" of the trinitarian persons in the "historical and eschatological history" of the Son.[20] Numerous trinitarian theologians say the same. The central challenge for such a barely qualified identity between God's being in Godself and God's being revealed in Jesus is torture and death as the defining event of Jesus' life. On the cross, Jesus shows what it means to be the divine Son. The implication is that the cross is the revelation of the Son's intra-trinitarian obedience and the appropriateness of suffering and death to his divine person.

This second problem of trinitarian theology has become especially acute in recent years due to a combination of factors associated with (post) modernity: the importance of history and the correlative interest in death, fragility, and change; attention to evil and suffering—heightened by the Holocaust—without trust that resurrection and eternal life offer adequate compensation; the turn to the subject; and modern sensitivity to the humanness of Jesus, which has rendered suspect once-definitional negations of his suffering—for instance, "he suffered impassibly." The outcome is a felt need to describe the immanent-eternal ground of the cross in ever more specific terms, to mythologize it as an event in the life of God.

Such theologies tie the self-gift of God on the cross ever more tightly to self-gift in intra-trinitarian relations of origin, often through focus on the Son's reception and sacrificial return of divinity in gratitude. The cross becomes the site where immanent and economic trinity coincide. While the sign-character of divine manifestation is taken for granted in scenes like the baptism of Jesus, with its appearance of a dove and a voice sounding from heaven, the cross seems to strip away signs to reveal the passionate anguish, the intimacy and distance, and the bond between Son, Father, and Spirit directly. The road to the cross, and particularly the agonized prayer in Gethsemane—"not my will, but thy will"—transforms Jesus' mission from proclaiming the arrival of the kingdom, teaching love of neighbor, and healing the sick and suffering, into one of mere obedience to the Father, some think. Here is fulfilled his mission as the one sent, corresponding to the "modality of his eternal personal being"[21] as the one who proceeds from the Father.

Such Christologies (kenotic in one sense of the term[22]) emphasize that Jesus' self-emptying nature, as the Son who eternally receives the Father's generous sharing of his divinity, makes possible his obedient and self-sacrificial death. The Son's eternal reception (giftedness) of "self" from the Father becomes that in the divine life of which the cross is an image. The Son's road to death, the death of God, becomes the crux and fulcrum of all revelation—not primarily because it shows that God-for-us overcomes death but because the intra-trinitarian drama of the cross is the clearest narratival exposition of relations among Father, Son, and Spirit. For example, the silence with which the Father greets the Son's anguished supplication on the cross shows how far the bond between them can stretch. That bond is the Spirit, who maintains unity in distinction and absolute distance (when the Son descends to hell). Even that absolute distance is not alien to God; it is an outward expression of the distance between God (the Father) and God (the Son). Distance becomes in this way a trope for and analogical expression of difference in the life of God. On that basis, interpenetration, emptying, and filling spatialize relations among the trinitarian persons in ways that—I will argue—are projectionist and incoherent and that illuminate the unexpected ways divine difference gets gendered and sexed, grounding the ultimacy of heterosexuality in the Christian imaginary.

A third problem of trinitarian theology reflects similar developments. Some charge Christianity with enforcement of the logic of the One against difference, diversity, and multiplicity.[23] In response, others emphasize that trinitarian relationality and difference underlie whatever might happen in the Godhead and elsewhere. Christianity is not about the logic of the One, they insist. Christianity offers the only possible approach to identity and difference: the unity of God is always a differentiated unity in which divine difference far surpasses—while grounding—human difference. Triune difference-in-identity reconciles the different, mediating between the sheerly different and the merely identical.[24] The optimism of this metaphysical vision is quite seductive. With occasional cautions about translating too directly between trinitarian constitution and human personhood,[25] theologians suggest the glorious possibilities such a vision of reality opens up, removing us from static self-presence, monadic self-enclosure, and all the other forms of metaphysics of presence that value the One over the Other.

Such moves were originally associated with so-called social trinitarians (among others, Moltmann, Pannenberg, John Zizioulas, Catherine Mowry LaCugna, and Stanley Grenz). Social trinitarians find significant analogies between the three trinitarian persons and human persons: the trinitarian persons make up a community of sorts; they are—in some sense—independent centers of consciousness and action; and they model what true human community in difference should be like.[26] In contrast, non-social trinitarians (like Barth and Rahner) find a single subject in God. Although the social/non-social trinitarian distinction was imprecise from the outset—reflecting emphasis rather than strict distinction—I will argue that some technically non-social theologians have come to share with social trinitarians the assumption that a major practical function of trinitarian theology is the critique of modern, Cartesian, or capitalist notions of selfhood and personhood. As Gijsbert van den Brink puts it in a recent article, "rather than uncritically adopting standard modern accounts of personhood, [social trinitarians] criticize these from the insight, derived from trinitarian doctrine, that to be a person does not mean to be an autonomous self-centered individual in the Cartesian sense but to find one's very identity in mutual relations with others."[27] Given that the defining project of postmodernity has been to make that point, one wonders who—other than perhaps certain analytic philosopher-theologians and economists (at least in their models)—considers the "Cartesian" notion of personhood standard. Given, too, that entire fields of study have managed to develop that insight apart from trinitarian doctrine, the anti-social trinitarian question remains: What do we learn from the trinity that we did not already know?[28]

A commonplace of contemporary trinitarian theology is that the doctrine of the trinity is a radically practical doctrine: It is neither abstruse speculation nor irrelevant dogma. Rahner's comment that "Christians are, in their practical life, almost mere 'monotheists,'"[29] suggesting the irrelevance of the trinity to most Christians, has been repeatedly answered by the claim that the trinity is a doctrine with deep and far-reaching practical implications—politically, ethically, socially, and (almost as an afterthought) soteriologically. Catherine Mowry LaCugna says the doctrine is "a practical doctrine with radical consequences for Christian life"[30] since it is radically critical of any monadic and self-enclosed accounts of the self. One sometimes wonders whether Christian theologians think they have *any* nontrinitarian resources for critiquing accounts of the self that emphasize self-seeking and self-possession over service to others.

The tendencies encapsulated in the van den Brink quotation above make up what I term *corrective projectionism*. Corrective projectionism identifies certain problems of human existence (e.g., delusions of autonomy, selfishness, self-possession, consumerism) and then generates a trinitarian theology that shows how the constitutive relationships of the trinity uniquely critique and overcome such human problems. In this way, corrective projectionism imports the very problems of human existence it intends to overcome. Corrective projectionism remains indebted to ideas of personhood that belong to a philosophy of the subject as the self-contained, self-possessed *noumen* that both determines and overcomes itself by positing itself as that which is not restricted to self-determination and self-possession, a bordered whole that cancels its own borders. Since—the assumption may be implicit or explicit—we live in a context that valorizes autonomy, self-possession, and self-sufficiency above all, a world where the "modern liberal subject of autonomy and self-determination" either always was or has been transformed into the rapacious subject of modern capitalism, the condition of possibility of the salvation of the world is to learn by inhabitation and faithful obedience the logic of the triune God that challenges and destroys self-seeking, self-enclosure, and self-possession and teaches us proper "wound-womb" (in my terminology) postures in relation to each other. Womb-wound language derives from the ancient image of the birth of the church out of the spear-wound in Jesus' side. I use the term "womb-wound" to indicate images of relationship that assume good relations between persons (divine or human) require making room for another (the spatialization of the womb, often associated with rendering "woman" into a place for the becoming of the other) through sacrificial forms of (something like) suffering. Womb-wound imagery is—as we will see—fundamentally heterosexual, and it sets up another "incarnation" of sexuality and sexual difference in God.

Why is it so important that the trinity be a practical doctrine? What do we see about ourselves and our way of understanding the world when we look in this mirror? The trinitarian theologies I discuss are correlative, at least implicitly, with accounts of modernity—accounts of modernity that most often devolve into a list of accusations against its flaws, flaws that the doctrine of the trinity is uniquely positioned to correct. Or in the decent idiom of contemporary theological conversation, the nihilistic logics of modernity are refused by the logic of the trinity. In the trinity, without speculation and with humble submission to the particular form of divine revelation, a revelation that refuses to seek God outside where God has shown Godself to be, we discover that it belongs to divinity also to obey and to sacrifice. We find that suffering is neither foreign nor strange to God, for the trinity does not describe a God who hovers impassibly above the world and its crucifixion. It describes a God who not only takes crucifixion onto Godself but who also contains and surpasses it already in God's own being.[31]

The glory of God's divinity is not an abstract glory in the way the world counts glory and power but a glory that fears not its own sacrifice: a glory whose content is sacrifice. God's glory, expressed toward us, is willingness to pour Godself out on our behalf. God's glory, expressed Godward, is that each trinitarian person seeks nothing for the self but places itself at the disposal of the other. The Father does not keep divinity but shares it with the Son and shares it at so fundamental a level as to not be antecedent to this act of sharing. The Son, whose divinity depends on relation to the Father, never had the option of keeping anything for himself in the first place. The Father's non-antecedence to self-gift is supposed to protect against a dangerous trinitarian monarchism while preserving the Father's status as origin and gift-giver. Admittedly, God is not subject to the same grammatical division between act and actor found in human reality. So there is no Father, and therefore no paternity, before—grammatically, logically—the act of sharing, of begetting, of procession, of *origin*. This act constitutes the Father as father. It makes the one who is father to be father. It introduces fatherhood and sonship. It makes the first divine person the first divine person. The person of the father does not underlie the act.[32] There is not a person who then acts. There is simply the act—*am Anfang war die Tat* indeed! This act—eternal, nontemporal—has no before. It is the before of all other befores, of all other firsts. Its ongoing character guarantees its self-identity throughout all transformation. It is the act, the emission, that never ends.

By so generating their theologies, I will argue, theologians betray fundamental trinitarian commitments: They insert an over-againstness between the Father and the Son that ultimately subordinates the Son to the Father and betrays the biblical insight that who has seen Jesus has seen the Father. These trinitarian theologies do not sufficiently consider the difference finitude and especially sin make to divine revelation, I contend. They threaten to collapse the immanent–economic distinction, and they operate with notions of personhood inadequate to *both* divine and human persons while forgetting the for-us aspects of God's action in Christ. Those who wish to dance in the gardens of trinitarian metaphysics offer increasingly detailed and specific accounts of the nature and significance of this relationality and its nature and order. Implicitly, the dubious axiom that human relations and practices are meaningful only insofar as they are reflective of some *specifiable* aspect of God's inner-trinitarian constitution underlies these attempts. These moves reduce trinitarian relations to ways of motivating proper human action and social order by writing such socialities into God.[33] Such trinitarianism fundamentally distorts human and divine personhood, and as I will show, those distortions are further gendered and sexed in surprising ways that are as difficult to diagnose as they are to combat—which brings us to the fourth problem of trinitarian theology that motivates this book.

I have discussed several aspects of (post)modernity that prompt the developments in recent trinitarian theology that I identify as problems. We live also in the age of sexuality and sexual difference; as Luce Irigaray says, "Sexual difference is probably the issue in our time which could be our 'salvation' if we thought it through."[34] On the one hand, Christianity has become associated with hatred of the body, women's subordination, and rigid, sex-negative regulations of human erotic relations. On the other hand, denominational and ecclesial bodies have raised gender and sexuality to ever greater importance by splitting over issues like women's ordination, female bishops, and—most prominently—the legitimacy of same-sex relationships.

Following these developments, the trinity has become a significant resource for demonstrating Christianity's ability to prefigure and surpass the accomplishments of "secular" approaches to gender and sexuality. Intimate relations between the trinity, sexual difference, and sexuality have come to seem axiomatic to some authors.[35] A recent book by David Jensen starts with the claim that "[s]ex is an expression of Christian faith" and rapidly moves from desire to God to the trinity: " 'The origin and home of this desire . . . is the triune life: a communion of persons who desire one another in love."[36] The ultimate human destiny is to become, "in a queer twist, brides of Christ"[37] so that our gendered identities are rendered unstable and impermanent.[38] In his zeal for his end, Jensen fails to note that *women* are not queered by becoming brides of Christ. The ease of Jensen's discussion exemplifies the expansive commonality such moves—in both liberal and conservative versions[39]—have gained in the last two decades.

A different kind of argument for the relationship between the trinity, sexual difference, sexuality, and the body is found in Eugene Rogers's *Sexuality and the Christian Body*. Rogers's work is innovative (and contestable) in its argument for the Christian acceptance of gay marriage via the unnatural status of Christian communion itself as well as through examination of the logic of racial and theological constructions of Jew–Gentile difference. Yet even Rogers falls victim to the pernicious form of projectionism that we will encounter in subtle variations throughout this book: "Precisely because love is incomplete *à deux*, it is the office of the Holy Spirit to witness, glorify, rejoice in, and bless the love between the Father and the Son."[40] Human love may be incomplete between two—at least that has been argued by many—but such assumptions cannot simply be imported into the trinity.[41] We will encounter this construal of the Holy Spirit as the third who completes or interrupts the otherwise narcissistic, unfulfilled, or self-enclosed relation between Father and Son repeatedly in the following chapters. It makes the "threeness" of the trinity a structural necessity based on assumptions about the nature of human love; it also heightens and exaggerates whatever analogies may exist between divine and human personhood in inappropriate ways. Trinitarian doctrine becomes generated in a straightforward manner by (often-contestable) ideas about how human beings (ought to) relate to each other, and those ideas are gendered and sexed in their divine versions at least as much as in their human variations.

Graham Ward beautifully sums up such a vision of relations between the different differences of trinity and created (sexual) difference:

> The doctrine of creation is founded upon a fundamental difference that opens up all possibilities for desire. It is a difference at the heart of any Trinitarian conception of the Godhead; a Trinitarian difference opened up by Christ, the second Person, and interpreted by the Spirit, the third Person. . . . Desire is built into the substructure of creation; and in that creation is the incarnation of desire and difference within the Trinity itself.[42]

The erotics of trinitarian love depend on processional difference and are reflected and incarnated in creation as sexual difference. Further, these erotics are space-making because difference must be held apart that it might not collapse. The Spirit holds this distance in place, distinguishing Father and Son while allowing them to interpenetrate each other. Unrestricted to heavenly speculation, trinitarian theologians have rendered all human practices—ecclesial, familial, and social—vulnerable to trinitarian interpretive penetration.[43] Many of the most interesting of these trinitarian sexualities have come from politically progressive theologians who have found the trinity a useful resource for thinking unity in difference. But although a minority have offered sophisticated accounts of the trinity, the majority have paid insufficient attention to the differences between divine and human forms of personhood and relationality and have failed to recognize problems related to importing death and suffering into the trinity.[44]

The intercalation of trinitarian and sexual difference that theologians with very different commitments have found productive in an age that is constitutively concerned with the question of difference (particularly in its sexual forms) fails to undo the masculinity of God. Indeed, many of the strategies theologians use to ensure that God is unsexed sex "him" more insistently than ever, a point I will make throughout, in part by examining what "bodies" trinitarian persons are given in contemporary theology.[45] Trinitarian theology takes place at a remove from bodies, it seems.[46] Yet even in so "immaterial" a practice, material bodies keep appearing unexpectedly, just out of sight: the body of the theologian writing about the trinity;[47] the church bodies that valiantly try to paper over the sex of Christian God-language by worshiping the Creator-Redeemer-Sustainer, imposing theological decency where there is none;[48] the loving bodies left outside the gates with Christ,[49] torn apart by issues of gender and sexuality. But trinitarian persons become bodied in other ways, too. The Father, Son, and

Spirit are given imaginary theological bodies as they relate to each other at a distance, touch each other, interpenetrate each other, deflect their attention from each other, give birth to each other, shatter each other, wound each other, speak each other, suffer, move apart from each other, and return to each other. All these bodies will appear in the following pages.

These four problems of trinitarian theology—the *even thoughs* and their relation to subordination and obedience; the tight connection between the cross, obedience, and revelation of the inner-trinitarian relations; the corrective projectionism of trinitarian theology regarding personhood and subjectivity; and the often unexpectedly sexed and gendered aspects of the former three problems—motivate this book. All are related to the supposed practicality of trinitarian doctrine.

The aim of this book is to unlearn every one of the lessons the practicality of trinitarian doctrine teaches: to untie divine and sexual difference from each other; to move beyond the need to overcome the self-possessed subject (fragmentation, vulnerability, and suffering are already fundamental to human existence in ways intensified by our current socioeconomic order); to avoid genealogy whether in positive or deconstructive form; to learn trinitarian ends rather than the origin of the trinity; and to release the doctrine of the trinity from its position as theological dogsbody and permit it to be no more than an impractical (yet essential) way to speak of the God who creates, reconciles, and brings us to eschatological transformation. Instead of reading elements of finitude and sin into the trinity, I will argue for the transformative work of a God who is not subjected to the same antinomies as humankind.

## OUTLINE OF THE BOOK

The first three chapters proceed in the standard idiom and conventions of argument in systematic theology. The interlude that follows summarizes the argument of the whole book, but readers unfamiliar with the genre conventions of queer theology may wish to reexamine that section after finishing the book in order to see how it does so. The fourth chapter returns to more familiar theological ways of speaking as it discusses three theologians who have sought to rethink trinitarian constitution for reasons similar to those that motivate this book (albeit not with respect to gender and sexuality). Of the three chapters that follow, the first and last make heavy use of queer theory in genre and content, while the middle chapter, which offers my own constructive trinitarian proposal, stays once more within the ordinary language of systematic theology.

The first two parts of the book are critical examinations of contemporary theologians. In the first three chapters, I discuss the kenoticists, who find the love of God in self-emptying: Hans Urs von Balthasar, Graham Ward, and Sarah Coakley. All have intentionally connected gender, sexuality, and desire to the trinity. I initially turned to Balthasar, who offers the most ambitious attempt to ground sexual difference in the immanent trinity, because so many theologians who interested me—including Graham Ward—found resources in his work, and I sought to discover what they found there. Instead, I found evidence for the conviction that increasingly gripped me: that trinitarian discourse funds (rather than solves) Christianity's tendencies toward sexism and heterosexism, and it does so for reasons internal to trinitarian reflection—not merely because the trinity is approached in distortive ways. That conviction was strengthened by engagement with Graham Ward and Sarah Coakley. The two of them are—from different directions—leading exponents of the intimate relation between trinity and sexual difference in feminist and nonhomophobic terms. I am thus in deep sympathy with much of their work, and my hope is that the depth of my engagement reflects how productive my readings of them have been to me. Nonetheless, I argue that their trinitarian theologies fail in different but interrelated ways. Ward and Balthasar ultimately erect the cross at the heart of the trinity, failing to take resurrection with sufficient seriousness while using trinitarian theology to correct mistaken accounts of human communities. Coakley does not distinguish adequately between sin and finitude, and her understanding of suffering and cruciformity betray dangerous assumptions about the nature of human personhood and the God relationship. Unlike the rest of the theologians discussed, the chapters on Ward and Coakley engage the entirety of their theological projects at the point of writing, partly because neither of them has yet received sufficiently expansive treatment in the secondary literature. More fundamentally, however, Ward and Coakley represent alternatives to the constructive moves regarding the transformation of finitude and the nonreproduction of the church that I make in chapters 6 and 7.

My conclusion, summed up in the interlude that follows part 1 of the book, is that the intimate relationship between the trinity, sexual difference, and the God-creation relationship, sought in diverse ways by Balthasar, Ward, and Coakley, exacerbates the theological translation mechanism by which difference entails competition (requiring kenosis as a corrective) and death.

As an alternative, I turn to three other theological allies, Jürgen Moltmann, Wolfhart Pannenberg, and Kathryn Tanner, who share the worry that animates this book: that trinitarian theology retains a subordinationism that undermines its intent. In order to prevent such subordinationism, all three rethink the nature of personal trinitarian constitution. Moltmann's concern is primarily patriarchal monarchy; Pannenberg finds unilateral relations of origin unsatisfactory and unable to capture the vitality of divine life and the varied patterns of trinitarian interaction found in the New Testament; Tanner seeks to describe the relation between Son and Spirit without subordinating the Spirit to the Son and Father. While each offers something to the project of rethinking trinitarian difference, I argue that Moltmann's attempt to disconnect divine and human paternity, and his distinction between the different levels of the constitution of the trinity, fail the tests of coherence and plausibility for trinitarian theology. Pannenberg's account of the kenosis of the Son reads difference as self-abnegation and ultimately death into the trinity, while Tanner's maintenance of "something" in the life of God that grounds the apparent submission of the Son to the Father threatens to undo her otherwise plausible account of trinitarian distinctions.

The fifth chapter, which introduces the constructive section of the book, makes trinitarian trouble using queer reading strategies. It examines what trinitarian rules of speech forbid, interpreting the trinitarian imaginary through the negations on which it depends. The aim is to make the overly familiar very strange while demonstrating the concrete means by which the trinitarian and theological imaginary is gendered. In the following chapter, the discoveries of previous chapters are brought together in order to generate a new account of trinitarian constitution without relations of origin. That account issues in a discussion of the way reconfigured materiality is inaugurated in the resurrection and in the eucharist. The final chapter returns to explicit engagement with queer-theoretical discourses to examine two basic ecclesiological types in relation to the temporality of the church and its self-understanding as the body of God. I argue for an apocalyptic temporality that establishes the church as a site of an abortive relation to time rather than as a sign of fidelity to temporal continuation of identity in relation to the handed-over body of God. Finally, the postlude brings the argument back to one of its inspirations, Friedrich Schleiermacher, whose refusal to import the antinomies of the world into God models one attractive approach to the question of God and difference.[50] Schleiermacher emphasizes the transformation of finitude wrought by a God beyond contrast and comparison with the world, yet to whom the human being is always intrinsically related.

## NOTES

1. Kathryn Tanner, *The Politics of God: Christian Theologies and Social Justice* (Minneapolis, MN: Fortress Press, 1992), ix.
2. Equality always raises the question of "equal to whom?" Who or what is functioning as the standard by which others may or may not be judged equal? As I argue that the Father's functioning as such a default threatens trinitarian theology at its deepest levels, I do not myself use the language of coequality for trinitarian (or for that matter, human) persons.
3. I assume rather than argue for a classical view of divine transcendence in this book. See Kathryn Tanner's *God and Creation in Christian Theology* (Minneapolis, MN: Fortress Press, 2005 [Oxford: Blackwell, 1988]) and her *Politics of God* for defenses of compatibilism, absolute dependence, and transcendence. Transcendence and immanence are not contrastive terms such that when one increases, the other decreases; the contrary is the case (i.e., immanence is enabled by transcendence).

4. I have not found arguments for excluding queer persons from full participation in church life convincing in any case.

5. For an accessible introduction to such critiques, see Ryan Conrad, ed., *Against Equality: Queer Revolution, Not Mere Inclusion* (Oakland, CA: AK Press, 2014).

6. New Revised Standard Version.

7. Marcella Althaus-Reid, *The Queer God* (London: Routledge, 2003), 94.

8. Although it is common to write Mary Daly off not only for valuing the essentially feminine, as well as for her (deeply misguided) trans-phobia, the former critique misses the sophistication and subtlety of the critique of masculinist idolatry that drives her work. As Daly's work demonstrates, even given the sophistication of a Thomist understanding or account of analogical language for God, a test may still be performed on analogical language to see whether the language, when used, brings with it the very implications that its theological adoption rules out. I perform such tests throughout this book.

9. See Martin Luther, *Lectures on Genesis 1–5*, in *Luther's Works*, vol. 1, ed. Jaroslav Pelikan, trans. George V. Schick (St. Louis, MO: Concordia, 1958), 14–15.

10. Althaus-Reid, *Queer God*, 128. See also my discussion of polyfidelity in "The Logic of Origin and the Paradoxes of Language: A Theological Experiment," *Modern Theology* 30, no. 3 (2014), 50–73, which incorporates part of ch. 5.

11. Althaus-Reid, *Queer God*, 98.

12. In the Thomistic picture, not all relations are person-constituting; only unshareable relations are. So the relation of active spiration, shared by Father and Son, does not constitute a further person.

13. Catherine Mowry LaCugna's introduction in Karl Rahner, *The Trinity*, trans. Joseph Donceel (New York: Crossroad Herder, 1997), xv.

14. Hence the now-common assertion that Karl Rahner's axiom about the unity of the immanent and the economic trinity holds only in one direction.

15. If we adopt a weakly Barthian version of God's self-determination to be God-for-us, which entails that the *logos asarkos* is always *incarnandus*, that is a higher-order statement of the same. In that case, creation is subsumed under mission, and mission is subsumed under God's self-determination to be God-for-us. Although creation and incarnation follow God's decision to be God-for-us, they only participate indirectly in the freedom of God's decision.

16. The assertion is not new, but the form in which it is used and the particular uncertainties it seeks to counter are characteristic of modernity and postmodernity rather than the classical tradition.

17. Gerard Loughlin terms this "Balthasar's surreal move" in his *Alien Sex: The Body and Desire in Cinema and Theology* (Malden, MA: Blackwell, 2004), 145, but the move has become increasingly standard in contemporary theology.

18. Kathryn Tanner, *Christ the Key* (Cambridge: Cambridge University Press, 2010), 211.

19. Friedrich Schleiermacher, *The Christian Faith*, ed. H. R. Mackintosh and J. S. Stewart (Edinburgh: T&T Clark, 1999), §171.2.

20. Jürgen Moltmann, *The Trinity and The Kingdom: The Doctrine of God*, trans. Margaret Kohl (Minneapolis, MN: Fortress Press, 1993 [1980/1981]), 65.

21. Hans Urs von Balthasar, *Theo-Drama: Theological Dramatic Theory*, vol. 3: *Dramatis Personae: Persons in Christ*, trans. Graham Harrison (San Francisco, CA: Ignatius, 1992), 201.

22. See Sarah Coakley's justly acclaimed tracing of various kenotic models in "*Kenosis* and Subversion: On the Repression of 'Vulnerability' in Christian

Feminist Writing," in *Powers and Submissions: Spirituality, Philosophy and Gender* (Oxford: Blackwell, 2002), especially 6–19. This model of kenosis comes closest to Coakley's fourth model (*"revealing* 'divine power' to be intrinsically 'humble' rather than 'grasping,'* " 11), although it differs slightly in its emphasis on the kenotic particularity of the Son.

23. For instance, Laurel Schneider critiques monotheism's "logic of the One" from a theological direction in *Beyond Monotheism: A Theology of Multiplicity* (New York: Routledge, 2008), 1.

24. See Catherine Pickstock, *Repetition and Identity: The Literary Agenda* (Oxford: Oxford University Press, 2014) for one example.

25. Karen Kilby has written several programmatic articles on this issue; see especially "Perichoresis and Projection: Problems with Social Doctrines of the Trinity," *New Blackfriars* 81, no. 957 (November 2000), 432–45. The so-called anti-social trinitarians have sounded this caution as well, but theirs is often based on a somewhat misguided faith in the ability of stipulation to rule the workings of language. In any case, the argument of this book problematizes a too-clean distinction between social and non-social trinitarians.

26. See Gijsbert van den Brink, "Social Trinitarianism: A Discussion of Some Recent Theological Criticisms," *International Journal of Systematic Theology* 16, no. 3 (July 2014), 336, for a useful summary of basic social-trinitarian positions.

27. Van den Brink, "Social Trinitarianism," 347.

28. See Kilby, "Perichoresis and Projection," 441–42; and Tanner, *Christ the Key*, 232–33.

29. Rahner, *The Trinity*, 10.

30. Catherine Mowry LaCugna, *God for Us: The Trinity and Christian Life* (San Francisco, CA: HarperSanFrancisco, 1993), 1.

31. The issue is not the much-discussed question of whether and to what extent God is a cosufferer with humanity. Rather, it has to do with construals of inner-trinitarian relations that import assumptions about the nature of self-sacrificial love that pertain either to finitude or to sin.

32. Note that this is why Aquinas prefers to say that the persons are distinguished by relation rather than by origin, although they are distinct in both, precisely because to say that they are distinct by origin seems to presuppose the preexistence of the Father (the begetter or generator). See Aquinas, *Summa Theologica* Ia Q. 40.2.

33. See also Kilby, "Perichoresis and Projection," 442–43.

34. Luce Irigaray, *An Ethics of Sexual Difference*, trans. Carolyn Burke and Gillian C. Gill (Ithaca, NY: Cornell University Press, 1993), 5. I disagree with both diagnosis and prescription, but the statement well reflects the regime of sexuality and sexual difference.

35. A recent example, Tina Beattie's *Theology after Postmodernity: Divining the Void—A Lacanian Reading of Thomas Aquinas* (Oxford: Oxford University Press, 2013), offers a plaidoyer for Aquinas's "maternal Trinity" over against his Aristotelian "One God." Despite Beattie's creativity and deep knowledge of Lacan, her engagement with Aquinas is not adequate to her intentions, particularly with regard to fundamental issues like divine transcendence. The maternal trinity turns out to mean no more than that Aquinas sometimes uses *birth* as one among several terms indicating divine paternal begetting (66). Other, more frequently used terms include *procession* and *generation*. From a very different direction, some evangelical circles have seen vociferous debate over whether the Son's subordination is ontological, eternal, or functional, and what the consequences of each position are for the roles of women in

the church. This connection will see further exploration (although not with respect to evangelicalism) in several following chapters. See, for instance, Wayne Grudem, *Systematic Theology: An Introduction to Biblical Doctrine* (Grand Rapids, MI: Zondervan, 1994), 249, 459–71; the response in Kevin Giles, *The Trinity and Subordinationism: The Doctrine of God and the Contemporary Gender Debate* (Downers Grove, IL: InterVarsity, 2002); as well as idem, *Jesus and the Father: Modern Evangelicals Reinvent the Doctrine of the Trinity* (Grand Rapids, MI: Zondervan, 2006), which has a helpful list of critical responses to the earlier work on 10–11.

36. David H. Jensen, *God, Desire, and a Theology of Human Sexuality* (Louisville, KY: Westminster John Knox, 2013), ix, 34–35.
37. Ibid., 59.
38. Ibid., 60–61.
39. Conservative versions include the Roman Catholic theology of the body and evangelical attempts to justify the subordination of women through the subordination of the Son.
40. Eugene F. Rogers Jr., *Sexuality and the Christian Body: Their Way into the Triune God* (Malden, MA: Blackwell, 1999), 196.
41. Contrast Richard of St. Victor, for whom the *fullness* of love between two, not its incompletion, makes a third particularly appropriate to love as such.
42. Graham Ward, *Christ and Culture* (Malden, MA: Blackwell, 2005), 145. Unlike most theologians who make this move, Ward recognizes that created sexual difference need not be heterosexual. The question is whether processional trinitarian accounts allow the same for God or whether procession guarantees divine difference in the way heterosexuality purports to do in humans.
43. For a few examples of practices that have received trinitarian illumination, see Daniel A. Helminiak, "The Trinitarian Vocation of the Gay Community," *Pastoral Psychology* 36, no. 2 (Winter 1987), 100–11; Bruce D. Marshall, *Trinity and Truth* (Cambridge: Cambridge University Press, 2000); Marc Ouellet, *Divine Likeness: Toward a Trinitarian Anthropology of the Family*, trans. Philip Milligan and Linda M. Cicone (Grand Rapids, MI: Eerdmans, 2006); Robert A. Pesarchick, *The Trinitarian Foundation of Human Sexuality as Revealed by Christ according to Hans Urs von Balthasar* (Rome: Editrice Pontificia Università Gregoriana, 2000); and Mary Timothy Prokes, *Mutuality: The Human Image of Trinitarian Love* (New York: Paulist, 1993).
44. Miroslav Volf has repeatedly drawn attention to such problems. See, for instance, "Enter Into Joy! Sin, Death, and the Life of the World to Come," in John Polkinghorne and Michael Welker, eds., *The End of the World and the Ends of God: Science and Theology on Eschatology* (Harrisburg, PA: Trinity Press International, 2000), 256–78; and " 'The Trinity Is Our Social Program': The Doctrine of the Trinity and the Shape of Social Engagement," *Modern Theology* 14 (1998), 412–19.
45. Human difference is signified by the body, particularly the skin. Trinitarian persons have multiple bodies of different kinds (the Spirit's dove, the Son's church, the Father's immaterial penetration of Mary, for instance) and trinitarian difference *appears* in a different way in each case. For instance, the kneeling body of Jesus in prayer may point directly as an arrow to the Father, identifying the Father in Jesus' bodied speech. Speech itself is a bodied act even if the speaking "body" is immaterial, for the voice is material (as in the Father's approbation of the Son at the latter's baptism): bodies that matter.
46. This is in contrast to the first-order place of trinitarian affirmations: in worship and glorification. Yet identifying worship and glorification as first-order trinitarian theology does not spare such practices from the need for theological

examination and analysis. Michael Welker points out that the doxological nature of trinitarian theology also requires consideration of lament and human hunger for justice. See Welker, "God's Eternity, God's Temporality, and Trinitarian Theology," *Theology Today* 55 (1998), 324 n.14.

47. That body experiences its own desires and negotiations in relation to God's body and other human bodies; those negotiations haunt the scene of writing.

48. See Marcella Althaus-Reid's discussion of decency in *Indecent Theology: Theological Perversions in Sex, Gender, and Politics* (New York: Routledge, 2000). These church bodies, like eighteenth- and nineteenth-century Europeans who gave clothes to so many of their glorious nudes, are actuated by admirable motives, but sadly, theological obscenity does not disappear merely by being covered over. The fig leaf over God's genitals only reiterates his insistent masculinity.

49. The image of "outside the gates" is Elizabeth Stuart's; Althaus-Reid uses it in *Indecent Theology*, 116.

50. Schleiermacher, *Christian Faith* §40.


## BIBLIOGRAPHY

Althaus-Reid, Marcella. *Indecent Theology: Theological Perversions in Sex, Gender, and Politics*. New York: Routledge, 2000.

———. *The Queer God*. London: Routledge, 2003.

Beattie, Tina. *Theology after Postmodernity: Divining the Void—A Lacanian Reading of Thomas Aquinas*. Oxford: Oxford University Press, 2013.

Coakley, Sarah. "*Kenosis* and Subversion: On the Repression of 'Vulnerability' in Christian Feminist Writing." In *Powers and Submissions: Spirituality, Philosophy and Gender*, 3–39. Oxford: Blackwell, 2002.

Conrad, Ryan, ed. *Against Equality: Queer Revolution, Not Mere Inclusion*. Oakland: AK Press, 2014.

Giles, Kevin. *Jesus and the Father: Modern Evangelicals Reinvent the Doctrine of the Trinity*. Grand Rapids: Zondervan, 2006.

———. *The Trinity and Subordinationism: The Doctrine of God and the Contemporary Gender Debate*. Downers Grove, IL: InterVarsity, 2002.

Grudem, Wayne. *Systematic Theology: An Introduction to Biblical Doctrine*. Grand Rapids: Zondervan, 1994.

Helminiak, Daniel A. "The Trinitarian Vocation of the Gay Community." *Pastoral Psychology* 36, no. 2 (Winter 1987): 100–11.

Irigaray, Luce. *An Ethics of Sexual Difference*. Trans. Carolyn Burke and Gillian C. Gill. Ithaca: Cornell University Press, 1993.

Jensen, David H. *God, Desire, and a Theology of Human Sexuality*. Louisville: Westminster John Knox, 2013.

Kilby, Karen. "Perichoresis and Projection: Problems with Social Doctrines of the Trinity." *New Blackfriars* 81, no. 957 (November 2000): 432–45.

LaCugna, Catherine Mowry. *God for Us: The Trinity and Christian Life*. San Francisco: HarperSanFrancisco, 1993.

Loughlin, Gerard. *Alien Sex: The Body and Desire in Cinema and Theology*. Malden, MA: Blackwell, 2004.

Luther, Martin. *Lectures on Genesis 1–5. Luther's Works*, vol. 1. Ed. Jaroslav Pelikan and Helmut T. Lehmann. Trans. George V. Schick. St. Louis: Concordia, 1958.

Marshall, Bruce D. *Trinity and Truth*. Cambridge: Cambridge University Press, 2000.

Moltmann, Jürgen. *The Trinity and the Kingdom: The Doctrine of God*. Trans. Margaret Kohl. Minneapolis: Fortress Press, 1993.

Ouellet, Marc. *Divine Likeness: Toward a Trinitarian Anthropology of the Family.* Trans. Philip Milligan and Linda M. Cicone. Grand Rapids: Eerdmans, 2006.

Pesarchick, Robert A. *The Trinitarian Foundation of Human Sexuality as Revealed by Christ According to Hans Urs von Balthasar: The Revelatory Significance of the Male Christ and the Male Ministerial Priesthood.* Rome: Editrice Pontificia Università Gregoriana, 2000.

Pickstock, Catherine. *Repetition and Identity: The Literary Agenda.* Oxford: Oxford University Press, 2014.

Prokes, Mary Timothy. *Mutuality: The Human Image of Trinitarian Love.* New York: Paulist, 1993.

Rahner, Karl. *The Trinity.* Trans. Joseph Donceel. New York: Crossroad, 1997.

Rogers, Jr., Eugene F. *Sexuality and the Christian Body: Their Way into the Triune God.* Malden, MA: Blackwell, 1999.

Schneider, Laurel. *Beyond Monotheism: A Theology of Multiplicity.* New York: Routledge, 2008.

Schleiermacher, Friedrich. *The Christian Faith.* Ed. H. R. MacKintosh and J. S. Stewart. Edinburgh: T&T Clark, 1999.

Tanner, Kathryn. *Christ the Key.* Cambridge: Cambridge University Press, 2010.

———. *God and Creation in Christian Theology: Tyranny or Empowerment.* Minneapolis: Fortress Press, 2005.

———. *The Politics of God: Christian Theologies and Social Justice.* Minneapolis: Fortress Press, 1992.

Tonstad, Linn Marie. "The Logic of Origin and the Paradoxes of Language: A Theological Experiment." *Modern Theology* 30, no. 3 (July 2014): 50–73.

Van den Brink, Gijsbert. "Social Trinitarianism: A Discussion of Some Recent Theological Criticisms." *International Journal of Systematic Theology* 16, no. 3 (July 2014): 331–50.

Volf, Miroslav. "Enter Into Joy! Sin, Death, and the Life of the World to Come." In *The End of the World and the Ends of God: Science and Theology on Eschatology,* ed. John Polkinghorne and Michael Welker, 256–78. Harrisburg, PA: Trinity Press International, 2000.

———. "'The Trinity Is Our Social Program': The Doctrine of the Trinity and the Shape of Social Engagement." *Modern Theology* 14 (1998): 403–23.

Von Balthasar, Hans Urs. *Theo-Drama: Theological Dramatic Theory,* volume III: *Dramatis Personae: Persons in Christ.* Trans. Graham Harrison. San Francisco: Ignatius, 1992.

Ward, Graham. *Christ and Culture.* Malden, MA: Blackwell, 2005.

Welker, Michael. "God's Eternity, God's Temporality, and Trinitarian Theology." *Theology Today* 55, no. 3 (October 1998): 317–28.

# Part 1

# 1   Dramas of Desire

No one has worked harder to connect the trinity with sexual difference than Hans Urs von Balthasar, so it is appropriate that a book on that connection begin with him.[1] One of the most influential theologians of the twentieth century, his astounding output has had significant impact across the theological field, particularly on theologies of the body and theological aesthetics. Although recent studies have recognized the centrality of sexual difference to Balthasar's theology,[2] critical assessment of his approach has focused primarily on whether and to what extent Balthasar is straightforwardly sexist,[3] without asking the further question of the adequacy of Balthasar's main object, the trinitarian theology that grounds sexual difference. Despite the challenges of Balthasar's account of sexual difference, some queer and queer-friendly theologians have found theological resources in him. Graham Ward, for example, reads him with Julia Kristeva in order "rethink [the] doctrine of the Trinity in terms of sexual difference."[4] Such a project, through and beyond Balthasar, will constitute the salvation of the world and of sexual difference: "There can only be salvation with Christ, through Christ, if there is sexual difference. Difference, thought theologically, is rooted in the difference of *hypostasis* in the Trinity."[5]

Rowan Williams's assessment is similar to Ward's.[6] For him, Balthasar's account of sexual difference takes "the genderedness of human existence with complete seriousness. . . . [W]hat makes [Balthasar's] analysis tantalizing is a central unclarity about how far sexual differentiation really can be said to partake of the differentiation of the trinitarian persons, a differentiation in which there is no unilateral and fixed pattern of priority or derivation but a simultaneous, reciprocal conditioning, a pattern of identity *in* the other without remainder." This "tantalizing unclarity" involves closer and more distant relationships between divine and sexual differentiation: if distant, Balthasar's hierarchy of male and female may not image the trinity very well, allowing Balthasar's sexual hierarchy to be dismissed as peripheral to his theology. If closer, sexual difference is given theological significance by its participation in trinitarian patterns of identity and difference, which would then allow Balthasar's trinitarian theology to overcome any apparently patriarchal remnants in his theology of sexual difference. Williams continues,

> To engage with this *aporia* in Balthasar, we need more than an enlight-
> ened outrage at a rhetoric of sexual differentiation apparently in thrall
> to unexamined patriarchy. Balthasar is not so easily written off. What
> is needed, rather, is a response within his own rhetoric, within the terms
> of the simultaneous and reciprocal difference that his account of the
> trinitarian relations and the relation of God to creation insists upon
> (and I say 'insists upon' rather than simply 'allows', because it is so
> clear that his entire theological enterprise falls if these relational dis-
> tinctions can in any way be reduced to a system of co-ordination and
> subordination).[7]

Williams ties together the relevant elements with admirable economy: Balthasar's theology stands or falls by the success of his intercalation of trinitarian relations, God–creation relations, and sexual difference.

Williams considers it unlikely that Balthasar's theology fails; after all, his project is great enough that "even a theologian of his stature is unlikely to realize it with uniform fidelity."[8] But note the assumptions that structure Williams's (and as we shall see, Ward's) assessment of Balthasar. First, the intercalation of trinitarian and sexual difference that the latter undertakes holds out the possibility of achieving a theological account of difference, particularly in terms of gender. Second, his intercalation will correct mistaken accounts of sexual difference *through* trinitarian difference, which demonstrates "no unilateral and fixed pattern of priority." Third, the promise of intercalating trinitarian and sexual difference is such that we must read charitably rather than critically when we encounter what merely seems like patriarchy. (We can only hope that theological patriarchs will be generous enough to inform us when we are encountering actual patriarchy and when some more subtle, nonpatriarchal analysis is in play in a theologian.) Fourth, it is possible but unlikely that Balthasar's project fails—but if it introduces coordination or subordination into the trinitarian order of difference, the whole system collapses.

These assumptions depend on the assumption that successfully achieved trinitarian difference can correct sexual difference if the latter turns patriarchal or hierarchical. Notably, the Christian theological tradition seems to have discovered the anti-patriarchal potential of trinitarian theology only at the point at which feminists discovered the patriarchal character of the Christian theological tradition. The basic assumptions in play in Williams are, importantly, just the sorts of assumptions that structure myriad attempts in the contemporary theological scene to relate the different forms of human difference to trinitarian difference.

Williams's challenge deserves a response—a response that reads sexual difference from the trinity, as Balthasar's theology requires. Rather than arguing—as do Balthasar's more appreciative readers—that any remnants of a hierarchy of sexual difference in Balthasar's theology depend on a natural or secular rather than theological order of sexual difference, I will argue in this chapter and the next two that sexual difference in the Christian imaginary is thoroughly theological, in ways that suggest the inadequacy of these theologies of the trinity and of difference more broadly. Balthasar serves as a first test case.

One form of testing described in the prelude—the use of over-literalization to make visible how a theology *works*, how it achieves its effects—can be applied to the illuminating character of Balthasar's use of metaphors and analogies of sexual difference in his trinitarian theology. Such testing uncovers the structures and associations—origin, paternity, personhood—that permit the trinitarian imaginary to function, and to function in ways that go beyond its stipulative content. Indeed, what is used as illustration or analogy may turn out to be as illuminating as what is stipulated.[9] Or in more technical terms, the identification of something as an analogue of the trinity may tell us more about the vision of the trinity in play than it does about the analogue. The second form of testing—for internal adequacy—depends on assumptions I share with the theologians in question: that there can be no degrees of divinity, that God is one, that the fundamental criterion of adequacy of a trinitarian theology is that it recognize the fullness of God in Christ. The second form tests probability rather than offering decisively probative evidence, since the affirmative structures of theology—the rules for coherent theological speech—offer a technical escape route: oppositions belonging to the created order should not be read as oppositional in God. For instance, whereas change and stasis are oppositional attributes in the created order, in the vibrant fullness of God, stasis becomes self-identity and consistency, whereas change indicates the liveliness of divine life.

I argue that there are some pairs in which one of the terms should not be read into the divine life, however stipulatively restricted; I will support that argument by showing the distortions of trinitarian theology that result when the paired terms are introduced and assigned to different aspects of trinitarian relationality. In Balthasar, for instance, versions of activity and passivity apply to the intra-trinitarian relations. The fundament of that distinction is the notion of passive spiration—that the Spirit is passively breathed out by the Father and Son. Passive spiration is a technical designation intended as a placeholder for a relation not directly named in scripture. It should not indicate anything like passivity on the part of the Spirit—but in Balthasar, terms like activity and passivity are read in over-literal ways to indicate the shape of intra-trinitarian relations, the modes of divine life. Activity and passivity also have gender connotations, made entirely explicit by Balthasar, but I contend that such gender connotations are symptomatic: the fundamental problem is not merely that Balthasar uses terms with gendered connotations but that contrasts between activity and passivity should not be applied to the immanent trinity.

## THE THEODRAMATIC NATURE OF DIFFERENCE

Balthasar's *Theo-Drama*[10] exhibits a mutual funding of a hierarchical ordering of the relation between "man" and "woman" and a hierarchical ordering of the relation between the Father, the Son, and the Spirit.[11] The two hierarchies explain, illustrate, and support one another. Balthasar's oscillation between hierarchy and equality, particularly in the divine case, results in a tortured understanding of personhood where being in relation means handing oneself over to another with the threat of death always present. Further, difference is reduced to repetition in the mode of reception, which poses a serious challenge to Balthasar's account of divine and human being. The point of connection between divinity and humanity is found in his account of the inner-trinitarian relations of origin and their extension into the world in the coincidence of infinite and finite freedom in the relation between Christ and Mary.

Kenosis and "supra"-sexual difference are coextensive in the relation between the Father and Son in the trinity. The nature of trinitarian decision-making shows that the order of the processions determines the concrete shape of the divine persons in their eternal relations to each other in such a way that "something like" death and sacrifice belongs to the very being of God; that "something like" intertwines with the distribution of activity and passivity, action and consent, supplication and command, and self-offering and obedience to different trinitarian persons in the divine life and its theodramatic enactment in the world. Balthasar's treatment of sexual difference illuminates and repeats the imagery of kenosis and submission that structures his account of trinitarian relations; it is thus a fundamentally theological account even though it also participates in biological literalism projected into God. Finally, the connections between sexual difference, trinitarian difference, and kenosis prefigure the cross; thus we encounter for the first time the cross that stands at the origin of the trinity.

Balthasar locates the possibility of difference—and its goodness—in the relation between the Father, Son, and Spirit. The Son proceeds from the Father and is his perfect image, equally divine, yet utterly different. The difference between the Father and the Son becomes the basis for the possibility of all other differences, specifically, the difference between God and creation which is imaged in the difference between men and women. Jesus connects divine–divine difference (the hiatus between the Father and the Son and their union in the Spirit) with human–human difference (sexual difference and its union in heterosexual marital fruitfulness). Balthasar's methodological starting point is the unity of Jesus' identity and work, which offers an epistemic ladder into the being of God.[12] Because Jesus is the performative presence of God in the world, both in his own identity and in his relation to the Father and the Spirit, it is in him that the eternal being of God is enacted and opened up to the world. Jesus is "the One Sent" (TD3:149–50). All other roles in the theodrama are secondary, as other human actors exist "before" they are given roles in the theodrama. Being an individual and a person are different: individuals are mere individuals, not yet significant in their difference. When God addresses one, one becomes a person with a role to play in the theodrama. But in the incarnate Logos, identity and role coincide: he *is* the Son of God present in the world.

Jesus, the only person whose role in the theodrama coincides with his identity, brings together human and divine in a single story: "the Son's *missio* is the economic form of his eternal *processio* from the Father" (TD3:201),[13] so he provides the *Anknupfungspunkt* between the biblical narratives of the life of Jesus and God's inner determination as trinity. The sending of the Son into the world is the extension into time and history of his eternal coming forth from or being begotten by the Father, while the Spirit guarantees their unity and thus the inclusion of the world in the theodrama. The patterns of the economic trinity follow from the immanent, although the two cannot be strictly identified with each other (TD3:157).[14]

This person, Jesus, acts as one who is utterly faithful to his mission. Jesus does not have a monadic identity with defined boundaries; his identity is from the beginning relational. His very identity depends on his relation to the Father and the Spirit: who Jesus is in history is determined by who he is as divine Son in relation to the Father. Jesus is "the eternal Son dwelling in time" (TD3:228); they are one, and his mission (sending) is "a modality of his eternal personal being" (TD3:201). Because the sending of the Son into the world is the temporal extension of the Son's eternal relation to the Father, the sending of the Son—and the Spirit in his wake—draws the world into the inner-divine relations.

Balthasar builds on the principle of the "ever-greater" found in Ignatius and Gregory of Nyssa. Jesus instantiates the "ever-greater" in pointing to his origin: "The Father is greater than I."[15] In response to the Father's initiative, there is a cycle of "surpassings" that point to the most "unfathomable" work of all: the divine surrender of the Son to death, a surrender motivated by love. The divine "ever-greater," which also applies to the missions of the Son and Spirit (thereby tying the ever-greater to analogy), is located in the eternal life of God. Methodologically, Balthasar allows ever-new aspects of God's greatness and being to come into view. But the ever-greater indicates also the greater dissimilitude contained in the Christological analogy between God and humankind: the dissimilitude within which the divine draws creation up toward itself, toward God's richly infinite ever-greater. The limit of analogy is the limit of philosophical analogy; it is not the limit of Christ's divine openness, which invites creation to follow into its own fulfillment. Jesus is the concrete *analogia entis*; abstract considerations of the relation between the infinite and the finite can never capture him.[16] The ever-greater God cannot be bounded by the static limit of philosophical-analogical thinking, nor by the "notion" of being; the ever-greater God is the God who in Christ unites Godself with humankind, opening the door for finite freedom to fulfill itself in the absolute and absolutely vibrant.

Analogy stands at the heart of Balthasar's account of the theodrama and its capacity to include the human being within itself. The analogy between divine and worldly drama is "no mere metaphor but has an ontological ground" (TD1:19) in the way the "drama of [human] existence" has been taken up into the divine. For finite freedom to fulfill itself in infinite freedom (which gives the finite its own identity and freedom), it must "get [. . .] in tune with the (trinitarian) 'law' of absolute freedom (of self-surrender)" (TD2:259). Divine freedom and bliss, revealed as love, show that absolute freedom involves self-surrender. The Father's act of surrender, in begetting the Son, elicits the Son's gratitude, which shows itself in "allowing the Father to do with him as he pleases" (TD2:256).

The world is located in the Son, which means that it is located in the "totality of the Godhead" (TD2:262). Although God is the author, actor, and director of the theodrama, a human[17] is "a spectator only insofar as he is a player . . . the involvement of man in the divine action is part of God's *action*, not a precondition of it" (TD1:18). In the theodrama, God acts in the space of the genuinely other and engages with a finite, temporal, and spatial creation. Through grace—the sending of the Son—humans are drawn into the divine life itself.[18] Balthasar argues that a monadic or undifferentiated God could not make room for an other within God. In that case, human community would have no value; it would be defective relative to divine unity (TD2:206). Revelation shows that God is internally differentiated as trinity. The greatest imaginable opposition, as it exists between the persons of the trinity,[19] is the basis of the difference that gives shape to the world of time and space. God's internal differentiation gives humans a space within which they can exist, but it also conditions their access to self-knowledge. The creature only knows itself through analogous participation in the trinity conditioned by the relations of origin; seen from that angle, procession and mission are one and the same.[20]

God's freedom demonstrates its greatness in its creation of free human beings.[21] The theodrama is the story of the confrontation of divine and human freedom on the same battlefield. Indeed, since Christ is the central event, revelation, and mystery of what it is to be both God and human, the difference of infinite and finite freedom constitutes the two foci around which all of human existence elliptically takes place. Although God is everything, humans are not nothing. Balthasar's account of relation and self-identity in God grounds the possibility of human differentiation without violent confrontation and identity and self-presence without staticity. Humans are not the other of God in an oppositional sense: We cannot conclude that "we are the 'others' as far as God himself is concerned" (TD2:193).

God creates human beings to be images of God. Differentiation in God is established by the relations of origin that constitute the persons as other: Those relations are " 'an eternal interplay of active generation and passive being begotten and being breathed forth' . . . From this standpoint we can already see that certain dualisms become possible within creation, between act and potency, for instance, between action and contemplation and between the sexes" (TD5:87–88).[22] A description of the exchange of love in the trinity can provide the *immediate* foundation for an understanding of sexual difference and the relation between act and potency—despite divinity's full actualization. Although the divine persons reciprocally interpenetrate one another "in the most intimate manner conceivable," they are not interchangeable, and the real distinction between them is not threatened. "[T]he triune God is neither indiscreet nor—on the contrary—prudish" (TD2:258). Each person has self-identity in letting the other be. The sexualized language—indiscretion and prudishness—is employed in a surprising way for the trinitarian relations. Human difference is paradigmatically imaged—even constituted by—sexual difference. From the beginning, sexual difference is tied to trinitarian difference.

Difference in the trinity reflects the processions. Balthasar terms the processions "kenotic": the Father's "expropriating himself by 'generating' the consubstantial Son . . . expands to a kenosis involving the whole Trinity. For the Son could not be consubstantial with the Father except by self-expropriation" (TD4:331).[23] To beget another (in the fullness of God's being) is to empty oneself, to surrender oneself to another. The kenotic act is the Father's willingness to share divinity with the Son by generating an image of himself—the Son—who responds in gratitude and, with the Father, breathes out the Spirit, who is the seal of their unity and differentiation. The Son's thanksgiving is "a Yes to the primal kenosis of the Father in the unity of omnipotence and powerlessness" (TD4:324). Thus kenosis belongs first to the Father—it is the mode of his ecstatic self-possession by self-expropriation. The Son's receptivity, the self-gift to him that constitutes his self as fully divine image, is also kenotic, since that is the content of the image of the Father. The Holy Spirit, in perhaps underdeveloped fashion, is breathed out as the ultimate seal of the non-self-seeking character of the trinity, since his role is to make room for the reality of the unity of Father and Son.

## THE ORDER OF THE TRINITARIAN COMMITTEE (GOD'S AGENDA)

The condition of love between persons is difference. Only the other can be loved as an other. This remains true also of the trinitarian persons, in whom difference is indicated by a certain distance or interval, which Balthasar terms a hierarchy.[24] The persons of the trinity "make room" for one another in "the hierarchical distance of the processions. There is a primal beginning in which the Father is 'alone', even if he was never without the Son, for ultimately it is he, unique and alone, who begets the Son'" (TD5:94).[25] This distance protects the distinction between the persons both immanently and economically. For the interval between the Father and the Son to be sufficiently great to allow them their personal distinctness, the Father must initiate the movement, which is nothing other than to say that he really is the begetter of the Son.

In the trinity, there is an infinitesimal moment, not of time but of distinction, where the Father is alone, but the Son is not *not*, because what the Father is doing is the Son. Without that moment, the distinction between the two would not be a distinction on the level of being, Balthasar argues. It is important to note the significance of his admission. The Father is never, by definition, without the Son, yet for the distinction between them to distinguish them from each another, the Father must make the "first" move. Once more, a surprising analogy is used: the relation between differentiation and unity "is like the relationship between the sexes" (TD5:94).[26] Balthasar specifies that "no doubt this image is only remotely approximate" (TD5:95), yet the relationship between sexual and trinitarian differentiation appears again.

Balthasar presents the decision to send the Son into the world to save as a decision made by divine committee that nonetheless reflects the order of procession in its genesis. Balthasar wants to avoid the implication that the Father pitilessly or alone determines that the Son must go—thus demanding a sacrifice, rather than allowing the Son to offer the sacrifice. He is impatient with mistaken attempts to criticize Anselm's theory of atonement for suggesting that the Father sacrifices his Son without regret and without attention to the wishes of the Son. Anselm lacks only "the link with the Son's trinitarian *missio*,[27] his 'sending' by the Father on the basis of his *processio*" (TD4:261), the link through which the Son offers himself in eucharistic gratitude to the Father for the gift of divinity. Divine decision making by committee happens "through the mutual integration of the Persons' 'points of view'." Although the Son's self-offering is as original as the Father's desire that the Son go (TD5:95–96), every trinitarian decision preserves "the hierarchy of the hypostatic processions" (TD3:199).[28] Balthasar's rule for determining the distribution of initiative, consent, self-offering, supplication, and so on seems arbitrary, although sourced in Adrienne von Speyr's insights.

Setting aside the speculative and mythological aspects of Balthasar's narrative, it is important for our purposes to note Balthasar's repeated struggles with the oppositional pairs he imports into the trinity. Freedom *and* obedience; initiative *and* response; action *and* consent; command *and* voluntarism: none of these pairs seems particularly applicable to the intra-trinitarian life in which the persons of the trinity share a single will and a single love.[29] Balthasar seeks to find the coincidence of opposites in God, to radicalize opposed terms to speak of the transcendent God without reducing God to something that stands in opposition to the world.[30] The move itself is familiar and legitimate; the coincidence of freedom and necessity in the trinitarian processions is an excellent example.

But Balthasar multiplies these pairs and assigns the opposed elements to different trinitarian persons. In one pair, the Father initiates and the Son responds; in another, the Son's eucharistic self-offering is as original as the Father's initiative. Balthasar's knowledge of these inner-divine patterns of over-againstness derives from the relation between Christ and the Father en route to the cross. Balthasar determines that much of the narrative of Jesus' road to the cross directly reflects his inner-trinitarian status as the Father's Son. When Jesus prays "not my will, but thy will," he achieves the utter availability, the "indifference that is ready to embrace whatever the Father wills" (TD3:522), that Balthasar radicalizes from Ignatian visions of mission. Balthasar expands further on the ways in which the cross can be prefigured in the inner divine life: " 'the Father, renouncing his uniqueness, generates the Son out of his own substance', which can be designated a 'pre-sacrifice' [*Voropfer*],"[31] "something utterly real, which includes the absolute and total exhaustion of the Cross" (TD5:510). The Father's pre-sacrifice *is* the Son. Suffering "must be something profoundly appropriate to [the Son's] divine Person" (TD3:226), since he proceeds from the Father. Jesus' actualization of the Father's original decision not to be God for himself alone reflects the law of self-surrender as freedom and letting be.[32] The temporal decision clings to a decision made in eternity, in which the Son "offered himself" for the task of atonement, which is "both accepted in free will *and* laid on him from without" (TD4:500).[33]

Yet when that eternal decision is projected into the temporal sphere, the aspect that appears to Christ is the pitilessness of the Father. Jesus the Son is obedient to the Spirit who mediates the Father's will to him. "[H]is obedience . . . is ultimately, that is, at the divine level, to rest on the equal-ranking initiative, now transformed into an indifference that is ready to embrace whatever the Father wills" (TD3:522). Such indifference—utter availability—is the highest possibility of response to God. Here, divine and human freedom coincide. The content of the Son's role is nothing other than to place himself at the disposal of the Father, even to utmost self-abandonment in death and descent into hell, and this content expresses his sonship in human form. Once more we find an oscillation: "it is not clear how the Incarnate One can receive and execute [the Father's] decision in pure obedience: for, just as eternally, it is his decision too" (TD3:510).

In infinite divine freedom, the Son offers himself in obedient responsive gratitude to the Father's unspoken supplication; in his finite freedom, Jesus remains faithful to the Father's command as mediated to him by the Spirit. "The Son, who is eternally subject to the Father, as man had to 'learn obedience through what he suffered' (Heb. 5:8)" (TD3:187).[34] Balthasar terms this shift in relationships the *trinitarian inversion*. In eternity, the Father begets the Son and the Father and Son together breathe out the Spirit. When projected into the temporal sphere, the trinitarian order becomes vertical rather than horizontal: Father to Son via Spirit, with the Spirit above the obedient Son. The Spirit mediates the unity of the wills of Father and Son as well as their distance: "It is as if the Spirit, now embodied in the form of a rule, says to them both: This is what you have wanted from all eternity; this is what, from all eternity, we have determined!" (TD3:188). The difficulty, however, remains: Why does Balthasar insist on creating such over-againstness within the trinity itself?

Three themes are at the root of Balthasar's reasoning. First is the consti- tution of each divine person. Second is the interplay between categories of personhood and of being, which implies that divinity, existing only as the three persons, can still do work as substance (although the divine substance is nothing other than the event of God). Third is Balthasar's configuration of the Father's begetting of the Son as self-surrender.

First is the "shape" of the divine persons and the way in which each of them possesses the single divine freedom and will. Balthasar's passage is worth quoting at length:

> It is extremely hard to see how the Son, who 'receives' Godhead, and hence eternal freedom, from the Father . . . can nonetheless possess this infinite freedom in the same sovereign manner (albeit in the mode of obedience) as the Father. . . . what the Father 'does' is nothing other than the Son himself. In receiving himself from the Father, therefore, the Son accepts the originless, self-possessing God, that is, that full- ness of being that must always be included and reflected upon in any *theologia*. (That is why it will not do simply to replace the so-called 'theo-ontological' categories of philosophy with 'personological' cat- egories, that is, to dissolve Being and its relationships.) (TD2:267–68)

The form of the Son's reception of self introduces a major difficulty acknowl- edged here. Balthasar asks how it is possible to possess "in sovereign form" what is given to one. This sets up a "serious clash between the philosophi- cal '*analogia entis*' (with its *maior dissimilitudo* between God and world) and the theological '*analogia fidei*' (which extends right up to *participatio divinae naturae*)." Here we find the divine ever-greater in transcendence of the merely human assumption that obedience indicates subordination: since there are no degrees of divinity, the Son's obedience to the Father does not indicate that he is less than the Father, even though he is divine "in the mode of readiness, receptivity, obedience and hence of appropriate response" (TD2:267). The gift of the "originless, self-possessing God" determines the Son's reception of divinity in the mode of obedience or receptive gratitude. The Son receives the divinity of the Father, but he has that divinity only in eucharistic thanksgiving for the gift itself, and his acts (like the Spirit's) are always "codetermined by the *ordo processionis* and the trinitarian unity" (TD2:258).[35]

Second, Balthasar highlights the interplay between "personological" and "theo-ontological" categories. The categories of Father and Son or giver and receiver in the abstract do not lend themselves to equality and shared sovereignty. Other considerations apart, a son is dependent on a father in various ways, and most particularly, in respect of his sonship and his existence. While a father depends also on a son to be what he is, the father's initiative and already existing selfhood (not yet qualified in respect of fatherhood) allow him to become father by begetting a son. Father and Son indicate precisely *what* and *who* God is. But without further qualification, this would seem to indicate that the Son is less divine than the Father, because the Father possesses divinity in an original manner while the Son possesses it derivatively. That result would be unacceptable. Thus Balthasar is unwilling to dissolve the being of God entirely into the intra-divine relationships of paternity and filiation. Remember, he has said that there is a primal moment when the Father is alone. Since the Father is God, in whom there is no "having," only "being," what the Father gives the Son can be nothing other than what the Father himself is. The Father gives the Son equality, the full divinity that is the Father's own, which the Son "has" in the mode of reception.[36] But the divine essence is not a static presence "behind" the trinitarian persons; it is always the case that the Spirit unites the Father and the Son in the former's initiative and the latter's response.

The third theme is the "utter" self-surrender of the Father-Origin in the generation of the Son and Spirit (TD2:287). *Begetting* is self-surrender. That the originless origin shares his divinity—he is never for himself alone but is always himself with and through another—shows that divinity is making room for the other, letting the other be.[37] The Father's "making room" for the other is thus the foundation of the Son's responsive obedience. "Inherent in the Father's love is an absolute renunciation: he will not be God for himself alone" (TD4;323–24). The coincidence in the Son of spontaneity and obedience is the image of the Father's generosity in begetting the Son and thus allowing himself to be determined by the Son. The Father "*is always himself by giving himself*" (TD2:256), so this is not a process of losing the self only to receive it back. Rather, the self is always already ecstatically shaped in the generation of the Son out of the Father's womb.

But doesn't the Balthasarean description of the Father's self-surrender depend on the conceptual possibility that the Father could have done otherwise?[38] Doesn't the interpretation of deciding to be with another as renunciation introduce the idea of difference as potential competition and suggest that the Father "could have," in some unimaginable act, chosen *not* to share his divinity?[39] Why else would the groundless generation of another to love—an other who is nothing other than loving response—count as renunciation and prefigure death? Another way of asking the question is to consider whether the Son, who is begotten, has any option in the matter.

And it turns out that, according to Balthasar, he certainly does—in the sense that God has freedom. Divine freedom is not, of course, a power for opposites but the power to truly be oneself and be present in and through one's actions. Balthasar requires the Son to offer an antecedent consent to being begotten. Following Bonaventure, he identifies a "passive generative potentiality" in the Son that "disposes" him to be begotten. "Divine conception has its roots . . . in the ability to 'let be' and . . . in the ability to allow oneself to be brought to birth, to separate oneself, really and in fact, from what is one's own" (TD5:85). Only so can the Son and Spirit come forth. Consent marks how the gift of self can be received: for a gift to be given, it must be received and received as gift. The "antecedent consent" of the Son is, it seems, necessary for the Son's offering up of himself in the world to be truly free.[40] If the Son had no "choice" in the matter (of his begetting), he would find himself *geworfen*, with no choice other than to act out his role in the theodrama. His action must (freely) spring entirely from the shape of his divine being, which is the form of gratitude and obedience for its begetting.[41]

The selves that are constituted by this Father–Son relation are selves vulnerable to each other. They are selves that can allow themselves to be utterly open to the other (that is, coinhere one another to the greatest imaginable extent without prudery) because their distinction from one another is secured by the procession of one from another. Here, rather disturbingly, Balthasar's language introduces something like death into the very notion and foundation of relations between persons.

> In giving himself, the Father does not give something (or even everything) that he *has* but all that he *is* . . . This total self-giving, to which the Son and the Spirit respond by an equal self-giving, is a kind of 'death', a first, radical 'kenosis', as one might say. It is a kind of 'super-death' [*Übertod*] that is a component of all love and that forms the basis in creation for all instances of 'the good death', from self-forgetfulness in favor of the beloved right up to that highest love by which a man 'gives his life for his friends'. (TD5:84)[42]

The shock of this passage is difficult to mute. A super-death introduced into God already in the relations between the persons? Before any consideration of sin and incarnation? A super-death a "component of all love"?[43] The problem lies in the introduction of the possibility and even, as it were, pre-reality of death into God. The possibility of competition may qualify every human relation, but why would we assume that the need to sacrifice oneself for an other, generated by the injustices and limitations of human existence, applies to the relation between God and God?[44]

Balthasar moves directly from difference to death, from begetting to renunciation, from the generation of a son to sacrifice. Balthasar's own view of personhood is becoming apparent. Following Ferdinand Ulrich, he suggests that "absolute love is only realized where there is this surrender of what is one's own, where this *separation* is taken seriously, where there is this 'going under' so that the Other can 'rise up' in himself" (TD5:85). Even, or perhaps especially, in the divine case, existence with another is founded on a prior sacrifice of self. The Father wills not to be God for himself alone. But in God, there is only being, not having. Why, then, does Balthasar consider what the Father does renunciation, kenotic sacrifice, and death?

Balthasar is, I submit, operating with an understanding of loving relations in which being in relation is possible only when one hands oneself fully over to another, holding nothing back. Surrender—handing oneself over—becomes the mode of love itself. If love can only be founded on surrendering to the other, if the begetting of an other is renunciation, then operating in the background is a concept of withholding or competition and the possibility that the Father might have been tempted to keep it all for himself.

Balthasar construes personhood in relation as requiring complete self-gift, or absolute self-expropriation. Selves are always in danger of overwhelming each other; therefore, distinction read as order or hierarchy appears as the necessary precondition of love. Love is intrinsically sacrificial because it involves the affirmation of difference. That affirmation of difference is the repetition of the Father's sacrifice. Only by building hierarchy into the being of God can Balthasar protect against his own instincts to see relation with another as destructive of the self; only so can the danger of being overwhelmed by the dangerous, different other be overcome. Availability to another means submitting to that one completely, and relation always requires withdrawal in order to let the other be. Balthasar's way to avoid rapacious subjectivity in God is to intensify the potentially rapacious subject in order to overcome it.

The consequences are considerable. The divine ever-greater shows itself in the coincidence of action and consent or initiative and response, which

> is expressed in the world in the duality of the sexes. In trinitarian terms, of course, the Father, who begets him who is without origin, appears primarily as (super-) masculine; the Son, in consenting, appears initially as (super-) feminine, but in the act (together with the Father) of breathing forth the Spirit, he is (super-) masculine. As for the Spirit, he is (super-) feminine. There is even something (super-) feminine about the Father too, since . . . he allows himself to be determined by the Persons who thus proceed from him; however, this does not affect his primacy in the order of the Trinity. The very fact of the Trinity forbids us to project any secular sexuality into the Godhead. It must be enough for us to regard this ever-new reciprocity of acting and consenting . . . as the transcendent origin of what we see actualized in the world of creation: the form and actualization of love and its fruitfulness in sexuality. (TD5:91)[45]

Associating initiative with super- (*über*—more than) masculinity and consent and determination with super-femininity certainly reflects a projection of secular sexuality into the Godhead on one level. But my primary concern is Balthasar's assignation of habits of initiative and consent to different persons of the trinity and the theological argument that derives sexual difference from these differentiated ways of being. Balthasar offers us a theological account of, and grounding for, sexual difference. It may seem that the solution to the problem Balthasar's account poses is simply to remove the essentialist and heterosexist aspects of Balthasar's argument and to say that initiative and consent, action and passion, are found in every sexual relation, not just heterosexual ones.[46] But that ignores the crucial imagery: The glory of a masculine, initiative-taking God is that He stretches Himself so far as even to allow himself to be determined by a feminized, consenting other. Birthing the Son leaves the Father's womb-phallus "empty" (TD3:518), demonstrating that divine masculinity is great enough to be able to humble itself; the humility only intensifies the greatness.[47] Generosity and being-with-an-other are connected from the very first (divine) moment with something like sacrifice and something like death. In order to deconstruct the logic of this move, it is necessary to consider Balthasar's understanding of sexual difference, which is grounded in divine difference.

## WHAT THEN IS SEXUAL DIFFERENCE?

Sexual difference in Balthasar "brings into view (engenders) the encounter between God and creature."[48] Yet Tina Beattie shows that Balthasar effectively identifies woman with "sex, death, and sin in a way that betrays a profoundly hostile attitude towards embodiment and sexuality."[49] Given that the entirety of the theodrama is an attempt to think about the encounter between God and creature, surprisingly little attention has been paid to the implications of Balthasar's trinitarian grounding of sexual difference.[50] Human beings present themselves in two modes of existence, which are irreducibly different at the level of "each cell . . . their whole empirical experience and ego-consciousness. At the same time both share an identical human nature, but at no point does it protrude, neutrally, beyond sexual difference, as if to provide neutral ground for mutual understanding" (TD2:365).[51] Sexuate existence *is* human existence. Sexual difference finds its meaning within a primary form of difference itself made possible only by the difference in God.

In order to understand how human finitude and transcendence can meet in sexual difference, Balthasar adopts Erich Przywara's designation of "the relationship between the image of God and sexuality [as] one of 'in-and-above'" (TD2:370), which captures the way human sexuality is both God-related and part of (while transcending) the spectrum of creaturely sexuality. Human sexuality, while related, differs from mere animality. The openness of human sexuality also points toward the divine ever-greater. Sexual difference is ultimately a theological reality. The Adam–Eve relationship is retroactively illuminated by the relationship between Christ and the church, of which it is a type. Until the relationship between Christ and the church has been made manifest, the relation between Adam and Eve does not shine forth in its full light.[52] Human sexuate existence is grounded in divine–human difference, which itself derives from the space opened up by the relation between the Father and the Son.

These analogical relationships are performed throughout the theodrama. The human Jesus, sexed male, is gendered feminine in relation to God, as is all creation. As the Son, he is "super"-feminine in relation to the Father. His role is to pour himself out in a kenotic self-emptying that constitutes the church as his body or his feminine counterpart in his life, death, and resurrection. By placing himself at the disposal of the Father in the mode of obedience (feminine mode of creaturely freedom), the Son is the one from whom all other theological personhood derives (masculine mode of divine freedom). He has to be male in order to represent the Father in the world, but he is divine in a feminine mode (the mode of receptivity). Indeed, the (fully active) passivity or indifference that is the mode of Jesus' mission translates into Balthasar's account of a *feminine* mission.[53]

So why does Jesus have to be male? The only visible remnant of his divinity ends up being his male-sexed body. His male body speaks of something that is always invisible—the male body is through and through a signifier, and in this case, a signifier of divinity.[54] This representational signification is extended to the priest such that a male-sexed body is the condition of the possibility of representing not only God but also Christ. The male body signifies what it is not: male bodies signify divinity even though all bodies are gendered feminine by being created. But there is no corresponding signification for the female body: She does not signify the creature; she *is* the creature. The sacramental function of the female body is "entirely negative." It is present only as that which is cancelled out.[55]

Mary, the feminine principle, "represents mankind (which, in relation to God, is female)" (TD3:288).[56] In the course of Jesus' linear mission (the straight road of the Word to the cross[57]), Mary develops in accordance with his needs. She, who is both the model of unrestricted creaturely consent to God as well as *the* woman, has to develop into Jesus' mother and his bride. Mary's "mission, in the feminine and creaturely mode, is to let things happen; as such it is perfectly congruent with the masculine and divine mission of the Son" (TD3:352).[58] Mary, watching Jesus on the cross, allows herself to be stripped bare by the agony he suffers, becoming useless to him. This stripping depends on her yes to God in the annunciation,[59] a yes that cannot be uttered.[60] Then God makes the " 'nothingness' of unfruitful virginity" into motherhood: "the Word is empowered to make his whole body into God's seed; thus the Word finally and definitively becomes flesh in the Virgin Mother, Mary-Ecclesia" (TD4:361).[61] The Father's impregnation of Mary with his Word (another *logos spermatikos*?) begets Christ's body, the church, which itself is the place or empty space that she has become. The church is constituted by Christ's fullness, so Mary's role is to allow her female bodily existence to be cancelled out, erased, and transmuted into his body and bride, the church.

We have discovered a sexed signification of creation, a locus of sexual difference—but one that cannot count as such. The interplay between divine fullness and human dependence, translated in sexed terms, continually eventuates as masculinity's full development inside and in relation to feminine self-evacuation. Such a relationship cannot engender real difference, and real difference is essential to Balthasar's project. We know that the divine–human relation takes its form from the relation between the Father and the Son. Perhaps, then, trinitarian difference can rescue sexual difference? Balthasar uses the second creation narrative, Eve's creation from Adam's rib, to illuminate three points that crystalize the mutual reinforcement of trinitarian and sexual difference. First, the man is primary: "he is alone before God and with God; although potentially and unconsciously he bears the woman within him, he cannot give her to himself" (TD2:373). "Woman" is thus subordinate to "man" in two ways: he stood alone before God at some point; and "she" was always already potentially in him.

Second, his loneliness shows that he is not a primal androgyne, who originally is complete with himself. He finds no complement to himself in the animal or divine realms. He names the animals and finds no partner; he finds himself alone with God. That move creates a problem for Balthasar. If "man" was alone with God and God then gave "woman" to "man," then "man" is complete when "woman" is added to him, but "she" is not originally other than "he," nor can "her" relationship to God ever match up to "his." To push the imaginary as far as it will go: God and "he" were alone together; "she" wasn't there yet.[62] God realized that there was some unfulfilled, unactualized potential in "him" that was crying out for more—a more that was already within "him" as "his" own *potentia*. So "he" (God) gave "him" (man) "her," and "she" is "his" (man's) answer. At no point is "she" permitted a question, nor does "she" even speak, because "she" "*is essentially* an answer (*Ant-Wort*)" (TD3:284).[63]

Third, woman comes from man. The conclusion Balthasar draws from this is an essential illumination of the way he repeatedly uses divine relations and human sexuate existence to illuminate one another: "the man retains a primacy while at the same time, at God's instigation, he steps down from it in a *kenosis*; this results in the God-given fulfilment whereby he recognizes himself in the gift of the 'other'" (TD2:373).[64] Adam's kenosis is a self-emptying that produces a partner made to fill his need, in whom he recognizes himself: his answer. Kenosis retains overtones of literal emptying since Adam's rib is taken out. His "self"-emptying issues in *his* fulfillment in an other who, from the first moment, is *his* other in a possessive sense. Further, "Balthasar's language implies that the creation of the woman is an act of divine violence against the man: he is 'overpowered' and 'robbed'."[65] How then is he stepping down from his (God-given and retained) primacy?[66] Again, we find that Balthasar reads being-with in terms of hierarchy and precedence. Someone must have precedence, even if he also quasi-sacrifices that precedence in service of his own fulfillment.

Woman's "fruitfulness" is not primary (the man's is, yet unable to fulfill itself by itself), so Balthasar finds "a kind of natural *vocation* on woman's part much more explicitly than in man's case . . . the woman's *missio* vis-à-vis Adam can be described as the extrapolation and continuation of her *processio* from Adam" (TD3:285–86).[67] Tying woman to nature (and, implicitly, man to culture and freedom) is a classic and questionable association.[68] The idea that childbearing constitutes a "natural vocation" for woman but not for man so that her vocation is to have his children is worrisome in its orientation of women's subjectivity and existence to the realization of men's and the reduction of women to their biological role in reproduction. Beyond such worries, Balthasar again discovers a surprising analogy between woman's relation to man and the trinitarian relations: The man retains primacy even while kenotically stepping down from it, by allowing an other to be generated alongside himself. From the first moment, in humanity as in the trinity, difference in itself never appears; we find only difference for which room has to be made, difference in which order, priority, and primacy remain.

Copresence requires a prior order in which one has primacy retained even in the sacrifice or renunciation of that primacy. The man gives the woman a mission that extends her procession from him, just as the Father gives the Son a mission that extends his procession from the Father. Being follows origin; woman, like the Son, is in the position of consenting to a mission given her by the father/man from whom she comes. Man has a persisting priority, just as the Father retains his primacy in the order of the trinity. Man kenotically empties himself for the generation of his own complement, just as the Father kenotically empties himself in the generation of his own image, the Son. The Son is allowed an antecedent consent denied to the woman, though, for she "is essentially an answer." Mary, the fulfillment of the promissory note represented by Eve, "had been given away to Joseph, which meant that she could not respond to God's choosing of her by any autonomous gesture of self-dedication: in any case, God took what was his, beyond all creaturely pacts. Furthermore, she had been given away to the overshadowing Spirit . . . [which made her consent] more like a natural self-giving arising from a long-accepted availability" (TD4:358).[69] The masculine aspect of the Son's divine freedom makes a difference here.

Those who—like Williams, Ward, Gerard Loughlin, and Gavin D'Costa—suggest that Balthasar's trinitarian theology can rescue his account of sexual difference fail to take their coimplication with sufficient seriousness. That does not simply mean that Balthasar's trinitarian theology exhibits hierarchically gendered patterns. Taking Balthasar on his own terms, as Williams requires, means reading the trinity as the transcendent determination of difference, beyond the projection of secular sexuality into the Godhead. Let us strip every explicitly sexuate image from Balthasar's trinity, leaving him the reciprocity of action and consent along with the primacy of the Father (reading Father as indicating begetter, not gender), and see what emerges.[70] There is a first—an actor—who brings a second—a "consenter"—into being, as it were. The second consents to the first, affirming the first just in "his" primacy as first. In that affirmation, the first and second join together as actors and generate a third, an other, alongside themselves. That third enacts the fulfillment of consent in affirming the first two. In the circulation of divine life, the first acts and the second consents; the first two act and the third consents; the second acts in concert with the unexpressed wish of the first, bringing together determination (command, obedience, mission) and consensus; and the second and third are given permission by the first to determine "him." Stripped to its barest essentials, we discover the following: coming from another and being added to another as an *and* (Father *and* Son, Adam *and* Eve) structures the relationship between trinitarian and sexual difference and introduces the hierarchical structure of the relationships in the analogy. Difference is intrinsically sacrificial, for it requires that the first "renounce" uniqueness. Difference is a matter of action and reception, activity and consent; cooperation or agreement always reduces to an initiator and a (spontaneous but always "second" in relation to a "first") responder. It turns out to be impossible to strip every remnant of secular sexuality from Balthasar's trinitarian theology because action and consent, determination and receptivity, initiation and derivation are the way heterosexuality and heterosexuate difference are constructed. They lie at the origin of heterosexuality, binary gender, and masculininty and femininity in the socio-symbolic order. The suggestive conclusion—which will be substantiated in later chapters—is that theological difference and "secular" sexuality may not be so different after all.

Is the Son less than the Father? No, Balthasar says, but his sexualizing of the trinity belies that claim. The Father is the origin of the Son, and is "super"-masculine in relation to the Son. The Son is "super"-feminine in relation to the Father, because the Father is the origin of the Son. The Son's answering love takes the concrete form that corresponds to his personal being: that of obedience. Balthasar continues to insist, almost despite himself, that the Son has divine freedom in the mode of obedience. Already at the inner-trinitarian level, hierarchy obtains: to be free, even a divine will must be part of a hierarchy—all this we have seen.

Is the Son less than the Father? No—because the personological categories of theology cannot supplant the theo-ontological.[71] Said crudely, the divine substance stipulatively guarantees their equality. The fullness of divine substance can perhaps rescue the Son's divinity, but at the cost of sacrificing the aspects of the correspondence between the appearance and the reality of God that Balthasar most wishes to preserve: the demonstration of the nature of intra-trinitarian relations given in the subordination of the Son to the Father in the road to the cross.[72] In the human case, there is no such protection—if sexual difference is irreducible and goes through all of human existence, there is no escaping a hierarchical ordering of men and women, where men have flexible roles while women are doubly tied to their biological determination toward men and children.

This brings us back to Balthasar's claims for the Father's vulnerability, kenosis, and "femininity" in relation to the Son. God the Father takes the ultimate risk by begetting an other, another self who is maximally other yet always along-with. But for Balthasar, the risk of love is only taken when the possibility of ontological dissolution is undercut by the secure differentiation of hierarchy. The giver, the Father, revels in a seeming threat—handing himself over entirely to another—yet never risks losing himself in this handing-over because he is always ontologically secured precisely in the event of handing himself over. Because the Father's mode of having or being divine is that of masculine initiator, his "self" is unaffected by his "riskily" begetting another divine person.[73] The Father can "safely" take on the feminine role, then, without risk to his fundamental (super-) masculinity. There is no generic concept of "person" in the trinity, Balthasar insists.

While Balthasar's language of the Father's utter self-surrender, his empty womb, his undergoing a kind of "super-death" may sound like a promising way to undercut masculine imagery for God, this language cannot stretch as far as Balthasar wishes it to. Despite the Father's "feminine" self-emptying, he is able to beget the Son out of his masculine fullness; this is why he is Father and why Jesus must be male. Masculinity is connected with origin and initiative. Femininity is an answering fullness that, in the end, is grounded, not so much in a natural (secular) account of gender but in a theological account of the relation between the Father and the Son in the Spirit. To make the point clear: the trinitarian theodrama hangs on what actual men and symbolic males can do—that is, become feminine, be squandered and poured out, without losing their primacy or their fullness. Their emptiness is only symbolic, because their fullness has feminine space, feminine wombs, and feminine bodies in which to realize itself.[74]

The Father overcomes his own masculinity, or expresses it in feminine mode, by permitting an-other beside him, one who interpenetrates him yet is ultimately distant from him, distanced by an interval or a hiatus that allows him to be alongside the Father, a being-with that Balthasar reads as vulnerability and "super"-death. This imaginary simply cannot separate being-with from pain and suffering. The Son too moves between activity and passivity, priority and receptivity. The Son's masculinity, expressed in his breathing out with the Father of the Spirit and in his divinity in relation to creation, is cancelled out or expressed in feminine mode already in his very being begotten by the Father. While Jesus is masculine, he is feminized by making himself subject even to the Spirit and responding to the Father's "reckless" squandering of himself by an equally divine reckless squandering of himself (TD4:328). Only the one who possesses himself (the creator–creature dissimilarity, "for even the highest creature lacks the most divine attribute: it lacks self-subsistence" TD3:525) can squander himself. The priest, in order to represent Christ to the community, has to be male but precisely as such can overcome his masculinity by representing femininity in relation to God on behalf of creation. Only the biological woman remains feminine throughout, and she does not recklessly squander herself; she never had the chance, for she was given away from the first moment. In the form of Mary, she allows herself to be stripped away.

Even in this cross-dressing, gender-bending theodrama, Balthasar cannot allow hierarchy, priority, and order to be upended forever. The economic modality of the trinitarian relations, where the Father's "pitiless rule" is mediated to Jesus by the Spirit, ends at the resurrection, when Jesus takes back control of the Spirit.[75] At the end of the Son's mission, "he subjects himself once again, in a new way, to the law of the triune life. Every act of obedience that distinguished the Son during his mission is now translated by the Father into that eternal form of subjection that will now enfold all the world's beings. It is as if the Son's final subjection is also the last condition for the world's eternal subjection to God" (TD5:521).[76]

## BALTHASAR AND DIFFERENCE

Recent discussions following Balthasar and Moltmann emphasize that God can abandon God to the depths of despair (to the utmost reaches of hell) in solidarity with sinners because God is trinity as Father, Son, and Spirit. The event of the crucifixion, as the depth-charge carried in the descending (kenotic) movement of incarnation, renders the moment of speechlessness (the silencing of the Word) into the revelation of the distances of intra-trinitarian movements of love. In its logic of epistemic justification, trinitarian theology proceeds from that moment (as a *theologia crucis*) and refuses to find God elsewhere than on the cross; the move from cross to trinitarian constitution (what must be the case about God for this distance to "speak" God) follows almost of itself. The crucifixion becomes an evidently trinitarian *event*—not in that the persons of the trinity are all involved in whatever the trinity does but in that the crucifixion is a drama of the enactment of trinitarian constitution. The subjectification of the trinitarian persons takes place through subjection. As Judith Butler asks, "How does the subjection of desire require and institute the desire *for* subjection?"[77]

The subjection of creation to the creator is not the problem with Balthasar's model. The problem is the way that creator–creature relationship, on the one hand, finds its origin in the Father–Son relation, and on the other hand, is mirrored and repeated in gender. Balthasar has allowed the unity of divine and human in Christ, and the repetition of that relation first in its origin within God (Father–Son relation), and second in its human analog (the relation between the sexes) to elide the differences among these differences. Divine–human difference, the difference between the wholly other beyond difference, God, and the object of creative love, the world, becomes enacted within the two other forms of difference, intra-divine and sexual.

It remains questionable whether Balthasar can secure the full divinity of the Son or think self-possession and love or risk together. In the end, Balthasar's gender-bending, masochistic, reckless God has risked nothing, has lost nothing, and has only flirted with transgender identification. His God remains a stable correlate of gendered human hierarchies—male over female, certainly heterosexual over inadmissible homosexual, priest over church—even as these hierarchies collapse under their own weight.

In this chapter, I have sought to answer Williams's challenge. I have argued that the "relational distinctions" in Balthasar can—not just in *any* way, but in *every* way—"be reduced to a system of coordination and subordination." It is a far more complicated system of coordination and subordination than a simple equation between divine fatherhood and human fatherhood, but it is such a system nonetheless. There are several modes in which coordination takes place that will reappear in different versions later in the book: space- and place-making for another in order to establish relation; difference as sacrifice; trinitarian over-againstness overcome through the total submission and (spontaneous) obedience of one trinitarian person to another; and the ease with which sonship transforms into subordination, obedience, and response. Each of these finds reflection and support in theories of sexual difference. That individual persons—like Jesus—can move through different positions in the theological-symbolic system (divine masculinity, divine femininity, creaturely masculinity, creaturely femininity) does not undo the coordinated aspects of the system; rather, that movement is the crucial stabilizing center of the system.

The correlative aspect of this argument will become especially important in the two following chapters: that there are terms belonging to the relation between God and creation that should not apply within created relationships and vice versa. Created reality exhibits contrasts between dependence and freedom and connections between dependence and vulnerability. I will argue that dependence on God does not contrast with freedom and that the kind of dependence that creation has on God (absolute dependence) should not be introduced into relations between created beings. Relations between created beings do not and should not directly image the relation between God and creation. The connection between dependence and vulnerability that relations between created beings exhibit also should not be read into the relation between God and creation: dependence on God should not be read in terms of vulnerability. Note that the contrast is *not* between vulnerability and invulnerability in relation to God; the contrast is between relations of dependence that can usefully be read in terms of vulnerability and invulnerability and relations of dependence that cannot. As Rowan Williams recognizes, the differences that Balthasar seeks to bring together—trinitarian difference, God-creation difference, and male-female difference—are different forms of difference, and I will argue that those differences matter for the nature and extensibility of the rules for theological speech in each case.

What does this mean for a trinitarian theology? At every point, Balthasar returns to the relation between the procession of the Son and the mission of Jesus. How else could one get from the narratives the New Testament tells about Jesus to an account of the relations of God *ad intra*? What is seen in the biblical account of the history of Jesus is a subordinate relationship between him and the one he calls God and Father. Jesus reveals the Father, prays to the Father, and has his authority confirmed by the Spirit. Since the earliest days of Christological reflection, theologians have struggled with how to understand the relation between Jesus and God. Eventually, Jesus' naming of God as Father and the New Testament use of the language of sonship for Jesus resulted in an account of the trinitarian relations of origin. The logical and epistemological underpinning of this move is something along the lines of a relation between procession and mission as Balthasar here describes. The question then becomes, if the relation between procession and mission, tied as tightly as in Balthasar, has undesirable consequences, what is the alternative? What sort of trinitarian theology would result if the two were disconnected from one another, if the cross no longer served as the ultimate revelation and enactment of the eternal trinitarian relations of origin?

In Balthasar, we have found notions of personhood as space-making, turning the self into a place in which the other may become—just the vision of femininity that masculinism most hopes to enact. At one point, Balthasar suggests that "woman" is dyadic because she is not merely bride but also mother.[78] One might assume that the male too would be dyadic, as he is also father. Not so, Balthasar explains in a footnote: "As a sexual being, the man is explicitly monadic, whereas the woman is dyadic: the area of woman that interests the man sexually is not the same that the child desires for its sustenance" (TD3:290). Invisible here, as throughout Balthasar, is another aspect of "woman's" sexual being: the primary site of her pleasure. Whereas phallic relations recur over and over in Balthasar's trinitarian theology, relations of nonpenetrative touch and nonbordered personhood—we might image such relations clitorally rather than phallically—are entirely absent. That absence (both actual and imagistic) is the more surprising because the genesis of trinitarian theology focuses heavily on the inseparability of trinitarian persons—otherwise, one would indeed have a subordinate God rather than God Godself in Christ.

Balthasar's position may be treated as uncovering while enacting certain haunting shadows that continue to bedevil contemporary trinitarian theology. The connection between trinitarian and sexual difference may not be as exciting and liberating as some queer theologians have wished to argue.[79] Instead, a trinitarian kenosis may serve to stabilize, now in divinity rather than humanity, theological imaginaries of sexual hierarchy. This rather startling assessment of Balthasar, and by implication of the liberating tendencies implied by many projects seeking to tie trinitarian and sexual difference together, will need further elaboration to convince. In the next chapter, we turn to a feminist- and queer-friendly appropriation of Balthasar: Graham Ward's trinitarian theology.

## NOTES

1. I will not engage Balthasar's thought in totality; my discussion is restricted to the *Theo-Drama*, as it best exemplifies the tendencies that are my concern in this book.
2. The best study remains Tina Beattie, *New Catholic Feminism: Theology and Theory* (London: Routledge, 2006), hereafter NCF.
3. For example, Jacob Friesenhahn alludes to Balthasar's assignation of attributes of "passivity, receptivity, submission, and kenosis" to the Son, which he assumes would meet few objections. He then correctly says that for Balthasar, these "feminine" attributes describe the form of relation that all human persons of whatever sex ought to have to God (ignoring the problems that gendering creation "feminine" brings) and suggests that one might then argue that "women are in a better spiritual position than are men," due, presumably, to their greater tendencies toward passivity, receptivity, and submission. Friesenhahn says that he will "*exclude* . . . [a]ny suggestion of sexism," which suggests that he has not yet considered the way accounts of sexual difference fail as much in their representation of women as in the absence of representation. Suggesting that women are especially passive and receptive does not exclude sexism, for instance; it is sexism. Friesenhahn, *The Trinity and Theodicy: The Trinitarian Logic of Von Balthasar and the Problem of Evil* (Burlington, VT: Ashgate, 2011), 112–13.
4. Graham Ward, *Christ and Culture* (Malden, MA: Blackwell, 2005), 215. In his article "In the Name of the Father and of the Mother," Ward suggests going beyond Balthasar to develop a "hermaphroditic Christology" that would "redescribe the operation of the Trinity." *Literature & Theology* 8, no. 3 (1994), 325.
5. Ward, *Christ and Culture*, 150.
6. Gavin D'Costa and Gerard Loughlin have also found ambiguity in Balthasar, approving his attention to gender and sexuality while deploring the unfortunately sexist aspects of Balthasar's analysis. See my article "The Limits of Inclusion: Queer Theology and Its Others," *Theology & Sexuality*, forthcoming, for more extensive discussion of their approach.
7. Rowan Williams, "Balthasar and Difference," in *Wrestling with Angels: Conversations in Modern Theology*, ed. Mike Higton (Grand Rapids, MI: Eerdmans, 2007), 82 (see also 79 and 84). Originally published as "Afterword," in Lucy Gardner, David Moss, Ben Quash, and Graham Ward, eds., *Balthasar at the End of Modernity* (Edinburgh: T&T Clark, 1999), 173–79.
8. Williams, "Balthasar and Difference," 84.
9. This may seem to contradict Kathryn Tanner's theory of theological language. She argues that theologians may borrow terms that are in circulation, "skewing" their usage to restrict some of the implications the terms would otherwise carry with them, and thereby determining their theological sense. The implication of my argument here is not that this theory of theological language use is false but that there are exceptions to it. It is too optimistic about the success of theologians in "skewing" the usage of *some* terms, particularly those with especially deep affective resonance in the constitution of human subjects and communities. This has to do with two elements not accounted for in her original theory: (1) that theological terms have a history after their original usage is specified (restricted); and (2) that some theological terms may activate such deeply embedded affective registers in human beings that they produce associations even if their stipulative theological function rules out such associations. Specifically, language of fatherhood and sonship: (1) has a history that rules out any active recovery of an "original" stipulative usage, even if

it could be shown that the original theological usage of these terms did not carry with it the implications of the priority of the Father over the Son; and (2) *works* for the sorts of uses to which it is put precisely *because* it activates these affective registers. Thus, to work again theologically, the language might need to be skewed once more, in a deeper way. See Tanner, *God and Creation in Christian Theology: Tyranny or Empowerment* (Minneapolis, MN: Fortress Press, 2005), esp. 54–55.

10. Hans Urs von Balthasar, *Theo-Drama: Theological Dramatic Theory*, vols. 1–5, trans. Graham Harrison (San Francisco, CA: Ignatius, 1988–1998). The titles of the individual volumes are I: *Prologomena*; II: *Dramatis Personae: Man in God*; III: *Dramatis Personae: Persons in Christ*; IV: *The Action*; and V: *The Last Act*. Volumes 4 and 5 in English correspond to the German vol. 4, parts 1 and 2. For simplicity, I refer to the theodrama without the hyphen in the text when discussing the category. Further references to the *Theo-Drama* are noted in the text as TD followed by volume and page number.

11. Much of the rest of this chapter originally appeared with minor differences as Linn Marie Tonstad, "Sexual Difference and Trinitarian Death: Cross, Kenosis, and Hierarchy in the *Theo-Drama*," *Modern Theology* 26, no. 4 (October 2010), 603–31. Significant changes include the material regarding contrastive pairs of attributes, which did not appear in the original article. I have also cut part of the discussion of sexual difference, and I reordered parts of the discussion to fit the trajectory of this chapter better.

12. Access to divine revelation is always participatory and Christoform. As theology's task is to "think after" Christ, it is both necessary and salutary to describe and retell what takes place in Christ; see Balthasar, TD2:128.

13. Referring to Aquinas, *Summa Theologica* I, q. 43.1.

14. Alyssa Lyra Pitstick elides this difference when she suggests that mission and procession are identical such that kenosis must be read as a univocal term. Pitstick, *Light in Darkness: Hans Urs von Balthasar and the Catholic Doctrine of Christ's Descent into Hell* (Grand Rapids, MI: Eerdmans, 2007), 215.

15. John 14:28, quoted in Balthasar, TD2:129.

16. See especially Balthasar, TD3:220–30.

17. Although the German *Mensch* is a masculine noun meaning "human," the word is generally rendered in English translation as "man." As discussed below, Balthasar rejects the idea of a generically (nongendered or androgyne) human being.

18. Balthasar, TD2:404. Further: "all this takes place in a mysterious, pulsating vitality, of which the creaturely community, at whatever level, can only be a pale reflection" (ibid.). See also Balthasar, TD2:42–44.

19. There is no category of "person" that all three divine persons fall under. Balthasar, TD5:84 n.14.

20. Balthasar, TD5:63–65, following Aquinas. The contingency of creation introduces the distinction between immanent and economic trinity that is a necessary condition of the preservation of the freedom of God. See also Silvia Cichon-Brandmaier, *Ökonomische und immanente Trinität: Ein Vergleich der Konzeptionen Karl Rahners und Hans Urs von Balthasars* (Regensburg: Verlag Friedrich Pustet, 2008), 236, 241–42.

21. Balthasar, TD2:260–71. God's refusal to overwhelm is gorgeously captured in the beginning of TD2: "the Beautiful never overwhelms those who resist it but, by its grace, makes prisoners of those who are freely convinced" (35).

22. Balthasar is partly quoting Adrienne von Speyr, *Achtzehn Psalmen* (Einsiedeln: Johannes Verlag, 1957), 55. The subject of Speyr's relation to Balthasar is controversial. Her influence is evident throughout his work, particularly in

vol. 5 of the *Theo-Drama*. Beattie finds parallels between Balthasar's theology of sexual difference and his relationship with Speyr in NCF, 170–79. All references to Balthasar quoting Speyr are taken from the translator's notes in volume 5.

23. This is what makes the cross a possibility for the trinity.

24. Michael Proterra emphasizes that "between the Father's 'eternal rest' and the Son's 'pilgrimage', there is not the slightest distance, since the Son can never be a lost son. And that because the Spirit never ceases uniting the Father and the Son. The distancing (*l'éloicement*) that does take place in *kenosis* is simply the mode of interior trinitarian life (*circuminessio*)." Proterra, "Hans Urs von Balthasar, Theologian," *Communio* 2, no. 3 (Fall 1975), 283–84.

25. The quotation is from Adrienne von Speyr, *The World of Prayer* (San Francisco, CA: Ignatius, 1985), 65–66. Note how metaphysical descent and epistemological ascent cross each other here. The "distance" seen on the cross has to have its foundation within God. Thus the relations within God *must* have a shape that allows for that distance. Thomas R. Krenski says that "Wenn [Balthasar] das trinitarische Entäußert-Sein Gottes as wesentliches Fundament seiner freien Entäußerung in Schöpfung, Bund und Kreuz zu verstehen sich bemüht und zugleich klarmacht, daß in dieser vorsichtslos-ungeschützten Entäußerung seiner Liebe die Möglichkeit seines Leidens eröffnet ist, gelingt es ihm, sowohl 'Gottes Freiheit in seinem Engagement in der geschaffenen Welt und insbesondere im eingegangenen Bund', das heißt aber auch in und über seinem Leiden, sicherzustellen als auch ,innertrinitarisch das . . . Fundament [aufzuzeigen], das so etwas wie Schmerz und Tod an Gott heranzutragen erlaubt'." Krenski, *Passio Caritatis: Trinitarische Passiologie im Werk Hans Urs von Balthasars* (Einsiedeln: Johannes Verlag, 1990), 193.

26. Quoting Adrienne von Speyr, *The Letter to the Ephesians*, trans. Adrian Walker (San Francisco, CA: Ignatius, 1996), 100.

27. Balthasar emphasizes that this link accounts for Jesus' obedience being directed to the Father rather than the trinity.

28. In contrast, Emmanuel Tourpe suggests that Balthasar lacks "a consideration of the order of the processions, which he in fact refers to only in passing, or in relation to the trinitarian inversion." Tourpe, "Dialectic and Dialogic: The Identity of Being as Fruitfulness in Hans Urs Balthasar," in *Love Alone Is Credible: Hans Urs von Balthasar as Interpreter of the Catholic Tradition*, vol. 1, ed. David L. Schindler (Grand Rapids, MI: Eerdmans, 2008), 325.

29. See Hans Urs von Balthasar, *Theo-Logic*, vol. 2: *The Truth of God* (San Francisco: Ignatius, 2004), for further discussion of the opposites that he discovers here.

30. See Tanner, *God and Creation*, 46–47 for a general discussion of this strategy.

31. Quoting Adrienne von Speyr, *I Korinther* (Einsiedeln: Johannes Verlag, 1956), 345.

32. See also Balthasar, TD3:153.

33. Pitstick reads obedience as the personal property of the Son, but that is not quite right. Responsive gratitude is transformed into real obedience when enacted under the trinitarian inversion. See Pitstick, *Light in Darkness*, 226–27.

34. See also Balthasar, TD3:516: he was "consulted when the original decision was made. His readiness to accept the mission cannot have been elicited from him by persuasion, as it were; rather, it must be in him a priori, he must spontaneously have declared his readiness 'before the foundation of the world'."

35. The "astounding" acts of the Son and Spirit reduce to the tenacity with which they enact the Father's will.

36. See Balthasar, TD5:66–67 and 84.
37. Balthasar's metaphor for the way divine generation involves an act of letting go (because the Father lets the Son be free) invokes male orgasmic emission: "So too, in the act of begetting, a man causes his seed to go on its way while he himself retires into the background" (a parenthetical assertion in TD5:86). Perhaps Balthasar's analogy should instead be compared to the ability of women to achieve multiple orgasms ("endless act"), but that would leave out the importance of the actual male emission in Balthasar's image (for female orgasm involves no separation or "going forth").
38. Steffen Lösel suggests a corrective: God's identity as love utters itself in the love of the Father for the incarnated Son. He goes on to specify that God cannot even potentially be thought as not-love, and that Balthasar's implied other possibilities verge on being so mythological as to be utterly incompatible with theological thought. Lösel, *Kreuzwege: Ein ökumenisches Gespräch mit Hans Urs von Balthasar* (Paderborn: Ferdinand Schöningh, 2001), 181–82.
39. "The processions in God are not free in any arbitrary sense, even though God is not subject to external necessity" (TD5:88); the processions "lie beyond freedom and necessity" (TD3:35).
40. Pitstick dismisses the idea of "antecedent consent" as conceptually incoherent, as a conditioning of the Father's existence, "who is supposed to be the principle without a principle," and as a conditioning of his own existence, which she reads as making him his own father (*Light in Darkness*, 126–27). The latter point is overliteral.
41. Balthasar, TD4:325–26; 329–30.
42. Pitstick charges Balthasar with introducing sin into God in the use of distance/kenosis/death that he employs here but elsewhere rejects. See Pitstick, *Light in Darkness*, 128–29. Lösel (*Kreuzwege*, 152) thinks Balthasar follows Speyr: "if death is undersood to mean the sacrifice of life, then the original image of that sacrifice is in God," an image Speyr contrasts with the death of sin. TD5:251.
43. In a letter to Thomas Krenski, Balthasar says that the inner-trinitarian kenoses belong in quote marks and refers to Philippians 2 and Colossians 1:17 for his justification; see Krenski, *Passio Caritatis: Trinitarische Passiologie im Werk Hans Urs von Balthasars* (Einsiedeln: Johannes Verlag, 1990), 140–41. Krenski terms this kenotic character of divine love God's joy (141). Robert A. Pesarchick rejects Jürgen Werbick's accusation that this use of kenosis tarnishes trinitarian love because Balthasar is reading the essence, processions, and relations off the revelation of God's love in Christ, which is what I identify as the problem. See Pesarchick, *The Trinitarian Foundation of Human Sexuality as Revealed by Christ according to Hans Urs von Balthasar* (Rome: Editrice Pontificia Università Gregoriana, 2000), 154. Lösel, like Moltmann and contra Balthasar, prefers to read the immanent trinity as an eschatological reality. "Erst die eschatologische Zukunft wird deutlich machen, daß Gott von aller Ewigkeit her derjenige war, als der er sich in Jesus von Nazareth offenbart hat. Damit erledigt sich allerdings die Notwendigkeit, vom Heilsdrama auf Golgotha auf ein vorgängiges Ur-Drama in der Ewigkeit analog zurückzuschließen," *Kreuzwege*, 178–79. Pitstick interprets Balthasar's passage to mean that "kenosis as such (i.e., as it is in its prime analogate, the Trinity) is love, because God is love, and love Balthasar understands essentially as the gift of self" (*Light in Darkness*, 211). The latter interpretation is the most plausible on Balthasar's terms: love and kenosis are self-gift without remainder, yet the connection between self-gift and death, the totality of the gift to the one who is established as other in the gift of self, and the renunciatory quality of begetting, constitute the problem. Pitstick goes on to argue that "the Son obeys the Father so perfectly as to be just an open space or medium for the Father's self-expression" (ibid.), which heightens the problem.

44. There is a difference between saying that there is no greater form of love than giving one's life for one's friends (which allows for the possibility of different, equally great forms of love, or that the love that gift expresses might also be expressed in different ways, without giving oneself up to death) and saying that such love is the *highest* and so paradigmatic form of love. Further, Balthasar finds death just where one might expect that one might find enjoyment of the beloved *without* death in the total positivity of divine difference.

45. Pesarchick says that analogy protects Balthasar from charges of projectionism in this passage. He refers to a line of Balthasar's that emphasizes the difference between the consent to generation of the Son and Spirit, in contrast to the female womb, which on earth is the condition of the possibility for the success of male generation. The latter argument hardly seems to support the case that no projection is involved, since it writes analogy to creaturely femininity out of God by cancelling out the female body. See Pesarchick, *Trinitarian Foundation*, 176–77. Commentators generally refer to this passage in the context of a discussion of sexual difference, but in the structure of Balthasar's theological imaginary, the trinitarian relations are the grounding problem here.

46. I do not consider initiative and consent or action and passion acts that are appropriately parceled out to different persons in a sexual (or other) relationship.

47. Thomas G. Dalzell, SM, suggests that Balthasar's use of terms such as suffering, joy, wonder, and surprise is metaphorical rather than properly analogical. He references Balthasar's acceptance in *Theologik* of Gottlieb Söngen's position that "metaphysics without metaphor is empty, and metaphor without metaphysics is blind" [*Theologik* II:248 n.3], quoted in Dalzell, *The Dramatic Encounter of Divine and Human Freedom in the Theology of Hans Urs von Balthasar* (Bern: Peter Lang, 1997), 170. Could the current study be accused of taking too literally what for Balthasar are "mere" metaphors? First, Balthasar himself uses the language as a way of describing what is taking place in God. The similarities he draws, as we shall see, between divine being and human sexuate existence apply the metaphors supposedly drawn from the divine life very concretely to human existence. Second, we are operating not merely in the realms of the philosophical and the theological, but also in the realm of the imaginary. Therefore, we accept the further dictum that the metaphors of metaphysics may tell us as much about the metaphysics as do the metaphysics themselves—indeed, to speak of metaphysics apart from metaphor is to lay oneself open to quite serious charges of projection. The idea that, for instance, procession might be spoken of analogically, while wonder and surprise are spoken metaphorically, is perfectly legitimate. That does not obviate the possibility of asking what *work* the metaphors are doing alongside the analogies, since they are present for a reason. Third, I assume the two-level operation of Balthasar's language. Balthasar intends sexual difference to receive its character as a created enactment of God's being, and in showing us how he understands sexual difference, he cannot but inform us of how he understands the trinitarian being of God as a result. Were the metaphorical terms being taken literally, Balthasar's theology would be so obviously unorthodox as to render him irrelevant to the dominant schools of theological thought, thus removing a need for this sort of analysis since he would be no more than a sport in theological history. His unproblematic use of such metaphors to illuminate what he thinks is an orthodox position is, however, telling; and the influence he has gained in the theological academy suggests that many find his imagery alluring and convincing.

48. Lucy Gardner and David Moss, "Something like Time, Something like the Sexes—an Essay in Reception," in Lucy Gardner, David Moss, Ben Quash, and Graham Ward, eds., *Balthasar at the End of Modernity* (Edinburgh: T&T Clark, 1999), 73.

49. Beattie, NCF, 149; see also 157.
50. The most significant treatment of sexual difference in Balthasar, Beattie's *New Catholic Feminism*, focuses on the human side of the relation. This book seems to be unknown or unnoticed by some commentators. See, for instance, Barbara K. Sain, "Through a Different Lens: Rethinking the Role of Sexual Difference in the Theology of Hans Urs von Balthasar," *Modern Theology* 25, no. 1 (January 2009), 71–96. Sain refers in passing to an earlier article of Beattie's in her first footnote, yet makes no reference to Beattie's book. This is especially strange because Sain argues that previous commentators have missed the deficiencies of Balthasar's account of created masculinity, deficiencies that Beattie treats at some length.
51. Pesarchick says that "male and female are ontological realities" for Balthasar, which overstates the case somewhat. Pesarchick, *Trinitarian Foundation*, 175.
52. Balthasar, TD2:373–374; Beattie, NCF, 104.
53. Mary's "potentiality" is "the highest act that a creature can perform in love of God": "perfect self-surrender to God" (TD4:354).
54. Pesarchick recognizes this point, although he does not consider it a problem: "Maleness is representational in nature, for it represents a 'primal originating principle' that it can never be. It is then symbolic of an originating generativity of which it is but a vague shadow" (*Trinitarian Foundation*, 255). He is not thinking of the distinction between the phallus and the penis in Jacques Lacan, but of the Son's reception of the Father's initiating generativity.
55. Beattie, NCF, 141.
56. Also quoted in Beattie, NCF, 110.
57. So too Ward, *Christ and Culture* 36 n.16: "Jesus's way criss-crosses through Galilee and only become straight when the direction is uniform and purposed (on the way to the cross)."
58. Also quoted in Beattie, NCF, 106.
59. Balthasar says that Mary consents to all that happens to Jesus when she consents in the annunciation, although it is not clear that she knows that is what she is doing (TD4:352).
60. Rachel Muers, "A Question of Two Answers: Difference and Determination in Barth and Balthasar," *The Heythrop Journal* 40 (1999): 276.
61. Note the transmutation of the body of Christ into the semen of the Father, which fructifies the mother-bride.
62. See also Lucy Gardner and David Moss: "All rhetoric of equality, complementarity and mutuality is severely threatened by this insistence on a spectral, retrospective sexual identity and security for man apart from woman." Gardner and Moss, "Difference—the Immaculate Concept? The Laws of Sexual Difference in the Theology of Hans Urs von Balthasar," *Modern Theology* 14, no. 3 (July 1998): 383.
63. My emphasis. Balthasar identifies woman's answer to man as "reproduction" on 286.
64. Also quoted in Beattie, NCF, 104.
65. Beattie, NCF, 105, referring to TD2:373.
66. Balthasar asserts that "the man's (persisting) priority is located within an equality of man and woman," TD2:373. Sain says that Balthasar "insists" on equality here, although it is more like a passing mention ("Through a Different Lens," 73). At this point, it is difficult to refrain from "outrage," despite Rowan Williams.
67. The significance of this passage does not seem to strike many commentators. An exception is Cichon-Brandmaier, who concludes that "Balthasar redet eindeutig einem hierarchischen Verhältnis das Wort" (*Ökonomische und immanente Trinität*, 268).
68. Balthasar shows some awareness of the problem in TD2:367.

69. This self-giving parallels the Son's antecedent consent and eucharistic self-offering.
70. Improper language cannot be avoided. The sequence is not temporal; the Son and Spirit are not brought into being in a strict sense; the Son is begotten without origin (beginning), and so on.
71. Yet the further this argument is pushed, the more work the divine substance does.
72. Balthasar arguably sacrifices such correspondence in a different sense in the trinitarian inversion, but the inversion exhibits the same logic that drives Balthasar to seek only ordered difference.
73. Lösel also accuses Balthasar of undercutting the meaning of the drama of salvation history for God on the basis of the lack of risk in creating the world. "Gott kann das Risiko der Liebe zur Schöpfung nämlich nur dann eingehen, wenn dieses Risiko in Ewigkeit inner-trinitarisch ,abgesichert' ist." Lösel, *Kreuzwege*, 179.
74. Leo Bersani offers an illuminating comment in this connection: "the sexual emerges as the *jouissance* of exploded limits, as the ecstatic suffering into which the human organism momentarily plunges when it is 'pressed' beyond a certain threshold of endurance. Sexuality, at least in the mode in which it is constituted, may be a tautology for masochism." Bersani, *Is the Rectum a Grave? And Other Essays* (Chicago: University of Chicago Press, 2010), 24. He adds that Georges Bataille "reformulates this self-shattering into the sexual as a nonanecdotal self-debasement . . . in which, so to speak, the self is exuberantly discarded. . . . [T]he self which the sexual shatters provides the basis on which sexuality is associated with power. It is possible to think of the sexual as, precisely, moving between a hyperbolic sense of self and a loss of all consciousness of self. But sex as self-hyperbole is perhaps a repression of sex as self-abolition. It inaccurately replicates self-shattering as self-swelling, as psychic tumescence. . . . For it is perhaps primarily *the degeneration of the sexual into a relationship that condemns sexuality to becoming a struggle for power*" (25). These connections between masochism, sexuality, power, and self-shattering may do much to illuminate why and how kenotic relationships between trinitarian persons become so crucial in contemporary theology for thinking the relation between the trinity and the erotic under the regime of sexuality. Interestingly, Bersani terms "the inability to think of desire other than as lack or loss" a heterosexual inability (55). For Bersani, the connection between homophobia and penetrative sex runs through "the sexual act [that] is associated with women but performed by men and . . . has the terrifying appeal of a loss of the ego, of a self-debasement" (27). The Father's supra-femininity and its relation to the Father's supra-masculinity has seldom been better expressed. In *Closet Devotions* (Durham: Duke University Press, 1998), 155 n.75, Richard Rambuss rightly raises the question of whether Bersani's position remains too closely tied to bottoming rather than topping—an appropriate question to Balthasar's erotics as well.
75. Balthasar, TD4:364.
76. Quoting Speyr, *Korinther*, 506.
77. Judith Butler, *The Psychic Life of Power: Theories in Subjection* (Palo Alto, CA: Stanford University Press, 1997), 19.
78. See Balthasar, TD3:287 (where man is identified as word or seed), 290, 292, 338, and 353.
79. For a particularly illuminating example, see Gerard Loughlin, "Sexing the Trinity," *New Blackfriars* 79 (1998): 18–25. While I share with Loughlin the desire for an account of sexual difference that moves away from both sex and gender, I doubt that even a trinity constituted by cycles of "donation, reception, and return" (25) can serve as a correlate of such an imaginary

without overcoming through careful theological reasoning the powerful and entrenched language of relations of origin or processions that undergird trinitarian difference along with the heterosexual logic of donation and reception. The relationship between "coming from" and "being given" (or initiative and consent) serves as the unifying thread between trinitarian and sexual difference in its theological form.

## BIBLIOGRAPHY

Balthasar, Hans Urs von. *Theo-Drama: Theological Dramatic Theory*, vol. 1: *Prologomena*. Trans. Graham Harrison. San Francisco: Ignatius, 1988.

———. *Theo-Drama: Theological Dramatic Theory*, vol. 2: *Dramatis Personae: Man in God*. Trans. Graham Harrison. San Francisco: Ignatius, 1990.

———. *Theo-Drama: Theological Dramatic Theory*, vol. 3: *Dramatis Personae: Persons in Christ*. Trans. Graham Harrison. San Francisco: Ignatius, 1992.

———. *Theo-Drama: Theological Dramatic Theory*, vol. 4: *The Action*. Trans. Graham Harrison. San Francisco: Ignatius, 1994.

———. *Theo-Drama: Theological Dramatic Theory*, vol. 5: *The Last Act*. Trans. Graham Harrison. San Francisco: Ignatius, 1998.

———. *Theo-Logic*, vol. 2: *The Truth of God*. Trans. Adrian J. Walker. San Francisco: Ignatius, 2004.

Beattie, Tina. *New Catholic Feminism: Theology and Theory*. London: Routledge, 2006.

Bersani, Leo. *Is the Rectum a Grave? And Other Essays*. Chicago: University of Chicago Press, 2010.

Butler, Judith. *The Psychic Life of Power: Theories in Subjection*. Stanford: Stanford University Press, 1997.

Cichon-Brandmaier, Silvia. *Ökonomische und immanente Trinität: Ein Vergleich der Konzeptionen Karl Rahners und Hans Urs von Balthasars*. Regensburg: Verlag Friedrich Pustet, 2008.

Dalzell, G. Thomas, SM. *The Dramatic Encounter of Divine and Human Freedom in the Theology of Hans Urs von Balthasar*. Bern: Peter Lang, 1997.

Friesenhahn, Jacob. *The Trinity and Theodicy: The Trinitarian Logic of von Balthasar and the Problem of Evil*. Burlington, VT: Ashgate, 2011.

Gardner, Lucy, and David Moss. "Difference—the Immaculate Concept? The Laws of Sexual Difference in the Theology of Hans Urs von Balthasar." *Modern Theology* 14, no. 3 (July 1998): 377–401.

———. "Something like Time, Something like the Sexes—an Essay in Reception." In *Balthasar at the End of Modernity*, ed. Lucy Gardner, David Moss, Ben Quash, and Graham Ward, 69–137. Edinburgh: T & T Clark, 1999.

Krenski, Thomas R. *Passio Caritatis: Trinitarische Passiologie im Werk Hans Urs von Balthasars*. Einsiedeln: Johannes Verlag, 1990.

Lösel, Steffen. *Kreuzwege: Ein ökumenisches Gespräch mit Hans Urs von Balthasar*. Paderborn: Schöningh, 2001.

Loughlin, Gerard. "Sexing the Trinity." *New Blackfriars* 79, no. 923 (January 1998): 18–25.

Muers, Rachel. "A Question of Two Answers: Difference and Determination in Barth and von Balthasar." *The Heythrop Journal* 40 (July 1999): 265–79.

Pesarchick, Robert A. *The Trinitarian Foundation of Human Sexuality as Revealed by Christ According to Hans Urs von Balthasar: The Revelatory Significance of the Male Christ and the Male Ministerial Priesthood*. Rome: Editrice Pontificia Università Gregoriana, 2000.

Pitstick, Alyssa Lyra. *Light in Darkness: Hans Urs von Balthasar and the Catholic Doctrine of Christ's Descent into Hell.* Grand Rapids: William B. Eerdmans, 2007.

Proterra, Michael. "Hans Urs von Balthasar, Theologian." *Communio* 2, no. 3 (Fall 1975): 270–88.

Rambuss, Richard. *Closet Devotions.* Durham: Duke University Press, 1998.

Sain, Barbara K. "Through a Different Lens: Rethinking the Role of Sexual Difference in the Theology of Hans Urs von Balthasar." *Modern Theology* 25, no. 1 (January 2009): 71–96.

Speyr, Adrienne von. *Achtzehn Psalmen.* Einsiedeln: Johannes Verlag, 1957.

———. *I Korinther.* Einsiedeln: Johannes Verlag, 1956.

———. *The Letter to the Ephesians.* Trans. Adrian Walker. San Francisco: Ignatius, 1996.

———. *The World of Prayer.* Trans. Graham Harrison. San Francisco: Ignatius, 1985.

Tanner, Kathryn. *God and Creation in Christian Theology: Tyranny or Empowerment.* Minneapolis: Fortress Press, 2005 (Oxford: Blackwell, 1988).

Tonstad, Linn Marie. "The Limits of Inclusion: Queer Theology and Its Others." *Theology & Sexuality*, forthcoming.

———. "Sexual Difference and Trinitarian Death: Cross, Kenosis, and Hierarchy in the *Theo-Drama.*" *Modern Theology* 26, no. 4 (October 2010): 603–31.

Ward, Graham. *Christ and Culture.* Malden, MA: Blackwell, 2005.

———. "In the Name of the Father and of the Mother." *Literature & Theology* 8, no. 3 (September 1994): 311–27.

Williams, Rowan. "Afterword: Making Differences." In *Balthasar at the End of Modernity*, ed. Lucy Gardner, David Moss, Ben Quash, and Graham Ward, 173–79. Edinburgh: T&T Clark, 1999. (Also published as "Balthasar and Difference." In *Wrestling with Angels: Conversations in Modern Theology*, ed. Mike Higton, 77–85. Grand Rapids: William B. Eerdmans, 2007.)

# 2 Suffering Difference
## Graham Ward's Trinitarian Romance

Graham Ward stands as one of the most creative and daring theologians on the Anglo-American scene. He deftly constructs his theology in conversation with the wide range of theoretical discourses in which he is fluent. Weaving desire and difference together, he incorporates human beings into the amatory relationships that constitute the trinity. Sexual difference lies at the very heart of his theology, yet he refuses to reduce sexual difference to (hetero)sexed relationships between men and women, whether in the theological, biological, or cultural sense. He uses insights from queer theory in the development of his transcorporeal Christology, which stretches the body of Christ beyond masculinity. His erotic ecclesiology places the story of the world in the space opened up by the trinity. Instead of the atomistic self of modernity, we find ever-expanding relationships between bodied persons who distend and fracture themselves in order to include the other.

Ward's account of the relation between divine and human desire has been greeted enthusiastically by many theologians who wish to overcome the homophobia, sexism, and apparent hatred of the body that drives so much distaste for Christianity. I share their appreciation for Ward's aims, as well as for his expansive and flexible interweaving of theological, philosophical, and theoretical resources. His sophisticated use of theories of gender and sexuality avoids the sometimes flat-footed approach of those who seek authoritative legitimation of same-sex relations in the Christian tradition. Upon closer examination, however, his theology suffers from significant problems, and his attempts to address them sometimes heighten them. Ward believes that grounding Christian accounts of sexuality, eros, and desire in the trinity moves theology beyond heterosexism and homophobia while valuing desire as the constitutive element of human existence.

But Ward's insistence that relation take the form of suffering, in the trinity as elsewhere, vitiates, I argue, God's power to save, while projecting elements of human existence into God in both univocal and equivocal ways. So eager is Ward to find resources for thinking human existence in the trinity that he imports the trinity's economic involvement in history's brokenness into the immanent trinity; he thereby fails to maintain the distinction between the immanent and the economic trinity with sufficient care. Finding suffering already in the immanent trinity, he tends not to distinguish well enough between different forms of suffering; an underdeveloped hamartiology results. Finally, Ward's spatializing of trinitarian relations by making distance a trope for difference threatens to tear apart the unity of the trinity.

These problems all stem fundamentally, I suggest, from starting the search for genuine difference-in-relation in the wrong place. Starting from difference understood as separation makes the other someone to be reached via negotiation of identity and difference. That negotiation requires an intermediate term that neither overcomes separation nor identifies one with the other. But such an intermediary term has to stay frustratingly vague in order to avoid a fixing of difference. Deriving difference and relation from inner-trinitarian relations also hampers recognition of the different *kinds* of difference that pertain to divine and human personhood, respectively. This problem becomes particularly acute in Ward's transmutation of dependence on God into vulnerability, which justifies his decision to narrate the Christian self in kenotic terms. Ward assumes that boundaries between persons can be overcome only if persons make room for each other, in a fracturing that permits extensibility or a penetrating of one another through consensual violence. Ward's trinitarian account of sexual difference tries hard to correct the mistakes he uncovers in (post)modernity; unfortunately, he brings such mistakes with him into God.

I start by analyzing what Ward says about trinitarian theology *per se*, then move through the different forms the God–world relationship takes in his theology to the anthropology of difference, desire, and the erotic that, according to him, are marks of the trinitarian God in creation. In this theology of sexual difference, I show that the only place for femininity is the womb-wound installed by a spear in Jesus' side. Finally, I demonstrate that challenges pertaining to Ward's account of human relations do not just reappear in his trinitarian theology; they are grounded there.

## DIFFERENCE, DESIRE, AND EXCESS

Ward's trinitarian theology centers on the dual themes of difference and desire, which tie together relations within the trinity, between God and world, and among human beings. (The latter two are grounded in the trinity; we will come to them in due course.) Trinitarian love is fundamentally about difference, about a desire for the other that generates cycles of trinitarian gift-exchange as God the Father begets the Son and the latter joins the Father in breathing out the Spirit. Trinitarian relations of origin involve the surrender of each divine person to the others as the cycle of divine love weaves the persons together. God is a community of sorts, a community constituted by movement.

This movement is simultaneously kenotic and pleromatic, "breathing out in order to breathe in," two aspects of the same circulation of the divine life.[1] Trinitarian, and therefore Christian, desire in this way abides by a logic of excess, lavishness, "more than."[2] So the Father lavishly surrenders himself in begetting the Son, a "diremption" that nonetheless does not split the unity of the divine essence. And the Father's self-surrender finds its response in the Son's total "givenness" to the Father. The unity of the two is held open by the second difference of the Holy Spirit, who ensures that their love does not become narcissistically self-enclosed.[3] Thus genuine difference is established through the self-abnegating moments that describe the "eternal suffering intrinsic to the plenitude of love itself" (CC, 263). Kenotic self-abandonment means that even in the immanent trinity, love involves distance and a kind of fracturing that reaches its height on the cross. "Motion is ecstatic and ultimately Trinitarian; and the condition for its possibility is distance. . . . [D]istance . . . gives intimacy and enables participation. . . . The ecstatic nature of motion requires continual self-abandonment" (CC, 82). We return later to arguments Ward makes for including incarnation and cross in this inner-trinitarian suffering of distance.

Perichoresis, the reciprocal interpenetration of trinitarian persons, allows them to be internal to one another in their differences; indeed, perichoresis "constitutes the impassable triune Godhead" (CC, 82–83).[4] Perichoresis thus serves as a way of avoiding the implication of lack or unfulfillment in the trinity while holding onto some notion of not-having. Ward retains classical assertions of the unity, infinity, and non-numerical multiplicability of the divine essence. Yet he insists that this "very equality-in-difference-of-one-substance expresses the creative tensions of loving communion" (CC, 262),[5] an "intradivine passion" between Father, Son, and Spirit that expresses an "infinite capacity for self-exposition" (CC, 261) that Ward understands as suffering.[6] "Wounding" is "intrinsic to the operation of love . . . between the Persons of the Trinity" (CC, 261). Trinitarian selves, who are nothing but difference, suffer their differences from each other in their differentiation and their love.

Since love requires difference and is an appetitive craving for the other, God just *is* desire (CC, 245).[7] The condition of love is difference. *Difference* is itself the object of love; indeed, love comes from difference, expresses difference, needs difference, and gives itself over to difference.[8] Difference becomes in this way the constitutive concept of the divine. Divine difference grounds human difference in trinitarian being.[9] In giving itself, and giving itself over, each trinitarian person receives itself from the other persons in a movement of desire reflected in humankind. Desire in human beings reflects "the divine appetite" that the persons of the trinity have for each other. The infinite is indeed the endless givenness of God in love.[10] Love propels the Father into the generation of the Son, and the Son's obedient reception of the divine essence expresses itself in the Spirit who is their unity; this is the wound of love. The trinity is thus constituted by gift, a constant giving that accompanies a constant reception of the other. Such gift-giving, like divine gift-giving in general, always goes beyond expectation and demand.

God's infinite plenitude means that God's gift-giving in the inner-trinitarian circulation of love is already excessive, already a more-than, and it expresses itself outwardly in the creation of the world.

## THE TRIUNE GOD AND CREATION

Ward remains ambiguous on the relationship between the immanent and the economic trinity. His embrace of divine immutability, divine transcendence, and creation *ex nihilio* suggests no simple equation of them. He adopts Rahner's dictum[11] and affirms "[t]here is no immanent trinity that is not economic—the Godhead holds nothing back in its desire for what it has created" (CC, 151). I understand this to mean that there is no God "behind" the economic trinity (that is, that the economy reveals God as God really is). Ward's position must, however, be more complicated, for I believe his grounding of human relationality, sociality, and desire in the trinity challenges divine transcendence.

Throughout his oeuvre, Ward tries to avoid the twin dangers of univocity and equivocity in speech about the divine,[12] dangers with implications for the relationship between God and creation and so for the relationship between economic and immanent trinity. How closely does creation resemble God in Ward's account? Ward recognizes the danger of tying God so closely to creation that theology becomes projection (idolatry), yet he wishes such a tie to creation to be as close as possible. Ward joins his radically orthodox colleagues in insisting that only participation-based analogy can prevent either disconnection between God and creation or their identification.[13] But to what degree do we participate in trinitarian and Christological ways of being? Ward never quite answers such questions, although he insists that his account of analogy is not one of proportion (or correlatively of resemblance).[14] Ward says that although there is a "profound difference" between divinity and humanity, there must "exist within the nature and self-understanding of the Trinity, a quality that has affinity with what it is to be human" (CC, 106). The scope of this claim remains undeveloped, but coherence demands that it be an epistemological rather than ontological claim. Ward himself frames the claim as an ontological claim with epistemological consequences; either way, the assertion of a "quality" in the trinity's "self-understanding" with an "affinity" to the human is a very strong one.

Ward approaches the relation between God and creation in three distinguishable but related ways: through the image of *diastema*, an image of separation he takes from Gregory of Nyssa; Christologically and pneumatologically, as the missions of the Son and Spirit cross the gulf or hiatus established by the diastema; and as a kenotic reflection of an inner-trinitarian kenosis. Diastema or diastasis is, first of all, a separation or distance between God and creation that arguably presumes creation *ex nihilo*.[15] The hiatus, distance, or separation that pertains between God and creation is grounded in God's willed ordering. Something must cross this hiatus or interval between God and creation, Ward says, in order to establish a relation between them (for example, in order for the latter to be taken up into the former); here Ward seems to be forgetting that being created itself entails a relation to God.

Ward generally limits use of the terms *diastasis* and *diastema* to the relation between God and creation. But the condition for that diastasis is an inner-trinitarian kenosis or hiatus (and Ward regularly uses hiatus as a synonym for diastasis).[16] Ward is following Balthasar on this point: The hiatus between God and creation is made possible by "a hiatus and kenosis within God himself. . . . Kenosis is the disposition of love within the trinitarian community," which "is a community constituted by differences which desire the other."[17] Thinking of difference in terms of distance or "diastema" "prevents any difference, sexual or otherwise, becoming a stable marker of a living body" (CC, 153). Distance is required for desire to operate at all, and distance creates the space necessary for love.[18] "Distance cannot in fact become an identifiable object. Perhaps the closest we get to distance as such is the identification of difference" (CC, 74).[19] These kenotic distances are trinitarian, ontological, and sexual. What "hiatus" in the trinity amounts to is unclear; in classical trinitarian theology, such a hiatus is just what trinitarian differences are *not*. Much of the development of trinitarian doctrine, indeed, focused on the inseparability of trinitarian persons and the absence of any interval between them.[20]

Ward never details what the relationship is between hiatus within God and hiatus between God and creation; presumably the relationship between the two is analogical since the unity of the divine substance means that no multiplication (and so no separation) can characterize inner-trinitarian relations. Yet because the persons empty themselves in order to receive themselves from each other, Ward does indeed have to distinguish between their existence as persons and their identification with the divine essence in ways that seem to jeopardize divine unity. He never clarifies whether he identifies the persons of the trinity with subsistent relations; the latter would rule out emptying and filling as constitutive movements of divine personhood.

In the second place, the missions of the Son and Spirit into the world traverse and bridge the distance between God and creation. The Son and Spirit cross the hiatus; they come "into" the world in order to bring the world to God. In going into what is other than God, the Son expresses his eternal relation to the Father by giving himself up without holding anything back, an extension outward of his inner-trinitarian givenness to the Father.[21] This becomes particularly apparent when Ward adopts Balthasar's understanding of Christ's descent into hell: The "displacement" between the Father and the Son—that the trinity is at its "most extended"—reflects the "eternal displacements of the trinitarian processions."[22] The trinitarian relations are spatialized again here as displacements.

The third aspect of the God–creation relation is the kenosis that crosses the distance between God and creation in the self-gift of the incarnate Son whose own self-giving expresses his kenotic inner-trinitarian relation to the Father. Kenosis names the relationship between loving human and divine subjects who empty themselves for one another while receiving themselves from one another. Kenosis permits the relation between God and creation to remain one of similarity-in-difference rather than identity. Without "continuity in difference" there can be no exchange between divine and human; kenosis therefore installs the "space" that is "a womb from which the Word of God and the word of being human are both birthed" (CC, 217–18). When humans respond to Christ, they are incorporated into Christ's relation to the Father[23] so that their form of life becomes kenotic as well, expressing the love that connects human beings across difference's fractures.

The Son's kenotic relation to the Father includes "incarnation (death and resurrection)."[24] Ward argues that if the kenotic aspect of Christ were only his death, he would remain bound by "the culture of necropolis" that Ward diagnoses as the condition of modernity.[25] Ward repeatedly dismisses alternative accounts of kenosis because they are "insufficiently trinitarian";[26] they fail to take account of the trinitarian shape of the kenotic relation that secures the mutuality of self-giving in the trinity. In Christ, human sign-making is crucified and the Word is silenced, but the same trajectory culminates in the speaking of a new Word in the resurrection,[27] which is "an eternal living beyond oneself."[28] The resurrection does not, however, reverse the crucifixion. Instead, resurrection continues the intra-trinitarian displacements that led to the crucifixion.[29] Through this kenotic-incarnational story, theological speech becomes participation in the work of redemption.[30] And this possibility is grounded in the distance, and the difference, between the Father and the Son.[31] The "wide-open" difference between Father and Son installed by the trinitarian processions founds this love that operates across distance (CC, 259). Love, to be operable, must be *opened up* to and by the other. And love, as we have seen, depends on difference.

In the incarnational trajectory of Christ, the held-open difference of the trinity finds itself repeated differently across difference, in the open womb of Mary's yes-saying to God and in the womb-wound in Christ's side from which the church is birthed. These differences bring human beings into relation to God. Difference among human beings means first and foremost sexual difference, which also mirrors the relation between God and creation, to which we now turn.

## SEXUAL DIFFERENCE, TRANSCORPOREALITY, AND THE WOMB-WOUND

Ward's account of sexual difference can be tested at several crucial junctures: his critique of Karl Barth's biological essentialism, his reading of

Irigaray's "Christology," and his account of the displaced body of Jesus Christ. The importance of sexual difference to Ward's theology appears in an early essay in which Ward advances a fiery critique of inclusive language in liturgical and theological contexts.[32] He claims inclusive language ignores the possibility that syntax is already male-sexed (so that the replacement of one pronoun with another will do no good). Inclusive language erases sexual difference and replaces it with "asexuality" that "excludes *both* men and woman [sic]."[33] Instead, Ward insists "[t]here can only be salvation . . . through Christ, if there is sexual difference. Difference . . . is rooted in the difference of *hypostasis* in the Trinity" (CC, 150). Sexual difference is grounded in the erotics of the trinity.[34] The move to inclusive language prioritizes reason over language, taking language to be a pellucid vehicle for communication rather than a way of constructing human beings.[35] But, contra Ward, doesn't the move to inclusive language assume just that? Language has the power to create what it describes.

One of Ward's highest priorities in his discussion of sexual difference is to avoid biological essentialism, against what he characterizes as the essentialism of much feminist theology. Sexual difference may pertain between any two people.[36] In Ward's assessment, the "number" of sexual differences is limited only by the "number" of human beings. He suggests three main ways of avoiding biological essentialism. We already encountered the first: the connection between difference and distance, which renders difference always relative and so—Ward hopes—unstable. If difference is always a matter of relative distance or proximity, difference takes no final or fixed form. Second, Ward makes sexual difference symbolic rather than biological, in analogy to the symbolics of sexual difference developed by Luce Irigaray via her critique of Jacques Lacan. No longer do phallic or nonphallic symbolics of sexual difference map onto sexed bodies with readily interpretable genital configurations. Third, based on the connection between Christology, trinity, and the God–world difference, he argues that sexual difference is first and foremost theological rather than natural. Sexual difference becomes a theological "trope" (CG, 194), a symbolism that can express God's relation to creation in a form derived from trinitarian difference and manifest in erotic attractions between human beings.

Sexual difference has, then, the following characteristics. As the primary way of understanding human difference, it is closely tied to human embodiment. But sexual difference—gender, sexuality, and their erotics—is ultimately a theological reality reappearing in different ways: in the trinity (as desire for difference); in Christ's relation to his disciples and to his church; in the relation between God and creation; in marital relations among human beings; and in the ecclesiological implications of such relations. Sexual difference not only points to and participates in trinitarian (and ontological) difference, it "constitutes human creatures as *imago dei*" through "its endorsement of both separation and relation. . . . In attraction-in-difference is reflected the difference-in-relation in the trinitarian God" (CG, 188).

Ward brings agape and eros together as "moments of giving and receiving where giving is also receiving, and vice versa" (CG, 201). Ward's "economy of response" makes reception-in-difference the condition of love's operation, such that even Christ's divinity becomes "meaningless" without such response from us (CC, 150).

Sexual difference expresses the always-relational nature of human beings who find themselves desiring each other in an intermixture of eros and agape that distantly reflects relations among the persons of the trinity and that is bound to Christological specificity in two different ways: in the concrete, bodied relationships between Christ and his followers and in the marital union between Christ the bridegroom and his bride the Church. No wonder, then, that Ward's account of sexual difference and embodiment is so exciting to many queer-friendly, postmodern, and some feminist theologians. Consonant with a much broader cultural-theological turn to desire, sexuality, and eros as primary sites of human naming and becoming, Ward connects sexuality with God so that Christian theology has a response to dominant, but unsatisfactory, cultural logics of sex and desire.

In developing his theological account of sexual difference, Ward pays especially close attention to the relations between the bleeding woman and Christ, between Christ and Mary in the garden, and between Christ and Thomas in the upper room. Ward reads the first using imagery of "touch, flows, and relations" (CC, 61). Jesus encounters a woman who "is being drained or undergoing a kenosis, an emptying out." Her body is thus in flow. Yet in her touch, in which she makes contact with Jesus, the mobility of power-knowledge becomes apparent as his healing power—on her initiative—moves through the conduit of his body into hers. Ward connects this encounter with the healing of the deaf man and the blind man in which Jesus goes even further—penetrating the body of one and smearing the other with his "own bodily fluids" (CC, 63–67). Ward calls attention to the maleness of both participants which makes such contact a cultural possibility. Such flows are always erotic and engender the body itself: "as if the body is brought into being by that touch" (CC, 71). These exchanges, distances, and interpenetrations of touch materialize the body while making its vulnerability evident (CC, 72). Touch is an "incarnat[ion] as the Word is incarnate" through which humans "become flesh as he became flesh" (CC, 76). In such enfleshment human sociality becomes an interchange of flows (via the spatial relation that touch is) so that relations of emptying and filling are established and "caught up," Christologically, into the motions of the Godhead (CC, 74–77, 82–83).

The next two encounters take place after the resurrection in the context of "an economy of response" (CC, 120). Mary seeks but does not recognize the Lord in the garden, and Thomas refuses to accept the Lord's bodily return. Mary's touch is refused or interrupted; in contrast, Thomas is invited to "penetrate" and "thrust himself into" the womb-wound in Christ's side (although he may or may not in fact do so) (CC, 121).[37] Ward characterizes these encounters as transactions or exchanges (CC, 121–22); *what* is exchanged is simultaneous recognition and alienation, presence and absence, although it becomes difficult to understand what exchange then means beyond communication. Perhaps the knowledge of Christ, which is carnal and a form of identification, is ultimately all that is offered (CC 122–23). For Ward, such response to Christ is already salvific. Engagement with Christ requires, however, more than preaching and hope for the future, which is all Mary is left with: Thomas's encounter involves "a new and more dramatic crossing of bodily boundaries." Ward even suggests that Thomas's penetration of the Lord's "vaginal lips" may heal the (ongoing?) pain of the resurrected Christ (CC, 126).

All these relations make clear Ward's intense focus on forms of contact that connect, invade, and transform differently permeable bodies, some marked by the womb-wound.[38] Christian embodiment makes the self a place, a space, for the other to exist. Humans empty themselves for God and for each other in imitation of Christ's self-emptying love, which creates a womb-wound, a place (the church) where God may be received in the world (CC, 149–50).[39] To be a human being in a loving relation is to make oneself into a space for the existence of the other; such place making constitutes the uniqueness of each body (CG, 95).

The boundary-crossing nature of these erotic encounters leads to a discussion of the sexuality of Christ. First, Ward asks whether "we [can] really speak of incarnation if we castrate the Christ"; from there he raises the question of Christ's sexuality (CC, 142–43).[40] The immediacy of Ward's move from castration to sexuality makes one wonder whether Ward consistently holds to his own account of sexual difference as a more-than or other-than biological reality. He tries to avoid any problem here by suggesting we cannot know the totality or truth of Christ's sexuality, although we ought not "deny that Jesus has the genitalia of a male" (CC, 143). Yet, as we shall see, Jesus' genitalia as well as Jesus' symbolic gender in the Christian theological imaginary play significant roles in Ward's theology.

Ward's second starting point is the trinity, although the starting point begs the question. As he puts it, "Since desire is integral to the Trinity, to creation and to being a sexuate creature, can we cordon off discussions of [Christ's] sexuality?" Once more sexuality reappears (redundantly); to know Christ we must examine Christ's desire. Because desire requires reciprocity, Christ "can only reconcile and redeem all to the extent he is responded to," as we are drawn to Christ erotically and desirously (CC, 149). Thus Ward argues that Christ, as "[a] male figure," cannot be "the focus for salvation," since Christology depends on responsivity and response requires difference. Yet it remains the biologically and chromosomally male Christ to whom we respond, and he retains priority in that we gain access to our "divinity" only through him (CC, 150).[41] Ward therefore needs to overcome Christ's maleness in some other way.

At this point, we perform our first test of Ward's account of sexual difference: with reference to his Christ of the phallus and two lips. Ward's justification for this reading of Christ depends heavily on Irigaray's quasi-Christology.[42] He argues that Irigaray's Christic representation entails a subtle destabilization of Christ's masculinity because the wound in his side installs, symbolically, a birth canal out of which the church emerges (CC, 140). Indeed, "[t]he cross is the final qualification and disruption of Jesus's male biological form," for the cross "is a profoundly feminine symbol" for Irigaray (CC, 150). Jesus' "chromosomal structure" fails to determine his "sexuate spirituality," which attracts and engages the men and women around him. Following the resurrection, Jesus' wounded body shows "the marks in his flesh of both the male and female sex, without him being androgynous" (CC, 150). This representation installs masculinity, and divinity, as that which is interrupted by femininity—in the form of elisions between a gaping wound, natality, and death—but overcomes it through internalization. The "Word" of the Father (his phallus) comes into the male body, where he is wounded (castrated) and killed. Yet the Word cannot be overcome; instead, he accepts death's castration, only to transcend it. Christ then outdoes Mary by birthing the church from his side without external divine insemination, while remaining the head of the church as man is the head of woman. Masculinity, interrupted by femininity, takes femininity into itself, outdoes it, and subordinates it. If this were Irigaray's project, the frequent appeal to her in many feminist Christologies would be inexplicable.

But Ward's use of Irigaray suggests an undecidability in her thought that, at least in the specific texts to which he refers, misrepresents her argument.[43] Ward mainly follows Irigaray's "Epistle to the Last Christians," where she says that "[i]n the body of the Son of Man there [re]appears, in the form of a wound, the place that, in women, is naturally open" (CC, 140).[44] Ward terms this "space . . . suggestively inclusive" (CC 140), but Irigaray actually identifies this Christ as "the Christ handed down to us by tradition," the one who "does not marry/make merry with women, for already he is bound to his heavenly Father." His recourse to the transcendently paternal deity closes off access to the body of the mother, "the means by which the (male) One passes into the other. Receptacle that, faithfully, welcomes and reproduces only the will of the Father." Mary becomes place, receptacle, "a dumb virgin with lips closed [who] occasionally receives the favor of a word." This is not a suggestively inclusive space. It is a critique of the transformation of woman-Mary into envelope-place of the becoming of the Son of the Father and the "erection of his passion" through the "double closure of her lips."[45] She is written out, closed off, in order to provide a site for his triumphant fidelity to the Father.

Irigaray identifies Mary's unrestricted consent to God, her *fiat*, as "a no to her own life. . . . No to everything, except the Word of the Father."[46]

Mary herself *has* no place; she just *is* place—a reduction of woman to the womb-place that births the ultimate man through the transcendent power of paternal reproduction. Instead of "a fascination with the precious paternal seed . . . that priceless *logos spermatikos* poured into her," Irigaray calls for what we might, mimetically, term a kenosis of Christianity that will "[l]eave the Christians to their crosses."[47] For Irigaray, and perhaps we will follow her here but no further, the difference is between an openness that is irreducibly present already in the morphology of two lips and the installation of rupture as violence that opens up, by crossing, a masculine shape that in resurrection will recover the phallus while maintaining the limitedly penetrable wound of difference.[48] Christ's male body is violated by the womb-wound, but when his Father resurrects him, he takes back control over his own body. But what is "wound" in Christianity's representation of Christ is "naturally open" in women—which means there is no need for a kenotic logic, no need for the wound-womb, in order to open up what is closed. Ward thus insists on rupture where an alternative symbolic order requires no such violation.

Yet this first examination of Ward's account of sexual difference does little to explicate his theological narrative. After all, sexual difference is intended to be a theological reality. To see what this means, we turn—in our second test case—to Ward's reading of Karl Barth.[49] Ward insists that Barth (and Balthasar), "more than any other twentieth-century theologians, recognised the importance of sexual difference for theology" (CG, 188).[50] His point of departure is Barth's understanding of marriage as a "covenant through desire for the other that constitutes the image in us of the nature of the Godhead itself and the economy of relations created by reciprocal desire within the Godhead" (CG, 193). This establishes the theological form of sexual difference by taking up ("by the power of God alone"; CG, 193) the erotic and sexual difference as an analogy of the gift-relationship within the trinity and of the covenantal relationships between Christ and church and God and Israel. Yet Barth's biological essentialism locks men and women into their anatomically specific roles despite Barth's better theological instincts, which recognize sexual difference's derivation from "more fundamental (because hierarchically arranged) contexts," in the following order: "I and Thou, Self and Other, Yahweh and Israel, Christ and His Church" (CG, 196). Instead of remaining with the theological form of sexual difference expressed in these analogical relations, Barth returns to biological, natural differences between men and women. Rather than expressing mobile positions in a theological-symbolic field, "woman" becomes the helpmeet of "man" and "he" "her" leader. Against his own, better, theological impulses, Barth rejects same-sex relations because they undermine the natural order (rather than the theological) (CG, 197).

What Barth gets right is tying church-Christ, Israel-Yahweh, and self and other together analogously. Ward applauds the fact that Barth wants the second term of each pair to "rupture . . . the autonomy of the former, questioning the authority and privilege of the former" (CG, 198). The problem, Ward thinks, is that Barth's account of sexual difference does not allow sufficient difference for "woman" to allow that rupture to take place. But the gendered distribution of these analogies is actually much more worrisome. The one whose autonomy is ruptured by the divine other is symbolized as female in the *theological* logic of these analogies (not the natural logic, whatever that might mean). The church is the bride of Christ the bridegroom. If male and female are tropes, then the theological logic of these analogies makes males tropes of God and females tropes of creation.

Since Barth reads the relation between "man" and "woman" naturally rather than theologically, "woman" "is in no position to question. She can only . . . answer. She does not stand *with* man, or *before* man as other; she stands *for* man" (CG, 198). Ward does not raise the crucial objection here that standing "with" or "before" "man" does nothing to disrupt a hierarchical economy of sexual difference. Merely raising "woman" to equality with "man" allows "him" to continue as the default against which "she" is measured. Ward argues that Barth's hom(m)osexual[51] erotic economy needs to be "taken up into, governed and transformed by . . . a trinitarian erotics in which true difference between the first and the second Person is maintained by the second difference of the Spirit" (CG, 198). Hierarchical sexual difference must be corrected by trinitarian difference. His assumption—and he is not alone in this—is that Barth does not rightly see the consequences of his trinitarian theology for sexual difference. There is some remnant of unacknowledged masculinism in his hom(m)osocial theology. Thankfully, Barth can be corrected through his own work (when framed in Ward's terms) by tying sexual difference even more closely to trinitarian difference. This correction will save both divine and human difference, rendering the latter significant by situating it in the former, and in so doing, constituting the salvation of our age's concern for sexual difference by showing forth a God who is no mere male—as Rowan Williams suggested regarding Balthasar in chapter 1.

Ward's reading of Barth culminates in the development of a more properly theological account of sexual difference via marriage and the church. Marriage "constitutes the basis for ecclesiology open to an eschatological horizon," and since marriage ("the becoming of 'one flesh'") grounds ecclesiology, marriage images the "intratrinitarian community" (CG, 187). This analogy, as Ward specifies, runs from above down (through Christ). But Ward does not justify what is in fact an odd claim. If marriage symbolizes and materially enacts the possibility of two persons becoming one flesh, and becoming one flesh is the form of ecclesial community in the nuptial relation between Christ and the church, then marriage participates in the Christ-church relation. But then marriage takes its significance from ecclesiology rather than the reverse. The ecclesial community is grounded in the intratrinitarian community, which is the condition of possibility for all kinds of union without the erasure of difference, so both ecclesiology and marriage should depend on the intratrinitarian community.

But none of these gets us an image of the immanent trinity, unless such images are found wherever difference is loved, since difference is "[w]hat is loved in love" (CG, 201). (If such a claim is to make sense, Ward must mean that the intervention of difference is the condition for love.) Ward specifies that his "teaching on 'marriage' here, . . . would only imply a radical critique against solipsism and ideologies of self-sufficiency" (CG, 235). One has to wonder who the implied others enamored of solipsism and an ideology of self-sufficiency are; given his critiques of capitalism in other portions of the text, perhaps he is thinking of his imagined capitalist subject. But in the current shape of capitalism, fractured subjects in relations to others are everywhere; indeed, the valorization of vulnerability and what Ward terms "frangibility" is very much of our cultural moment. So the theological contribution that Ward is making—relationality is good, identities are not self-enclosed—appears rather anemic.

Ward argues that seeing same-sex marriages as relations that maintain genuine (heterosexual)[52] difference will dismantle theological tendencies toward heterosexism and biological essentialism. Same-sex relationships, without the distortions of heteronormativity, point toward the graced nature of the divinely established analogy between trinitarian, ontological, and sexual difference (CG, 200–01).[53] The work of the church is to "sanctify" and "discern difference in all the relationships it sanctifies" (CG, 202). (What work the church's "discernment" of difference adds to its sanctification of marriage remains unclear.) The church must do this work for same-sex relationships as well as those recognized as heterosexual. "The labour of trinitarian love—of difference, in difference, from difference, to difference—prescribes the relation of the Godhead to creation and the relation that is possible between two women, two men or a man and a woman" (CG, 201–02), establishing difference beyond the biological. This nonbiological sexual difference becomes the salvation of the world as it "participates analogically in trinitarian difference, while maintaining the ontological difference which enables the suspension of all that is and becomes in this world within the perfection of God's own transcendent being" (CG, 202). Sexual difference constitutes human creatures as the image of God because sexual difference "endorses" separation and relation at the same time, so reflecting trinitarian difference.

The story Ward tells is surprisingly familiar—a standard theology of marriage in which marriage reflects the nuptial union between Christ and the church, which itself is the Christian specification of the union between Yahweh and Israel. Ward adds more erotic language and permits such union to be imaged by same-sex couples as well as by heterosexual ones, but otherwise nothing has shifted. Ward even adopts perhaps the most contestable aspect of such accounts, the implication that the creator–creation relationship is gendered and sexed: "the Christian tradition provides overwhelming evidence of thinking through divinity and sexuality in 'marital terms' " (CC, 146 n.65).[54] These marital terms include the covenant relationship between

Israel the whore/bride and her husband/master YHWH; the marital relation between Jesus and his mother, Mary, enacted when the risen Christ, the bridegroom, takes the church he births as his bride; and the incorporation of the church into a body of which Christ is the head—all relationships whose expression of the relation between creator and creature depends on a hierarchical relation between (a) man and (a) woman. Ward valiantly hopes to show that the destabilization of heteronormativity in same-sex unions will undo the symbolic effect of these images, especially when combined with the transcorporeal nature, and therefore unstable sex, of the body of Christ. So to Christ's body we must now turn—in our third examination of Ward's use of sexual difference.

Ward's examination of the body of Christ starts from desire for Christ. Christology depends on response, and such response includes the erotic, which embraces the gendered and the sexual, "the very mark of embodiment itself." Yet in encounter with the divine, the sexual is reordered. The category of embodiment broadens as the body becomes "a temple of the Spirit . . . holy . . . graced . . . transcending our understanding" (CC, 160–61). On this basis, "the gendered relations . . . *are* queered. For they render unstable the categories of sexual difference." Ward refers back at this point to his discussion of Irigaray, returning us to Christ's phallic, two-lipped body. He continues, "It is not that gender disappears. Gender is not transcended. It is, rather, rendered part of a more profound mystery: the mystery of relation itself between God and human beings. Given over sacrificially to God, I am subsequently found in God to be most myself, my sexual, gendered and gendering self. But I have to be taught what it means to be such a self by the Christ who draws me into a kenotic relationship with him. It is then the very maleness of the body of Jesus Christ crucified and resurrected that comes to determine how I understand my own embodiment" (CC, 161). Given his argument so far, the abrupt confrontation with the biological, transhistorical, resurrected masculinity or maleness of Christ draws one up short, especially when it becomes apparent that Christ's *circumcision* is the mark of embodiment, and so of incarnation.

Circumcision "marks a boundary of inclusion and exclusion"; it joins theological and theoretical accounts of the body and marks the fullness of incarnation—Christ's "gendered corporeality" (CC, 165). Lukan circumcision, serving first as assurance of Christ's faithfulness to Jewish law, comes in patristic and liturgical contexts to imply self-sacrifice, redemption, and resurrection (CC, 171). This transformation, Ward suggests, *erases* the materiality of the body so that "we are no longer talking about . . . the mutilation of sexual organs" or about "the cutting of male flesh, an incision into masculinity itself" (CC, 172). These ways of characterizing the act of circumcision once again disturb, given Ward's symbolic rather than biological sexual difference. Here, masculinity stands reduced to the relation between the foreskin and the penis.

Ward holds onto the symbolic and political nature of embodiment; ultimately, reflections on the body of Christ are forms of participation in the triune God, "that which constitutes the very participation of the human in the divine" (CC, 177). The Word, the condition of interpretation, is always on the move throughout history in the continual expansion and transformation of the church (the body of Christ). Since the church conditions theological reflection on the body of Christ, such reflection becomes a form of response to the divine and as such it participates in the very movements of the triune God. These reflections depend on return to, and relation with, "the actual physical body of Jesus Christ" in its eucharistic dissemination (CC, 177–78).[55] Bodies are fractured and fissured; in such fracturing, they are opened up to further expansion and growth. "Only as such can the wounding, can the differences, image the intradivine wounding, the intradivine differences, of the Godhead" (CG, 95). Pursuing the embodiment of the Logos leads us into "the profound mystery of embodiment itself," since we never encounter a body that can be fixed and held in place as a fully knowable object of our inquiry. Such inquiry "is an incarnational act itself, a theological materialism in which the body of Christ is constituted" (CC, 178). While Ward rightly wants to avoid materialist reductionism, this body is rendered ethereal, created only by the theological imagination. As an alternative to contemporary cultural obsessions with the body, perfectible and disappearing (CC, 179), Ward offers a "return to the wounded and violated body of Christ: the body as always in some sense circumcised and in need of circumcision. What knowledge issues . . . from the wounded body about the wounded gendered body?" (CC, 180).

We need to consider for a moment the various transpositions and elisions in the argument we have just recounted. The gendered body is equated by Ward with the circumcised body; all bodies need circumcision; participation in the unfolding hermeneutics of the triune God's relation to creation depends on a connection to the physical materiality of Jesus, which, we have seen, centers on the violated penis, masculinity's wound. Ward worries that an uncircumcised body lends itself to visions of perfectibility rather than fragmentation and laceration. The transgression and sacrifice of perfectibility take place in the dual images of the circumcised and crucified body. In each case, visible fragmentation is the violation of masculinity—in the first case, via the cut performed on the penis, and in the second case via the installation of the wound-womb in Jesus' side. The symbolic positions available reduce to identification with phallic plenitude or the laceration of phallic plenitude via femininity's cut. Invisible once more is the symbolism of a body neither identifiable with plenitude nor in need of circumcision—a female body.

If Ward reduces embodiment to our theologizing in response to the Logos, the body becomes dematerialized. If he instead reduces Christ's embodiment to the biology of his violated male organ, he transgresses his own strictures about the nature of gender, sexuality, and sexual difference. (Arguably, the identification of maleness and masculinity with the organ of the penis has already done that.) Ward's transcorporeal body of Christ intends to avoid the trap of these alternatives. Transcorporeality permits the expansive transformation of multiple bodies without the disappearance of any of them. Transcorporeality names "a series of displacements or assumptions of the male body of Jesus Christ such that the body of Christ . . . become[s] multi-gendered." Eventually, "the particularities of one sex give way to the particularities of bodies which are male and female."[56]

Ward assumes here that the displacements in which Jesus' body and bodied identity participates derive from and mirror the "eternal displacements of the trinitarian processions." These displacements (Ward uses expansion, transformation, and cancellation equivalently) entail "[d]isplacement [without loss] of identity itself," so displacement constitutes "the mark of God within creation."[57] Such displacement, Ward maintains, allows for the transformation of gendered and bodied specificity without final loss of earlier forms of identification. As with his understanding of analogy, displacement suggests simply "similar but different," without any further specification of what those similarities and differences amount to (since specifying suggests an analogy of proportion). Yet newer forms must overtake earlier ones if Ward is to achieve what he wants, especially given the importance of the church's genetic connection to Jesus' circumcised penis. More worrisome for his argument is that trinitarian "displacements" are *not* the displacement of the identity of trinitarian persons (as he suggests) but what constitutes the very identity of those persons. The Father simply *is* fatherhood; the Son simply *is* sonship, and so on. Trinitarian personal identity is entirely relational—it is relation as identity.

Ward wants to undermine the fixity of Christ's masculinity. Christ has no "male progenitor"; instead, God is his Father.[58] His "XY *chromosomal maleness . . . issues from the XX chromosomal femaleness of his mother as miracle.*"[59] The destabilization of Christ's maleness depends on the *true*— "formal, rather than material"—Fatherhood of God, yet even here Ward cannot resist making use of a reductive notion of the biological.[60] Ward traces further series of transformations that broaden Jesus' masculinity via transfiguration, eucharist, crucifixion, resurrection, and ascension.[61] In the transfiguration, Christ's body serves not as an object of our attraction but as a medium of our desire for God. This "erotic economy" may include a sexual element, although he insists that "this man cannot be fetishized, because he exceeds appropriation." His physical body points beyond itself to God (when we "view . . . him through God as God").[62] But the transfiguration of the body (and it is worth noting that Moses and Elijah appear as well, although Ward has nothing to say about their embodiment[63]) engenders *fright*, even *terror*, not desire, in the disciples who witness it. Attraction disappears, along with other details of the text difficult to square with Ward's own position ("we are silenced, like James and John, before this Christic sublime"[64]—no mention of the ambiguities of Peter's response).

The second form of displacement is a surrender in which the body extends to incorporate bread within itself, although the relation between surrender and extensibility is unclear. The body becomes both male and neuter, Ward suggests, thereby eliding the difference between Jesus' body and the bread-body Jesus assumes.[65] Either Jesus' body extends to incorporate the bread-body (in which case, might not the bread-body be transformed so that the revelation is not of the displacement of Jesus' masculinity but of the sexing of things?), or Jesus transmutes the bread into his own body, in which case, in order to be *his* in his specificity as Ward defines it, the bread would have to become masculine. Alternatively, a separation between Jesus as person and his body must be assumed in which the *person* may be unsexed while having both a male and a neuter body—but we have learned that it is just in his chromosomal male embodiment that we encounter Jesus' full humanity.

In the third form of displacement, Jesus becomes passive, naked, and vulnerable in the erotic and sexual power play of crucifixion.[66] Jesus' maleness is again displaced: "This is a man among men; no sexual differentiation is taken account of."[67] Ward grounds this displacement in the objectification of Jesus' body, but of course objectification does not entail the erasure of gendered specificity, especially if Jesus is a man among men. (The hom(m)o-sociality of this scene *is* masculinity, not its erasure.[68]) Ward also bases the displacement of maleness on the reduction of Jesus to "mere flesh" on the cross. Yet only as Jesus remains identified with his body is *he* crucified; unless Christ is materially dehumanized before his death (undoing incarnation), his mere flesh remains that of the male Jesus Christ.[69] We have already examined problems with the way Ward establishes a hermaphroditic Christ[70] through the violent installation of a wound-womb in his side; the same worrisome logic returns when Ward genders the "pain and suffering of the crucifixion" as "the labour pains of birthing."[71] Brought into the space of crucifixion, Christians cross the boundaries of gender: "Men will become mothers . . . [and] women will become virile."[72] Ward admits (in a footnote) that transition from male to female is not valued as highly as transition from female to male in the patristic and medieval contexts from which such imagery derives, but he wishes to endorse the transformation of gender while leaving privileged masculinity behind.[73]

Ward's ideal Christian self is always "fissured."[74] Even in resurrection, it participates in the eucharistic fracturing of the church; *to be created*, to be made "out of" nothing, is to be fissured. The human problem is that we do not belong to ourselves, for all that we are depends on and is given us by God. The human must be disciplined, broken apart, fissured, forced into the recognition of the "lack of foundations within oneself which requires and enables the reception of divine plenitude."[75] The self, it seems, can have divine plenitude added to it only if it recognizes that it does not have it, but here Ward confuses the effects of sin with those of finitude. To have one's foundations outside oneself would not, for a merely finite creature, be a problem or a loss, and neither would it require breaking: One might walk and talk with God in the cool of the evening. Finitude still involves forms of limitation that union with God transcends, but such losses turn into evils only under conditions of sin.[76] Under sin, finitude turns into desire for self-possession and unwillingness to admit one's dependence. Neither condition is endemic to finitude.[77] Ward does not adequately consider the difference that sin makes to finitude, and derivatively, to the work of Christ.

In the resurrection, Ward suggests, the "ability to . . . walk through walls . . . is countered by a corporeality which is tangible and able to eat." These bodies of Jesus are "not literally identical";[78] the relation between them is analogical. How, then, does Jesus' masculinity disappear or find itself replaced? Or differently, to *what* are these bodies analogical? Analogy requires analogues *of* something. In a later addition to the "Bodies" essay, Ward discovers another gendered displacement. Since the body of Christ is replaced by the witness of the church, and the first witnesses are female, Ward suggests that "those gendered feminine [may] more easily recognize the analogical nature of embodiment than those living within and practising the patriarchal logics of Aristotelian identification."[79] Such a suggestion, with its implication that women live outside patriarchy (rather than inside and under it) and so develop a deep wisdom unavailable to male logic, may not be the best way to combat sexism.

In the last displacement of ascension, the "gendered body of Jesus Christ" becomes "the multi-gendered body of the Church." And it is from the church's reflection on Jesus that we need to think the body of Christ: "we can only examine what the Church is and what it has to say concerning the nature of that body."[80] But it is of course *the church's reflection on the body of Christ* in word and act that has created the problem Ward's essay seeks to dissolve: the male God and his reflection in the Christian prioritization of male over female in priesthood and practice. Ward says that "[t]he Church is now the body of Christ,"[81] but given his understanding of identity, displacement, and deferral, this cannot mean simple replacement. Since the church in the power of the Spirit continues to live out of Christ (that is, its origin in Christ does not reduce to the once-upon-a-time loss of his reductively identified material body), the male, circumcised body of Christ remains its head. Ward's attempt to claim Christian orthodoxy for his vision of Christianity and sexuality fails to grapple with the complexity of Christian assertions and practices in this regard, and his high ecclesiology cannot account for the intensity with which the church continues to hold onto the significance of the maleness of Christ's body—a significance that Ward retains as well.

Ultimately, all bodies are "permable, transcorporeal and transpositional" in their unification into a single body, following Galatians 3:28.[82] But the oneness offered in Jesus is either *not* multigendered (for now there is neither male nor female[83]), or else it is a unity that does not erase the specific differences of religious insider and outsider (Jew/Greek), slave and master, and male and female, in which case Jesus' own specificity would have to be "analogously" maintained. The addition or incorporation of female bodies in Jesus' male body (which remains the genetic progenitor of the church as well as its head) would not undo the maleness of that body unless the logic of transposition were one of replacement. Even if his "church"-body incorporates members of multiple genders, the church remains also his theological bride—producing again the very problem that Ward intends to solve.

Ward grants surprising significance to the biological maleness of Christ even as he asserts that the transcorporeal body of Christ becomes multigendered in a way that overcomes the hierarchical relation between "man" and "woman" in the Christian imaginary. In practice, his assertion that there may be as many genders as persons has little theological heft. But his reading of the theological nature of sexual difference might rescue him, and it is to that we now turn.

## ALLEGORICAL SEXES, THEOLOGICAL TROPES, AND TRINITARIAN DIFFERENCE

Ward's enemy in theological accounts of sexual difference is essentialism, not the gendering of the God–world relation—indeed, he needs the latter. Sexual difference images trinitarian difference across ontological difference, without the two becoming identical. The relation focuses on the person of Christ, whose erotic relations encompass both. But gendering the God–world relation will have to be based, for Ward's account to work, in the theological symbol-set available,[84] and that theological symbol-set is heterosexual in quite specific ways.

Sexual difference signifies (analogizes or allegorizes) trinitarian and ontological difference: sexual difference has theological significance because it is "about" the trinity and participates in the trinity's establishment of difference. As Mark Jordan says, in contemporary Christian theology, "male-female complementarity becomes not only a universal moral regulation but a cosmic fact and a key to the inner life of the Trinity."[85] Jordan assigns this development to the "incestuous" Christian discourses about sex that happen under the regime of sexuality after the death of God, who was replaced by "a better-sexed divinity" and the divinization of "better-managed *human* sex."[86]

The acknowledgment that the regime of sexuality begins after the death of God may raise suspicion among well-read and historically sensitive theologians that this connection is a local theological mistake that could be corrected by better catechetical education,[87] by recognizing and restricting the scope of sexed (paternal-filial) language in the trinity,[88] or as in Ward, by removing human, male–female complementarity from the equation. The intercalation of divine and human difference through an encompassing erotics promises, Ward suggests, to unveil the true face of the new deity who rules under the aegis of sexuality: He is the dead-now-living God, the trinitarian God who has difference already within himself, and from whose self-constitution, self-expression, and self-expropriation sexual difference is to be thought in theological terms.

Yet the oneness of the trinity is quite different from whatever possibilities of union pertain to intra-human relations, so the relationship between these analogates must be a distant one indeed, especially if *any* attraction-in-difference reflects the triune God. Ward's assumption must be that there are no two persons of the "same" sex because humankind through grace reflects the infinity of trinitarian difference. Personhood in the trinity indicates incommunicability or particularity, so reading sexual difference as a trope for the particularity of any human being means that to be in relation with any particular other is a way to image the God who is always in relation with the other in Godself. But the sexual aspect plays no role, theologically or otherwise, in such an account—and the theology of relation sketched here is so desiccated as to be virtually empty. The sexuality of difference disappears, and that is in no way what Ward is after, precisely because he sees sexual difference as a symbolic and theological reality. If sexuality, eros, and desire become such expansive categories that they name any type of human relating, they become useless for all purposes of distinction. If sexuality and eros remain specific to sexual difference, Ward would have to argue for the priority of sexuality over other forms of human desiring and relating, rather than simply assuming it.[89] Why, for instance, is marriage (as the foundation of ecclesiology) granted priority over adoptive relations specifically, over parental relations more generally, and over siblinghood? After all, the "first" inner-trinitarian relation is between Father and Son, and Christ's "marital" union with the church extends his "sonship" to the rest of his adopted siblings, with whom he becomes one flesh. Nor can Ward's expansive erotics account for the priority of marriage over friendship rather than the reverse. Further, the nature of trinitarian difference is that each trinitarian person "has" the others—love as *having*, enjoying, in fullness.

Theologically speaking, imaging God in creation through sexual difference depends on symbolism that is gendered in ways irreducible to the biological essentialism that is Ward's primary fear.[90] The available theological symbol set offers only a limited number of positions. The symbolics of sexual difference are hierarchically heterosexual everywhere. The relationship between Christ and the church is a heterosexual relationship, as is the relation between Yahweh and Israel. Christ's transcorporeally inclusive body never cancels out his circumcision. These are not only heterosexual relationships; they are heterosexual relationships in which priority is given to the male over the female, and heterosexual relationships in which—even more—masculinity signifies, symbolizes, divinity. Allowing same-sex relationships to stand in for these theological symbolics of gender only serves to emphasize that heterosexual difference is a theological rather than a natural logic. In this logic, it is not by nature that men are ordered above women;

it is by grace. It is not by nature that women are oriented to men; it is by grace and election.

The very nature of the symbolic order of sexual difference is that the terms of symbolization themselves are already hierarchically ordered. The nature of symbolization of "woman" is one in which "she" is excluded just where "she" is represented. "Woman" is represented either as unrepresentable or as the mysterious "other" of "man"; both representations fail to represent difference. The "rupturing" of the autonomy of one by the other heightens rather than undoes this problem. The relations between Yahweh and His Israel, and Christ and His Church, authorize this hierarchically ordered symbolics of sexual difference theologically and reinforce it culturally. This is true not only in the natural or cultural (as opposed to "Christian") order of sexual difference, but most of all in the very symbolic logic of the Christian theological tropes that Ward finds so promising.

The theological problem does not lie in reversion to naturalized sexual difference grounded in biology; the problem lies in the symbolics of sexual difference, which cannot be used to signify ontological difference without masculinizing God and rendering "Him" an idol while gendering creation feminine in relation to "Him." Sexual difference cannot simply be reinvented theologically to get us beyond heterosexuality, for it is the theological ordering of sexual difference that grounds and authorizes the hierarchical ordering of "man" and "woman" in the Christian imaginary. Opposition to the ordination of women or same-sex marriage is, in many forms of Christianity, grounded in a *theological* rationale that derives sexual difference from the relationship of Christ and the church. Heterosexual difference in the Christian imaginary is already theological all the way down. Trinitarian difference-in-relation, equality-in-hierarchy, order-without-inequality does not *challenge* the logic that allows for hierarchical sexual difference; it *exhibits* and *grounds* it in a logic of origin and in an account of trinitarian difference that sees distinction always as the threat of violence, the need for sacrifice in a debt-economy of scarcity, and the necessity of suffering death. Ward optimistically assigns the failure in theological thinking of gender to importation of "secular" gender theory, but—at least inside the Christian imaginary—this gets the relationship precisely wrong.

In the architectonic structure of the Christian imaginary, the relationships between Christ and His Church, Yahweh and His Israel, Jesus and His Mary, Adam and His Eve, and the Father and His Son exhibit and generate hierarchically gendered orders of sexual difference. The conjunction *"and"* in the theological symbolics of sexual difference seen in this list means that the second term *comes from* the first, and at the top of the list we find the Father.[91] Even if all these men are not male—if these iterations of God are not "man"—and are made transcorporeally inclusive of sexual differences, a floating and transforming (purportedly nonphallic) paternity (*comes from*) continues to structure the Christian theological imaginary of sexual difference. This is true twice over in the trinity, as the Son, the Spirit, and even the Father move around and through the various positions allowable inside a symbolic imaginary of sexual difference that depends on "coming from" for difference and on self-emptying for relation. Even the servanthood of Christ, which makes obedience proper to God, belongs to Christ the Son as the one who *comes from* God the Father.

Ward writes as though the theological deconstruction of heterosexual difference is an accomplished fact. Adding same-sex unions, an oddly straight outcome of divine "genderfucking" (CC, 262), is the only missing piece of the Christian symbolics of sexual difference. The establishment of genuine difference beyond essentialism or hom(m)osociality has been accomplished in God, through the second difference of the Holy Spirit, and this difference is imaged in the infinity of human sexual difference. Therefore, theology must advance a closer account of the relationship between trinitarian and sexual difference, he thinks. And so it is time for us to go in search of the trinitarian "body," the textual incarnation[92] of the divine relations. Ward's account of sexual difference has its problems, but those mistakes are in large part grounded in his trinitarian theology. Trinitarian "bodies," the spatial and relational logics of the divine persons, are the ground of all other analogical bodies in Ward. In their bodies, we find the womb-wound of trinitarian relationality.

Ward wants to preserve the "differences of difference"—that is, he does not want to identify humankind with God, nor does he want to say that the differences between God and God, between God and humans, and between human beings are the same kind of thing; they are analogously related through participation. As we have seen, how strong this participation is cannot be discovered directly from Ward's text, since he never quite addresses the question.[93] And in practice, that question may be the wrong one to ask him.

## SUFFERING DIFFERENCE

In testing Ward's trinitarian theology, it becomes apparent what form of personhood he grants the Father, Son, and Holy Spirit, and how difference comes to be deployed as a relation of suffering. Ward holds that trinitarian love involves a form of eternal suffering in the very being of God. In an astonishing passage, he explains the nature of that suffering.

> [W]e need to explore the economy of that loving which incarnates the very logic of sacrifice as the endless giving (which is also a giving-up, a kenosis) and the endless reception (which is also an opening up towards the other in order to be filled). The suffering and sacrifice which is born of and born by passion is the very risk and labour of love; a love which is profoundly erotic and, to employ a queer theory term, genderfucking. It is a suffering engendered by and vouchsafing difference; first

Trinitarian difference, subsequently, ontological difference between the uncreated Godhead and creation, and finally sexual difference as that which pertains most closely to human embodiment. But here is not the valorisation of difference as such, only difference in relation to the oneness of God. . . . For the suffering and the sacrifice participate in a redemptive process; they are moments in what is finally a doxological movement. . . . *The primordial suffering is the suffering of loving and being loved.*[94]

The nature of erotic love involves a suffering connected to passion; that suffering establishes and maintains trinitarian difference as well as the relationship between God and creation and between human beings; the movements of love involve the reciprocity and simultaneity of giving up and opening up; and there is an eternal suffering of love that grounds all other forms of suffering. Ward's apparent derivation of this trinitarian structure from his account of erotic love goes understandably unmarked in the text, as it would fundamentally threaten the analogical order that he seeks. But his description of eros is the missing link. Eros makes one "vulnerable because receptive. . . . an eros that classically cannot be entirely divorced from suffering and subjection" (CC, 109).[95] *Receptivity* entails *vulnerability* and *dependence* (even in reciprocity) involves vulnerability; thus love itself is suffering.[96]

Ward figures this vulnerability as "the demands of being absolutely dependent that touch fosters" (CC, 109). So touch renders the body vulnerable, and refusal of such vulnerability turns erotic relations into relations of consumption. Schleiermacher is the source of the concept of absolute dependence. But Schleiermacher distinguishes between absolute dependence as a relation to God and relative freedom and dependence in relation to the world. Schleiermacher argues that, because we have the experience of relative freedom in relation to the world, we can never find ourselves absolutely dependent on anything within the world—indeed, to do so would be the grossest form of idolatry. To be created means precisely that no dependence on anything other than God can be absolute. Rather, in our experience of relative freedom and determination in relation to the world, we find that we have not made ourselves, what Schleiermacher terms the element of *Sich-selbstnichtsogesetzthaben*.[97] For him, absolute dependence on God is strictly distinguished from the relative dependence we experience in the world. To be absolutely dependent on God means precisely *not* to be absolutely dependent on anything else, even on those who would destroy the body, in biblical language. Instead, such dependence permits, in Søren Kierkegaard's terms, resting tranquilly in the power that established us, the deep wellspring underlying the quiet pond that overflows in an always-more-than-enough relation of dependence that permits free giving.[98]

Ward goes in almost exactly the opposite direction. He does not maintain a strict distinction between dependence on God and dependence on others.

Instead, he brings the experiences of dependence's (potential and actual) distortions that are endemic to finite and especially sinful human existence into the constitution of the trinity. Ward subsumes even inner-trinitarian "giving" and glorification into an economy of debt relationships and scarcity where love entails a vulnerability that constitutes suffering. Suffering "adheres" to love "and seeks . . . the glorification of the other" (CC, 262). But under what conditions might glorifying another be "suffering"? Only under conditions where there is not enough glorification to go around, where glorification of another comes at the expense ("expenditure"?) of the self. Glorification is costly in an economy of scarcity, it is true. Glorification of God, in contestation with idols who also seek glory, may also be costly. But in the "infinite plenitude" of the divine being, what cost pertains to the *inner-trinitarian* relations?

Distinction itself—difference itself—*is* suffering, on Ward's account. "The primordial suffering, then, is a passion of utter givenness through the excess of contact[99] within the Godhead itself, which is given expression in the very act of creation so that a certain suffering is endemic to incarnate living, a *suffering that always made possible the sacrifice on the cross*" (CC, 262; emphasis added). Note the sequence: utter givenness is connected with touch—which in the trinity means interpenetration, intelligibility, and handing oneself over to the other—and with begetting and (via the *filioque*) spiration. Difference becomes intrinsically a form of suffering; thus the differences of difference collapse into a single story of suffering across the "hiatus" between God and the world. To be different from another is to suffer, a suffering that in incarnate living entails sacrifice. When Ward distinguishes between suffering "which undoes the economics of sin through a therapy of desire," and suffering as a consequence of sin, "which undoes the orders of grace that sustain creation in its being" (CC, 254), he recognizes that these moves tread "dangerously close to a theological justification for suffering" (CC, 262). That is a severe understatement, since Ward connects both forms of suffering to the cross and argues that there is "a foundational giving" that is "extravagant and costly"—namely, the origin of the Son and Spirit in the Father (CC, 255).[100] These inner-trinitarian differences express themselves in handing oneself over to another: the Father to the Son in the Son's begetting, and the Son to the Father in eucharistic thanksgiving, a thanksgiving that renders the Son the eternal sacrifice. Expressed outwardly, even "[c]reation . . . issues from a certain kenotic giving, a logic of sacrifice that always made possible the Passion of Jesus Christ on the cross" (CC 255).[101]

To render creation kenotic violates its utter gratuity. The utter gratuity of creation, its *ex nihilo* status, entails that the world is not made out of God's kenotic self-emptying. Nor could creation somehow encroach on God (requiring God to move aside in a kenotic or withdrawing move) since it is just in its relation *to* God—its utter dependence on God—that creation exists at all. Yet more surprisingly (to introduce a distinction without a separation), it is not merely *Christ*, on this kenotic account, who is utterly given to the Father: it is the *Son*. Indeed, *sonship* is to be so given, a radical-ization indeed of the eternal election of Jesus Christ that misses the central point of such an eternal election (God-for-us, no God who did not already love the world).

Ward argues that "givenness, that comes with recognising that all is gift, each thing is given-over-to, announces a sacrificial logic distinct from a suffering that is the effect of sin." The first intimations of this logic are connected to the body which finds itself "exposed, naked to the world . . . perpetually kenotic and impassioned" (CC, 254–55). This sacrificial given-ness or primordial suffering "concerns the divine economy with respect both to its internal relations and its creation" (CC, 255). What bodies experience, in the vulnerability that makes up their intimately distant relations with others, expresses not a characteristic of creation's frangibility and finitude but the specific particularity of distinction that belongs to the totality of the Son's givenness to the Father.[102] The givenness of the Son requires a logic of gift belonging to the immanent trinity in which being given oneself (that is, being begotten) engenders gratitude's obligation in the trinitarian order. More strongly, though, if the Son's givenness bespeaks his trinitarian consti-tution in the order of origin, we find that the hiatus of trinitarian distinction is the subjugation of all under the logic of nothing for free and so nothing for grace.[103] So the persons of the trinity are textually embodied in just the ways in which human beings are embodied, and their relations to each other are construed in a manner derived from the spatiality and destructibility of the finite body.

To be given over to is to suffer, and to be given (even oneself)—as gift—is to suffer. *Givenness* joins these elements to each other, and givenness belongs to the inner-trinitarian relations of glorification, begetting, and emptying in order to be filled. This implies that *sonship* itself constitutes sacrifice. To be a son is to have one's origin outside of oneself. To be given oneself is *already* to be made into a sacrifice in virtue of the costly extravagance of differentia-tion; thus, inner-trinitarian processions are sacrificial. To owe one's being to the love of another already makes (one) a sacrifice; to be a son is to be a sacrifice. One could interpret the Son's eucharistic sacrifice to the Father on the cross as the enactment of one of love's myriad possibilities,[104] an emer-gency measure in response to the scarcities that constitute human existence under conditions not only of finitude but also of sin. Instead, such sacrifice becomes the nature of (even trinitarian) love itself. Sin may have suffering as one of its consequences, but there is also, primordially, a trinitarian suf-fering that began prior to the fall (and it is clear, this suffering is not merely a retroactive side effect of a certain future fall) (CC, 255). Suffering belongs to the nature of God's own being; it is enacted in the multiple dynamics brought together in Christ's straight road to the cross. There is no free gift in this economy.

Ward, like many contemporary trinitarian theologians, believes that the trinity grounds a concept of selfhood that can resist the monadic, nihilistic, death-driven, consumptive, and fictively autonomous subjectivities installed by modernity. The common critique of so-called social trinitarianisms is that they require divine persons who are autonomous centers of rational action and so necessitate three distinct divine beings related in some under-specified or incoherent way.[105] Ward's trinitarianism, which is a reworked social trinitarianism, maintains the unity of the divine *ousia* though insisting on trinitarian "community." The problem of the divine community in his case (and increasingly in the field of contemporary trinitarian theology) is not that he writes autonomy, rationality, and subjectivity in their now-pejorative Enlightenment senses into the trinity, nor even in concerns about the multiplication of substances in God. Instead, the problem is the strong relationship between the being of God in the concrete hypostases of the trinity and the ideal relations between human beings that his theology seeks to advocate. This trinitarianism seeks to forestall self-seeking and self-enclosure on the human *and* on the divine side.

The mistake Ward makes comes from a laudable desire to look to the cross for the revelation of the nature of divine love and to ensure that Christian accounts of love do not seem too far removed from the material conditions under which human beings exist. This, though, is where a stronger focus on resurrection and a better distinction between economic and immanent trinity—the condition of recognizing the "for us and for our salvation" of divine action in the world—would help Ward. He could then more adequately distinguish between the nature of divine, trinitarian love; its nature when extended into a world of finitude and sin; and its transformative capacity in humans. Instead, Ward's trinity is a corrective projection based on what he believes is necessary to generate the ethically and imaginatively constituted *human* subjects he hopes to produce.[106]

We recall at this point that Ward seeks a Christian account of reality that can counter what he sees as the nihilism of the modern age, an age that is not ontologically founded on a reality greater than itself but in which finitude's limitations and sin's perversions appear to be the best that humankind can hope for. Modernity, on his reading, flattens out all logics of difference into a single immanent plane; therefore, Christianity counters by reestablishing participation as a form of relation between the infinite and the finite that seeks to overcome any simple opposition between them. Affinities, similarities, likenesses, and analogies make up such differences-in-relation. In so countering, however, Ward's fears generate his theological claims. He tells the Christian story in ways that he hopes will provide an alternative, but the way he develops the alternative simply turns the assumptions he discovers in the current secular order on their head—an odd, but by no means unprecedented, form of projectionism.

The kenotic form of all relationality, the relationship between difference, distance, and suffering, and the connection between sonship and excessive "givenness" to another that constitutes the trinitarian relations, ground thrice over a concept of the self that is anything but "naturally" open to the other, and establishes the nature of bodied personhood (divine and human[107]) as a practice of making room for the invasion of the other. A distinction between forcible and consenting penetration remains, but that distinction comes to lie in a conscious consent that implies a self-possessed, autonomous, choice-making self at precisely the point where one wishes to ground the opposite. The resurrection in which one lives beyond oneself assumes that the self must be subjected, given up—he who loses his life will gain it: the assumption is that to have a self is to grasp oneself, and it is this willed self-enclosure that must be (in a consent beyond possibility) given up to God for life to be returned to one. Again, given the connections between sinfulness and self-enclosure, between sinfulness and idolatry, such sacrifice may be necessary for sinful selfhood (although even in that case, the sacrifice was accomplished *once*-for-all and once-for-*all* on the cross). But is this the nature of the trinitarian relations?

This mythology of trinitarian property relations, where the glory of God is that, despite having every right, God sacrifices God's rights (Godself) and yields eternally to the otherness that is within God and temporally to the otherness that is outside God when God is externalized in the Spirit-overseen Christological operation, writes the autonomous property rights of the liberal Enlightenment body into God as that which God must overcome in God's own being. The only counter to its fear of a self-enclosed self that a theology like Ward's can find is to call for the squandering of the self as the mode of the self's establishment. But—as the employment of this imagery for the intradivine relations makes clear—heightening the demand on the self while inverting it (the self is not to assert itself; it is to cancel itself out) establishes rather than threatens the self-enclosed self as the basic nature of selfhood. The self then has to be pierced, flayed, reminded of its vulnerability (which, apparently, it is like to forget)—*penetrated* (emptied in order to be filled) as trinitarian persons always already are, for in no other way will it be brought to the life beyond itself that true selfhood requires. (An infinite capacity for self-exposition: glory.) Father, Son, and Spirit—in their intradivine community—live just such lives beyond themselves.

Ward's account of suffering distinguishes between suffering that "undoes" sin and suffering that "undoes" grace but offers no space for an image of relation that is not suffering. Indeed, Ward considers a distinction between good and evil suffering "Gnostic."[108] Since only difference allows for enjoyment, and difference is imaged as suffering, Ward's critique of sadomasochism as the "cultural logic" of late capitalism appears as a narcissism of minor differences: In Ward's account, suffering may have an eschatological end (although how that end can be made consistent with the primordiality of suffering and the sacrifice of the Son in his givenness to the Father is unclear),[109] but that end is an inverse correlate of how highly he raises suffering into the inner-trinitarian "community."[110] Although both economies "internalis[e] a pleasurable pain . . . only God can discern and distinguish what is true suffering" (CC, 260). But true suffering, the kind that belongs to love itself, belongs also to God as trinity, eternally and constitutively. Despite Ward's claims to the contrary, suffering has no end, for the genesis and location of suffering is distinction itself.

At the end of the cross is a new word, Ward suggests—the word of resurrection as an eternal living beyond the self. But what new word may be spoken in the givenness of the Son to the Father, when distinction's suffering installs the cross in the immanent trinity? Reading inner-trinitarian love in such a way reads the price of the cross ("expenditure") into the very existence, being, and "operation" of the Son in the trinity.[111] Where is the transformation of the world grounded when difference always means sacrifice? What transformative word can the Father speak when his only Word is already the word of distinction's suffering?[112] No positivity of difference and distinction is made available here. Indeed, how can the Son give what he himself does not have, a distinction from the Father that does not mean suffering but the absolute positivity of God's own life? If we think through the analogy of bodies that Ward draws on, it might seem that bodies must make room for each other, must stretch to incorporate each other—must, indeed, *penetrate* each other in order to relate to each other—because matter signifies irreducibility, thus protecting the particularity of bounded and finite identities (although such a reading ignores the vast possibilities and pleasures of nonpenetrative touch; conversely, the need to overcome a boundary to be in relation installs the very boundary it intends to overcome—skin, the "border" of human matter, is never such a boundary to begin with). So his logic of relational penetration requires that room be made for the other. The body of Christ remains wounded even after the resurrection (CC, 150 n.77).

But in the nonbounded and nonbodied trinitarian relations, where the persons are relational all the way down, space-making, wounding, and self-emptying language verges on the mythological. It denies just what trinitarian relationality allows: intimacy without distance, differentiation without fracture, difference without competitive multiplicity, and gratuity without sacrifice or suffering. If instead the Father's penetration of the Son entails the eternal sacrifice of the Son (as an eternal election for suffering), then God indeed holds nothing back in God's love for God's creation. God's love then means that the distinction of the Son from the Father is what makes the world the site of difference's intolerability, since the suffering of incarnate life derives from that distinction. There can be no eschatological end to suffering in such an account, for God's *ousia* is not then infinitely plenitudinous; divine difference too is a threat that can only be met by self-sacrifice.

In wrapping up our consideration of Ward, there is one final aspect of his trinitarian bodies that invites examination: his use of distance imagery as a way to protect against fixed difference. Distance spatializes relation; further, if distance stands as a proxy for relation itself, the trinitarian relations—the origin of all relation—may themselves be approached in spatial terms: excessive intimacy and touch, interpenetration, making room for another. "[D]esire is both the creator and the creation of space" (CC, 145), and this trinitarian spatiality grounds the spatiality of creation. The body thus makes its way into trinitarian discourse at precisely the points where the spatial limitations and boundaries both carried and symbolized by our bodies do not apply. These divine bodies have side-holes whose outlines are difficult to discern: Are they the marks of wounding (and violent penetration) or the marks of a place "naturally open" (thus inviting, perhaps, nonviolent penetration)? The persons of the trinity are theologically embodied in such descriptions of their relations to each other and in the spatialization of such relations. They live in such intimate closeness that they penetrate each other. They live at a distance—giving themselves up to each other in their relations, allowing for the separation that incarnation expresses—in their differences from each other.[113] Such spatializations of trinitarian bodies and persons serve as the ground that justifies the corrections of distance (self-sacrifice) engendered by the spatializations themselves.

Ward's interweaving of trinitarian relations with difference, desire, and embodiment seeks to value the body by grounding it in the trinity. The analogical relations between God and creation describe the ways in which God is made available to us in the Christ-event. Yet Ward's inadequate distinction between sin and finitude and his practice of theology as a corrective to the failures and nihilism of the contemporary context in which he writes combine to generate a trinitarian theology that heightens rather than solves the problems Ward seeks to address. These connections between sexual difference, personhood, sacrifice, penetration, and distance exhibit possibilities that derive from the inner-trinitarian relations. It is as "deflections" in Rowan Williams's memorable term,[114] or as "differences that desire the other," in Ward's own language, that the distinctions among trinitarian persons constituted by the relations of origin turn into distance and suffering. Because desire—apparently in God as well as in humans—requires the simultaneity of having and not-having, and since trinitarian persons are the desire for each other that propels them into their differentiation, their bodies appear wounded by the excess of love that overcomes "masculinity's" fixity in their reciprocal "feminization" as space in which the other might appear. Their self-sacrificial relations to each other are, in the end, no more and no less than the very selves they are. A laudable commitment not to go behind God's self-revelation on the cross has, via an entanglement of desire, difference, and bodied existence, erected a cross in the very heart of God's eternal being.

## NOTES

1. Graham Ward, *Christ and Culture* (Malden, MA: Blackwell, 2005), 83, 261 (hereafter CC).
2. See Graham Ward, *Cities of God* (London: Routledge, 2000), 77 (hereafter CG). Ward derives this language from Balthasar's construal of the Ignatian principle of the divine "ever-greater."

3. Ward names the Holy Spirit the second difference in a reinterpretation of Karl Barth in CG, 198; in CC, 145, he suggests that "Trinitarian difference [is] opened up by Christ, the Second Person, and interpreted by the Spirit, the third Person." See also CC, 172.

4. Ward must mean that the trinity just *is* that perichoresis, not that the Godhead is *constituted* in the technical trinitarian sense by perichoresis.

5. It is odd to apply such a reading to the God who Ward recognizes is "one in substance" (ibid., 261).

6. In n.35 on the same page, Ward makes explicit that this "passion" is "the condition for the possibility" of Christ's passion.

7. Presumably, Ward sees desire as another term for love.

8. Ward, CG, 201–02.

9. Ward, CC, 150.

10. Ward, CG, 172. In CC, 77, Ward terms this "the infinite plenitude of God's *ousia.*"

11. Graham Ward, "After Ascension: The Body of Christ, Kenosis, and Divine Impassibility," in Robert MacSwain and Taylor Worley, eds., *Theology, Aesthetics, and Culture: Responses to the Work of David Brown* (Oxford: Oxford University Press, 2012), 208.

12. These twin dangers engender somewhat hyperbolic rhetoric. On the one hand, Ward insists Christian speech is authorized by the "inner operation of God" (CG, 6; see also CG, 115, 188, 254; and CC 31, 42, 177, 215, 218, 220). But in almost the same breath, he admits that "the discourse of Christian theology is itself a cultural product . . . a sign of the times and part of the market" (CG, 13; see also CG, 70, 226; and CC, 19). Ward dramatizes the necessity for Christian participation in cultural contestation (as, for instance, CC, 178, and throughout *The Politics of Discipleship: Becoming Postmaterial Citizens* [Grand Rapids, MI: Baker Academic, 2009]), which generates an implicit (and sometimes explicit) assertion of the first point over against the second. That is, while admitting that his version of Christianity is not Christianity absolutely, his descriptive (rather than argumentative) theologizing combines with his derivation of Christian speech from inner-trinitarian knowledge (called revelation or illumination) and his understanding of redemption as something that happens via human sign-making to render his own project difficult to critique.

13. Ward moves inconsistently between analogy and allegory. In *Cities of God* (2000), the central task of the book is an attempt to give "a theological account of analogy and analogical relations" (22). Yet in *Christ and Culture* (2005), Ward calls for a move from the "stasis of analogy and symbol" to allegory (220). Allegory's temporality, its power to historicize and spatialize, grounds Ward's preference of it over analogy (CC, 230); indeed, "[a]llegory as such forestalls what otherwise would be idolatry" (CC, 237). At this point, analogy takes its place *within* allegory, and allegory becomes the very nature of revelation, which is replaced by the term "disclosure" when the relevant essay is republished in *Christ and Culture* (see 242–43). However, this essay was first published in 1999 and reprinted in 2000, around the time the development of an analogical worldview was his primary aim in CG. See Graham Ward, "Allegoria: Reading as a Spiritual Exercise," *Modern Theology* 15, no. 3 (July 1999), 271–96; idem., "Allegoria: Reading as a Spiritual Exercise," in Gerhard Sauter and John Barton, eds., *Revelation and Story: Narrative Theology and the Centrality of Story* (Burlington, VT: Ashgate, 2000), 99–125. In recent work, Ward returns to the language of analogy without quite clarifying at what degree of resemblance analogy slides into idolatry, or why he has changed his mind on the issue. See Ward, "How Literature

Resists Secularity," *Literature & Theology* 24, no. 1 (March 2010), 77; and Ward, "After Ascension," 206. Perhaps the key to Ward's underdevelopment of the relation is found in a comment from *Cities of God*: "given an analogical world-view, I have no need to argue *for* a relationship between the ecclesial body and the civic. The relationship is already there; a participation already exists on the basis of the intratrinitarian community which causes other analogies of itself, however fallen and however remote, to be. A doctrine of analogy is also a doctrine of participation and causality" (236). This may be why Ward never finds it necessary to identify the type, conditions, extent, and limitations of such participation with any precision. Ward's aim in the creation of an analogical worldview is to change the material conditions of existence; he believes not only that political and economic processes *reflect* worldviews but that political and economic changes are *generated by* shifts in worldviews (*Politics of Discipleship*, 74; see also CG, 54). Ward discusses the relationship between transformation and the imaginary in *Cultural Transformation and Religious Practice* (Cambridge: Cambridge University Press, 2005), 148–60.

14. Ward, CG, 164–65, where he critiques John Calvin for assuming some fit between sign and signified. On 165, Ward comes as close as he ever does to a definition of analogy: "analogy defines the mediation between similarity and difference, univocity and equivocity." He may be following Hans Urs von Balthasar, *Theology of Karl Barth* (San Francisco, CA: Ignatius, 1992), 109.

15. Ward's use of *diastema* generally follows Hans Urs von Balthasar's in *Presence and Thought: An Essay on the Religious Philosophy of Gregory of Nyssa*, trans. Mark Sebanc (San Francisco, CA: Ignatius, 1995). But Ward probably follows Julia Kristeva in this particular case. In his early, programmatic essay "In the Name of the Father and of the Mother," Ward makes use of a line from Julia Kristeva (from *In the Beginning was Love*, trans. Arthur Goldhammer [New York: Columbia University Press, 1987], 31) to which he repeatedly returns: "In reality, it is the biblical God who inaugurates separation at the beginning of creation [by His Word], He creates division which is also the mark of his presence," *Literature & Theology* 8, no. 3 (September 1994), 311–27, at 323. See also CC, 211–12.

16. As in Graham Ward, "Kenosis: Death, Discourse and Resurrection," in Lucy Gardner, David Moss, Ben Quash, and Graham Ward, eds., *Balthasar at the End of Modernity* (Edinburgh: T&T Clark, 1999), 44.

17. Ward, "Kenosis," 44. Ward adopts these moves for himself; see CC, 145, 206, 218, and esp. 254–66.

18. Ward, CC, 145.

19. See also Jean-Luc Marion, *The Idol and Distance: Five Studies*, trans. Thomas A. Carlson (New York: Fordham University Press, 2001).

20. The "infinite plenitude of God's *ousia*" (CC, 77) is crucial. Yet if that plenitude is truly infinite, the pleromatic must always overcome the kenomatic, as Ward recognizes in CC, 257. Ward's account of difference, love, and distance offers no resources for envisioning that possibility. His description of the oneness of God assumes that each person is utterly oriented toward the differences of the other persons, which implies that oneness is secondary to difference, and since—as we will see—Ward reads difference as suffering, the question of the relation between diastasis and a kenotic hiatus becomes pressing enough to pose a challenge to the coherence, and attractiveness, of Ward's project.

21. Creation is "Christ's Eucharistic confession to the Father" (CC, 189), so the sacrificial aspect of Christ is woven into creation itself.

22. Graham Ward, "Bodies: The displaced body of Jesus Christ," in John Milbank, Catherine Pickstock and Graham Ward, eds., *Radical Orthodoxy: A New Theology* (London: Routledge, 1999), 169. See also "Kenosis," 48–49.

23. Ward reads Christology as "a chain of substitutions—from the Father to the Son, from the Son to the Twelve, from the Twelve to the Church" that operates "without any beginning and without any end" so that Christology becomes a form of "constitutional representation—the standing-in of an official substitute for the actual presence of another"; Jesus becomes the *substitute* for the absent Father (CC, 44). The equivalence of these substitutions makes it seem as though no direct access to the Father is available to us, and our relations to each other become analogies of the relation of the Father to the Son—generating theological problems in both directions. We are left finally with a series of displacements and representations that "are searching for a legitimating fatherhood or origin" (CC, 57), something that must be found in the inner-trinitarian processions. But this is a narrative of loss and devolution rather than of incorporation and expansion. Ward's later editing of his essays rightly downplays language of loss—this is especially evident when "Bodies" is republished in CG.
24. Although Ward exegetes the Philippians hymn in order to discover "the kenotic economy," he skips directly from there to modernity's turn to kenosis, starting from Lutheran orthodoxy. This may be why he fails to note how far his own reading of kenosis is from that of the early church, where it—in most cases—expresses the act of assumption of humanity (the appearance of the God of glory in human form), rather than a general economy of sacrifice or representation. See Ward, "Kenosis," 22–25.
25. Ward, "Kenosis," 21; the latter quotation is in n.13. Thomasius also reads the incarnation itself as the kenotic act. Gottfried Thomasius, "Christ's Person and Work," in Claude Welch, ed. and trans., *God and Incarnation in Mid-Nineteenth Century German Theology* (New York: Oxford University Press, 1965), 51–52.
26. See "Kenosis," 29, 30, and 43. Balthasar's adequate understanding of kenotic trinitarian logic is presumably where these criticisms lead; see, for instance, ibid., 41–42. Ward also asserts that an inadequate theology of kenosis characterizes the death-bound logic of modernity, leading "directly" to the Holocaust; ibid., 37–38.
27. Ibid., 47.
28. Ibid., 21 n.13; CC, 184.
29. Ward, "Bodies," 172–73. The "self-emptying" that "reaches its nadir in death" is "reversed in a final coronation" (CC, 261).
30. The desire to give significance to human creating (*poeisis*), which drives many of Ward's arguments, values the task of the theologian too highly.
31. Jean-Luc Marion also informs Ward on this point. Marion writes, "Poverty coincides with overabundance in the divine because God admits—what is shown by the Spirit—the distance of the Son," *Idol and Distance*, 111; see also 114, 174. For Marion, distance protects against idolatry; paternal withdrawal generates otherness and so communion in the trinity. Ward has written a number of essays on Marion, the earliest of which appeared in 1995, although never a sustained reflection on Marion's trinitarian theology.
32. In one case, Ward insists he uses masculine language for God simply "because of Barthian precedence. It is a metaphor" (CG, 189). The disclaimer appears nowhere else to my knowledge; Ward generally uses masculine terms for God.
33. Ward, "In the Name of the Father and the Mother," 313.
34. Ward makes two different claims in these texts: that trinity needs to be thought in terms of sexual difference and that sexual difference must be thought trinitarianly. The relation between the two claims is never satisfactorily clarified.
35. Ibid., 312–14.
36. As such, the statement is correct, but he limits its ultimate scope by reverting to the symbolics of sexual difference. He says, "kinship is a symbolic, not a

natural arrangement, and . . . there are [as] many genders as there are performances of being sexed" (CG, 183). See also "Bodies," 177 n.1, where Ward mentions his doubt about whether there are only two sexes in connection with the suggestion that he, unlike the feminist theologians he critiques, rearranges "a masculinist symbolics" so that Christ may be seen to save all.

37. Ward prefers to assume that both touches do take place—see n.26 on the same page.

38. This is particularly relevant because of numerous other examples of relations that could have been examined without working inside economies of penetrative touch. Perhaps the best example is Jesus' invitation to Peter to walk to him on the water.

39. See also "Bodies," 176, where Ward says that the "withdrawal of the body of Jesus" in the ascension is the Logos's creation of "a space within himself, a womb, within which the Church will expand and creation be recreated."

40. Ward makes a similar move at the end of the "Bodies" essay: "We have no access to the body of the gendered Jew. So all those attempts to determine the sexuality of Jesus are simply more recent symptoms of the search for the historical Christ" (176–77). Ward's direct movement from body to sexuality (implying that if we did have access to the body of the gendered Jew, we might be able to determine his sexuality) is surprising.

41. In "After Ascension" (206–207), Ward maintains the difference between us and Christ, but the tendency throughout—partly, but not only, due to his emphasis on response—is toward the replacement of Christ by the church (and so by implication by us).

42. The relevant essay was first published as "Divinity and Sexuality: Luce Irigaray and Theology," *Modern Theology* 12, no. 2 (April 1996), 221–37, and reprinted in slightly different form in CC, 129–58. My citations of the essay follow the CC version. The prompt comes from Irigaray's critique of Elizabeth Schüssler Fiorenza's *In Memory of Her* (CC, 136–38). Irigaray's essay, "Equal to Whom?," can be found in *The Postmodern God: A Theological Reader*, ed. Graham Ward (Malden, MA: Blackwell, 1997), 198–214. Ward is rightly known as a subtle reader of the French feminists, but the work their thought performs in his theology is more ambivalent than this might suggest. For Ward, the "French feminists" sometimes serve as shields against feminists who propose more radical projects than he approves. Ward critiques patriarchy and heterosexism, but the way he discusses feminist theologians sometimes undermines his intentions. Notable is Ward's use of Rosemary Radford Ruether's question (a chapter title from her classic *Sexism and God-Talk* [Boston: Beacon, 1983]) about whether a male savior can save women. Ward doesn't consider what the question is doing in her work, how she answers it (yes), and whether and how the question is taken up by other theologians (for instance, the debate about Jesus, blood, and substitution among womanist theologians like Delores Williams in *Sisters in the Wilderness: The Challenge of Womanist God-Talk* [Maryknoll, NY: Orbis, 1993] and JoAnne Marie Terrell in *Power in the Blood? The Cross in the African American Experience* [Maryknoll, NY: Orbis, 1998], is particularly interesting in this regard). See Graham Ward, "Bodies," 177 n.1. Ward opts to use Ruether's (rhetorical) question as an example of a tendency toward essentialism in feminist theology. Reference to Ruether's question without engaging its function in her argument has unfortunately become a standard trope in anti-feminist theologies. "Bodies" is framed by two references to this question, on 163 and 177. Ward's theological method is based on close reading; the decision not to offer that close reading to feminist theologians is worrisome.

43. Amy Hollywood shows that Irigaray eventually "rejects the claims to gender fluidity on which her reading of Christ as a feminized divinity are based . . . arguing that divine women are required if women are to achieve full autonomy of freedom"; *Sensible Ecstasy: Mysticism, Sexual Difference, and the Demands of History* (Chicago: University of Chicago Press, 2002), 181. But even in "The Crucified One: Epistle to the Last Christians," in *Marine Lover of Friedrich Nietzsche*, trans. Gillian C. Gill (New York: Columbia University Press, 1991), Irigaray troubles Ward's point.
44. Ibid., 166. Ward's version of the quotation does not include the "re" of reappears.
45. All quotations ibid., 166.
46. Ibid., 167.
47. Ibid., 170.
48. See Irigaray's identification of the transformation of wound into belief: "wounds inflicted . . . of bodily humiliation in order to *believe* in the resurrection" (ibid.).
49. Ward discusses both Barth and Balthasar, but since I consider Balthasar in ch. 1, I focus on Barth here.
50. By implication, feminist and womanist theologians do not sufficiently recognize the theological significance of sexual difference.
51. Ward adopts the term "hom(m)osexual" from Irigaray, for whom it expresses a social economy of masculine sameness. The term is a punning elision of *homme* and homosexual.
52. Ward insists that "God-ordained desire can only be heterosexual" (CG, 201). Thus "heterosexual" relationships may have "homosexual" (narcissistic) forms of desire, while "homosexual" relationships may have "heterosexual" (conditioned by true difference) forms of desire.
53. Ward's appropriate worries about heterosexism sometimes cause him to underplay worries about sexism.
54. Ward is disagreeing with John McIntyre, who rejects the nuptial analogy. Ward emphasizes that language of sex with Christ is neither metaphorical nor symbolic, since "sexual intimacy" is "an intimation of the divine relation that operates between God and human beings" (CC, 108–09).
55. Ward suggests that eucharistic fracturing comes to an eschatological end (CG, 237), but as we will see below, he cannot follow up on that eschatological promise.
56. Ward, "Bodies," 163. In an important addition to the version of the essay found in CG, 112, Ward says, "displacement is not the erasure but the expansion of the body"—perhaps indicating recognition that displacement might indeed suggest erasure.
57. Ward, "Bodies," 170.
58. Ibid., emphasis added.
59. Ibid.
60. Presumably, he assumes that Jesus had XY chromosomes because of circumcision. Since Mary's pregnancy is a miracle, there is no reason to assume anything about her chromosomes.
61. Ibid., 166.
62. Ibid.
63. Neither appears in the original version. Ward adds a reference to Moses and Elijah in CG (101), but they are merely symbols of the temporality of recollection and expectation.
64. Ward, "Bodies," 167.
65. Ibid., 167–68.

66. The discussion of crucifixion in CG replaces or redefines the language of lack in "Bodies" in order to remove the implication of a fundamental loss or absence.
67. Ibid., 169.
68. See also Eve Kosofsky Sedgwick, *Epistemology of the Closet* (Berkeley: University of California Press, 1990), 15, 72, 87–88, and 184–87.
69. In the CG version, Ward adds that "[t]he body hangs as neither woman nor man, but meat; . . . as the body raped. Death degenders," 103–04. After death, there may be no sexual difference. But even in the later version, the body is an object in this way before death, and rape terminology does not degender; see CG, 104.
70. "In the Name of the Father and the Mother" ends with a call for a "hermaphroditic Christology which would necessarily redescribe the operation of the Trinity" (325).
71. Ward, "Bodies," 170; and again on 174.
72. Ibid., 171.
73. See my "Limits of Inclusion," *Theology & Sexuality*, forthcoming, for a critique of such distinctions.
74. Ward, "Bodies," 172.
75. Ibid., 173; CG, 108.
76. See Friedrich Schleiermacher, *The Christian Faith*, ed. H. R. MacKintosh and J. S. Stewart (Edinburgh: T&T Clark, 1999), §66, §69, and especially §§75–76.
77. Otherwise the saving effect of Jesus Christ would be impossible.
78. In the later version of the essay, "Aristotelian identification" replaces "literally identical," CG, 109.
79. Ward, CG, 109–10.
80. Ward, "Bodies," 177.
81. Ibid.
82. The text is misattributed as Philippians 2:12 in both versions. Ibid., 176–77.
83. In *Politics of Discipleship*, Ward says that the image of the church as a body in Paul, filtered through this text, is both "sexed," since it has genitals, and "sexless," since it is not male or female (253).
84. Ward recognizes this elsewhere when he emphasizes that "key . . . symbols" install a hierarchical priority of symbolic interpretation inside any cultural (or I suggest, theological) framework. See CC, 168.
85. Mark D. Jordan, "The Return of Religion During the Reign of Sexuality," in Linda Martin Alcoff and John Caputo, eds., *Feminism, Sexuality, and the Return of Religion* (Bloomington, IN: Indiana University Press, 2011), 51.
86. Ibid., 41.
87. Kathryn Greene-McCreight, *Feminist Reconstructions of Christian Doctrine: Narrative Analysis and Appraisal* (New York: Oxford University Press, 2000), 124.
88. Kathryn Tanner, *Christ the Key* (Cambridge: Cambridge University Press, 2010), 178–79; idem, "The Use of Perceived Properties of Light as a Theological Analogy," in Gerald S. J. O'Collins and Mary Ann Meyers, eds., *Light from Light: Scientists and Theologians in Dialogue* (Grand Rapids, MI: Eerdmans, 2012), 122–30; and idem, "Gender," in Mark Chapman, Ian Douglas, Martyn Percy, and Sathi Clarke, eds., *The Oxford Handbook on Anglican Studies* (Oxford: Oxford University Press, forthcoming).
89. The closest he comes to such an argument is on CC, 153–54: "difference, to the extent that it treats the bodies of other responsive beings, is always erotic and therefore sexually charged . . . because it is only constituted in relation, and relations between responsive bodies become increasingly eroticised through proximity. . . . Is it in the moment of sexualisation, in the arrival of

attraction, that bodies take on a sexual difference? . . . Sexual difference is always an 'achievement'[.] . . . [T]here is no theology of sexual difference, then, only the production of sexual difference in a theological relation." On 155, Ward makes explicit that he intends this analysis to apply to *any* organic body (see also Ward, "Theology and Cultural Sadomasochism," *Svensk Teologisk Kvartalskrift* 78 [2002], 9). But this assumes what he seeks to prove: that *any* bodied relation is necessarily sexual; that all bodied relations are relations of attraction or repulsion; that to be close to another body entails an erotic relation to it. None of these assumptions are givens.

90. Ward images sexual difference by "the symbolics of the phallus and the two lips" (CC, 158), so neither the theological nor the theoretical symbol set can serve to get him what he wants.

91. Therefore, replacing "Father" and "Son" with nongendered terminology indicating origin remains within the same terms, because the stabilization of sexual difference in hierarchical form in the Christian imaginary lies in origin rather than in paternity (or: what makes it paternity is origin).

92. Ward repeatedly emphasizes that the body is a textual reality, as for instance in "Bodies," 174; CG, 93; *Politics of Discipleship*, 228.

93. See also Kevin Hart, "Response to Graham Ward," in Lieven Boeve and L. Leijssen, eds., *Sacramental Presence in a Postmodern Context, Bibliotheca Ephemeridum Theologicarum Lovaniensium* CLX (Leuven: Leuven University Press, 2001), 205–11. Hart's concern about participation holds for Ward's work as a whole.

94. Ward, "Theology and Cultural Sadomasochism," 9–10, my emphasis. Sections of this essay, including this one, appear in *Christ and Culture* in the chapter "Suffering and Incarnation," 262–63. In "Kenosis," 51, Ward distinguishes between ontological difference (Being/existence) and theological difference (God/creation) in Balthasar, but he does not himself carry through that usage consistently.

95. Ward then refers the reader to the section containing the long quote above.

96. See also CC, 73, where Ward connects intimacy with fear and vulnerability, and so with desire and distance. Desire entails suffering the otherness of the other and the dread of being absorbed by the other. Since Ward maintains this model for both divine and human persons, neither the reception-response model of trinitarian relations that Ward develops, nor the plenitude of the divine essence, can answer the following critique. Although Ward maintains that self-gift and kenotic emptying result from an ongoing gift, so that "what I am being emptied of is that which I am being given" (CC, 79), his insistence that givenness, love, and distinction are themselves forms of suffering, his projection of these models into the immanent trinity in the lavish and costly giving that "is" the inner-trinitarian processions, and the translation between desire, displacement, and distance, combine to overcome his attempt to maintain the fullness of gift and goodness in God.

97. Schleiermacher, *Christian Faith*, §4.

98. Søren Kierkegaard, *Works of Love: Some Christian Reflections in the Form of Discourses*, trans. Howard V. Hong and Edna H. Hong (New York: Harper, 1962), 27.

99. Ward defines this contact as "[a] theology of touch in which the Father eternally begets the Son, and through that contact with them the Spirit born of them both endlessly makes known the intelligibility of what they share," but he does not explain what that means.

100. Ward also specifies that origin provides legitimation, and that a search for origin is a search for fatherhood (CC, 53–57).

101. See also CG, 172, where Ward specifies that he reads creation as kenotic because it otherwise would have no relation to God. But creation *is* already

a relation, even as God remains wholly other from the direction of creation. Ward mistakenly assumes that reading God as wholly other would render God irrelevant to creation and render the infinity of God the negation of finitude. The reverse is the case, for the wholly other is also the non-other.

102. Ward may be following Marion, who reads the givenness of the Son as the Son's loss, and so reception, of his life from the Father (*Idol and Distance*, 175). Crucially, Marion argues that this trivializes what we know as death, since it is "almost nothing" when set inside trinitarian distance.

103. Marcella Althaus-Reid, *The Queer God* (London: Routledge, 2003), 104; idem, "A Woman's Right to Not Being Straight," in *From Feminist Theology to Indecent Theology: Readings on Poverty, Sexual Identity and God* (London: SCM, 2004), 96.

104. Although I do not read the cross as the Son's self-offering to the Father, such a reading is common in contemporary theology.

105. See, for one much-cited example of such an argument, Brian Leftow, "Anti Social Trinitarianism," in Stephen T. Davis, Daniel Kendall, SJ, and Gerald SJ O'Collins, eds., *The Trinity: An Interdisciplinary Symposium on the Trinity* (Oxford: Oxford University Press, 1999), 204–50.

106. Ward comes close to recognizing this (although not as a problem) when he says that "an exploration of the relationship between kenosis, love, difference-in-relation and the Trinity might provide a model for a Trinity and therefore the operations of a God who offered a transcendental horizon for both male and female subjectivity" (CC, 152).

107. Ward emphasizes that "the body is always an imagined thing," *Politics of Discipleship*, 228.

108. Graham Ward, "*Kenosis, Poiesis* and *Genesis*: Or the Theological Aesthetics of Suffering," in Adrian Pabst and Christoph Schneider, eds., *Encounter Between Eastern Orthodoxy and Radical Orthodoxy: Transfiguring the World Through the Word* (Aldershot, UK: Ashgate, 2009), 173–74.

109. Ward says suffering comes to an end but insists that he is exploring an "eternal suffering intrinsic to the plenitude of love itself" (CC, 263), so it must be only the suffering that is the result of sin that actually ends.

110. Ward critiques Balthasar on this count, since Balthasar thinks redemption overcomes suffering. Ward argues that "subsequent suffering . . . participates in a true and ongoing suffering; a . . . passion located in the very Godhead itself" (CC 259–60).

111. Such a reading may have interesting consonances with Bruce McCormack's hotly debated theses, first published in the *Cambridge Companion to Karl Barth*, regarding Barth's account of God's self-constitution in the eternal election of Jesus Christ. See Kevin Hector, "Immutability, Necessity and Triunity: Towards a Resolution of the Trinity and Election Controversy," *Scottish Journal of Theology* 65, no. 1 (February 2012), 64–81, for a useful bibliography and consideration of the state of the question as of this writing (although it is not clear that Hector's revision of Barth and McCormack avoids subordinationism in its embrace of subordination). Ward cannot avoid the mistake of prioritizing cross over resurrection for revelation of the intra-divine differences. The cross becomes as it were retrospectively instead of prospectively eternal.

112. Or, as Karl Barth develops the dangers of subjecting God to suffering's necessity, "God gives Himself, but He does not give Himself away. . . . He does not come into conflict with Himself. . . . He frees the creature in becoming a creature. . . . He is not untrue to Himself but true to Himself in this condescension, in this way into the far country. If it were otherwise, if in it He set Himself in contradiction with Himself, how could He reconcile the world with Himself? Of what value would His deity be to us if—instead of crossing in that deity

the very real gulf between Himself and us—He left that deity behind Him in His coming to us[?] . . . A God who found Himself in this contradiction can obviously only be the image of our own unreconciled humanity projected into deity." *Church Dogmatics* IV/1, *The Doctrine of Reconciliation, Part 1* (Edinburgh: T&T Clark, 1956), 185–86. Ward cites the point preceding this passage on CC, 201, but does not draw out the implication. I do not draw the same conclusions as Barth regarding how to avoid alienating God from Godself.

113. See Graham Ward, "Hosting the Stranger and the Pilgrim: A Christian Theological Reflection," in Eric Boynton and Martin Kavka, eds., *Saintly Influence: Edith Wyschogrod and the Possibilities of Philosophy of Religion* (New York: Fordham University Press, 2009), 72.

114. Rowan Williams, "The Deflections of Desire: Negative Theology in Trinitarian Disclosure," in Oliver Davies and Denys Turner, eds., *Silence and the Word: Negative Theology and Incarnation* (Cambridge: Cambridge University Press, 2002), 115–35.

## BIBLIOGRAPHY

Althaus-Reid, Marcella. *The Queer God*. London: Routledge, 2003.

———. "A Woman's Right to Not Being Straight." In *From Feminist Theology to Indecent Theology: Readings on Poverty, Sexual Identity and God*, 95–102. London: SCM, 2004.

Balthasar, Hans Urs von. *Presence and Thought: An Essay on the Religious Philosophy of Gregory of Nyssa*. Trans. Mark Sebanc. San Francisco: Ignatius, 1995.

———. *Theology of Karl Barth*. San Francisco: Ignatius, 1992.

Barth, Karl. *Church Dogmatics*. Vol. 4, pt. 1, *The Doctrine of Reconciliation*. Ed. G. W. Bromiley and T. F. Torrance. Trans. G. W. Bromiley. London: T&T Clark, 2004.

Greene-McCreight, Kathryn. *Feminist Reconstructions of Christian Doctrine: Narrative Analysis and Appraisal*. New York: Oxford University Press, 2000.

Hart, Kevin. "Response to Graham Ward." In *Sacramental Presence in a Postmodern Context*. Bibliotheca Ephemeridum Theologicarum Lovaniensium CLX, ed. Lieven Boeve and L. Leijssen, 205–211. Leuven: Leuven University Press, 2001.

Hector, Kevin. "Immutability, Necessity and Triunity: Towards a Resolution of the Trinity and Election Controversy." *Scottish Journal of Theology* 65, no. 1 (February 2012): 64–81.

Hollywood, Amy. *Sensible Ecstasy: Mysticism, Sexual Difference, and the Demands of History*. Chicago: University of Chicago Press, 2002.

Irigaray, Luce. "Equal to Whom?" In *The Postmodern God: A Theological Reader*, ed. Graham Ward, 198–214. Malden, MA: Blackwell, 1997.

———. *Marine Lover of Friedrich Nietzsche*. Trans. Gillian C. Gill. New York: Columbia University Press, 1991.

Jordan, Mark D. "The Return of Religion During the Reign of Sexuality." In *Feminism, Sexuality, and the Return of Religion*, ed. Linda Martin Alcoff and John D. Caputo, 39–54. Bloomington: Indiana University Press, 2011.

Kierkegaard, Søren. *Works of Love: Some Christian Reflections in the Form of Discourses*. Trans. Howard V. Hong and Edna H. Hong. New York: Harper, 1962.

Kristeva, Julia. *In the Beginning was Love*. Trans. Arthur Goldhammer. New York: Columbia University Press, 1987.

Leftow, Brian. "Anti Social Trinitarianism." In *The Trinity: An Interdisciplinary Symposium*, ed. Stephen T. Davis, Daniel Kendall, SJ, and Gerald O'Collins, SJ, 203–249. Oxford: Oxford University Press, 1999.

Marion, Jean-Luc. *The Idol and Distance: Five Studies.* New York: Fordham University Press, 2001.
Ruether, Rosemary Radford. *Sexism and God-Talk: Toward a Feminist Theology.* Boston: Beacon, 1983.
Schleiermacher, Friedrich. *The Christian Faith.* Ed. H. R. MacKintosh and J. S. Stewart. Edinburgh: T&T Clark, 1999.
Sedgwick, Eve Kosofsky. *Epistemology of the Closet.* Berkeley: University of California Press, 1990.
Tanner, Kathryn. *Christ the Key.* Cambridge: Cambridge University Press, 2010.
———. "Gender." In *The Oxford Handbook on Anglican Studies,* ed. Mark Chapman, Ian Douglas, Martyn Percy, and Sathi Clarke. Oxford: Oxford University Press, forthcoming.
———. "The Use of Perceived Properties of Light as a Theological Analogy." In *Light from Light: Scientists and Theologians in Dialogue,* ed. Gerald O'Collins S.J. and Mary Ann Meyers, 122–30. Grand Rapids: Eerdmans, 2012.
Terrell, JoAnne Marie. *Power in the Blood? The Cross in the African American Experience.* The Bishop Henry McNeal Turner/Sojourner Truth Series in Black Religion, vol. 15. Maryknoll, NY: Orbis, 1998.
Thomasius, Gottfried. "Christ's Person and Work." In *God and Incarnation in Mid-Nineteenth Century German Theology,* ed. and trans. Claude Welch, 31–101. New York: Oxford University Press, 1965.
Tonstad, Linn Marie. "The Limits of Inclusion: Queer Theology and Its Others." *Theology & Sexuality,* forthcoming.
Ward, Graham. "After Ascension: The Body of Christ, Kenosis, and Divine Impassibility." In *Theology, Aesthetics, and Culture: Responses to the Work of David Brown,* ed. Robert MacSwain and Taylor Worley, 197–210. Oxford: Oxford University Press, 2012.
———. "Allegoria: Reading as a Spiritual Exercise." *Modern Theology* 15, no. 3 (July 1999): 271–95.
———. "Allegoria: Reading as a Spiritual Exercise." In *Revelation and Story: Narrative Theology and the Centrality of Story,* ed. Gerhard Sauter and John Barton, 99–125. Burlington, VT: Ashgate, 2000.
———. "Bodies: The Displaced Body of Jesus Christ." In *Radical Orthodoxy: A New Theology,* ed. John Milbank, Catherine Pickstock, and Graham Ward, 163–81. London: Routledge, 1999.
———. *Christ and Culture.* Malden, MA: Blackwell, 2005.
———. *Cities of God.* London: Routledge, 2000.
———. *Cultural Transformation and Religious Practice.* Cambridge: Cambridge University Press, 2005.
———. "Divinity and Sexuality: Luce Irigaray and Christology." *Modern Theology* 12, no. 2 (April 1996): 221–37.
———. "Hosting the Stranger and the Pilgrim: A Christian Theological Reflection." In *Saintly Influence: Edith Wyschogrod and the Possibilities of Philosophy of Religion,* ed. Eric Boynton and Martin Kavka, 63–81. New York: Fordham University Press, 2009.
———. "How Literature Resists Secularity." *Literature & Theology* 24, no. 1 (March 2010): 73–88.
———. "Kenosis: Death, Discourse and Resurrection." In *Balthasar at the End of Modernity,* ed. Lucy Gardner, David Moss, Ben Quash, and Graham Ward, 15–68. Edinburgh: T&T Clark, 1999.
———. "*Kenosis, Poiesis* and *Genesis*: Or the Theological Aesthetics of Suffering." In *Encounter Between Eastern Orthodoxy and Radical Orthodoxy: Transfiguring the World Through the Word,* ed. Adrian Pabst and Christoph Schneider, 165–84. Farnham, UK: Ashgate, 2009.

————. "In the Name of the Father and of the Mother." *Literature & Theology* 8, no. 3 (September 1994): 311–27.

————. *The Politics of Discipleship: Becoming Postmaterial Citizens.* Grand Rapids: Baker Academic, 2009.

————. "Theology and Cultural Sadomasochism." *Svensk Teologisk Kvartalskrift* 78 (2002): 2–10.

Williams, Delores. *Sisters in the Wilderness: The Challenge of Womanist God-Talk.* Maryknoll, NY: Orbis, 1993.

Williams, Rowan. "The Deflections of Desire: Negative Theology in Trinitarian Disclosure." In *Silence and the Word: Negative Theology and Incarnation*, ed. Oliver Davies and Denys Turner, 115–35. Cambridge: Cambridge University Press, 2002.

# 3 Speaking "Father" Rightly
## Kenotic Reformation into Sonship in Sarah Coakley

Sarah Coakley is the leading Anglican theologian working at the nexus of sacrificial selfhood, desire, sexuality, and the trinity.[1] Her expansive knowledge of the Christian tradition, engagement with analytic philosophy and theology, and distinctive combination of analytic clarity with creative positions that run counter to conventional opinion have gained her a sterling theological reputation and wide influence. Her programmatic essays often achieve a higher level of clarity in a few pages than many authors do in a hundred—see, for instance, her delightfully pointed discussion of ontologies of relation in intertwinings of science with trinitarian reflection,[2] her exemplary critique of Yves Congar's gendering of the Holy Spirit,[3] or her dryly witty appraisal of the masculinism of analytic philosophers.[4] Her classic discussion of the varied kenotic Christological models arguably remains unsurpassed in the literature.[5]

Yet the deservedly high estimation she enjoys in the theological academy also reveals some of the ongoing challenges to mainstreaming feminist concerns in Christian discourse. While Coakley identifies as feminist, her primary antagonists are often other feminist theologians who, she claims, do not have the necessary "perceptive," "profound," and "subtle" understandings of the nuances of Christian traditions[6] and of the importance of shared rationality and analytic philosophy of religion.[7] Rhetorically, she is established as the exception among feminist theologians, the one who need not be relegated to the margins of mainstream theological conversation due to the combination of force and subtlety in her thought.[8] Just this aspect of her style, combined with the compatibility of her project with typical forms of resistance to the theological importance of feminist concerns, makes her the favorite feminist of those theologians and analytic philosophers of religion most hostile to or uninterested in gender concerns.[9]

Despite its wide popularity and influence, Coakley's work has yet to receive adequate critical assessment from either feminist or systematic theologians; in this chapter I undertake just such an assessment. The problems I uncover in Coakley are in some ways quite different from those of Ward and Balthasar. Strictly speaking, Coakley does not gender intra-trinitarian relations, although she does symbolically sex the God–world relation. But like Ward, Coakley has difficulty distinguishing between sin and finitude, and she, too, interprets dependence on God as vulnerability. The suffering purgation required for human beings to be united with God (in some ways the very nature of the God-relationship) stems from finitude as much as sin. Correlatively, Coakley elides the differences among the suffering of prayer (the loss of noetic and idolatrous certainties, which combines with expansion of the self's capacities), suffering in its more ordinary sense (tragedy, horrendous evil, and injustice), and self-sacrificial suffering that entails loss rather than gifted and expansive transformation. Humans practice self-erasure so that God may move in, for true humanity means ceding to the divine. Yet the human being's free practice of contemplation also conditions the movement of God in significant ways. The self-erasing human being in this way comes to stand at the very center of her theological project. Coakley asserts the goodness of the relations with others that result from contemplation, but although prayer purportedly has cosmic significance, its theological function is to confront the individual pray-er with her particular desires, especially in their sexual form, thus proving the relationship between sexual desire and desire for God. The psychoanalytically inflected desires of which the pray-er is reminded in silent prayer are to be redirected in an ascetical direction toward God and in marital continence.

United with Christ through prayer, the human being *becomes* the Son; as a result, the significance of Christ's work and the trinitarian activity of the Son both disappear under the weight of Coakley's eagerness to recover the priority of the Spirit. She construes the God–world relation in dangerously competitive ways for someone committed to classical transcendence: divine threeness "ambushes" human twoness, incarnation "transgresses" the difference between God and creation, and creation's dependence on God is redefined as vulnerability and submission. Throughout, Coakley explicitly advances heterosexist symbolics of sexual difference while insisting that the contemplative (alone) names the Father rightly as she overcomes patriarchy "on her knees." Coakley's program adds to the mounting evidence that drawing connections among sex, gender, and the trinity is not as promising as its proponents claim. Our concerns about suffering and sacrifice, spatialization, theological symbolics of sexual difference, and corrective forms of projection are heightened rather than ameliorated in encounter with Coakley. As my cumulative case for a revision of trinitarian relations grows, Coakley's project helps pinpoint where trinitarian theology goes wrong and therefore how it can be corrected.

## CONTEMPLATION, PATRIARCHY, AND FEMINIST FATHERHOOD

In the first volume of her systematic theology, *God, Sexuality and the Self: An Essay "On The Trinity,"* Coakley develops the method of *théologie totale* as a way to draw systematic theology beyond its tendency to ignore the affective, imaginative, and symbolic registers of theological reflection. She also wants theology to be in dialogue with other "sciences," particularly sociology, analytic philosophy of religion, and feminist thought. Using iconography, interviews with church members, and readings of patristic sources alongside Ernst Troeltsch's typology of the Christian churches, Coakley seeks to reinvigorate Christian Platonism through application of the biblical text that stands at the center of her theological *oeuvre*, Romans 8—particularly verses 14–17 and 26. Silent, contemplative prayer is the heart of her theological method, for it is in such prayer that the pray-er makes room for the Spirit to reform her, enlighten her, reshape her into the Son, and bring her to the Father. Such prayerful waiting on God is a form of power-in-vulnerability. The four central elements of Coakley's theology come together in these verses from Romans: (1) the Spirit prays in us; (2) when the Spirit prays in us, we learn to call God "Abba"/Father and what that name means; (3) the "flesh" (in the Pauline sense) must be overcome for the sake of life in the Spirit; and (4) overcoming the flesh means becoming conformed to Christ by the power of the Spirit through suffering. Coakley adds to the Romans text that these four elements are descriptions of what happens particularly and primarily in contemplative prayer.[10]

Silent, contemplative prayer is the primary site of theological formation; indeed, deep theological and philosophical reflection is simply unavailable to those not engaged in that practice (GSS, 16). Contemplative prayer also enacts the material connections among sex, gender, sexuality, and God. Desire, more fundamental than gender or sex (GSS, 6), is the trace God has left in the human being, the "ineradicable root of human longing for God" that organizes the self as a singular entity (GSS, 26). It is the mark of God in the human; its telos is to be identical with divine desire (GSS, 10, 15). Divine desire is the trinitarian "plenitude of longing love" expressed as God's desire for creation's full participation in the life of God; desire is primarily divine and only derivatively human (GSS, 10).[11] Gender is defined as embodied difference that draws human beings toward union. Gender need not be limited to the fixed and fallen binary of heterosexist twoness, although male and female remain. The process of divine desire's transformation of human desire unfixes gender, making it "labile." While gender as twoness does not disappear eschatologically, its significance is relativized in the priority that divine threeness has over human twoness. Already Coakley's use of the trinity to correct gender and sexuality becomes apparent.

Although Coakley retains a classical understanding of God's transcendence, she locates herself within a Christian tradition that sees the proper posture of the human in relation to God as one in which the human being needs to be painfully cleansed of her sin and finite limitations through a divinely delightful purgation ("batter my heart") found only in contemplative prayer and performed by the only Other to whom the human being can submit with no safe word.[12] This cleansing will "empower" the person to work toward the transformation of the world and to resist her own idolatries and those of others. The condition of possibility of Coakley's position is that God successfully purges the individual pray-er over time of her paternal idolatries: when she now refers to God as Father, she (alone) means the *only* one who is in a nonmetaphorical sense the Father of the Son, neither of whom are "male" in any *real* sense (GSS, 325–27).

This is not, as Coakley rightly insists, a subjectivist argument, but neither is it publically testable. Each pray-er has to test the power of contemplative prayer for herself and examine whether she, too, finds herself caught up by the Spirit into responsive engagement with the one to whom all desire is directed and from whom all desire comes (the Father), thus becoming Christic through suffering. The tradition of contemplative prayer offers the "dark night of the soul" or language of spiritual dryness, sterility, and aridity to explain why some may not immediately, or ever, experience these delights of idolatry purgation, although such a dark night of the soul is an essential stage in human transformation into the "(cruciform) Son" (GSS, 14).

We tested Graham Ward's positions by examining the uses to which he put them. Coakley's are open to additional forms of testing. Before that testing, however, we must untangle the fundamental "nexus" of the trinity, sexuality, and gender that Coakley does so much to promote. It is on grounds of attentiveness to gender that Coakley is a feminist theologian; and it is on grounds of a particular account of the trinity that Coakley sees gender becoming fluid inside divine desire. These themes combine to provide Coakley with the theological means of destroying patriarchy, divine and otherwise.

Contemplation undoes patriarchy in three ways. I already mentioned the first: the way contemplation—and nothing else—ensures the correct sense of divine fatherhood and gives the pray-er the strength to resist her own idolatries and those of others by opposing patriarchy and other forms of injustice. Second, contemplation renders the pray-er gender-labile so that she is no longer trapped by fixed societal gender roles. Third, contemplation teaches the pray-er the correct "place of the Spirit in the Trinity," knowledge of which is the only way to "resist the (ever-seductive) lure back into patriarchal hierarchy" (GSS, 333). Let us consider these in order.

First, the practice of silent prayer is a locus of transformation in which the self is broken down and remade through a process in which the Spirit prays to the Father in the pray-er, thus transforming the pray-er into an adopted "son" in the shape of Christ. For Coakley, this sacrificial and kenotic self-emptying purges the self of her idolatries through a practice of willed un-mastery in silent prayer, thus allowing her to learn the correct meaning of fatherhood as it applies inside the trinity: "in the same silence we learn to use 'Father' *proprie*, and *only* as 'Father' in Trinity" (GSS, 326). Since the Spirit prays in us, and the Spirit "knows" the Father intra-trinitarianly, the Spirit gives us that knowledge in ways irreducible to propositional claims. Coakley therefore maintains, following Thomas Aquinas, that if God is referred to as Father in any way other than as "Father" in trinity, such usage is improper (GSS, 324). The distinction between the linguistic and referential registers of divine and human fatherhood is given over to God, whose responsibility it becomes to enlighten the pray-er through the "dazzling darkness" in which the pray-er's cognitive abilities are surpassed and transformed. As she becomes transformed into a Christ, she is made able to call God "Father," in the *proper* fashion. " 'Can a feminist call God Father', then? One might more truly insist that she, above all, *must*; for it lies with her alone to do the kneeling work that ultimately slays patriarchy at its root" (GSS, 327).[13]

Interestingly, the purgative work of kenosis installs different truth relationships for the same linguistic terms. "Father" both *means* and *refers* differently for the person whose purgation process is successful. The contemplative, in contrast to the noncontemplative, recognizes that right use of fatherhood removes it from its merely human usage: "Its appropriateness inner-trinitarianly means that the *true* meaning of 'Father' is to be found in the Trinity, not dredged from the scummy realm of human patriarchal fatherhood" (GSS, 324). Ascetic purgation and sanctification lead almost inexorably to expanded and enhanced cognitive as well as sensory faculties (the spiritual senses) as the pray-er's reason, imagination, and will are ecstatically transformed and incorporated into God.[14] But further, must not these noetic consequences be recognized by the pray-er? Otherwise how would Coakley know that her idolatries were being eradicated? Here Coakley's argument stretches thin: the dazzling darkness in which the pray-er learns to use "Father" correctly is also (but not only) a cognitive reality for the pray-er. In contemplation, "our presumptions about 'Fatherhood' strangely start to change [as] we follow Jesus into an exploration of the meaning of 'Fatherhood' beyond all human formulations" (GSS, 326). This exploration teaches us that "Father" refers to "*the* source of infinite tenderness and joy" (GSS, 326)—a surprising return to paternal tenderness as an unfixing of divine masculinity, given her own criticism of motherly fatherhood.[15] The relation between trinitarian naming and gender—the Spirit's teaching of a nonpatriarchal fatherhood that undoes human patriarchy—thus continues to project gender onto inner-trinitarian relations. The Father remains marked as masculine even "after" the purgative success of contemplative prayer in that the pray-er must know that, when she says Father, what she does *not* mean is specifically *father*, rather than anything else. Speaking Father rightly in this way retains rather than undoes a relation to human fatherhood, a point to which I return in chapter 5.

Second, gender takes its shape and meaning from divine desire. Divine desire renders gender fluid; the praying submissive discovers that her Christic transformation "feminizes" her into the "masculine" Christ. Fixed, binary gender roles represent the problem of patriarchy and the fallenness of gender as we actually experience it. In "Woman at the Altar," an exploration of the significance of female priests in liturgical settings, Coakley makes clear the importance of retaining the theologico-symbolic order that genders the God–world relation. Like Ward, she finds the nuptial metaphor of crucial significance for thinking church, Christology, and gender, because the only alternative is to "repress" or "de-essentialize" it. The key is that, "in representing *both* 'Christ' *and* 'church,' the priest is not simply divine/'masculine' in the first over human/'feminine' in the other, but *both* in *both*."[16] The priest's gender fluidity both "summons" and "undermines" gender binaries.[17] But the fluidity of the priest is not limited to movement between masculine and feminine symbolic positions. The priest's gender fluidity moves across the boundary between divine and human as well. The priest symbolically enacts the "*transgression*" of the distinction between divine and human that takes place in the incarnation; this transgression purportedly undoes gender binaries.[18]

The ambiguity here must be noted. Coakley wishes to argue that the "feminization" of creation and the pray-er in relation to God is not to be considered an essentialist assertion about the nature of femininity itself. Rather, this assertion is to invert cultural stereotypes about whether the human who relates to God is "man" in the image of God. The person becomes, as it were, woman, in entering that "dark continent" of willed submission and vulnerability to the only "Father" (of the "Son") who can be trusted to batter the sinful submissive into the only kind of chastity that frees her from her sexed vulnerability to sinful human structures of patriarchy. "She" (and "he," who must become like "her"), must abandon herself to the control of the Spirit in analogy to the way in which the self loses control to the other in the darkness of sexual desire and relationship. But can femininity be installed (even nonessentially) as the human shape of a God-relation without installing masculinity on the divine side of the relationship?[19] Further, the affective life of binaries, as I term it, may not be so easily displaced, for their power often depends on their associative, symbolic relations, which are not overcome. That differently sexed persons move through different positions in a theologico-symbolic order may rather demonstrate the expansive capability of that order to retain its fundamental hierarchies in the face of social transformations.

Construing human, binary gender inside the wider space of divine desire may seem a promising way to destabilize human "twoness." But it brings human and divine personhood into relation closer than they can support: divine persons are fundamentally unlike human persons in that they are the *same* in a very strong sense (the numerical non-multipliability of God). On this issue, there may be some unacknowledged remnants of a now-abandoned position on Coakley's part. In a much earlier version of what becomes chapter 6 of *God, Sexuality and the Self*, Coakley says, "It is axiomatic for me that visions of God as Trinity see the inner-trinitarian relationships . . . as a prototype or charter for right relationships *tout court*. . . . If God's inner relationships are the prototype for our human relationships . . . [then] [t]he perfect relations found in God will be reflected in the relations found at these other levels."[20] In *God, Sexuality and the Self*, she no longer holds this position (GSS, 270).[21] Instead, the Son alone becomes the prototype, or identity, of the human being rightly reformed. Nonetheless, finding the solution to a distinctly *human* problem of relationships in the constitution of the *trinity* remains at least as crucial for Coakley as for the social trinitarians she critiques.

Coakley assumes only two alternatives are available to the Christian and the feminist: either admit, and celebrate, the gendered nature of the God–world relation and the necessary intertwining of (specifically) sexual desire and trinitarian theology or repress it.[22] She finds the former alone viable—understandably, if the alternative is repression. Contemplation's tendency to throw up sexed and sexual ghosts from the unconscious serves as the primary warrant for the assertion that trinity and sex, sexuality, and gender are necessarily entangled.[23] But this does not necessarily follow. Coakley recognizes that the replacement of masculine terms with feminine or non-gendered ones is unlikely to undo Christianity's patriarchal tendencies. But in her readings of gender fluidity, valorization of "vulnerability" and "submission" to God, and hypersexualized trinitarian theology, she strengthens rather than weakens the symbolic-theological order of gender that trinitarian theology helps hold in place. The elevation of gender continues the focus on marital relations as paradigmatically and particularly indicative of the divine–human relation, which is—in some sense—a hierarchical relation. Eschatological gender fluidity promises redemption of gender, but Coakley's insistence on the importance of gender and sexuality now is matched only by her reticence about what such gendered redemption means.[24]

In conversation with Gregory of Nyssa, Coakley also reads the relation between the humanity and divinity of Christ in gendered terms.[25] In one example, Gregory analogically interrelates the intimate mingling between Christ's two natures, the relationship between Christ and the soul, and heterosexual marriage.[26] Coakley argues that, since Gregory designates the divinity of Christ by the image of a bridegroom, "it follows that the human nature of Christ is figured as feminine, as the bride. But it is by no means clear from this that she . . . is simply passive." She continues, "There is . . . an erotic sliding-scale here that moves downward: first the primary mingling between the divine and the human in Christ, then the union between Christ and each human soul in the church, then sexual union between husband and wife."[27]

Two aspects of this are important to Coakley: there is mutuality rather than passivity and activity when Christ becomes the bridegroom, and the "erotic sliding-scale" helps us see "human sexual union" as a "proper, albeit finally mysterious, metaphor for the workings of the incarnate life."[28] Of course, this metaphor is one of heterosexual union, even if no merely passive femininity is assumed, and the kenotic relationality that undergirds this series of metaphors is one in which a divine bridegroom, without lack or self-emptying, pours his fullness into the actively desirous receptacle of his human bride (Christ's human nature).[29] One wonders how non-heterosexual unions could figure the incarnate life, for the image requires that difference between God and humanity be figured by some particular element of the erotic union. The union between divinity and humanity is, after all, a union between what is dissimilar, not a union between two exemplars of the same kind. Nor are Christ and the human being on the same level, even when they are united. In union both with the church and the individual soul, Christ remains the head; this is why we worship him rather than our divinized selves.

If the feminized humanity of Christ is supposed to be, as Coakley suggests, analogous to or even identical with the feminine contemplative, then feminine or human activity is active self-emptying of one's noetic faculties, an active passivity of waiting on God by willfully choosing to make space for the God whose emission fills one. She creates the conditions that permit God's presence, even though she cannot command that presence. This emerges as an odd and unsatisfactory corrective to the problem of passive femininity, and it is not motivated by convincing theological reasons. Images of divinity, the trinity, and sexuality that are generated by the need to correct some problem of human existence or of the construal of personhood remain entirely within (by reversal) the terms of possibility that they seek to overcome. In this case, understanding kenosis as outpouring allows for a sliding scale that moves downward, and implicitly upward, so as to install femininity in the Son *qua* incarnate and masculinity in divinity. Feminine control, the free choice to lose control, means making the self an empty vessel desirous of infusion by divine masculinity.

As Coakley develops the "bafflement" of literalistic gender imagery[30] and the complicated relationships between trinitarian and sexual desire in Gregory, she focuses especially on the way that male "eros" in the believer's submission to God "tips over" into a feminine "dark womblike receptivity" (GSS, 286) as the believer penetrates the darkness of Mount Sinai and waits on the bridal bed to be penetrated by God. Coakley finds sexual symbolism even in the believer's "penetration" of "the invisible and incomprehensible" (GSS, 277).[31] If that really is sexual symbolism, the phallicized believer penetrates the dark, unknown continent of a feminized God. She conjoins this with a never-arriving perfection that she equates with "*loss* of control" and so with male orgasm (GSS, 286, 277). Gender literalism is "baffled" in such moves, perhaps—Coakley's own literalism of "penetration equals sex" goes unremarked—but binary heterosexism certainly is not. Moving between "male" phallicism and "feminine" receptive activity does nothing to undo either their human ordering in relation to each other or the primary heterosexism that such imagery encodes. Again, the theological symbolic order of sexual difference turns out to be far more powerful than the sort of biologically or socially reductive "twoness" that worries Coakley the most, just as in Ward.

Lost is precisely what Coakley would seemingly desire: the theological significance of more expansive and varied relationships among human beings. Further, because idolatry purgation is explicitly and continually an individual act (GSS, 45, 325), albeit with cosmic consequences, what Coakley terms "secular" gender presumptions (the symbolic order of sexual difference[32]) are left untouched. Undoing gender hierarchies means no more than permitting and working toward liberal goals of equality and justice (GSS, 80–81) while valorizing the bodied and affective dimensions stereotypically associated with the feminine and derogated in some Christian and Enlightenment traditions. Coakley remains trapped in what she believes to be feminist aporias of equality and difference, and of conflict between sexual desire and desire for God. Neither gets at the fundamental feminist conviction (as I see it) that the very social order itself needs to change, and that feminism serves as a diagnostic and partial prescription for what such change entails. Remaining within gender, as it were, or heightening gender (even in a fluid form), *distracts* from feminist goals, just as an obsessive focus on homosexuality—pro or con—distracts from the true challenges queer relationships and ways of thinking pose to the symbolic and material orders of church and society.

It is not surprising to find that the various gender transformations the believer undergoes, and that take place in the Son's assumption of a human nature, remain structured around imagery of heterosexual penetration. What is surprising is that theologians not tied to the ultimacy of heterosexuality, whether as orientation or gender identity—Coakley and Ward among them—find such imagery so promising for both trinitarian theology and theologies of sexual difference. Neither of them engages what remains absent from these theologies of sexual difference and divine desire: the significance of clitoral rather than phallic pleasure—that is, of surface touch or copresence rather than penetration. The trinitarian bodies—the images, symbols, and vivifications that theologians use to explicate the shape of these relationships in order to coordinate sexual desire with desire for God and ultimately with inner-trinitarian desire—remain penetrated and penetrating bodies, bodies that must make room for each other since they cannot be in the same place at the same time, their transformations amounting to no more than cycles of penetrating and being penetrated. One of them must give itself over to make room for the other: There is no place for the human being in the trinity unless she willfully and deliberately evacuates herself and becomes ontologically identical with the incarnate Son in the process. The infusion of divinity into the contemplative paradoxically elevates her too highly while reinforcing the figuration of the God–creation relationship in hierarchically and heterosexually gendered terms.

The final way contemplation undoes patriarchy is by prioritizing the Spirit. Seeing how that is the case requires consideration of the constitution of the trinity. The trinity transgresses binaries between two, since the Spirit "interrupts" the relation between Father and Son. The Spirit not only invites human beings into the divine life, but it also "distinguish[es] hiatus: both within God, and in God's relations to creation. It is what makes God irreducibly *three*, simultaneously distinguishing and binding Father and Son and so refusing . . . the mutual narcissism of even the most delighted of human lovers" (GSS 24).[33] The priority of the Spirit in contemplative prayer breaks and checks any assumption that the Father-Son "dyad" takes priority over the Spirit (GSS, 56). To the contrary, the Spirit's experiential priority over both of them (as the "incorporator" of the human into God), reflects the ontological status of the Spirit. The Spirit's priority becomes evident also in that it makes the incarnation possible, enabling the "sonship" into which humans are called and formed. Christology intensifies the sense that trinitarian threeness "ambushes" and "interrupts" human twoness, for we encounter not only the threeness of the trinity but also the incarnational "transgression" of the "ontological binary difference" between God and creation.[34]

Coakley fails to recognize that the difference between God and creation is not a binary difference. Binaries entail the definition of one term by the exclusion of the other. Making the difference between God and creation a binary difference of that sort produces a bad infinity, as it would define (and so limit) the divine by its opposition to the finite, negating transcendence. But Coakley also falls into a kind of theological numerology. It is one thing to argue that any human relationship must be transfigured by the divine as an intermediate "term." It is another to say that divine "threeness" resolves all dyadic fixations—how could such fixations even have arisen in God? Further, what inner-trinitarian hiatus the Spirit maintains and spans becomes unclear; trinitarian difference is arguably "absolute difference"[35] rather than a distinction that needs to be maintained and transcended. As in Ward, the argument seems driven by human-oriented concerns—in this case, the need to interrupt narcissism and allow the trinitarian constitution to solve human conflicts without falling victim to social-trinitarian temptations. But God would not need to be triune in order to interrupt inter-human narcissism, nor does it seem justified to read the Father–Son relation as potentially narcissistic; the latter is a classic instance of the sorts of assumptions that Coakley critiques so ably in analytic-philosophical discussions of free will (i.e., assumption of a zero-sum logic).[36] The orientation of humankind to God redirects destructive inter-human fixations without involving the further posit of metaphysical ambush by divine constitution.

The Spirit's priority extends from the economic trinity into the immanent trinity. Coakley seeks to solve the problem of the filioque in two ways. The first is by fiat: "even to *say* 'filioque' " suggests "a remaining subordination of the Spirit" since it assumes "that a privileged dyad of Father and Son is already established and that the Spirit then somehow has to be fitted in thereafter" (GSS, 330).[37] While Coakley does not show that such is the case, it is a plausible reading of the way doctrine functions beyond the stipulative. The second is by following Thomas Weinandy's reconstitution of the trinity in *The Father's Spirit of Sonship*, including the adoption of some of its more speculative and mythopoetic aspects.[38] That the priority of the Spirit entails its "mutual infusion *in* Son and Father" would seem to entail that the Spirit remains a third. But Coakley goes further: there is "no Sonship which is not eternally 'sourced' by 'Father' *in the Spirit* (in such a way, in fact, as to query even the usual and exclusive meanings of Fatherly 'source')" (GSS, 332). Coakley does not clarify how the latter holds, for the effect on the Father is his "reception back of his status as 'source' from the other two 'persons'" in a process involving eternal "ecstatic . . . deflecting" (GSS, 333).[39] This would establish rather than destabilize his status as source. Moreover, the means by which this reconstitution of the trinity effectively undoes patriarchal idolatry is left unexplained; all we get is that "we humans have to cleanse our hearts and minds of any suggestion that the paternal divine 'source' could ever involve . . . rivalry" between the Father and the Spirit (GSS, 334). But if we could do that, perhaps our other idolatries might be overcome in this way as well; we could "cleanse our hearts and minds of any suggestion" that the Christian God has anything to do with patriarchy and so say nothing more on the topic.

## KENOTIC FEMINIST SELFHOOD

One of the most discussed aspects of Coakley's *oeuvre* is her recovery of vulnerability, submission, and self-emptying—kenosis—from a feminist direction. Yet despite Coakley's careful distinction between different kinds of kenosis, I will show that the meaning of kenosis and its sacrificial implications remain ambiguous in her work and challenge her contention that her recovery of sacrifice has feminist implications.

In a rather strange essay, Coakley reads the binding of Isaac (the *"akedah"*) as "the type of feminist selfhood," in which the "'sacrificial' ordeal" Isaac undergoes involves paying the "costly . . . price of freedom in the richest sense."[40] Isaac is an "honorary woman" who, like "feminist women in the contemporary workplace," moves "between submission to the logic of a *false* patriarchal sacrifice" and "an authentic and discerning 'sacrificial' posture . . . (in which genuine consent is given to the *divine* call to purge and purify one's own desires in order to align them with God's)."[41] Patriarchal sacrifice excludes a "feminist presence in the sacrificial site."[42] Coakley introduces such a presence through Isaac, who freely consents to Abraham's binding. The intense, narcissistic father–son relationship[43] is then ambushed by the angel, who frees Isaac from "human powerlessness . . . through . . . a transformative, divine *interruption*."[44] Reading the *akedah* through the lens of idolatry shows that "[i]t is about the primal sin of the false direction of desire." Thus, sacrifice is required "if I am to unite my desires with God's desires."[45]

It is difficult to follow the logic of Coakley's moves here. Sacrifice is costly—but Isaac ultimately pays no cost. Sacrifice involves submission to God rather than to a patriarch—but it is to Abraham that Isaac submits.

The *akedah* is about idolatry—in that it teaches Abraham not to worship a God who tells him to kill? Sacrifice and submission are required because of sin—but what is *Isaac's* sin? That he obeys his father? But that is just the act that Coakley recommends to the feminist: that act *is* Isaac's submissive sacrifice. The oddity of this account already dramatizes some of the tensions of Coakley's recovery of rational sacrificial kenosis for feminist purposes.

Prayer is Coakley's preferred site of kenotic sacrifice. The pray-er's kenosis is required by her fundamental problems: idolatry and sinfulness. Her desires are wrongly directed. Idolatrously, she prays "Father" and thinks "father." Sinfully, she resists reformation into the shape of Christ, wanting instead to retain her self with its distorted relationships and desires. She wants to hold on to her false knowledge of God and of the other, rather than allowing God to perform the painful reformation of self, knowledge, and relationships that she needs. The practice of contemplative prayer, a freely willed waiting on God that takes the form of self-emptying, permits God to forge her anew by the power of the Spirit so as to bring her to the Father in the form of the crucified Son. In contemplative prayer, "the Spirit progressively 'breaks' sinful desires, *in and through* the passion of Christ" (GSS, 14). The kenosis of the pray-er entails her reformation into "sonship."

The result of contemplative prayer is "distinctive ways of knowing" achieved through willingness "to endure a form of naked dispossession before God; . . . surrender control; . . . accept the arid vacancy of a simple waiting on God in prayer; . . . at the same time to accept disconcerting bombardments from the realm of the 'unconscious': all these are the ascetical tests of contemplation without which no epistemic or spiritual deepening can start to occur" (GSS, 19).[46] The dispossession of the self is simultaneously an achievement of the self: It is a decision freely made, an almost Promethean submissiveness.

This freely willed submissiveness has extraordinary outcomes. The "very capacity to think, feel, and imagine" is transformed by "a constant and disciplined self-reminder" of idolatry's temptations helped along by "the Spirit's simultaneous erasure of human idolatry and subtle reconstitution of human selfhood in God" (GSS, 23). Systematic theology's "insights" are grounded in "intentional practices of un-mastery" that permit one to "consciously guard against the 'onto-theological' danger" (GSS, 46–47). Coakley even "strategically dispossess[es]" herself to the Spirit on occasion.[47] In this transformation, God takes up the pray-er into God's own life. Over time, elite practitioners[48] are joined to the Father and Spirit in the position of the Son through their participation in the suffering of Christ's crucifixion. Although Coakley is somewhat coy about it, the most frequent depiction of this suffering is as a loss of noetic certainty and of idolatrous assumptions of control. Why these amount to *suffering* is never quite explained. Like Ward, Coakley construes the dependence of the human on God as a form of vulnerability. She seeks to distinguish different forms of dependence from each other[49] but never explains her decision partially to conflate dependence with vulnerability in the divine–human relation.

## KENOSIS AND THE CHRIST

The kenosis of the pray-er is conditioned by a prior "Christic" kenosis (PS, 34), which heightens the difficulty of making sense of the ultimate referent of kenosis and sacrifice.[50] Christ is our model: His "frailty, vulnerability, and 'self-effacement'" in Gethsemane and on Golgotha "shows us 'perfect humanity'" (PS, 30). Coakley prefers a broadly Antiochene Christology, since she worries about a separation of natures (threatening the unity of the hypostasis) that assigns suffering to the human nature of Christ or that holds that Christ suffers impassibly.[51] Instead, "Christ's personal identity (his *hypostasis*) is *confected out* of the 'concurrence' of the human and the divine, not simply *identified with* the invulnerable pre-existent Logos. . . . Christ . . . instantiates . . . the very 'mind' that we ourselves enact, or enter into, in prayer" (PS, 38). Christ represents the perfect coincidence of human and divine, although how confection affects the model of divine-human union remains unexplained.

In Christ, we find "the normative concurrence . . . of non-bullying divine 'power' *with* 'self-effaced' humanity," which is Coakley's preferred kenosis: "choosing *never to have* 'worldly' forms of power" (PS, 31).[52] Coakley wants the kenosis of Christ's humanity to be the refusal of false, worldly forms of power, but it seems rather to mean the self-emptying obedience of the human Jesus to the divine will—whether his own or the Father's, for the will of God is also Jesus' *own* divine will, a point emphasized by his "confected" hypostasis. But grasping worldly power is sin, and not sinning must be a genuinely human possibility. Jesus' refusal of false powers must be a human refusal that he is capable of *in* and *by* his humanity. If his humanity "alone" can refuse such power, it becomes unclear why we could not do so also—why we are necessarily sinners while he is not.

Following Gregory of Nyssa, Coakley elsewhere suggests that the "kenosis" of Christ is the infusion into humanity of as much divinity as it can hold.[53] The frailties and limitations of human existence are thus overcome as his humanity becomes suffused with his divinity. As she puts it, using Nyssa's famous image of a drop of vinegar in an ocean, "the divine characteristics are progressively absorbed by the human."[54] She mentions but makes nothing of the fact that Gregory's image is about the divine absorbing the human rather than the reverse. It is not clear how this position is consistent with her earlier claim that Jesus' frailty and vulnerability instantiate perfect humanity, since frailty is here overcome.

These statements combine to raise questions about the character of Christ's kenosis and its relation to his person. Christ did not suffer his own idolatries and sins from which he had to be purged; as Coakley recognizes, he suffered the consequences of the idolatries and sins of others. So his human kenosis cannot be the kenosis into which the pray-er is shaped unless the need for kenosis, theologically, goes *beyond* one driven by sin and idolatry and becomes a need driven either by humanness itself (apart from sin) or by sonship itself (again apart from sin). I contend that both are the case.

Coakley emphasizes that "when one thinks rightly of God as Trinity, the Spirit cannot bypass the person of the Son, or evade thereby his divine engagement in Gethsemane and Golgotha" (GSS, 14). Despite Coakley's distaste throughout for the "linear" model of the trinity, some version of that model is in play here. *Sonship* once more becomes sacrificial, for the content of the Son's person just *is* cruciformity. But—I shall argue—the Son need not be divine on her model, since, granted that the Spirit always returns to the Father, the crucial element Coakley needs is that the Spirit reforms us and carries us up with itself to the Father. What we cannot do independently of the Spirit is reshape our wills so that the desire we have given up may be returned to us after passing through the "crucible" of divine desire. But giving up our own wills is an act of free will, a bodied practice into which grace simply invites us.

Coakley's Christology combines the "concurrence" of human and divine power with the insistence that contemplation—the precondition for salvific transformation—is a freely chosen human possibility. The result is a tendency toward an understanding of deification in which the human enables and initiates divine activity, for the proper human posture is the posture of *making room* for God in the self (PS, 35). That practice of making room is itself not identical with God's action in the human being. God's action is the result of such space-making; just that space-making permits the Spirit to do its work in us. If giving the Spirit permission to work in the human being joins Christ's kenosis to ours, there may be experiential pressure toward hypostasizing the Spirit, but there is neither experiential nor theological pressure toward hypostasizing the *Son*. No reason remains why Christ could not, for instance, have been adopted by God as a result of his extraordinary vulnerability to the Spirit's leading. The human Jesus clings so closely to God that he becomes entirely transparent to the divine. In obedient crucifixion, he sacrifices his own will to God's, thus achieving perfect human freedom. The resurrection is the entirely natural result of this conformity.[55] We are reformed into Christ's shape as we learn to crucify our own wills as he crucified his, and such self-crucifixion is a human ability, a waiting on God.

Since Coakley's earliest trinitarian writings, she has been concerned (in response to Maurice Wiles) to demonstrate the necessity of hypostasizing the Spirit. As a result, the Spirit is—as we have seen—given priority and a multitude of tasks throughout. The Son is, however, given much less to do: He is left nothing but a "creative effulgence," of which the Father is the ultimate source in any case (GSS, 333). In the incarnation, it is the Spirit that "destabilizes [the] 'certainty' of ontological difference" (GSS, 331). Within the circulation of the divine life, the "*primary* divine power" of the Spirit destabilizes even the monarchy of the Father (GSS, 330–32). While the Father is the source and telos of desire, and the Spirit enlivens the pray-er from within, the pray-er *is* the Son, as in the image that Coakley calls "a near perfect visual representation" (GSS, 258) of her trinity.

In an early essay, Coakley describes what is learned about the Son in prayer, which we may mine for reasons to hypostasize the Son. The first and strongest reason is that the experience of prayer is "an experience of a God who actively and always wills to be amongst us," which "immediately focuses attention on the second person in the Godhead."[56] But experience of God's will to be among us might just as easily indicate the work of the Spirit who "incarnates" the Son and lures creation to God. The second argument equates becoming Christoform with "allow[ing] oneself to be shaped by the mutual interaction of Father and Spirit," which entails "entering into his divine life itself."[57] This, too, can be equally well accounted for by an adoptive Christology or by the shared will of the Father and Spirit to make room for humanity in the divine life.

The third argument is that suffering in prayer brings us back to the "grace of divine hiddenness" while reminding us that glorification cannot be achieved without suffering, but that point pertains to the presence of God to the suffering Christ rather than Christ's own divinity.[58] The fourth insight is of the unity of soul and body, that God wants us with our bodies (and sexualities) as well as all the rest.[59] Again, the return of creation as a whole to God along with the adoption of the firstborn of all creation would be enough to account for that element. Fifth, we learn that as individuals we are not cut off, separate, and disjoined from one another, but all part of the body of Christ.[60] That body may just as well be the Spirit-enabled expansion of his transformed materiality following the resurrection; it does not depend on Christ's divinity. Finally, all of creation comes "along" into union with God, but what is necessary is again the bodied materiality of human beings, *some* human one's complete transparency to God, and the way that any union of humanity with God brings the rest of creation with it in the ascent to the Father that the Spirit enables.[61]

Christ's sacrifice is redemptive because, as the climax of evolutionary processes, it represents the completion (my term) of humanity and so of creation as a whole.[62] In him, we see what the human being really is intended to be: "Christ's agony in the garden, or his submission to divine will on the cross, [is] the hallmark and pattern of achieved human freedom."[63] True human freedom *is* "submission" to God.[64] Submission to God means freely willing what God wills through alignment of divine and human desire. Christ's submission is utter and total (expressing the full coincidence of divine and human). He does not resist God at any point; even his Gethsemane experience cannot really be reluctant. Instead, he is led and guided throughout by the Spirit. His utter transparency to the Spirit enables his return to the Father, the source and goal of all desire. His return to the Father realizes the possibility of so returning; the existence of such Christoform humanity

(Christ's humanity, that is) provides the template into which the Spirit molds us. Being molded into that template just *is* redemption, and it makes us (along with the rest of creation) into the Son. The Spirit's purgation repeats the crucifixion in all of us.[65]

Once more, there is no reason why the Son must be hypostasized. A Spirit-led human will—an especially graced human will—is a distinctly human possibility as well as a form of union with God (the Spirit and the Father) as a "son." In fact, an adoptive sonship may cohere better with Coakley's project than the alternative. It avoids potential conflict between Christ's own human and divine wills, which would require the constant evacuation of the former by, or for the sake of, the latter; the difficulties of construing the proper human posture in relation to God as submission when Christ as incarnate Son *is* God and has God's "own" will for his own; and the over-againstness between Father and Son that such a position entails. It would also avoid the erasure of the uniqueness of Christ entailed by her understanding of the Son.

Discussing Troeltsch, Coakley distinguishes between the quantitative ("total interaction of the divine and human") and qualitative ("no other person could ever be like this again, or convey God in this way"—a loose definition) revelation of God in Christ, it may be that she wishes to abandon the latter while retaining the former.[66] But significant problems would then result. The human being could presumably become like Christ, but would have to be "personed" by the second person of the Logos (the reason for the anhypostatic/enhypostasized distinction, although Coakley may intend her confected hypostasis to avoid such a distinction) unless the only condition of the unification of God with human nature is that the human being chooses to make it so (perhaps with divine help, returning us to the question of the actor and mode of union in a confected divine-human hypostasis).[67] The "ownness" of the human will of Christ in relation to the Logos is an important differentiating condition between him and us, one that can explain his sinlessness in contrast to our sinfulness. The explanatory differendum between us and Christ must then yield. Otherwise, the question of why hypostasizing the Logos is necessary becomes unanswerable.

## THE SUFFERING BODY: EVOLUTION, INCARNATION, AND FINITUDE

But Coakley's recovery of vulnerability, submission, and sacrifice for rationalist and feminist purposes raises further questions of the relation between God and finitude, the kind of suffering she enjoins, and the nature of bodied being. Her recovery depends on two fundamental elements: first, that the control given to God is voluntarily ceded to a noncoercive divine power; and second, that the expansion and "empowerment" of the self (cognitively, affectively, spiritually, politically, and sexually) are the result of such sacrificial submission, even though the submission continually, inextricably, and intrinsically involves suffering.

Sacrifice, in other words, must not be enjoined for its own sake; sacrifice may be prescribed to the feminist because it has desirable results for the feminist and for the world. Sacrifice also needs to be made rational rather than violent or patriarchal, Coakley believes. She holds that humans have true freedom;[68] combined with her high valuation of reason, this is why motivation matters so much for the evaluation of altruistic actions. Coakley rationalizes sacrifice through a complicated interweaving of evolutionary theory and Christology with an account of the spiritual senses. The spiritual senses enable the human being to see the world with new eyes. Using those senses, she recognizes the Christological nature of sacrifice at the apex of the evolutionary process in acts of excessive altruism, as well as the preparations for that sacrifice that are laid down in evolutionary processes themselves. Excessive altruism is rational: it leads to greater fitness for entire populations, provides new evidence for a creator (in rendering evolution teleological), and drives the most significant breakthroughs in the evolutionary process.[69] Examining Coakley's rationalization of sacrifice demonstrates unexpected ambiguity in the motivations and effects of sacrificial suffering, however. This ambiguity stems from Coakley's difficulty with envisioning difference in non-agonistic ways.

In recent work, especially her 2012 Gifford lectures,[70] Coakley mounts a case for God's existence through examination of the metaphysical, teleological, and mathematical assumptions and discoveries of contemporary evolutionary biology, specifically in the work of her former Harvard colleague Martin Nowak. Her argument depends on the discovery of trinitarian and Christological aspects of evolution that serve to make plausible (rather than prove) the intimate involvement of an explicitly trinitarian God in every moment of the evolutionary process.[71] Contemplation results in the development of enhanced cognitive faculties as well as "spiritual senses," bodied ways of experiencing the world truthfully in the way that saints do. When applied to the nature of bodied life, the patterns of evolutionary breakthroughs, the potentially fitness-enhancing properties of activities like cooperation and altruism, and the motivations of particularly self-sacrificial persons, the spiritual senses combine with the enhanced cognitive faculties of the contemplative to render visible God's (ordinarily invisible) providential involvement in evolutionary developments. The whole cosmos is set up as a school for self-sacrifice so that all of creation may be divinized by participation in the crucifixion of the Son. God's presence in precultural evolution takes the form of the Holy Spirit's "perpetual invitation and lure of the creation to return to its source in the 'Father', yet never without the full—and suffering—implications of incarnate 'Sonship'."[72] Ultimately, God's constant involvement in the evolutionary process—while hidden most of the time—entails that even Christ's resurrection becomes the "*entirely* 'natural' " climax of "alignment between divine, providential will, and evolutionary or human 'cooperation'."[73]

Competition is endemic to sinful finitude, and suffering and pain are endemic to bodied life. Cooperation is built into creation by evolutionary processes both as a form of fitness-advancement (when sacrifice benefits others) and as a countervailing force to competitive pressures. Cooperation is the evolutionary preparation for altruism, which is participation in Christic agony.[74] The corrective to competition is altruism,[75] willed self-sacrifice on behalf of another, as (she claims) in pregnancy and childrearing.[76] Under conditions of scarcity, altruism requires freely choosing loss and suffering. Such choice is built into the conditions under which human beings exist as part of the evolutionary process,[77] but it is also—and this is Coakley's emphasis—religiously motivated.

The "excessive" altruism of the saints provides evidence that God has set up the evolutionary process so that the teleology of the cosmos is to become a self-sacrificing Christ in its and his totality. This cosmic teleology constitutes a new argument for the existence of God. The argument proceeds in the following fashion. Immanuel Kant's restriction of proofs for God's existence contains some haunting remnants of a teleological argument: regularity in the world alongside the idea of a final cause serves as a "propaedeutic" to belief.[78] Kant's principles disallow the ascription of such teleology to the world as such—but Coakley wants to discover teleology in the world as such. On the other hand, Thomas Aquinas's five ways include a teleological argument requiring a creator to account for regularity. Evolutionary science has no such requirement, even though Aquinas's "natural law ethic . . . coheres perfectly with the deliverances of evolutionary cooperation and altruism."[79] So a teleological argument irreducible to the existence of order, regularity, or fit—for which ateleological evolution can account—is required.

Teleology asks what X—excessive, "supernormal" altruism—is "for" in the case of the saints. Coakley answers that excessive altruism is "for" union with a self-sacrificial God by way of Christic imitation (sacrifice). Deeply self-sacrificial acts are "a manifestation of response to a transcendent realm of grace and 'supernormality'."[80] These self-sacrificial acts lead to a loss of genetic or cultural fitness.[81] Such loss of fitness must be evaluated in evolutionary and rational terms. The current state of evolutionary science recognizes five mechanisms that drive the cooperative aspects of evolution: "kin selection," "direct reciprocity," "indirect reciprocity," "spatial selection (clusters of individual cooperators do well)," and "group selection (groups of cooperators out-compete other groups)."[82] These mechanisms lend themselves to demonstrating that cooperation is an essential evolutionary strategy, even if it is not fitness-enhancing for the individual cooperator. However, significant aspects of human altruistic practices simply *cannot* be accounted for by evolutionary mathematics: that is, they are not reducible to easily codifiable cost-benefit analyses, whether on the individual or group level.[83] Evolution cannot account for " 'genuine', well-motivated altruism," which requires "some means of accounting for the absolute *purity* of altruistic intention, as opposed to a merely strategic self-interested weighing of pros and cons for myself and the group."[84] Either the saints are " 'abnormal' or even mad," or we are rationally forced to recognize that we cannot account for the saints in any way other than Christologically.[85] Judging the saints this way is a "noetic" and "affective" response that we "trust" via an "ecstatic" motion of reason.[86] Such response is enabled by the spiritual senses, which serve "epistemological deepening" activated by an infectious quality that she terms "catch[ing] the halo" of the saints.[87] Using the spiritual senses with the enhanced noetic capacities given in contemplation makes apparent that creation's end is incorporation into God via self-sacrifice.

Coakley's ethico-teleological argument thus intends to account for such *pure* altruism. But here we run into significant definitional trouble. The problem is that excessive altruism has now been defined in such a way that it cannot be "for" the very thing that it is "for." Evolutionary mathematics can currently account for the five behaviors above and may continue to discover new cooperative mechanisms. Further, cultural evolution and the complexity of human social organizations necessarily involve the expansion of group identification beyond close biological kinship. But by defining pure altruism against "merely strategic self-interested weighing of pros and cons," Coakley has definitionally excluded any altruism that evolutionary mathematics could ever account for from "pure" altruism.[88] Calculation indicates a cost-benefit analysis that would render altruism rational in a reductive sense, rather than in the "superrational" sense that Coakley desires.[89] But her contrast between cost-benefit analysis and pure altruism effectively renders impure any altruistic act in which the benefit to another is greater than the cost to me—at least if I am aware of that difference; alternatively, her contrast requires that I effectively forget the interrelatedness of all humankind (a recognition contemplation is often thought to engender).[90]

Notably, Jesus' own practices and ethics of sacrifice are "a fulfillment and completion of" pre-human evolutionary processes that, in the resurrection, result in "a completely *new* form of 'cultural evolution' . . . in the 'excessive', uncalculating mode of a new type of cooperative community."[91] But in what sense is such altruism beyond cost-benefit analysis? Jesus' altruism gives others *maximum* benefit: eternal life in union with God. His altruism has significant cultural impact in its creation of a new community of saints. Coakley too wants altruism to benefit the poor.[92] She also emphasizes repeatedly that death and suffering are nothing in light of the resurrection: Might not Christ have weighed his suffering against its benefit to others and found it almost nothing? The translation away from cost-benefit analysis entails redefining cost-benefit reductively to mean only the immediate genetic and cultural success of the individual who sacrifices; the community on behalf of which the individual sacrifices has disappeared from view in order to avoid the appearance that such sacrifice makes sense on naturalistic evolutionary terms.[93] And since such altruism is Christoformity, the outcome of that altruism is only temporally and derivatively the benefit of another; ultimately, its outcome is one's own benefit (since the "value" of eternal life transcends even the most costly sacrifice). Sacrifice is both the precondition and the mode of one's own divinization, the transformation of one's cognitive, affective, bodily, and sensory capacities beyond ordinary human limitations already in this life. The expanded self thus remains at the very center of the altruistic project.

Coakley continually insists that our kenotic, purgative, prayer-driven suffering is sacrifice of our distorted desires for the sake of flourishing—including our own. The necessity for sacrificial altruism results from sin.[94] Christ's inbuilding in the evolutionary process represents God's providence and responsiveness to contingency rather than God's "direct" will.[95] The reality of sin requires the existence of human freedom, but in evolutionary terms, human freedom is a late development. God knows that human beings will use the freedom built into the evolutionary process to sin, so God also builds a climactic corrective to the results of such sin into the evolutionary process. The climactic nature of the corrective (altruism in its most extreme Christic form) reflects the preparatory developments for it found in the phenomenon of cooperation. The whole cosmos must be conformed to a self-sacrificial God by its suffering and death; humans also have the mandate to choose excessive suffering beyond that enforced by bodied life itself. Coakley dismisses concerns about the extent and qualitative intensity of such suffering through the promise of resurrection.[96] Incarnate life is equated with crucified and sacrificial life: All of creation is disciplined by its own futility so that it might be transformed by a God who can now do what God did not in creation, namely overcome the suffering inherent to bodied life.

On this account, it becomes impossible to argue that sacrifice is necessary because of sin. Finitude must be the driver of self-sacrifice's necessity; better, the driver is material, bodied existence, which serves as a vale for soul-making (not only for humans; for the cosmos as a whole). Implicitly, Coakley operates with something like an Irenaean theodicy transformed into evolution's Christological teleology. Coakley does not wish to offer a theodicy, nor to justify unnecessary suffering, yet she ends up doing both. Although Christ suffers agony and death, the Spirit promises resurrection to everything that suffers like Christ, for to be incarnate (material) is to suffer. Extinction, death, and competition in the evolutionary process do not ultimately constitute a reproach to God, for God is intimately involved throughout, albeit in a hidden way that only occasionally becomes apparent.[97] The evolutionary process is not then wasteful in the amount of suffering and death it involves, for its reality is justified by its end and by its redemption; bodied existence is taken along into resurrected existence, but bodied existence is also in itself the generator of self-sacrifice, pain, and suffering.

It turns out, then, that the body is the human, indeed the cosmic, problem—a surprisingly unfeminist conclusion. Lack is the driver of the evolutionary process in this way, for the necessity of sacrifice along with its fitness-enhancing properties results from the scarcity endemic to finitude. In this sense, the condition of human and evolutionary development is the problem that human and divine sacrifice must overcome. The entire order of creation has been set up in this way because God knows that human beings will sin, so God builds in a corrective to sin: a school for self-sacrifice. That corrective establishes the teleology on which Coakley's argument for God's existence depends.

Coakley defines altruism so that it is always costly (the same goes for cooperation at lower evolutionary levels); economies set up to benefit all participants in those economies are thus consigned to lower, premoral levels of development. The goodness of creation lies therefore in its finite capacity to provide opportunities for the kind of self-sacrifice that reforms the human being into the image of God. Its goodness lies not in itself but in the material for soul-making it provides, for excessive altruism overcomes the merely natural by transforming nature into God. The affirmation, value, and fulfilment of material creation requires entering into a crucified state, freely in the case of humans, inevitably in most nonhuman creation. All of creation may, through its bodied and suffering existence, return to God, but only by affirming its existence *as suffering* and *through suffering*. In so doing, creation becomes divine, for the Son is "divine and perfected creation" as a whole (GSS, 114).[98]

## ATTENTIVENESS TO THE OTHER

I have argued that Coakley's struggles with difference reflect problems in her trinitarian theology as well as her account of the God-world relation. Another form of testing of Coakley's attentiveness to difference is available. The transformations the pray-er undergoes should not bring with them silence in the face of oppression and injustice. Silent waiting on God should not lead to complacency in the face of evil, and neither ought it to entail acceptance of pain and suffering grounded in injustice rather than in the painful justice of God. To the contrary, the pray-er finds the strength to resist injustice in waiting on God. Indeed, *only* the contemplative is properly able to attend to the other without imperialism (GSS, 47–48).[99] We follow Coakley as she tests the merits of contemplative prayer for social transformation through fieldwork. Coakley uses fieldwork to provide empirical evidence for her sexually focused trinitarian theology as well as for the transformative effects of contemplation. In published work so far, she gives two examples of such fieldwork. The first structures the engagement with "lived religion" (GSS, 68) in the first volume of her systematics, while the second will provide the ground for arguments in later volumes.

In GSS, her fieldwork takes the form of qualitative ethnography: eighteen interviews, lasting up to ninety minutes each, with white Britons from a town in northern England during the mid-1980s.[100] The character of the evidence brings the generalizability of her findings into question.[101] This question intensifies when one sees how Coakley describes occasions on which her fieldwork fails to comport with her theological views. Nearly all her informants think the Spirit's activity of praying in the pray-er leads to joy and an uplifted affect, for instance. Coakley strongly believes, to the contrary, that mature contemplative prayer entails pain and participation in "genuinely Christlike dereliction." The decision whether to consider such dereliction and pain either a Spirit-willed condition or a sign of the Spirit's absence or "inactivity" becomes the "theological crux" of the maturation and true Spirit-directedness (the orthodoxy) of her informants (GSS, 178–79).[102] When congregants insist on "joyousness" as the "norm," Coakley presses them until they admit "phases of dryness themselves" (GSS, 176). In contrasting the more "fundamentalist" charismatics among her informants with the increasingly intellectual Anglicans (GSS, 175, 183),[103] Coakley suggests that maturation entails "a nudging towards reflective trinitarianism" combined with "[q]uieter worship [and] a greater respect for 'tradition'." Most important, these more mature Christians develop a chastened understanding of the Spirit in which they "are more truly affected by implicitly christological issues of prayer and pain, prayer and desolation, prayer and apparent failure." As a result, they are "emerg[ing] into conscious trinitarianism." *Why* is conscious trinitarianism necessary for a mature prayer life? Because "life in Christ" necessarily means an "intimate relation to the Father" and therefore "must be consistent with life in the Spirit too, otherwise the 'persons' would be divided" (GSS, 181). These themes did not, apparently, emerge in her interviews until she introduced and pressed them.

In the second example of fieldwork, performed while teaching at Harvard and training for the Anglican priesthood, Coakley spent an hour a week for a semester teaching the practice of silent prayer to jailed prisoners in the Boston area.[104] Coakley vividly describes her astonishment at encountering the harsh realities of the racialized prison system in the United States (in implicit contrast to a less-racialized British context).[105] Her descriptions of the prisoners and her reactions to them are worrisome, however. She never "felt under threat from the men, nor was [she] ever subjected to any inappropriate sexualized remarks, as [she] had expected"—apparently this might be "beginner's luck."[106] One wishes she had thought more deeply about power and the way prison regulates prisoners and punishes transgressions: How could these prisoners possibly be threatening to her? She expresses surprise at the insight of a "bright and articulate Latino-African-American prisoner"[107] who had "instinctively grasped," without the "language of asceticism," how asceticism works. She compares the "position a young African-American man is apt to adopt when sitting informally" to the posture of heschyastic prayer.[108] She then hastens to reassure the reader she is "fully aware of the violent and criminal capacities" of the prisoners, even as she expresses her newfound sympathy for the reasons why they might wish to return to lives of crime after their sojourn in jail.[109] Coakley enthusiastically describes the transformative effects of silent prayer on the prisoners in prayer's production of "[g]entleness, poise, peace and solidarity,"[110] but she fails to reckon too with a deeper challenge the experience poses to her thesis regarding sociopolitical transformation. The prisoners reportedly become calmer and less resistant as a result of their contemplative activities—a desirable transformation, perhaps, in the context of a just order. But the prison system in the United States is, as Coakley comes to recognize, decidedly not a just order. To conform prisoners more thoroughly to the parody of nonviolence required by the prison arguably belies rather than supports Coakley's thesis regarding the sociopolitical effects of contemplative prayer.

One might think Coakley's expectations in the prison reflect nothing more than (inexcusable) thoughtlessness, or perhaps a certain level of ignorance of racial, class, and power dynamics in the United States to be remedied in future writing; white feminist theologians teaching at elite institutions, like Coakley and myself, have often shown ourselves lacking in this regard. Forthcoming volumes of her systematic theology promise a deeper exploration of these issues, but hints already present suggest little cause for optimism. Following Cornel West's (and others') insights about the invention of race in the Enlightenment, Coakley introduces a "speculative" connection between that invention of race and the Enlightenment suppression of the "dark continents" into which transformative silent prayer brings the pray-er, suggesting that a " 'dark,' subversive divine power" unleashed through silent prayer might therefore provide an antidote to modern practices of racialization. Her reversal here of the negative associations of divine "darkness" is an instance, however, of the sort of inversion—good associations replacing bad—whose efficacy Coakley herself strenuously questioned in cases where maternal images replace paternal ones in divine gendering. An inversion of the associations of darkness will foment the recovery of the potential for "penitential reformation" in prison rather than punishment.[111] Little consideration is thereby given to the actual, concrete ways in which the modern prison system in the United States is sustained by economic practices, cultural ideologies of criminality, and racially unequal enforcement of laws. Coakley suggests she in future offer "a Christian theological response" to Michel Foucault's "cynical views of repressive power . . . in prison and asylum" since "[t]hese institutions are a mark of our civilization or lack of it."[112] Although Foucault was not a cynic who understood power as repressive, time spent with him may well lead to more thoughtful engagement with sociopolitical otherness (and hopefully race) in her later work.

In conclusion, let us look at Coakley's interpretation of Matthew 25, which shows the way in which she misses, I believe, the fundamental nature of transformed existence in Christ. As Coakley recognizes, the story of the sheep and the goats must be the absolute center of any representation of the risen and returning Christ. Jesus says that on the day of judgment, those chosen for the kingdom say to the Lord that as they served others, they did not know him. Even as Christ identifies himself with those whom they served, they cry out that they did not see him in the poor, needy, hungry, and imprisoned. By implication, they simply shared of their goods with those in need, thinking neither of Christ nor of themselves. Their actions determine their fate, but they did not know what they were doing. Coakley, however, interprets this text in opposite fashion. "[T]he true recognizers of Jesus are precisely the ones who are unaware of it; yet presumably their moral antennae have in some sense been trained, spiritually if unconsciously, and by repetitive breakage, to respond to the identity of Jesus in those whom they serve."[113] That repetitive breakage is the effect of kenotic creation of "the 'space' in which non-coercive divine power manifests itself" (PS, 5). Such self-withdrawal, and a constant policing of the self to ensure that withdrawal, make up the heart of Coakley's theology. No delighted presence to and with the other is permitted in this life. The self constantly monitors itself to make sure it is adequately lost; it seeks the good of the other for the sake of its own transformation. Only on that basis is the self found, expanded, made better than ever—in fact, made divine. In sum, there are *selves* all the way down. Self-perfection is here raised not only to a, but to *the*, religious duty. And once more the gratuity of creation is abrogated: "gifts to the poor are . . . the paying back of an initial debt that God lays on us even as we are created. Since life itself is a gift, all of life is also a repayment."[114] Perhaps such fundamental indebtedness—the utter absence of gratuity—can explain the obsessive focus on "dispossessing" a possessive self in Coakley's work.

## NOTES

1. See Linn Marie Tonstad, "Sarah Coakley," in Staale Johannes Kristiansen and Svein Rise, eds., *Key Theological Thinkers: From Modern to Postmodern* (Burlington, VT: Ashgate, 2013), 547–57, for a brief overview of her biography and work.
2. Sarah Coakley, "Afterword: 'Relational Ontology,' Trinity, and Science," in John Polkinghorne, ed., *The Trinity and an Entangled World: Relationality in Physical Science and Theology* (Grand Rapids: Eerdmans, 2010), 185–99, esp. the discussion on 195–97.
3. Sarah Coakley, "'Femininity' and the Holy Spirit?," in Monica Furlong, ed., *Mirror to the Church: Reflections on Sexism* (London: SPCK, 1988), 124–35.
4. Sarah Coakley, "Feminism," in Philip L. Quinn and Charles Taliaferro, eds., *A Companion to Philosophy of Religion* (Cambridge, MA: Blackwell, 1997), 601–606.
5. See Sarah Coakley, "*Kenosis* and Subversion: On the Repression of 'Vulnerability' in Christian Feminist Writing," first published in Daphne Hampson, ed., *Swallowing a Fishbone? Feminist Theologians Debate Christianity* (London: SPCK, 1996), 82–111.

6. Sarah Coakley, *God, Sexuality and the Self: An Essay 'On the Trinity'* (Cambridge: Cambridge University Press, 2013), 2, 19, 20, 23 (taking examples just from the prelude); hereafter GSS.

7. Looking only at GSS, see xiv, 6–7, 9, 10, 34, 74–76, 84, 273–74, 291, 296–98, 320–22 (where we encounter the specter of "an enforced feminist rearrangement of God and the world"), and 326.

8. The warrants for Coakley's theological moves heavily depend on the character of her spiritual life. In contrast to other academics who "engage in self-aggrandizing polemics" (GSS, xvi), her work "involves a complex range of interdisciplinary skills" in "a task of some considerable spiritual and intellectual delicacy" (GSS, xvii). She practices "trinitarian thinking of a deep sort" thanks to her practices of prayer (GSS, 16). Indeed, her *"contrapuntal relationship"* to contemporary philosophy is not "a merely human product" but grounded "in response to God's prior tuning" (GSS, 18). Her task requires "historical, religious, and political sophistication" alongside "distinctive spiritual strengths of self-knowledge and humility" (GSS, 80). Although I critique certain aspects of Coakley's understanding of the effects of contemplative prayer in this chapter, no part of the critique is directed at the practice as such.

9. In recent years, some feminist theologians have also begun finding resources in Coakley. The primary critical question they raise is whether advocacy of vulnerability to God is bad for women. The theologically dubious character of construing dependence on God *as* vulnerability does not arise. See Carolyn A. Chau, " 'What Could Possibly Be Given?': Towards an Exploration of Kenosis as Forgiveness—Continuing the Conversation Between Coakley, Hampson, and Papanikolaou," *Modern Theology* 28 (January 2012): 1–24; Anna Mercedes, *Power for: Feminism and Christ's Self-Giving* (London: T&T Clark, 2011), esp. 30–34 and 106; and Janice Rees, "Sarah Coakley: Systematic Theology and the Future of Feminism," *Pacifica* 24 (October 2011): 300–14. Jason Byassee's "Closer Than Kissing: Sarah Coakley's Early Work," *Anglican Theological Review* 90, no. 1 (Winter 2008): 139–55, shares with Rees's article the disadvantage of repeating Coakley's claims without analysis or critique. Anne-Louise Eriksson prefers dependency to submission as the site of vulnerability in relation to both God and other in Eriksson, " 'Behold, I Am the Lord's Handmaiden, Not the Lords'!' On Sarah Coakley's Powers and Submissions," *Svensk Teologisk Kvartalskrift* 85 (2009): 73.

10. The Carmelites John of the Cross and Teresa of Ávila are her primary sources for the nature of contemplative prayer and its purgative effects.

11. Intra-trinitarian love need not be construed as desire for union, which is Coakley's designation of good desire. The distinct trinitarian persons simply *are* their union; in contrast, Coakley suggests that the Spirit "sustain[s] the difference between the persons, thus preserving a perfect and harmonious balance between union and distinction" (GSS, 24). We are reminded of Ward's "differences that desire the other."

12. See Sarah Coakley, " 'Batter My Heart . . .': On Sexuality, Spirituality, and the Christian Doctrine of the Trinity," in G. Gilbert, ed., *Papers of the Henry Luce III Fellows in Theology* (Atlanta: Scholars Press, 1996), 49–68; a version of the discussion appears in GSS, ch. 6.

13. In the late 1980s, Coakley occasionally used both masculine and feminine pronouns for the trinity (e.g., in "Femininity and the Holy Spirit," 128 and *passim*).

14. In GSS, Coakley identifies six implications of her method, which "represent the human, cognitive correlate of what we have here taught about the Trinity": recognition of the relation between sexual and divine desire, the need to keep the Holy Spirit in the lead and "guard" its "distinctness," the lability

and decentralization of gender that contemplation entails, the transformation and expansion of reason that contemplation performs, the ascesis of desire in which contemplation results, and the achievement of a "trinitarian model of power-in-vulnerability" (340–43).

15. Coakley, "'Femininity' and the Holy Spirit?" 124–35, esp. 126 and 132. See also her critique of Leonardo Boff, which focuses on his Mariology but includes brief reflections on the Spirit. Sarah Coakley, "Mariology and 'Romantic Feminism': A Critique," in Teresa Elwes, ed., *Women's Voices: Essays in Contemporary Feminist Theology* (London: Marshall Pickering, 1992), 97–110, esp. 109.
16. Sarah Coakley, "The Woman at the Altar: Cosmological Disturbance or Gender Subversion?" *Anglican Theological Review* 86, no. 1 (Winter 2004): 76.
17. Ibid., 76–77.
18. Ibid., 87–88, esp. n.31.
19. Part of this paragraph also appears in my chapter on Sarah Coakley in *Key Theological Thinkers*, 551.
20. Coakley, "Batter My Heart . . . , " 51. In GSS, the claim becomes more modest: the trinity is "charter and paradigm of perfect *relationship*"; "reflections" in "Batter my heart . . . " now become mere "associations" (266).
21. In GSS, 271–72, she charges some versions of feminism with a similar problem.
22. Coakley, "Woman at the Altar," 75; GSS, 74–75, 276, and *passim*.
23. Coakley also avers that a number of patristic authors demonstrate the necessity of sexual metaphor in exploring the trinity. Many of those metaphors are found in commentaries on the *Song of Songs*; this weakens the evidence since the text, not the trinity, requires the metaphors. Others derive from imagery of reproduction rather than sexuality. Further, such metaphors are almost always accompanied by a variety of other images; Coakley privileges those relating to sexuality over the rest.
24. In Sarah Coakley, "Ecclesiastical Sex Scandals: The Lack of a Contemporary Theology of Desire" (forthcoming as ch. 1 of *The New Asceticism* [London: Bloomsbury Academic, 2015]), it becomes clear the options are restricted to lifelong marital fidelity (straight or gay) or erotic chastity (i.e., celibacy).
25. Coakley has published multiple essays and chapters on Nyssa, often with only minor variations. This discussion focuses only on "'Mingling' in Gregory of Nyssa's Christology: A Reconsideration," in Andreas Schuele and Günter Thomas, eds., *Who Is Jesus Christ for Us Today? Pathways to Contemporary Christology* (Louisville, KY: Westminster John Knox, 2009), 72–84.
26. Coakley, ibid., 75. On 78, she refers to her essay, "Does Kenosis Rest on a Mistake? Three Kenotic Models in Patristic Exegesis," in C. Stephen Evans, ed., *Exploring Kenotic Christology: The Self-Emptying of God* (Oxford: Oxford University Press, 2006), 256–59, with respect to the pouring out of divinity by the bridegroom, implying that she adopts an infusion model.
27. Coakley, "'Mingling'," 78–79.
28. Ibid., 79.
29. Ibid., 78.
30. Coakley shares with Janet Martin Soskice, Rowan Williams, and to some extent Graham Ward the belief that as long as sexed theologico-symbolic positions do not map directly and straightforwardly onto sexed bodies, sexed and gendered imagery is entirely appropriate to relations between God and the world.
31. The first image refers to Gregory of Nyssa's *Life of Moses*; the second comes from his *Commentary on the Song of Songs*.
32. Which, as we have seen in Balthasar and Ward, is at least as theological as it is secular.

33. The Spirit is clearly a "third" here.
34. Sarah Coakley, "The Trinity and Gender Reconsidered," in Michael Welker and Miroslav Volf, eds., *God's Life in Trinity* (Minneapolis, MN: Fortress Press, 2006), 139; also in GSS, 57.
35. As Kathryn Tanner argues in "Absolute Difference," in Chris Boesel and S. Wesley Ariarajah, eds., *Divine Multiplicity: Trinities, Diversities, and the Nature of Relation* (New York: Fordham University Press, 2014), 217–33.
36. See Coakley, "Feminism," 604.
37. Her earlier construal of the Spirit as the interruption of the narcissistic relation between Father and Son does exactly what she here rejects.
38. See Thomas Weinandy, *The Father's Spirit of Sonship: Reconceiving the Trinity* (Edinburgh: T&T Clark, 1995), 73, where Weinandy claims that the Spirit "persons" the Son and Father.
39. Coakley seems to adopt Rowan Williams's language of ecstatic deflection as a designation of trinitarian relations. Williams describes how John of the Cross's understanding of the union of the soul with God entails participation in the way divine love never rests on a single "object" but is always deflected onto another: Word to Father to Spirit to Father ("The Deflections of Desire: Negative Theology in Trinitarian Disclosure," in Oliver Davies and Denys Turner, eds., *Silence and the Word: Negative Theology and Incarnation* [Cambridge: Cambridge University Press, 2002], 123). Williams shares with Coakley the assumption that in some way, divine relations must exhibit (in order to overcome) the same potential problems as human relationships do. Both also write as though trinitarian relations take place primarily as one-to-one relations, as if the Father focuses only on the Son, but then has "his" gaze deflected onto the Spirit, and so on—seemingly ruling out simultaneous attention to *both* of the other trinitarian persons.
40. Sarah Coakley, "In Defense of Sacrifice: Gender, Selfhood, and the Binding of Isaac," in Linda Martín Alcoff and John D. Caputo, eds., *Feminism, Sexuality, and the Return of Religion* (Bloomington: Indiana University Press, 2011), 20.
41. Ibid., 25.
42. Ibid., 23.
43. Ibid., 27.
44. Ibid., 18.
45. Ibid., 29.
46. The unconscious functions primarily in the Jungian sense; see Sarah Coakley, *Powers and Submissions: Spirituality, Philosophy and Gender* (Malden, MA: Blackwell, 2002), 51–52 (hereafter PS). The danger for the human being is "a too sudden uprush of material from the unconscious, too immediate a contact of the thus disarmed self with God" (PS, 35). The view of selfhood, and of the unconscious, entailed by such statements has never quite been explicated in Coakley's writing.
47. Sarah Coakley, "Stories of Evolution, Stories of Sacrifice," Gifford lecture 1, Apr. 17, 2012, https://web.archive.org/web/20130514032332/http://www.abdn.ac.uk/gifford/documents/Gifford_Lecture_1_-_lecture_text.pdf (accessed Dec. 14, 2014), 7 (hereafter Gifford 1).
48. Coakley holds both that contemplation is a practice available to anyone, and that real advancement happens as the person ascends from stage to stage in a deepening purgation before God. It is only as the latter takes place that the deep noetic and suffering consequences of contemplation become available. While all are *in via*, some are much further along than others, and it is from them that we are to learn. Seeing the risen Christ, for instance, is the effect of such differences: "reception of religious truth does not occur *on a flat*

*plane* . . . even within the ranks of 'believers' the understanding or perception of the 'risen Christ' will have variations of depth" (PS, 132).

49. Sarah Coakley, "Creaturehood before God: Male and Female," *Theology* 93 (1990): 57–58.

50. Coakley's full Christology and soteriology await further development in later volumes of her systematics. In *Punish and Heal*, vol. 3, she intends to treat sin and atonement, and in vol. 4, *Flesh and Blood*, she will exposit Christ and the Eucharist. Further indications of her Christology, which fit well with this discussion, may be gleaned from her work on Ernst Troeltsch; see especially the distinctions in *Christ Without Absolutes: A Study of the Christology of Ernst Troeltsch* (Oxford: Oxford University Press, 1988), 104–107, and ch. 4 *passim*.

51. Coakley, "Does Kenosis Rest on a Mistake?" 251–56.

52. Coakley makes clear that *divinity* is not kenotic, although it is gentle (PS, 38). However, in "Providence and the Evolutionary Phenomenon of 'Cooperation': A Systematic Proposal," in Francesca Aran Murphy and Philip G. Ziegler, eds., *The Providence of God: Deus Habet Consilium* (London: T&T Clark, 2009), 187, Coakley equates divine kenosis with "effusive pouring out" and with "self-hid[ing]," which she considers peculiarly appropriate to divinity.

53. Coakley, "Does Kenosis Rest on a Mistake?" 258–59.

54. Ibid., 258.

55. Coakley, "Providence and the Evolutionary Phenomenon," 189.

56. Sarah Coakley, "God as Trinity: An Approach through Prayer," in *We Believe in God: A Report by the Doctrine Commission of the General Synod of the Church of England* (London: Church House Publishing, 1987), 109.

57. Ibid.

58. Ibid., 109–110.

59. Ibid., 110.

60. Ibid., 110–111.

61. Ibid., 111. See also GSS, 114.

62. Coakley intends the entire cosmos to be carried "back up" to the Father by the Spirit as all of creation in its groaning suffering becomes Christoform, but she intends the volitional aspects of response to God to remain human, rational, and free. The latter has to be the case in order to protect her against the criticism that her kenotic humanity entails unfreedom. The mechanism for bringing the cosmos "along" with the elevation of the human, beyond something like the retention of (transformed) bodied materiality, is unclear, although the Eucharist will clearly play a central role.

63. Coakley, "Providence and the Evolutionary Phenomenon," 188. Here again we see that Christ's kenosis may actually be his obedient submission to the "Father."

64. As I have argued throughout, there is no need to construe human dependence on God as submission or vulnerability.

65. Coakley wants to hold the crucifixion as a once-and-for-all event; this is true in the sense that at least one human being "successfully" returning to the Father is required for the "creation" of the form of true humanity. But in a derivative sense, the crucifixion is to be repeated in each of us as the condition of possibility and indeed the mode of access to the form of true humanity. See Coakley, "Reconceiving 'Natural Theology': Meaning, Sacrifice and God," Gifford lecture 6, May 3, 2012, https://web.archive.org/web/20130514032332/http://www.abdn.ac.uk/gifford/documents/Gifford_Lecture_6_-_lecture_text.pdf (accessed December 14, 2014), 18 (hereafter Gifford 6).

66. Coakley, *Christ Without Absolutes*, 105. Coakley points out that Troeltsch's Christology does not permit Christ to be unsurpassable, but she approves the capacity of Troeltsch's Christology to "democratiz[e] . . . revelation," which allows "a much more positive appreciation of all the saints" (ibid., 117). Coakley's natural theology and her theological epistemology depend heavily on a kind of democratic elitism of the saints (the saints are spiritual elites, but anyone may participate in the practices that make them so and hope to become saints themselves). Coakley generally affirms some version of the sixth type of Christology she identifies in ibid., 106, Chalcedonianism, but as she explains in "What Does Chalcedon Solve and What Does It Not? Some Reflections on the Status and Meaning of the Chalcedonian 'Definition'," in Stephen T. Davis, Daniel Kendall, S.J., and Gerald O'Collins, S.J., eds., *The Incarnation: An Interdisciplinary Symposium on the Incarnation of the Son of God* (Oxford: Oxford University Press, 2002), 143–63, that affirmation leaves quite a bit of leeway.

67. The theological rationale for the immanent trinity would almost disappear in such a case. Christ would not even be necessary for salvation; he might simply be a coincidence, an exemplum of what might happen in any human being.

68. In PS, 26, she rejects a libertarian view of freedom. Her quasi-theodicy in "Providence and the Evolutionary Phenomenon" depends on indeterministic freedom (188). Coakley insists throughout that contemplation is "freely willed."

69. See her inaugural Norris-Hulse lecture: "only the production of moments of evolutionarily stable 'cooperation' could have brought about the *breakthrough* events in the whole upward thrust of evolutionary development. At those key moments . . . cooperation can be shown to have been creatively and sustainingly vital." Sarah Coakley, *Sacrifice Regained: Reconsidering the Rationality of Religious Belief* (Cambridge: Cambridge University Press, 2012), 23–24.

70. The text of the six lectures, collectively titled "Sacrifice Regained: Evolution, Cooperation and God," is available at https://web.archive.org/web/20130514032332/http://www.abdn.ac.uk/gifford/about/ (accessed December 14, 2014).

71. Coakley, "Providence and the Evolutionary Phenomenon," 187.

72. Ibid., 186–87.

73. Ibid., 189.

74. Ibid., 191.

75. Writing with Martin Nowak, Coakley distinguishes between cooperation, which they define as "a form of working together in an evolutionary population, in which one individual pays a cost (in terms of fitness, whether genetic or cultural) and another gains a benefit," and altruism, which requires also intent: "an individual is motivated by good will or love for another (or others)," "Cooperation, *alias* Altruism: Game Theory and Evolution Reconsidered," Gifford lecture 2, Apr. 19, 2012, https://web.archive.org/web/20130514032332/http://www.abdn.ac.uk/gifford/documents/Gifford_Lecture_2_-_lecture_text.pdf (accessed December 14, 2014), 6–7 (hereafter Gifford 2). Although Coakley insists on the importance of careful definition (Gifford 2: 8), her position on altruism is slippery. On the one hand, altruism is part of evolutionary processes in at least the human case. It *is* altruism, by definition, because it imposes a cost on the individual for the intended benefit of another—or so we must read "good will or love." Yet in other cases (as in "Ethics, Cooperation and the Gender Wars: Prospects of a New Asceticism," Gifford lecture 4, April 26, 2012, https://web.archive.org/web/20130514032332/http://www.abdn.ac.uk/gifford/documents/Gifford_Lecture_4_-_lecture_text.pdf

[accessed December 14, 2014], 1, hereafter Gifford 4), she wants to investigate altruism that surpasses any benefit to another.

76. Willed pregnancy is a recent development (presuming effective contraception as well as other forms of female reproductive control). Coakley's interpretation of the voluntarily submissive and sacrificial aspects of childrearing appears already in "'Femininity and the Holy Spirit," 130, where she suggests that while women raising children are "battered into submission," forced to give up their abilities to control and plan their lives, men avoid the same so that their recognition of vulnerability is postponed until later in life. The problem for Coakley here is merely that "spiritual surrender of this sort also involves economic surrender and subjugation." Coakley's use of such imagery, with its direct translation of submission to other people into spiritual gain, raises questions about her insistence that she advances only the latter, not the former.
77. Gifford 1:15–16.
78. Coakley, "Teleology Reviewed: A New 'Ethico-Teleological' Argument for God's Existence," Gifford lecture 5, May 1, 2012, https://web.archive.org/web/20130514032332/http://www.abdn.ac.uk/gifford/documents/Gifford_Lecture_5_-_lecture_text.pdf (accessed December 14, 2014), 14–16 (hereafter Gifford 5).
79. Gifford 5:18.
80. Ibid.
81. Gifford 5:19. Coakley does not note the reduction from her earlier, more expansive definition of altruism.
82. Gifford 2:14.
83. Gifford 3:4–5.
84. Gifford 3:10.
85. Gifford 6:11; 5:20. These disjunctions may fall victim to the fallacy of the excluded middle.
86. Gifford 6:9–12.
87. Gifford 6:14.
88. Thus her insistence that her argument is not a God of the gaps argument also falls apart, since she has simply defined the saints as something that science cannot account for (Gifford 5:19). Coakley follows Alexander Pruss ("Altruism, Normalcy, and God," in Martin A. Nowak and Sarah Coakley eds., *Evolution, Games, and God: The Principle of Cooperation* [Cambridge: Harvard University Press, 2013], 329–42), on this issue, who says that an explanation must be found for the surprising fact that for human beings, "what is biologically cooperative and what is morally altruistic by and large coincide." Since science cannot explain normative facts, another explanation must be found: God wanted it to be so (333). Such cooperation must be explained by a cause that can generate new natural kinds, and God is such a cause (335–39). Science can account only for such a development if it indeed (which Pruss admits is possible) already contains normative concepts in some sense. Presumably Pruss and Coakley assume that all normativity requires a transcendent source and so the posit of a God. Unsurprisingly, Pruss develops his teleological argument into a defense of reproductively-oriented, exclusively heterosexual sexual ethics in *One Body: An Essay in Christian Sexual Ethics* (South Bend, IN: University of Notre Dame Press, 2012).
89. Coakley, Gifford 6:17.
90. Coakley's examples of pure altruism, which (partly following Pruss) include Jean Vanier, Mother Teresa, and Dietrich Bonhoeffer, emphasize that the altruistic actors are not gaining any genetic or cultural fitness advantage *themselves* in what they do (Gifford 5:19). But Nowak's rules of cooperation seem perfectly capable of accounting for situations in which I do not myself benefit

(whether genetically or culturally) from my own sacrifice, especially if my group identification is expanded (as cultural evolution permits and indeed requires) beyond close biological kinship.

91. Coakley, " 'Ethics, Cooperation and Human Motivation: Assessing the Project of Evolutionary Ethics,' " Gifford lecture 3, Apr. 24, 2012, https://web.archive.org/web/20130514032332/http://www.abdn.ac.uk/gifford/documents/Gifford_Lecture_3_-_lecture_text.pdf (accessed December 14, 2014), 18.

92. This theme emerges most clearly in Gifford 4. At the end of Gifford 6, Coakley argues for benefitting the poor, although the Cappadocian material she cites in Gifford 4 focuses on seeing Christ in the poor rather than on assisting them. Elsewhere, she mentions that her essays on the resurrection and on seeing Christ in the poor are the preliminary moves toward the work she will do in the second volume of her systematics, *Seeing Darkly: An Essay 'On the Contemplative Life'*. Sarah Coakley, "Gregory of Nyssa," in Paul L. Gavrilyuk and Sarah Coakley, eds., *The Spiritual Senses: Perceiving God in Western Christianity* (Cambridge: Cambridge University Press, 2012), 55 n.63.

93. This is a reason gender—discussed almost exclusively in Gifford 4—plays no real role in the lectures. Coakley points out the well-known association between sacrifice and femininity in the history of evolutionary biology (Gifford 4:3–8). Her discussion of the gendered aspects of evolutionary cooperation (especially in meerkats) in Gifford 4:9–16 mentions Sandra Blaffer Hrdy in passing but ignores much work in feminist evolutionary biology, perhaps because it often argues that such cooperation is fitness-enhancing among kin (as, for instance, in the grandmother hypothesis). Macrina, as the Christian culmination of gender fluidity, is fluid because she is not "concerned in any way with *genetic* reproductive success" but rather with "cultural reproduction," Gifford 4:19. Later, however, Coakley contrasts concern for cultural reproduction with excessive altruism (Gifford 5:19) while insisting that excessive altruism (contra Timothy Jackson) does have cultural impact (Gifford 5:6). It is not clear how to square these points with each other. After all, the outcome of such sacrifice in Christ's case is a community of cooperators that institutes an entirely new order of reality.

94. Coakley, "In Defense of Sacrifice," 23.

95. Coakley interprets Thomistic secondary causation in terms she explicitly derives from Molinism (despite their incompatibility), so that the existence of "contingent variables and choices" does not entail God "directly *causing* what occurs" although God knows what will occur; "Providence and the Evolutionary Phenomenon," 187.

96. Ibid., 188.

97. Ibid., 188–89, 192.

98. Coakley's reluctance to distinguish between us and Christ emerges already in Sarah Coakley, "Can God Be Experienced as Trinity?" *The Modern Churchman* 28 (1986): 22: "the Spirit is what *makes* humanity divine, whereas 'Christ' *is* divine humanity."

99. The same claim is found in Sarah Coakley, "The Deepening Life of a Silent Prayer Group," *Harvard Divinity Bulletin* (Spring 2002): 24.

100. The work took place in connection with Coakley's term on the Doctrine Commission of the Church of England.

101. Coakley assumes that one can examine "social connections and *patternings* in doctrinal and spiritual expression" that transcend radically different social and historical contexts. She asks what trinitarian theologies accompany which social orders, along with particular views of women, gender, and sexuality (GSS, 157). The many different ways in which doctrines and

church practices relate in different contexts render the assumption of consistent regularity questionable, especially since the most contemplation-focused traditions have not historically demonstrated the consequences (particularly regarding gender) that Coakley believes must necessarily result. Coakley discovers similar patterns in a variety of patristic conflicts, particularly Montanism, the Arian controversy, and the "Origenist" crisis (see GSS, 121–41; and Sarah Coakley, "Prayer, Politics and the Trinity: Vying Models of Authority in Third-Fourth-Century Debates on Prayer and 'Orthodoxy'," *Scottish Journal of Theology* 66 [November 2013]: 379–99). Throughout, Coakley heavily depends on suggestive rhetorical tropes and rhetorical questions, thus rendering her argument difficult to pin down or assess on the merits.

102. In the earlier version of this chapter, published as "Charismatic Experience: Praying 'In the Spirit'," in *We Believe in the Holy Spirit: A Report by The Doctrine Commission of the General Synod of the Church of England* (London: Church House Publishing, 1991), Coakley connects Christ's dereliction to Balthasar's question whether "the Spirit may not only on occasion drive one into a sharing of Christ's desolation, but actually be that in God which spans the unimaginable gulf between despair and victory?" (31). In a footnote, she reads William Blake's "throne of grace" representation of the trinity which adorns the cover of GSS (and serves as one of her two preferred visual images of the trinity in ch. 5 of GSS) this way.

103. Coakley somewhat condescendingly excuses the lack of technical and traditional theological knowledge among her informants (GSS, 174, 177, and esp. 184–85). In "Deepening Life," 23, she clarifies that she agrees with Thomas Keating that silent prayer is impossible unless one has a genuine attraction or aptitude ("attrait") for it, and that the practice will "inexorably" lead to the adding on of "*lectio divina*, imaginative, scriptural meditation, liturgical prayer, intercession, and so on."

104. Sarah Coakley, "Jail Break: Meditation as a Subversive Activity," *Christian Century* (June 2004): 18–21.

105. See ibid., 18. Great Britain is not, however, less racialized, only differently racialized: the seemingly endless recalcitrance of the Metropolitan Police in London to deal effectively with racial issues is only the internationally best-known example of the intertwining of police practice with British racialization.

106. Ibid., 19.

107. Ibid.

108. Ibid. She here elides a classed and gendered bodily habitus with racial categories. Bodily ownership and the claiming of space, and the ways posture signals power, have complicated connections to age, class, race, and gender.

109. Ibid., 21.

110. Ibid., 19.

111. Ibid., 20.

112. Ibid., 21. It is worrisome to see the use of language of "civilization" in a piece on race, given the role ascription of civilization and its lack plays in dehumanizing racial others.

113. Sarah Coakley, "The Identity of the Risen Jesus: Finding Jesus Christ in the Poor," in Beverly Roberts Gaventa and Richard B. Hays, eds., *Seeking the Identity of Jesus: A Pilgrimage* (Grand Rapids, MI: Eerdmans, 2008), 316–17. Coakley also contrasts the knowledge of Christ shown by the elect with the ignorance shown by the damned.

114. Ibid., 317.

# BIBLIOGRAPHY

Byassee, Jason. "Closer Than Kissing: Sarah Coakley's Early Work." *Anglican Theological Review* 90, no. 1 (Winter 2008): 139–55.

Chau, Carolyn A. " 'What Could Possibly Be Given?': Towards an Exploration of Kenosis as Forgiveness—Continuing the Conversation Between Coakley, Hampson, and Papanikolaou." *Modern Theology* 28, no. 1 (January 2012): 1–24.

Coakley, Sarah. "Afterword: 'Relational Ontology,' Trinity, and Science." In *The Trinity and an Entangled World: Relationality in Physical Science and Theology*, ed. John Polkinghorne, 184–99. Grand Rapids: Eerdmans, 2010.

———. " 'Batter My Heart . . .': On Sexuality, Spirituality, and the Christian Doctrine of the Trinity." In *Papers of the Henry Luce III Fellows in Theology*, ed. Gary Gilbert, vol. 1, 49–68. Atlanta: Scholars Press, 1996.

———. "Can God Be Experienced as Trinity?" *The Modern Churchman* 28, no. 2 (1986): 11–23.

———."Charismatic Experience: Praying 'In the Spirit'." In *We Believe in the Holy Spirit: A Report by The Doctrine Commission of the General Synod of the Church of England*,17–36. London: Church House Publishing, 1991.

———. *Christ Without Absolutes: A Study of the Christology of Ernst Troeltsch*. Oxford: Oxford University Press, 1988.

———. "Creaturehood before God: Male and Female," *Theology* 93, no. 755 (September 1990): 343–54.

———. "The Deepening Life of a Silent Prayer Group," *Harvard Divinity Bulletin* 30, no. 4 (Spring 2002): 23–24.

———. "Does Kenosis Rest on a Mistake? Three Kenotic Models in Patristic Exegesis." In *Exploring Kenotic Christology: The Self-Emptying of God*, ed. C. Stephen Evans, 246–64. Oxford: Oxford University Press, 2006.

———. "Ecclesiastical Sex Scandals: The Lack of a Contemporary Theology of Desire." In *The New Asceticism: Sexuality, Gender, and the Quest for God* (London: Bloomsbury Academic, forthcoming).

———. " 'Femininity' and the Holy Spirit?" In *Mirror to the Church: Reflections on Sexism*, ed. Monica Furlong, 124–35. London: SPCK, 1988.

———. "Feminism." In *A Companion to Philosophy of Religion*, ed. Philip L. Quinn and Charles Taliaferro, 601–606. Cambridge, MA: Blackwell, 1997.

———. "Feminism and Analytic Philosophy of Religion." In *The Oxford Handbook to Philosophy of Religion*, ed. William J. Wainwright, 494–525. Oxford: Oxford University Press, 2005.

———. "God as Trinity: An Approach through Prayer." In *We Believe in God: A Report by the Doctrine Commission of the General Synod of the Church of England*, 104–121. London: Church House Publishing, 1987.

———. *God, Sexuality and the Self: An Essay 'On the Trinity.'* Cambridge: Cambridge University Press, 2013.

———. "Gregory of Nyssa." In *The Spiritual Senses: Perceiving God in Western Christianity*, ed. Paul L. Gavrilyuk and Sarah Coakley, 36–55. Cambridge: Cambridge University Press, 2012.

———. "The Identity of the Risen Jesus: Finding Jesus Christ in the Poor." In *Seeking the Identity of Jesus: A Pilgrimage*, ed. Beverly Roberts Gaventa and Richard B. Hays, 301–19. Grand Rapids: Eerdmans, 2008.

———. "In Defense of Sacrifice: Gender, Selfhood, and the Binding of Isaac." In *Feminism, Sexuality, and the Return of Religion*, ed. Linda Martín Alcoff and John D. Caputo, 17–38. Bloomington: Indiana University Press, 2011.

———. "Jail Break: Meditation as a Subversive Activity." *Christian Century* (June 2004): 18–21.

———. "*Kenosis* and Subversion: On the Repression of 'Vulnerability' in Christian Feminist Writing." In *Swallowing a Fishbone? Feminist Theologians Debate Christianity*, ed. Daphne Hampson, 82–111. London: SPCK, 1996.

———. "Mariology and 'Romantic Feminism': A Critique." In *Women's Voices: Essays in Contemporary Feminist Theology*, ed. Teresa Elwes, 97–110. London: Marshall Pickering, 1992.

———. "'Mingling' in Gregory of Nyssa's Christology: A Reconsideration." In *Who Is Jesus Christ for Us Today? Pathways to Contemporary Christology*, ed. Andreas Schuele and Günter Thomas, 72–84. Louisville: Westminster John Knox, 2009.

———. *Powers and Submissions: Spirituality, Philosophy and Gender*. Oxford: Blackwell Publishers, 2002.

———. "Prayer, Politics and the Trinity: Vying Models of Authority in Third-Fourth-Century Debates on Prayer and 'Orthodoxy'." *Scottish Journal of Theology* 66, no. 4 (November 2013): 379–99.

———. "Providence and the Evolutionary Phenomenon of 'Cooperation': A Systematic Proposal." In *The Providence of God: Deus Habet Consilium*, ed. Francesca Aran Murphy and Philip G. Ziegler, 179–93. London: T&T Clark, 2009.

———. "Sacrifice Regained: Evolution, Cooperation and God." The Gifford Lectures. University of Aberdeen. Aberdeen, Scotland. April 17–May 3, 2012. https://web.archive.org/web/20130514032332/http://www.abdn.ac.uk/gifford/about/. Accessed December 14, 2014.

———. *Sacrifice Regained: Reconsidering the Rationality of Religious Belief*. Cambridge: Cambridge University Press, 2012.

———. "The Trinity and Gender Reconsidered." In *God's Life in Trinity*, ed. Michael Welker and Miroslav Volf, 133–42. Minneapolis: Fortress Press, 2006.

———. "What Does Chalcedon Solve and What Does It Not? Some Reflections on the Status and Meaning of the Chalcedonian 'Definition'." In *The Incarnation: An Interdisciplinary Symposium on the Incarnation of the Son of God*, ed. Stephen T. Davis, Daniel Kendall, S.J., and Gerald O'Collins, S.J., 143–63. Oxford: Oxford University Press, 2002.

———. "The Woman at the Altar: Cosmological Disturbance or Gender Subversion?" *Anglican Theological Review* 86, no. 1 (Winter 2004): 75–93.

Eriksson, Anne-Louise. "'Behold, I Am the Lord's Handmaiden, Not the Lords'!' On Sarah Coakley's Powers and Submissions." *Svensk Teologisk Kvartalskrift* 85 (2009): 70–74.

Mercedes, Anna. *Power for: Feminism and Christ's Self-Giving*. London: T&T Clark, 2011.

Pruss, Alexander. "Altruism, Normalcy, and God." In *Evolution, Games, and God: The Principle of Cooperation*, ed. Martin A. Nowak and Sarah Coakley, 329–42. Cambridge: Harvard University Press, 2013.

———. *One Body: An Essay in Christian Sexual Ethics*. South Bend, IN: University of Notre Dame Press, 2012.

Rees, Janice. "Sarah Coakley: Systematic Theology and the Future of Feminism." *Pacifica* 24, no. 3 (October 2011): 300–14.

Tanner, Kathryn. "Absolute Difference." In *Divine Multiplicity: Trinities, Diversities, and the Nature of Relation*, ed. Chris Boesel and S. Wesley Ariarajah, 217–33. New York: Fordham University Press, 2014.

Tonstad, Linn Marie. "Sarah Coakley." In *Key Theological Thinkers: From Modern to Postmodern*, ed. Staale Johannes Kristiansen and Svein Rise, 547–57. Burlington, VT: Ashgate, 2013.

Weinandy, Thomas G. *The Father's Spirit of Sonship: Reconceiving the Trinity.* Edinburgh: T & T Clark, 1995.

Williams, Rowan. "The Deflections of Desire: Negative Theology in Trinitarian Disclosure." In *Silence and the Word: Negative Theology and Incarnation*, ed. Oliver Davies and Denys Turner, 115–35. Cambridge: Cambridge University Press, 2002.

# Interlude

The kenotic theologies that we have examined in Coakley, Ward, and Balthasar connect difference—particularly sexual difference and sexuality—to inner-trinitarian relationality. All three, for diverse reasons, assume that difference continually requires making room for the other. In each case, the differences of difference keep collapsing into each other. In Ward and Balthasar, the connection between difference, suffering, and (self-)sacrifice introduces the cross into the eternal relations of origin and places the cross at the origin of the trinity. In Coakley, gratuity disappears in an economy of dispossession that elides different forms of suffering and continues to symbolically sex the God–world relation. These kenotic theologies make use of theological translation mechanisms in which coming from someone installs submission to that someone: obedience under the sign of sin, humanity, or sonship; eucharistic gratitude under the aegis of an economy of debt grounded in the gift.

## UNDOING THE MATCH: DEATH AND TRINITARIAN *TAXES*[1]

Karl Rahner's famous axiom sets up the basic problem of the relationship between the history of the Son and the immanent trinity: "the 'economic' Trinity is the 'immanent' Trinity and the 'immanent' Trinity is the 'economic' Trinity."[2] Rahner's interest is in the implications of the axiom for experience and knowledge of God. If incarnation is not proper to the divine person who becomes incarnate, but is merely appropriated to the Son,[3] what existential significance will the doctrine of the trinity—grounded in just that incarnation—have for humankind? Theologians typically worry that Rahner's axiom, taken to its fullest extent, makes the world necessary to God. Rahner himself does not read the axiom that way. It is not intended to violate the contingency of creation but to express the reality of God's self-revelation in the economy. He wants to avoid installing a hidden God whose self-revelation is untrue to God's own being. At least in intention, Rahner's axiom expresses the fundamental truth-condition of trinitarian theology: God shows Godself as God truly is in the history of Jesus.

Yet the death of Jesus and his apparent subordination to the will of the Father require that there be *some* differences between who God is eternally in God's own blessed being, and the way and means by which God reveals Godself in history's fractures and fragmentations. Jesus is not simply identical with God (though he is fully God), for he is also human, and his humanity alone cannot itself become the direct object of worship.[4] These differences are also required by the fact that the mission of the Son takes place in a finite world marred by sin and death, all of which, in some way, render the world a nontransparent place for the enactment of his eternal relationship with the Father and the Spirit.[5]

An oft-told account of the relationship of the Son to creation assumes that creation takes place in his image and (if supralapsarian) for the sake of his incarnation within it. Creation *qua* finite may thus be a near-transparent vessel for his embodiment, since that embodiment was intended from the first. But creation cannot be equated with divinity and remain creation. Although the infinite must never be thought in competition or direct contrast with the finite, it must conversely not be reduced to a magnified version of finitude. As human, Jesus is finite, even if his personal particularity as a human being is that he is the eternal Son incarnate (i.e., that he is enhypostasized by the Logos).

Sin and death make the differences more apparent and more challenging. The rule of sin in the world means that creation lives fundamentally at odds with itself. This self-contradiction, the *in curvatus se* of the human imaginary, means that even if the Son assumes humanity untouched by sin, the untwisted character of his humanity is not shared by those around him, and they act on him as much as they are acted on by him. Further, the imagery of a humanity untouched by sin reflects assumptions about the relationships between persons, and between persons and natures, that have little meaning in a world in which the interdependency of all persons on each other and on the social, material, and cultural environment stands in the foreground of historical consciousness. The sinfulness of the material and relational context affects the mode of revelation even if Jesus himself is the full shining forth of God in his every act, a tension heightened by the centrality of his suffering and death. The majority opinion in the history of Christian theology is that subjection to death is an effect of sin, although immortality cannot belong to human or finite creatures by right, as their own possession: even in the garden, Adam and Eve depend for their immortality on access to the fruit hanging from the tree of life (or in drier imagery, on their relation to God). Conversely, death cannot belong to God, and—I would argue—should not be made the translation of *any* aspect of inner-trinitarian relations. Death is, in the theological sense, what stands opposed to God, what has no being. It ought not be made internal to God, especially in some sacrificial or deflectionary account of the relationship between the Father and the Son.[6] Any modification of that thesis that makes death appropriate to the Son threatens his absolute divinity even if it is modified by the assertion that there is nothing generic in the trinity and that the three persons are not persons in the same way.

Some account must be given of how Jesus' history relates to the glory he had with the Father before the world began. The solutions we have examined make something of the contingency of creation but allow for very little other difference; in different ways, Balthasar, Ward, and Coakley all ground the cross in the trinity. I have argued that they are unable to distinguish with sufficient clarity between what belongs to the particular form of the revelation of the Son in history and what belongs to his eternal relation to the Father. Indeed, to a significant extent, they refuse to draw that distinction; when and where they do draw it, they weaken it as much as possible. They collapse difference across God–world economies in order to interpret sonship or coming from another as death, submission, and suffering. These trinitarian theodicies reflect the concerns of the contemporary cultural moment: difference, suffering, and sexuality. In opposition to imagined liberal, autonomous subjects, they construct subjugated divine and human subjects of desire. The theological justification for these connections lies in the way the cross must be made possible by "something" in the eternal life of a God now understood as the ultimate desir-er. The result is that characteristics belonging to the economic history of the Son are written into the eternal relations between trinitarian persons.

## TRINITARIAN ORIGINS

> The call to become a follower of Christ is in the first instance a call to accept the obedience of the Son to the Father.[7]

Depending on the direction from which the trinity is viewed, cross and Father variously stand at the origin of trinitarian theology. The Father's origin status may seem unproblematic: The Father is the ingenerate origin. The claim that the cross stands at the origin of the trinity is much less familiar. Yet in the order of knowing rather than the order of being, the claim approaches the trivial. For it is at the cross that Jesus transforms himself into God's word-seed, his flayed speaking body the word of love, forgiveness, condemnation, identification; his final silence the most eloquent speech of the Father. We might then ask with Marcella Althaus-Reid about "the economy of God's exchange-rate mechanism,"[8] or what, in this theo-economy, counts as exchangeable for what. Revealed is the ineffable God, yet it was the Son and not the Father who suffered on the cross—patripassianism is among the oldest heresies. So the Son represents the Father, a doctrine of absence rather than presence.[9] Whence this hidden God, this God who withdraws and in hiding stands out as most visible—or does He? Hence Irigaray: "Sublime and unattainable distance of a God-Father, intolerable brazier to which anyone comes who does not overcome passion."[10]

The Mediator. The In-Between. Behind the cross stands the Father's word, expressed in his Word. When mission is tied to cross, when the Son comes to die, and when this death belongs to him by virtue of his status as Son, the cross stands at the origin of the trinity, for the cross is read back into the Father–Son relation from its first moment. In receiving himself from the Father, the Son receives the possibility—indeed, the reality, the *Voropfer*, the eucharist—of death. In non-owed gratitude to the one to whom he owes his being, he offers himself up in kenotic submission to the Father whose very begetting of another alongside himself stands as the Father's own sacrifice. So God contains within Godself the possibility, indeed the reality (in superscript we write: given creation, but in eternity we have but one act) of death. And death is at the moment of distinction. Death and difference meet and kiss. The embrace of difference grounds death. Not just that: in *this* difference, in receiving oneself from another, there is death. For death belongs to the Son and not the Father: to be begotten ultimately contains death within itself. To beget another is to give that one death: begetting installs difference, gift, gratitude, and consent to the grateful self-sacrifice contained in the reception of self, or in the receptive self. Eucharist (the gift of death). And this begetting grounds the goodness of difference itself, of creation, and of sexual difference. Death and difference are thus read backward into the constitution of the trinity and forward into the cross.

Exchange rate: difference equals death.

When kenosis is tied to crucifixion and the road to Calvary, and is read into the nature of the divine being as such, the self-emptying of God does not escape the logic of that which it opposes: the victory of death in love. At the heart of the trinity one finds the eternal cross.

The analogical imagination that ties together these theological relationships—differences in relation that do not collapse into identity—remains tied to theologico-symbolic heterosexuality. The symbolic order of these theologies of sexual difference—Father–Son, God–man, Christ–church, Yahweh–Israel, and Adam–Eve—contains within itself no reciprocity between and among women. This symbolic order spatializes kenosis by thinking it as a space-making in which the self must move aside to make room for the other, to be filled by the other, for self and other cannot be in the same place at the same time, as it were. It is no wonder, then, that the emissary logic of this symbolism ties begetting to the imagery of male climax. In contrast, clitoral pleasure does not proceed; it does not penetrate or need penetration. There is no need to make space where there is surface. The skin's surface that reveals and hides need neither be broken nor invaded for the enjoyment of relation—a phenomenology of touch without violence.[11] There need be no coming-from (no *and* as the installation of symbolic masculinity) in this imaginary.

What would trinitarian theology look like, what would phenomenologies of difference or theological symbolics of difference look like, if they were thought under the aegis of the clitoris instead of the phallus? This is an oblique way to get at the question of relation without procession.

## DISAFFILIATION AND DISFILIATION

> [T]o become multiple may mean only one thing: to disown the name of
> the Father, or the name of the heterosexual dyadic family.[12]

In the final moment of this tour of kenotic turns in recent theology, let us
consider the queer theologian Marcella Althaus-Reid. Althaus-Reid's work
borrows without repayment from a wide variety of discourses and represents
an experiment in form, in theological writing without final responsibility to
a Father-God and his consensually sacrificed Son. Althaus-Reid commends
critical bisexual theological reflection: both-and, not either-or (QG, 1). Her
two major books, *Indecent Theology* and *The Queer God*, examine the
interrelation of theology, economy, and sexuality. Althaus-Reid (with Lisa
Isherwood) describes queer theological thinking: "Queer Theology takes its
place not at the centre of the theological discourses conversing with power,
but at the margins. It is a theology from the margins which wants to remain
at the margins." Asking for equality requires rendering oneself legible for
the center, which distributes the privilege of recognition. "Terrible is the fate
of theologies from the margin when they want to be accepted by the centre!
Queer Theology strives, instead, for differentiation and plurality."[13]

Althaus-Reid brings together liberation theology with feminist theology
and theory, queer theory, and Marxist thought, and goes beyond all in a
heady mixture of allusive genre-play, brilliant flashes of theological insight,
and turns of phrase that linger long after the reading is complete. For
Althaus-Reid, theology at its best is a practice of transformation: "theology's
main function is to be fictitious. It aims to lie in the sense that its mission is
to express the inexpressible, . . . utopia" (QG, 130). Where authorized theology claims purity and self-transparency, in language and sexual practice,
queer theology recognizes that "[t]o regulate sexuality in the name of divini-
ties means to regulate the order of affectionate exchanges but also other
human exchanges such as the political and economic systems. . . . Queering
theology is not a rhetorical pastime but a political duty."[14] Queer theology
is written differently: its genre is camp, irony, humor, indirect communication, and self-disclosure, theology written while not wearing underwear,
in Althaus-Reid's famous image from the beginning of *Indecent Theology*.
Or again, "Queer Theology is the theology of baring behinds as an act of
protest and defiance against ways of thinking which must be dis-authorised
and discredited" (QG, 149). Importantly, "Queer holiness . . . is always the
holiness of the Other" (QG, 134). Queerness does not insist on the logic of
the same, that is, that the other must be just like me, must be acceptable and
decent according to my standards for living and loving.

Queer theology is not only for those identified by the ever-expanding acro-
nyms of non-straight existence, for "[h]eterosexual women need to come out
of their closet like anybody else, speaking the truth about their lives, heavily
domesticated by patriarchal definitions of what it is to be a heterosexual,

monogamous, faithful woman with a motherly vocation."[15] The strictures that ideal-type theology—T-Theology, as Althaus-Reid terms it—imposes are so narrow, and so contrary to lived existence, that "heterosexuality makes of every courageous human being a Queer, indecent person. Only very hypocritical people may claim to live according to the rules, *contra natura*, of heterosexual politics and theology. Deep in our hearts, we are all 'Queer Nation' needing to come out" (IT, 120). Althaus-Reid sees T-Theology as a practice of ideological mystification, a naturalization and codification of rules that ground exploitative economic orders and ensure that there are always ways to condemn those who live and love differently for their indecency. She challenges the isolation of women and queer theologians, in which "their voices are not heard questioning serious issues on the construction of the Trinity or Christology,"[16] even as Althaus-Reid's queer theology does not assume the stability of categories of gender, sex, or sexuality.

Althaus-Reid's influence runs throughout this project, albeit often at a subterranean level, although as should also be obvious—given the genre and some of the postulates found in previous chapters—this project is also far more deeply engaged with T-Theology than she would approve. In the rest of this interlude, I summarize the argument of the book from within Althaus-Reid's queer-theological discourse. The summary may be difficult to follow for those unfamiliar with the hermeneutical practices of queer theory generally and of Althaus-Reid specifically; for those unfamiliar with queer theology, it may also be startling in language and genre.

> [T]o be a theologian is to respond to urges of parental divine ingratitude, and in a way, nothing could be more true.[17]

The profoundly absurd theological logic of Althaus-Reid's lobster God recognizes the position of God between regulation and undoing (QG, 65). This God "liberates us from finding in God 'the source' of sexual identities such as God the Lesbian or God the Genderfucker. No, instead of these 'premature ejaculations', sexuality becomes part of the articulation of God in history, of people and Trinitarians" (QG, 68). As we saw in our analysis of Graham Ward and, in a different sense, Sarah Coakley, "the Genderfucker may also be straight" (QG, 68), for the straight road to the cross may be a phallic logic. We seek no warrant in God Godself for abandoning heterosexual thinking and the privileging of heterosexual practice. Nor do we look to the cross as the instantiation of the meaning of divine difference. Instead, we seek non-ordered logics of difference, grounded in resurrection as transformative nonrepetition.

The faithful are invited to infidelity, to a refusal of the logic of betrayal that structured Rahab's disidentification with her people and re-identification with the colonial other (QG, 107). Rahab joined "the patriarchal economy of 'nothing for free' (or for grace) [so] she has been redeemed in the (hetero) sexual exegesis of the text," a redemption the queer theologian must refuse for herself (QG, 104). God needs human infidelity; God needs to be led astray on a leash held by the queer theologian (QG, 46). To "obliterat[e . . .] filiations," as we seek to do, is costly for the woman philosopher (and theologian), many of whom live with "broken hearts" (QG, 48). Of course, kenotic emissions come from fullness when they spurt out with the theologian's generative creativity; there is no lack in the moment in which the penis asymptotically approaches identity with the phallus,[18] except for the lack installed by time itself. But since theology takes place not in time but in ideal-space, or so it seems, the theologian's emission, like God's, may be eternal or near-as-makes-no-difference.

Queer theology's kenosis of representation comes from theologians on the move, across borders, "[n]omadic Queers [who] are searching for God's nipples and soft lips and trying to bite them in oblique ways in order to achieve some oblique transcendence in their lives" (QG, 49). Nomadic queers pay the cost of disaffiliation and disidentification; they become lost in the God who, even when led astray, may continue to direct the action consensually. Most significantly, the nomadic queer theologian follows two rules (and she does not repay her debts): "First, never repeat and second, keep decency at bay (in order to fight the theological vocation of normalising discourses about God)" (QG, 51). But the logic of trinitarian theology as rule-bound invocation is nothing other than the vocation of repetition and normalization: normalization of the one-and-only-ness of the transcendent Father whose generous begetting of the other Son renders him consensually sacrificed, given up, before the foundations of the world were laid, installing the cross at the very heart of the trinity and death in the womb and vaginal canal of woman theologically construed. (The areas of the woman that Balthasar suggests do not interest the heterosexual man sexually are forgotten.) So the nomadic queer theologian must betray the trinity.

This betrayal begins in Althaus-Reid's work in the kenosis of representation that is God the orgy. The kenotic debate, as Althaus-Reid recognizes, has been an attempt to "find in Jesus the imperial power of God which is not self-evident, and make of it a grandiose theological speech of power" (QG, 56); as we have seen, reinstalling the Father as identical with the only God and rendering difference collapsed across gendered economies. For Althaus-Reid, the trinity offers promise at this point, because two representative economies collide and embrace here.

First, the trinity installs "an immoderate, polyamorous God, whose self is composed in relation to multiple embraces and sexual indefinitions beyond oneness, and beyond dual models of loving relationships." While superficially reminiscent of Coakley's attempt to destabilize sexed "twoness" through the "ambush" of the interruptive third, Althaus-Reid sees that there may be "more than three in this triad" since other loves and lovers may still be stashed in various closets (QG, 58). The "statistics (or logic of three)"—the work that the concept *threeness* does—might also have to be given up (but not in favor of two or four) (QG, 61). This moves us outside an attempt to prioritize known (to the extent necessary), revealed, and regulated divine difference over known (to the extent necessary), constructed, and regulated heterosexual difference, a move that repeats without removing the structure of visions of God-human relations that either elide difference or make difference competitive.

Second, an "omnisexual kenosis" commits to "destabilise sexual constructions of heterosexual readings of heterosexuality itself," and of all other sexual identities in "a truly genderfucking process" (QG, 57)[19] that, we can now see, will have to refuse a genealogy of patriarchal difference as quickly as it refuses a genealogy of sexual difference. The "sameness" of the sexed identities of the trinitarian persons' nonsexed selves refuses ultimacy to regulated difference (sexual difference) while installing the possibility of omnisexual kenotic movement for trinitarian and human persons alike, precisely in the refusal of "trinitarian and human persons alike."

Significantly, Althaus-Reid's concept of kenosis focuses not on an operation of the self on the self, a paternal or filial self-emptying that installs a regulated ecstatic relation requiring mythologies of difference and distance, but instead on the necessity for humans to lead God astray. Theologically speaking, it is we who have jailed God, locking God up in eternal Father-Son relationships that transform into "hypostasized transcendence" rather than recognizing in God a nomad capable of multiple nonfidelities.[20] For "Queer theologians are the ones who consider to what excesses God takes God's love for humans, that is, which are God's transgressive desires and how we have sadly tamed or limited these villainies" by locking together "the ruling of economic orders, those of divinity, and the ruling of intimate relationships" (QG, 23, 25). Divine economies reveal and enact the ultimacy of economies themselves. Keeping *theologia* and *oikonomia* together will be legitimate only if and when we unregulate the *oikonomia* and allow *theologia* to follow (unleashed). Althaus-Reid transposes kenosis, saying instead that "Queerness is something that belongs to God, and . . . people are divinely Queer by grace" (QG, 34). The whole kenotic order is here inverted. Althaus-Reid's project is against "T-Theology," colonial theology operating on the level of ideas and idealism while refusing its own intercalation with material bodies. Our current project extends Althaus-Reid's critique in order to show the specific refusal (and installation of regulation) that drives trinitarian theology down the straight road to the cross to stand before the door of the law of sacrifice and submission. We show just how it was possible "theologically speaking to merge the God-Father's self-referential monogamous love with the polyamorous love of God in community which is the Trinity" (QG, 37), for although Althaus-Reid considers this merge the "real mystery," the details of the project and the conditions of its success *are* the ideal-theological project that, in its very success, loses sight of the God of whom it attempts to speak. And this project is *very* successful.

The God of the cross is a "dissolute" God who "repl[ies] to our horror by redistributing frontiers and allocations, in an exercise of an economy of horror where God's self needs to be sacrificed in order to continue exist-ing" (QG, 36). Rather than reading Althaus-Reid into a regulated kenotic economy on this point, let us instead think of the cross with no Godself remaining hidden behind the cross, no distant Father enthroned even if his embrace of the Son is loving, for the Father loves you himself. A kenosis of patriarchy "could theoretically still pay at least some of the bills left in theology by the colonial orders, by producing an effectual relocation of assumed landmarks" (QG, 38).

If we move from dick-sucking[21] to clit-licking in touching God's transcendence—if we no longer arrange ourselves kneeling around God's Son-phallus or the priest-theologian's asymptotic possession of it (QG, 10)[22]—we will no longer gag on God's fullness nor be forced to swallow an eternal emission. Instead we may find there already the differences of pleasures "outside the law."[23] Let us grant that "the historical (public) acts of the Trinitarians cannot differ too much from their private ones" (QG, 59) and thus ask about the temporality of acts directed toward the estab-lishment of a nonrestricted community of what Althaus-Reid, referring to God, calls polyfidelity, although even polyfidelity may not be enough as we need infidelities also (even if infidelity to divine paternal revelation leaves us with broken loving hearts) (QG, 58). After all, "God's back is made of difference" (QG, 16), which means that neither sameness nor difference can ultimately predominate in our stereoscopic trinitarian visions. Preventing domination will require enlisting specific forms of contradiction rather than the installation of distanced super-intimacies. Disaffiliation, and disfiliation of God, initiate a new relationship to both past and future, for "the filial always looks at the past in search of traditions of authority," and an apoca-lypse in theology (the unveiling of the veiled Father) will refuse an eschatol-ogy that is "the science of postponement" (QG, 45). We must redistribute the frontiers of theological bodies to show the truth that "the Trinitarian formula expresses the material reality of the intimate reunion where God is not expected to coincide with Godself" (QG, 54). But before we can get to climaxes, we must pay the *taxes* of the gift.

## NOTES

1. A *taxis* (plural: *taxes*) in trinitarian theology indicates a pattern of trinitarian action or order.
2. Karl Rahner, *The Trinity*, trans. Joseph Donceel (New York: Crossroad, 1997), 22.
3. Trinitarian reflection often appropriates divine acts or appearances to differ-ent persons. They are appropriations because *opera trinitatis ad extra sunt indivisa*. Rahner's particular target is the assumption that any person of the trinity could have become incarnate.
4. See Wolfhart Pannenberg, *Systematic Theology*, vol. 1, trans. Geoffrey W. Bromiley (Grand Rapids, MI: Eerdmans, 1991), 311.

5. As Miroslav Volf emphasizes; see "'The Trinity is Our Social Program': The Doctrine of the Trinity and the Shape of Social Engagement," *Modern Theology* 14 (1998): 403–23, esp. 413–15.
6. This is especially true when the first super-death is the Father's generation of an other alongside himself, as we have seen in previous chapters.
7. Peter Casarella, "Experience as a Theological Category: Hans Urs von Balthasar on the Christian Encounter with God's Image," *Communio: International Catholic Review* 20, no. 1 (Spring 1993): 125.
8. Marcella Althaus-Reid, *The Queer God* (London: Routledge, 2003), 94 (hereafter QG).
9. See Graham Ward, *Christ and Culture* (Malden, MA: Blackwell, 2005), 33.
10. Luce Irigaray, *Marine Lover of Friedrich Nietzsche*, trans. Gillian C. Gill (New York: Columbia University Press, 1991), 186.
11. I am not intending here to set a pure and perfect clitoral pleasure against fallen phallic pleasure but, rather, to suggest that the imaginary failure to consider clitoral pleasure is a sign of the limitations of theological accounts of sexual and trinitarian difference. In chapter 7, I argue for nonreproductive pleasure in Christianity.
12. Althaus-Reid, QG 61.
13. Marcella Althaus-Reid and Lisa Isherwood, "Thinking Theology and Queer Theory," *Feminist Theology* 15, no. 3 (2007): 304.
14. Ibid., 305.
15. Marcella Althaus-Reid, *Indecent Theology: Theological Perversions in Sex, Gender and Politics* (New York: Routledge, 2000), 46 (hereafter IT).
16. Marcella Althaus-Reid, "*¿Bien Sonados?* The Future of Mystical Connections in Liberation Theology," *Political Theology* 3 (2000): 55.
17. Althaus-Reid, QG, 44.
18. See ch. 5.
19. The "genderfucking" terminology is adopted from Ward, who Althaus-Reid follows in disloyal fashion at this point. Thanks to Hannah Hofheinz who helped me to see her disloyalty.
20. Hypostasized transcendence is Mary Daly's terminology in *Beyond God the Father: Toward a Philosophy of Women's Liberation* (Boston: Beacon Press, 1973), 19.
21. "We are all Marys with gigantic divine phalluses stuffing our mouths, and not necessarily by our own will" (IT, 102–03).
22. As Althaus-Reid emphasizes, a position in relation to the priest's (or God's) phallus is also about a social and ecclesial relation that reflects material causes and consequences—in her case, Argentine patriarchy (QG, 17).
23. So Althaus-Reid (following Jacques Derrida): "How might the Trinity lead us into the kenosis of heterosexual practices, within justice but outside the law?" QG, 46; see also 78.

## BIBLIOGRAPHY

Althaus-Reid, Marcella. "*¿Bien Sonados?* The Future of Mystical Connections in Liberation Theology." *Political Theology* 3 (November 2000): 44–63.
———. *Indecent Theology: Theological Perversions in Sex, Gender and Politics.* New York: Routledge, 2000.
———. *The Queer God.* London: Routledge, 2003.
———, and Lisa Isherwood. "Thinking Theology and Queer Theory." *Feminist Theology* 15, no. 3 (May 2007): 302–14.

Casarella, Peter. "Experience as a Theological Category: Hans Urs von Balthasar on the Christian Encounter with God's Image." *Communio: International Catholic Review* 20, no.1 (Spring 1993): 118–28.

Daly, Mary. *Beyond God the Father: Toward a Philosophy of Women's Liberation.* Boston: Beacon Press, 1973.

Irigaray, Luce. *Marine Lover of Friedrich Nietzsche.* Trans. Gillian C. Gill. New York: Columbia University Press, 1991.

Pannenberg, Wolfhart. *Systematic Theology*, vol. 1. Trans. Geoffrey W. Bromiley. Grand Rapids: Eerdmans, 1991.

Rahner, Karl. *The Trinity.* Trans. Joseph Donceel. New York: Crossroad, 1997.

Volf, Miroslav. "'The Trinity Is Our Social Program': The Doctrine of the Trinity and the Shape of Social Engagement." *Modern Theology* 14 (1998): 403–23.

Ward, Graham. *Christ and Culture.* Malden, MA: Blackwell, 2005.

# Part 2

# 4 Patterns of Personhood in Three Variations

## ECONOMIC EXCHANGES: CHRISTOLOGY BEYOND OBEDIENCE AND DEATH

As we have seen repeatedly in previous chapters, trinitarian theology faces a serious problem in its tendency to translate the Father–Son relation into gendered versions of death, wounding, space-making, self-emptying, and eternal sacrifice. The Father–Son relation, understood as willing obedience, is turned into feminine acquiescence that genders the God–world relation or erects the cross in the womb-wound of trinitarian relationality. Each of these ways of thinking the trinity reads sexual difference and death into the trinity itself or into the God–world relation in ways that threaten the goodness of either.

In this chapter, we turn our attention to theologians who modify the logic of trinitarian space-making (procession). Jürgen Moltmann, Wolfhart Pannenberg, and Kathryn Tanner all reconstruct the single-patterned, unidirectional processional logic of trinitarian doctrine in favor of richer, more complicated patterns of person-constitution. They seek to relate the Son and Spirit to each other without reducing either to an adjunct of the other. They also consider the contribution Son and Spirit make to the constitution of the Father's personhood. Each of them is driven in part by concerns about the subordination the trinitarian relations may entail, and each contributes something to the constructive account of trinitarian differentiation I develop in chapter 6.

The theologians to whom we turn our attention in this chapter avoid the most obvious gendered pitfalls in their immanent trinitarian theologies, with the exception of an occasional romantic but misguided comment from Moltmann about motherly fathers or the like. My concern here is not, then, to show that there are gendered resonances to the trinitarian patterns of personhood in these theologians despite their own intentions and protestations.[1] Pannenberg shows no interest in such gendering, and Tanner refuses to grant any significance to the gendered aspects of trinitarian reflection. Moltmann's and Pannenberg's trinitarian theologies depend on space-making logics that have gendered side effects, but the specifically gendered aspects of their projects are not the central focus at this point. Instead, the focus is on their (biblically based) patterns of trinitarian person-hood, the concomitant conceptualization of the relation between the imma-nent and economic trinity, and the rethinking of the immanent trinity that each undertakes. Moltmann's, Pannenberg's, and Tanner's solutions reflect different assessments not only of the problem of the connection between begetting, subordination, and death but also of the nature and seriousness of the problem.

Some important strategies for avoiding the translation mechanism between begetting, subordination, and death are common in contemporary theology. For instance, Delores Williams holds that what is salvific about Jesus is not his death; it is the ministerial quality of his presence, which offers a new vision for human flourishing.[2] This strategy displaces death from the center of Jesus' work but does little by itself to address other aspects of his apparent subordination to the Father. One might also argue that Jesus' apparent subordination to the Father is an expression of the appropriate human relation to God rather than an expression of his status as eternal Son. Successfully pursuing this particular strategy requires *every* aspect of subordination in the economy to be assigned to Jesus' humanity rather than his sonship, thus suggesting that what is being enacted in these subordinationist moments tells us absolutely *nothing* about the Son's rela-tionship to the Father in the eternal life of God. Jesus' explicit invocations of the Father's superiority to him, his willing or reluctant obedience to the Father, and so on all belong to the way he models true humanity for us in a world of sin and death. This requires a greater distance between the par-ticularity of sonship and the shape of humanity (at least in its sinful state) than would otherwise be the case. Another alternative posits that whatever the meaning of the apparent subordination of Jesus to the Father in the road leading to the cross, any suggestion of subordination is overcome in the resurrection of Jesus in which he is translated to the right hand of the Father, thus demonstrating the coequality of the divine persons. The Son's equality with the Father is made evident by the Father's vindication of the Son's message and mission in the resurrection. The resurrected one seated at the right hand of the Father cannot himself be other than divine, or so the argument would go.

But why not? Jesus might be no more than the first fruits of all cre-ation, vindicated by his faithfulness to God. Adoptionist Christologies are perfectly commensurate with this approach as well. By itself, arguing the vindication of Jesus and the priority of resurrection does little to remove intimations of inferiority in the relation between Jesus and the Father. When combined with a standard account of the begetting of the eternal Son, the vindication of Jesus means no more than a repetition of his origin in a dif-ferent mode as he continues to receive everything from the Father.

Although these strategies for avoiding the translation of begetting into obedience and death are helpful, they are ultimately insufficient. They only work around the edges to address the problems of trinitarian predication. Overall, these ways of revising the connections between procession, subordination, and death leave procession untouched. In the order of knowing, procession derives from the way the Son calls his God "Father" while praying to him, glorifying him, and obeying him, even unto death on a cross. *Even though* the Father apparently sacrifices Jesus; *even though* he has come forth from the Father; *even though* he says "not my will, but thy will"; *even though* the Son only does what he sees the Father doing; and so on, the Son is *not less than* the Father (who is the ever-greater). Those constitutive repudiations, the "even thoughs" of trinitarian theology, are moved around a little bit but continue doing much the same work as before because the condition that requires the addition of an "even though"—sonship—remains unmodified.

The theologians we examine in this chapter offer revised accounts of the relationship between procession and mission that expand the trinitarian constitution beyond sonship. Without leaving sonship behind, they modify its scope and meaning in service of avoiding its subordinationist qualities. They open the door to variability in the trinitarian relations of origin. This might require developing a more differentiated analysis of the missions than allowed by a single *exitus-reditus* pattern along the Father-Son-Spirit-Son-Father *taxis*, as Moltmann does. It might mean paying attention to the other ways, beyond the relations of origin, in which the persons are constituted by and in their distinctions from each other, as in Pannenberg. Tanner emphasizes the difference that finitude and sin make to the revelatory quality of the history of Jesus while resolving the *filioque* problem through the mutual contributions of the Son and Spirit in their procession from the Father. Each version is an experiment in trinitarian theology that allows us to see what happens if *this* or *that* decision is made differently.

## THE TRINITARIAN PATTERNS OF JÜRGEN MOLTMANN'S SPATIAL PERSONS

> The promise which announces the *eschaton*, and in which the *eschaton* announces itself, is the motive power, the mainspring, the driving force and the torture of history.[3]

Jürgen Moltmann is one of the most influential theologians of the twentieth century. In *Theology of Hope* and *The Crucified God*, he develops a theology of a God who does not stand apart, untouched by the suffering of the world, but who is intimately engaged in bringing transformation out of death and suffering. By the time he publishes *The Trinity and the Kingdom* in 1980, he sees the trinity as the most significant Christian resource for avoiding political monotheism and the patriarchal rule of the fathers. Moltmann reflects several of the tendencies critiqued in previous chapters, particularly the imagery of trinitarian persons "making room" for each other and an understanding of the constitutive role of the cross that places it at the origin of the trinity. But he also discovers grounds in the biblical economy for reconfiguring the relations between trinitarian persons according to patterns other than a single, straight road to the cross. These contradictory impulses render Moltmann's trinitarian metaphysics conceptually incoherent. Yet Moltmann's idea of different levels of unity in the trinity, each centered on a different person, offers a differentiated description of the curlicues of divine patterning that structure God's action in the world to save.

The typical problems of trinitarian theology include several to which Moltmann offers innovative, albeit dubious, solutions. How is the Son different from, yet related to, the Spirit if they both come forth solely from the Father? How does the revelation of God in salvation history (the economic trinity) relate to God's being in Godself (the immanent trinity) with respect to time, death, suffering, and subordination? How does the shape of trinitarian relationality offer possibilities for envisioning human community, and how does the trinity "make space" for human participation in it?

Moltmann believes that classical accounts of the trinitarian relations of origin install subordination in the being of God, for they are unilateral relations that derive all from the Father. In response, Moltmann repatterns the trinitarian relations on the basis of their enactment in the history of the Son, arguing that the persons constitute both their unity and their differences. An example of such repatterning is Moltmann's attempt to solve the problem of the *filioque* clause, which was added to the Western version of the Nicene creed. It states that the Holy Spirit comes forth from the Father *and* the Son. While Moltmann shares the concern for distinguishing Son and Spirit that justifies the addition, he also recognizes the validity of the Eastern concern that the Father's uniqueness as the source of the life of the trinity disappears if the Son is set up as a second origin within the trinity.

In response, Moltmann argues that the existence of the Holy Spirit is attributable solely to the Father, but the Father is always already the Father of the Son; this is what makes him a concrete "Father" rather than an abstract "Principle" or "Source." Therefore, the "Son is the logical presupposition and the actual condition" of the breathing out of the Spirit.[4] The Spirit also receives something from the Son: the form of the Spirit "is moulded by the Father *and by the Son*" (TTK, 186). This introduces a distinction between "existence,"[5] given by the Father as the only source and principle in the Godhead, and form, given by Father and Son. The gift of form renders the Spirit a seal of their unity and introduces a constitutive relation—yet not a relation of origin—between the Son and the Spirit. This constitutive relation secures both their distinction from each other and their relation to each other. This differentiation between existence and form rests on Moltmann's interpretation of the distinction between hypostasis and *prosopon* ("person having form"). He understands hypostasis as the divine being in its sheer existence, while the *prosopon* is given form by its relations to the other divine persons (TTK, 186).[6]

The distinction between existence and form parallels and enables another distinction that Moltmann introduces between the constitution of the trinity and its inner life (TTK, 177). On the level of constitution, the Son and Spirit both receive their being from the Father. The Father is the source of the trinity—not as cosmological monarch but as the Father of the Son (TTK, 183).[7] On the level of life, the persons interpenetrate one another perichoretically, as equals.[8] The distinction between the level of constitution and the perichoretic inner life of the trinity protects the latter from turning into an indissoluble hierarchy. *Even though* the Father is the origin of divinity, the persons are equal in the life of the trinity (TTK, 175–76).

The distinction between the level of constitution and the level of life does not correspond to a distinction between the ontological and the salvation-historical aspects of divine existence (immanent and economic trinity). The perichoretic unity of the divine persons has ontological status and is definitive of the persons.[9] However, the concurrent ontological validity of these two levels of existence raises a difficulty. In being (level of constitution), God the Father is the source of the divinity of the other two persons and constitutes them through the relations of begetting and procession. In life, the three persons mutually coinhere one another while enacting completely reciprocal (yet asymmetrical) relations. The level of constitution requires, according to Moltmann, that the Father be thought of as logically prior to the other two.[10] There has to be a single logical (not, of course, temporal) moment at which the Father is thought of "alone": the logical moment in which the Father generates the other two. This follows from Moltmann's understanding of the Father as ingenerate origin, but it departs from the basic Thomist understanding of the persons as substantial relations by requiring relata that are only subsequently in relation.[11] Ascribing equal ontological status to the level of constitution and the level of life thus becomes difficult. Either the level of constitution trumps, since the Father has to be thought of by himself at one logical moment, or the level of life trumps, and the Father can at no logical moment be thought of by himself (since he is always-already ontologically-perichoretically penetrated by the others) and thus cannot truly generate the other two. Moltmann attempts to avoid the logic of the single divine subject, but depending on how seriously we take the idea of full perichoresis, there would be no Father who could generate apart from the already-existence of the Son and Spirit, thus threatening on the level of constitution just what Moltmann considers essential for distinguishing the persons from each other.

Moltmann's distinction between person and hypostasis introduces a further difficulty. He understands the term *hypostasis* ontologically, in terms of being, and the term *person* or *prosopon* aesthetically, in terms of "form" or "shape" (TTK, 183, 186–87). The form is the relational, perichoretic aspect of the hypostasis. The level of constitution guarantees the hypostases:

there are three and all three are divine. The monarchy of the Father—his role as the source and origin of the trinity and its unity—applies on the level of constitution. The level of constitution reflects the Father's priority: "If one does not want God to disappear into Sabellian obscurity, then one must see the eternal origin of the Trinity in the Father" (TTK, 165). But the personhood of the divine beings belongs to the level of life, "for the existence of the receiver logically precedes the reception" of form (TTK, 187). This requires the building of shape upon shape in the trinity: these hypostases are constituted in existence, but subsequently (ontologically *and* logically) shape each other into the specific "forms" ("person") that each of them is.

Divine personhood is thus reshaped from its linear form determined by a single *taxis*. Rather than reducing fatherhood to origin, sonship to reception, and spirit to unity and distinction (or expansion outward), Moltmann recognizes a variety of patterns in the trinity. We have already seen that Moltmann distinguishes between the level of constitution and the level of life. More complicated yet, Moltmann introduces a third level of unity in the trinity: the doxological level, which is the mutual manifestation of the persons in glory (TTK, 176). Each of these levels centers on a different trinitarian person: the level of constitution, on the Father; the level of life, on the Son; and the doxological trinity, on the Spirit (TTK, 177–78). Importantly, the immanent trinity is identified only with the doxological trinity, so that the immanent trinity belongs, strictly speaking, to the "end" rather than the "beginning" of God's history with the world.

If we sketch the different levels of divine existence and unity, we find equivalences between the level of constitution and the origin of the trinity, on one hand, and doxological trinity and eschaton, when God shall be all in all.[12] What remains unclear is how each of these levels relates to the economy of salvation, the history of the Son in which the distinctions and relations between the persons appear. Although perichoresis probably ought to belong to the level of constitution, Moltmann assigns it to the level of life (concentrated on the Son) of the trinity, since perichoresis is the totality of the circulation of divine life (TTK, 65, 177).[13] On the level of life, the three persons form their unity, and on that level, their equality is apparent. For this to be the case, it seems that the economy, specifically the history of the Son, would have to be a history of mutual glorification and reciprocity, enacting and demonstrating the perichoretic equality and mutuality of the trinitarian persons. Moltmann has identified the Son's history as the justification for distinguishing and relating the three persons. Presumably, that history exhibits the qualities of reciprocity and mutuality, especially since the Son is the focal point of the level of life. Surprisingly, though, Moltmann's history of the Son is a history of obedience—*eternal* obedience at that.[14] The aesthetic form of the Son must then be his obedience to the Father. That obedience extends and repeats the origin-relation between the Son and Father and thus can do nothing to dismantle the unilateral and subordinationist character Moltmann says the relations of origin introduce. This can be seen in three ways.

First, the relationship between hypostasis, distinction, and shape turns out rather confused when interrogated. The hypostases must be fully distinct at the "moment" (level, in Moltmann's terms) of generation.[15] But granted that the "form" of personhood could be given after the "being" of hypostasis, the "being" of hypostasis would retain its unilateral character (in order to secure distinct hypostases) while "form" would only follow as an additional and arguably unnecessary and contingent shape given to the divine persons. The unilateral priority of the Father would therefore belong to the level of being, while the equality and mutuality given to the persons in their "form" would, in a sense, just happen to be the case—beautiful flourishes added to substantial (unilateral) distinctions. Given that the persons are already distinct on the level of "being," the source of these additional mutual shapings would, it seems, have to lie somewhere in what distinguishes them, namely, in the relations of origin—which are also *sufficient* to distinguish them from each other. What *constitutive* power could any further shaping of their relations with one another have, and what particularity of the persons could be the source of that further shaping? Since everything in God is one with the exception of what distinguishes the persons, only their (constitutive) distinctions could originate the distinctions of form. Separating being and beauty (ontology and aesthetics) in this way renders beauty superfluous.

Second, the level of life of the trinity is seen in the economy—Moltmann strongly emphasizes that the history of the Son is the only basis for a trinitarian theology (TTK, 65). But if the economy is subordinationist, what justifies the assertion that there is mutuality in the level of life of the trinity? Further, what then is the connection between the level of constitution and the level of life of the trinity? If they contradict each other—hierarchy contrasted with mutuality—and mutuality wins out, the level of constitution is at best the positing of a distinction that has no significance for salvation history, for the assumption of humanity into God, or for the life of the trinitarian persons themselves. In fact, the level of constitution becomes an abstract posit, for the "being" of the persons at the level of constitution gives no "shape" to them in their relations either with one another or with the world.

Third, Moltmann specifies that "ultimately Christ's whole lordship serves the purpose of glorifying the Father" (TTK, 93). That does not seem right, however—Moltmann here introduces a competitive relation in which the glory of the Father supercedes and subsumes the lordship of Christ. But the recognition that "Jesus is Lord" cannot and need not be subsumed into "the glory of God the Father"—the two are part of the same confessional moment, a moment that points toward an entirely noncompetitive relation between the two. Moltmann's decision to assign ultimacy specifically to the Father introduces a competitive relation even at the eschatological level, where there should be none on his own account.

It seems that the level of life and the level of constitution would have to contradict one another for Moltmann's argument to work—mutuality correcting hierarchy—but it turns out that the priority of the Father is retained within the level of life in yet another way, since "the logical priority of the Father" appears from the "interpersonal relationships" themselves (TTK, 189). Moltmann thus repeats the elision between the various forms of the Father's monarchy that he is so critical of in other contexts. This correspondence between the role of the Father in the level of constitution and the role of the Father in the level of life removes the very distinction that Moltmann introduced to guard the inner-trinitarian life from hierarchy.

The difficulties of sorting out the (onto)logical relationships between hypostasis, person, and relation are insuperable in Moltmann's account. His separation of the level of life from the level of constitution is a valiant endeavor to conceive of the inner-trinitarian relations without the all-enveloping monarchy of the Father. However, Moltmann's connections between person, relation, and form, where form follows the level of constitution both in structure and content, obviates the initial distinction between the level of constitution and the level of life. Moltmann either would need a stronger distinction between the being and form of the divine persons (with the concomitant problems of a stronger distinction), or else the distinction collapses and inner-trinitarian hierarchy remains.

Moltmann's discussion of the "form" is restricted to the Holy Spirit. Presumably, the Son has a form as well,[16] a form solely given by the Father, since the begetting of the Son logically precedes the procession of the Spirit. At the level of life, then, there is also another kind of priority. Causal or constitutive proceedings are not limited to the level of constitution, which further challenges the suggestion of absolute mutuality or equality in the level of life. And what of the Father's form, since form is the perichoretic aspect of the persons?

The distinction between "being," given solely by the Father, and "shape" or "form," the relations of reciprocal love and exchange, requires a too-strong analogy between divine and human persons. Human persons receive being in birth and are then shaped by a variety of other relationships throughout their lives; that's how they become what and who they are. But trinitarian persons are distinct in and through their relationships to one another (for only those relationships share the eternity of God). Even if Moltmann's account were made coherent, the content of his added relations makes the problems of priority and hierarchy more, rather than less, pressing, since the relations actually seen in the history of the Son are relations of subordination. The obedience of the Son to the Father belongs precisely to that history. For our purposes, Moltmann's repeated introduction of hierarchical subordination through the very means he uses to correct such subordination suggest the difficulty of the task he undertakes.

Yet a closer look at Moltmann's understanding of the relations seen in the history of the Son will help us to understand why, despite his own account of the Son's eternal obedience, he finds some reason to posit reciprocity on the level of life of the trinity. Reciprocity's epistemological ground appears in the various patterns (*taxes*) that the trinity displays in the enactment and establishment of economic distinctions among the persons. For instance, the form of the trinity found in the early stage of Jesus' ministry has the following three patterns: F(ather) sends S(on) through Sp(irit); S comes from F in power of Sp; Sp brings us into S's relation to F (TTK, 75).

Note how Moltmann understands these patterns: all three share a basic form, grounded in the relations of origin, but each pattern centers on a different person. The same can be seen in other examples that Moltmann gives. In the passion, the giving up of the Son, F gives up S to death "for us"; S gives self up "for us"; while Sp "joins and unites" F and S in S's forsakenness (TTK, 83). In resurrection's trinitarian form, F raises S through Sp; F reveals S through Sp; and S is enthroned through Sp (presumably by F, although Moltmann does not specify; TTK, 88). Then follows the sending of the Spirit: F "raises the dead" S through Sp; F "enthrones" S; and S sends Sp from F (TTK, 89). With the exception of revelation (F revealing S), the relations between the Father and Son follow the familiar pattern of origin-repetition or origin-reflection (or superior-subordinate). At the same time, these patterns are a bit more expansive than are the bare relations of origin, and they exhibit some variability.

In the eschaton, even enthronement and revelation disappear, since "the Father subjects everything to the Son; the Son transfers the consummated kingdom to the Father; the Son subjects himself to the Father." Moltmann continues: "the Son . . . is the real actor in this consummation of salvation and in this glorification of God; and the Father is really the one who receives" (TTK, 93). Moltmann argues that such a sequence establishes God's lordship as a communally shared rather than singularly paternal property,[17] for the Father becomes the *recipient* of the kingdom, the one to whom the kingdom is given. In this return, the activation of the lordship of the Son allows for the reciprocity Moltmann's account of salvation history needs in order to demonstrate the antihierarchical thrust of the patterns of trinitarian relations. But what the Father receives is the return of all that is his, the kingdom that he originally transferred to the Son, mediated now as ever through the eternal obedience of the Son. Although the ideas of paternal revelation of the Son and paternal reception from the Son are suggestive, the Father's revelation takes the form of raising the Son from death and effectively seating him at his own right hand, and the Father's receptivity takes the form of being enthroned, finally and forever, as cosmic-trinitarian monarch. Although Moltmann is right to highlight elements of paternal receptivity in this logic, ultimately, this is a return to the Father of all that was his already, and put playfully, the Son still sits only *beside*, not *on*, the throne. The receptivity of the Father turns out to mean his status as the one to whom all glory finally belongs. Moltmann's attempts to avoid hierarchy founder on his own terms.

In *The Spirit of Life*, Moltmann expands and revises the distinctions and patterns we just examined into four levels of unity: monarchial, historical, eucharistic, and doxological.[18] Moltmann reads the monarchial trinity as an expression of the West's tendency to collapse the immanent trinity into the economic trinity (here, the monarchy is of a subject in salvation history and of a hierarchical ecclesiology, not of the Father within the trinity).[19] Moltmann's revision of the monarchical trinity is twofold: the monarchial trinity for him corresponds to "the Trinity in the sending," which expresses the openness of the trinity to the world on both the immanent and economic levels; it is a sort of "primordial trinity."[20] The historical level of the trinity is a periodization that reflects the association of the Father with creation, the Son with reconciliation, and the Spirit with sanctification. This periodization is a matter of appropriation and focus, not a splitting of salvation history between the persons. The historical level expresses diachronically what the monarchical level expresses synchronically.[21] The eucharistic level reverses the monarchial movement, since it returns to the Father what is originally given by him.[22] The crucial question again will be whether the Father becomes the one to whom something is *returned* eternally or the one who eternally *receives*, thus allowing the logic of the transfer of the kingdom to meet and reverse the logic of origin. Moltmann needs the receptive character of the Father as an enactment of reciprocal relations in salvation history, but he may in the end achieve nothing more than return. The movement of grace downward in the monarchial trinity is now reversed by the movement of praise upward to the Father (via the Son).[23] The eucharistic trinity is now the "goal" of the monarchial trinity,[24] which is a revision of Moltmann's original correction of the level of constitution by the level of life. The doxological level is still identified with the immanent trinity. The doxological trinity is perichoretic and eternal; the movements of the trinity are no longer linear but circular.[25] The doxological level of trinitarian identity "completes" the movements of the other levels, yet it cannot contradict them.[26] It is difficult to see how that can be the case. The circulation of perichoretic life, with its mutuality beyond origin and its reciprocity beyond gift and return/reception, seems quite clearly and necessarily to contradict the overtly linear patterns of both the monarchial and historical levels of the trinity.

As perichoresis has taken an increasingly prominent place in his theology, Moltmann's conceptualization of trinitarian personhood as space-making for the other has grown in importance. This imagery, found in his work quite early on, moves front and center as his interest in ecology, with its concomitant valuing of space, develops. In exploring this theme, Moltmann identifies two images of trinitarian perichoresis: movement and rest. Both types are presented as forms of space-making. Movement "means that the trinitarian Persons reciprocally offer each other the inviting, open room for movements to develop their eternal livingness. There can be no personal freedom without free spaces in social life." The imagery of rest suggests that "the Persons are . . . also Spaces, wide rooms for each other. . . . We should talk not only about three trinitarian Persons, but also about three trinitarian Spaces or Rooms" in which each person gives and receives itself.[27]

This space-making language needs further examination. Moltmann offers a fascinating combination of imagery in which active space-making for the other expresses one side of trinitarian interpenetration, while a passive architecture of trinitarian personhood empties out any content the rooms might have had as they form themselves into spaces for the becoming of each other. Moltmann depends heavily on the analogy to the sociality of human personhood when he suggests that personal freedom requires free spaces; undergirding that analogy is the assumption that the (distinct) perichoresis of human personhood enacted in ecclesial communion must have a trinitarian basis.[28]

It is impossible not to recognize yet again the return of what Moltmann himself would consider a "bad" Enlightenment subjectivity (a monadic concept of personhood as self-possession, self-determination, and self-constitution) precisely at the points where Moltmann is most concerned to combat such subjectivity. Moltmann seeks language for the possibilities engendered (in both senses) by perichoretic personhood, which designates an "unmixed and undivided community . . . a community without uniformity and personhood without individualism."[29] It would be difficult to come up with imagery less conducive to these aims than Moltmann's designation of trinitarian persons as those who not only make room for each other—already a problem—but who *are* Rooms. Perhaps we might connect this discussion to his distinction between hypostasis and *prosopon* and suggest that the rooms are the hypostases, while the *prosopon* is the decoration and perhaps also the shape of the Room each trinitarian person is.

By now it should be clear that the way Moltmann attempts to avoid a single cosmic divine Monarch-Subject-Father-Ruler of All is to stretch out personhood so that to be a person is to make room for the other. Moltmann assumes that space-making is required for personal relationality because the boundaries of persons are so distinct and definitive that they would have to be violently breached for relation to take place any other way. Although he does not make this explicit, the evidence is the lengths to which he goes to allow for the salutary possibilities of free sociality in the trinity, and by extension between the trinity and human persons. To disallow the violence of breaking and entering another person, *to be a person* must be *to make/ be room for another person*. In such room-making, the trinitarian persons come to consciousness of themselves in one another. Their "selfless love" gives them themselves in one another[30]—but what selves has Moltmann left them? The analogy that comes to my mind is the last cookie in a circle of very polite people. As each person defers to the next, no one ends up with the cookie.

Despite Moltmann's claims, the ultimate authority for the development of a trinitarian theology of reciprocity, mutuality, and equality cannot lie as directly in the relations enacted in the history of the Son as Moltmann would like. Too many of the explicit or overt relations on display, particularly between Father and Son, remain hierarchical. More significantly, Moltmann's struggles to develop a trinitarian theology of multiple patterns out of the relations as demonstrated through their interactions in the history of the Son repeats and extends a mistake common to trinitarian theologians: relying too heavily on explicit relations in the history of Jesus without considering the aim of the economy of salvation with sufficient care. Moltmann thus introduces a contradiction at precisely the wrong point between what God achieves when God acts to save and who God is and how God relates to Godself in that action. God brings human beings into the life of God, not only as adopted children but even as friends of God who encounter one another around an abundant banquet table at which there is more than enough room for all. The end that God seeks is the upending of hierarchy, the undoing of logics of first and last, of desert and merit, of sacrifice and obedience. Yet the God who acts toward such ends is read by trinitarian theologians in terms contradicting the ends that God seeks. That God appears to use subordination, obedience, hierarchy, and order as means in the economy of salvation—means that directly reflect some aspect (specifically sonship and spiration) of God's own being—while acting toward an end that undoes such elements of human and divine communion. In seeking to ensure that God corresponds to Godself in the economy of salvation, theologians introduce a contradiction between God's being and God's ends. Moltmann rightly holds the important axiom that God is as God does ("God is in himself as he appears to us"[31]). But Moltmann is also right to raise concerns regarding simplistic applications of that axiom, even if his revisionary trinitarian levels of unity and patterns of life fail to gain the conceptual clarity or consistency they would need to convince.

Since the history of the Son necessitates speaking of distinct persons in God, there are two implicit motivating assumptions that need to be examined in trinitarian methodology: the salvific and the epistemic. The salvific assumption is that only God can save. The salvific assumption is grounded in the logic of the economy of salvation as something that God does on our behalf that we could not do for ourselves, an achievement that could belong to no one who is less than God absolutely. The epistemic assumption says: only God can reveal Godself as God really is, and God does so in Jesus. Because this epistemic assumption has taken a distorted form, attention must be drawn to it. If the epistemic assumption paralleled the salvific assumption more closely, it would be God's saving attitude—what we come to know of God through the communion God establishes with us—that would bear the weight of the epistemic assumption. As John Calvin never tires of reminding us, God's attitude to humankind interests us, not God's nature considered in the abstract. But increasingly, the epistemic assumption has overtaken the salvific assumption. The for-us character of God's action and the character of the God who reveals Godself in so doing—one who creates friendship relations even with those who are not God's equals—disappears in favor of a focus on the concrete materiality of the revealed intra-trinitarian relations.

The salvific assumption underlies Moltmann's assertion that the level of life and the doxological trinity involve no hierarchy. The epistemic assumption underlies his use of eternal trinitarian distinctions as well as his repeated recourse to the repetition of the patterns of origin in the level of life. These assumptions might appear to be one and the same, as salvation-related concerns partly underlie the epistemic assumption. They are not, as we see in Moltmann's own collapse into hierarchy and subordination. However, Moltmann makes an essential contribution to a satisfactory account of the relations between trinitarian persons. Moltmann moves the full weight of the trinitarian relations away from the cross to the doxological trinity, or the trinity in glory: the trinity reconciled to the world and "reunited," as it were, with us and with one another (TTK, 152).[32]

## MAKING ROOM FOR THE FATHER'S DEITY: RECIPROCAL SELF-CONSTITUTION IN WOLFHART PANNENBERG[33]

God and not nothing is the end of time.[34]

Wolfhart Pannenberg offers one of the most ambitious attempts in contemporary theology to rethink the relation between the eternity of God and salvation history. He explicitly disagrees with Moltmann on the distinction between the level of constitution and the level of life, arguing that the monarchy of the Father belongs both to the relations of origin and to salvation history. Otherwise, there would be no link between Jesus' preaching of the Father's kingdom and the life of the trinitarian persons (ST1:325).[35] Pannenberg wishes to retain the relations of origin while holding that the mutual self-distinction of the persons is also constitutive of the shape of trinitarian personhood. The primary differences between his position and Moltmann's are twofold: First, while Moltmann restricts the monarchy of the Father to the relations of origin, Pannenberg expands it to include also the mutual self-distinctions of the trinitarian persons, where it provides the link between the immanent and economic trinity. Second, Pannenberg's model uses the historical and ultimately metaphysical establishment of the monarchy of the Father in the world to do something like the work done by Moltmann's level of life in order to establish reciprocity and mutuality among the trinitarian persons. But Pannenberg's "level of life" turns out utterly to correspond with the "level of constitution,"[36] so that Pannenberg's account becomes consistent through sacrificing the gain of reciprocity in personal constitution that mutual self-distinction was to have added to the picture. Although Pannenberg shows that the Son and Spirit contribute to the constitution of the personhood of the Father, they do so through relations that ultimately collapse in upon themselves into hierarchy and submission. I shall argue that making room for the deity of another becomes the mode of unification of the economic and immanent trinity, and of the infinite and the finite, beyond, across, and despite the differences of sin, death, and time.

For Pannenberg, the object of theology is God, so all of theology takes place in the "relationship between the eternal trinitarian life of God in himself and his presence in salvation history, the so-called economic Trinity" (ST1:6). The question of the relation between the economic and immanent trinity is therefore the central theological question. The immanent and economic trinity must be distinguished from one another (ST1:327), although they should be neither contrasted nor separated. This means that the move from the economic relations between Jesus and the Father to the immanent relations between Father and Son is legitimate, for the latter are read off the former. Pannenberg insists that "the existence of a world is not compatible with [the Father's] deity apart from his lordship over it. Hence lordship goes hand in hand with the deity of God. It has its place already in the intra-trinitarian life of God, in the reciprocity of the relation between the Son, who freely subjects himself to the lordship of the Father, and the Father, who hands over his lordship to the Son" (ST1:313). Pannenberg's repeated emphasis on an inner-trinitarian monarchy spares him from adducing anything like a trinitarian inversion (Balthasar) or a "level of life" set apart from the hierarchy of the relations of origin (Moltmann), since the form of the divine monarchy in the economy is the enactment of its inner-trinitarian shape.

The immanent and economic trinity are joined by an "inner dynamic" of God expressed and enacted through the "common action" of the persons of the trinity (ST1: 392). The power of love, and the dynamic of spirit, are expressed in the self-giving characters of the trinitarian persons: "The Spirit is the power of love that lets the other be" (ST1: 427). The Spirit is both "the love by which the Father and Son are mutually related" and "a hypostasis [that] stands over against both as the Spirit of love who unites them in their distinction" (ST1: 429). This twofold character of Spirit expresses the absolute identity of God as spirit as well as the particularity of the hypostasis of the Spirit.

Like Moltmann, Pannenberg enriches classical accounts of trinitarian distinction. He wants to describe the distinctions of the divine persons as mutual rather than unilateral (ST1:320).[37] In the typical picture, the Son and Spirit make no contribution to the personhood of the Father even as they receive everything from him.[38] In response, Pannenberg argues that reciprocal self-distinction is the form mutuality takes in the trinity. He wishes the "richly structured nexus of relationship that binds together the Father, Son, and Spirit" to "constitute the different distinctions of the persons" (ST1:321). That richly structured nexus of relationship names the ways in which the persons distinguish themselves from each other, particularly in the history of Jesus. His understanding of self-distinction is crucial and quite specific: self-distinction means that "the one who distinguishes himself from another defines himself as also dependent on that other" (ST1:321). This definition is helpful in interrogating how mutuality and dependence are construed here. In order for the trinitarian relations to be genuinely mutual, the Father must depend on the Son and the Spirit in some fashion, just as they depend on him in being begotten and being breathed. This distinction of the self from another is not to be thought of as an alienation from the self but as self-identity through the mediation of another (ST1:377).[39] This dependence gives shape to the persons who have come into existence (in a nontemporal sense) through the relations of origin.[40] Pannenberg's connection between dependence and distinction implies that relational distinction cannot be thought without a form of dependence. Even divine persons exist only through the acceptance and enactment of a love that requires dependence and a form of making room for the other (in this case, for the Father's claim to deity).

The self-constitution of the persons in their active relations to one another is materialized in their adoption of a common aim. In other words, the voluntary identification of a divine person with a particular goal ties together the immanent and economic trinity. The economic trinity's goal is the existence of independent finite beings who can be given a share in the trinitarian life to redound to the glory and praise of the Father; that goal externalizes what is already the case in the immanent trinity. In the immanent trinity, the monarchy of God the Father is established by the Son's distinction of himself from Father who, for the Son, is the one God (ST1:313, 326). Given creation and the existence of the world, God's deity stands and falls with the enactment of God's deity in the world, as the very concept of deity implies rule and lordship.[41] God's rule—the Father's monarchy—thus has to be established in the world. In the asymmetrical relations between trinitarian persons, the Father's gift of divinity to Son and Spirit returns to him through their establishment of his cosmic monarchy.

God creates genuinely independent finite creatures alongside God. God intends for those creatures to affirm their independence in dependence on God—that is, to use their independence in praise of the God who gives them that independence. Instead, however, creatures choose to affirm their independence against God. In so doing, they cut themselves off from the source of their being and deny their own fundamental nature—that is, their createdness. The incarnation of the Son for the purpose of salvation follows God's creative will "that the creature should live" (ST1:421). Omnipotent divine resourcefulness overcomes the creature's antagonism toward God in the position of the creature.

The Son's successful distinction of himself from the Father is also the establishment of God's lordship in the world: "This self-emptying of the Son (Phil. 2:6–7) is also to be understood as the self-actualizing of the deity of the trinitarian God in its relation to the world that comes into being thereby." As part of that establishment, the Son becomes incarnate in the human history of Jesus, who is the "self-created medium of his extreme self-actualization in consequence of his free self-distinction from the Father, i.e., a way of fulfilling his eternal sonship" (ST2:325). The incarnate Son renders to God the Father what is owed him by all: recognition of his lordship. The Son "takes the place of the creature . . . so as to overcome the assertion of the creature's independence in the position of the creature itself" (ST1:421). As the Son moves out of the unity of the trinity by "distinguish[ing] himself not merely from the person but also from the deity of the Father," the inner-divine law of free distinction expands to include finite existence, since "subjection to the monarchy of the Father is the basic law of the relation of creatures to the Creator" (ST1:421). This subjection is the condition of the possibility of fellowship with God, for it brings creatures into the very relationship the Son enjoys with the Father (a relationship fulfilled in the Spirit). Finitude takes its shape from the relation of the Son to the Father: the Son's eternal self-distinction from the Father is the ground of the goodness of creation in its otherness from God, the shape of creation in its ordered reality, and the ability of the pinnacle of creation, humankind, to appropriately distinguish itself from God (at least potentially) and to distinguish other finite existences from each other. Humans are given the potential to distinguish themselves from God so that the Son-Logos may enact his own self-distinction from the Father in humankind (ST2:385–86).

Subjection for the sake of communion is also the way in which God's love affirms the being, reality, goodness, and limitations of what is distinct from God: "the finite shows itself to be affirmed by God precisely in its limitation and in acceptance of [its limitation]," and God's affirmation of the creature "gives the creature the opportunity by accepting its own limits to transcend them and in this way itself to participate in infinity" (ST1:422). In affirming themselves against God, however, sinful human beings deny their limits—they seek to elevate themselves to the position of God. In denying their finitude—denying that their finite independence exists only in dependence on the infinite—human beings themselves tie their existence to death. Finite existence is ambiguous: "as finite beings and in spite of all our independence, we are inescapably subject to death" (ST2:390). That subjection follows creaturely denial of finitude.

Pannenberg makes a difficult and decisive decision: to attach death to sin rather than finitude,[42] since the "eschatological hope" of Christianity claims the possibility of a finite existence no longer subject to death. When time encounters eternity, when creatures have themselves entirely in the eternal present of the life of God, finitude without death will be realized (as already in the resurrected existence of the Son Jesus) (ST2:271–72). Finite existence has to go through death in order to be given the totality of its existence in the eternal presence of God, since, like all essences, finite existents achieve their actual existence over time. But once a finite being has become the center of its own activity and established its particular existence, "a being can be preserved or renewed as it participates in the eternity of God" (ST2:95). The temporal duration of finite creatures is therefore a contingent fact of their pre-eschatological condition, not an intrinsic consequence of finitude itself.[43] Post-eschatological transformation creatures have the totality of their lives in a single, eternal "moment."

The basic situation, then, is that finite beings, created open to transcendence or to the infinite, cut themselves off from it by affirming their own freedom over-against their dependence on God. Reconciliation to God requires personal affirmation of finitude—that is, the affirmation of finitude in dependence on God. The Logos becomes incarnate in Jesus for such affirmation. The history of Jesus is the medium of the presence and action of the eternal Son, and Jesus is unified with the Son by way of personal union. Pannenberg explains that the "*noetic* basis for [Jesus'] eternal sonship" is found in the self-distinction of Jesus from the Father. But the "*ontic* basis" (*Seinsgrund*) of the human existence of Jesus, and of all creation, is the eternal Son (ST2:22–23). The Son exists "before" incarnation in unity with the Father[44] but moves out of that unity into the world in incarnation.

In sending the Son and the Spirit, the Father hands over his kingship to them so that they may realize the Father's kingship in the world—they become the fully authorized deputies of the Father's divine lordship. In handing the kingdom to the Son, the Father makes himself dependent on the Son for his deity, given the connection between deity and actualized lordship. The sending expresses and fulfills the relation between Jesus the Son and the Father (ST1:312). The Son's fulfillment of the sending has its basis in the immanent trinity, so the handing over and back of the kingdom is constitutive for the personhood and as well as the deity of the Father. The trinitarian relations involve not only the "personal being" of each of the three persons but also their deity (ST1:329). Pannenberg heavily depends on a single text, 1 Corinthians 15:28, in which the final consummation of the Son's lordship is handing the kingdom back to the Father, "that God may be all in all" (ST1:312–13).[45] Through all of this the Spirit mediates their fellowship (although ultimately the Spirit's personal distinctness is seen through the Spirit's glorification of—and so self-distinction from—both Father and Son) (ST1:358, 315). Because the lordship of God is established only by the cooperation of Father, Son, and Spirit, the "totalitarian implications of a single divine subject acting without restriction" are vitiated (ST1:388). As a consequence, the Son's self-distinction from the Father as the only God is not an economic expression of the failure of finite existence to grant God's exclusive claim to deity. The Son's self-distinction from his Father, the only God, expresses the nature of the Son's divinity. He has it only by not claiming it.

Jesus preaches the coming of the kingdom of the Father—the material establishment of the Father's lordship in creation. The suffering and death of Jesus were the necessary result of the content of his message (ST2:341). The suspicion of those who put Jesus to death was that he was trying to escape his own finitude; in reality, however, he embraced death "as the bitter consequence of his mission": his death seals his finitude, his self-distinction from, and thus his unity with, God (ST2:433). When Jesus is put to death, the deity of the Father is at stake because Jesus claims that access to the kingdom of the Father can be had only through Jesus himself, and that is *why* he is put to death (ST1:329). The Father "suffers with the suffering of the Son" because he has "made his deity dependent on the success of the mission of the Son" and in the (apparent) failure of the Son's mission, the "kingship of the Father" becomes doubtful (ST2:391). In the resurrection, the Father vindicates the Son; he affirms that the Son remained obedient to the will of the Father throughout his earthly history. "In his extreme humiliation, in his acceptance of death, Jesus took upon himself the *ultimate consequence* of his self-distinction from the Father and precisely in so doing showed himself to be the Son of the Father" (ST1:314).[46] The kenosis of the Son is the "activation" of his deity in its refusal of any equation of himself with the Father (ST2:377). Pannenberg specifies that the kenotic love of the Son is "not directly related to the world, but to the Father in expressing his obedience to him".[47] The Son's kenosis is "an expression of the love of God for us. For by the self-distinction of the Son from the Father, God draws near to us. The *kenosis* of the Son serves the drawing near of the Father" (ST2:379). Pannenberg denies that kenosis can be attributed to "God himself" because "nowhere is it said that the Father emptied himself . . . To the contrary, this kenotic action on the part of the Son is described as obedience to the Father." Thus, although "the redemptive love of God includes an element of sacrifice . . . the Son is sacrificed, not the Father." Pannenberg specifies that the Son's obedience "is not the alien obedience of the slave," but is the "expression of his free agreement with the Father" (ST2:316)—but in what sense is free agreement best characterized as obedience?

If the cross is the ultimate consequence of the Son's self-distinction from the Father, then the cross is not the result of sin. Pannenberg is explicit about this: the nonaccidental offense caused by Jesus, which led to his death, was essential to his mission. As a result, "all these consequences flow from the divine sending of Jesus and ultimately from God himself" (ST2:343). Most tellingly, Pannenberg distinguishes the cross from the "traces and consequences of evil" that have to be "purged" in the establishment of the essential identity of all as it passes through the fires of eschatological judgment, thus requiring a distinction between the cross on the one hand and sin and death on the other (ST3:606). Presumably, the cross can remain (without sin and death?) precisely because it expresses the essential relationship of free subordination between Father and Son. Since the cross is remembered in eternity, the relation between self-distinction and death is part of the concrete self-distinction of trinitarian persons that constitutes them as who they are (that gives "content" or "shape" to their personhood).

The concrete self-distinctions of the trinitarian persons take place in the history of Jesus. In developing the "richly structured nexus of relations" that binds them together through distinguishing them, Pannenberg enumerates a number of relations between Jesus the Son, the Father, and the Spirit. For example, Jesus subordinates himself to the Father, obeys him, glorifies him,

receives the Spirit from him, establishes the monarchy of the Father in creation, and is the locus in eternity of the monarchy of the Father that seals the
unity of the trinity.[48] The Father hands his rule over to the Son and receives
it back, begets the Son, and gives the Spirit to the Son. The Spirit glorifies
the Son and in him the Father raises Jesus from the dead, manifests Jesus
as Son so as to reveal the Father, is breathed, glorifies the Son in obedience
to the Father, and so on.[49] As this list suggests, every relation between Jesus
and the Father that Pannenberg picks up is a variation on a single theme:
hierarchical subordination, which translates into obedience and results in
in death and humiliation. Jesus teaches us to know the Father as the only
true God by subordinating himself to him in obedience. Similarly, all the
Father's actions are variations on the theme of hierarchical superiority and
command or deputizing. Finally, the Spirit's relations are all oriented toward
the hierarchical Father–Son relation, so that this "richly structured nexus of
relationship" becomes a single pattern that extends and repeats the relations
of origin, rendering them materially hierarchical in a way that even exceeds
their inner-trinitarian determination.

Attempting to make concrete distinctions as seen in salvation history
constitutive for triune divinity is laudable, but in practice, the structural
contribution the Son makes to the personhood of the Father—establishing
the monarchy of the Father in the world as it is already established inside the
trinity—amounts to a catastrophic failure of the theological imagination. If
the self-distinction of Jesus from the Father is constitutive for his existence
as Son (ST1:310), and the relation between Jesus and the Father (epistemo-
logically) leads to the thought of the eternal Son (ST1:311),[50] and the history
of Jesus is (ontologically) the expression of what is already the case in the
eternal trinity, then the need for the existence of Jesus to be consumed in the
service of God lies already in the relation between the Son and the Father.
At this point, the connection between eternal sonship (immanent) and its
historical, incarnate form (economic) is apparent.

> The self-emptying and self-humbling that we find when we compare the
> eternal deity of the Son to his incarnation must not be seen as a limita-
> tion but as an expression of the eternal deity. But this is possible only if
> we understand it in relation to the eternal self-distinction of the Son as
> the basis of the possibility and reality of creaturely existence in general.
> The eternal self-distinction from the Father contains already the ele-
> ment of self-emptying. (ST2:320)[51]

In God's immanent being, there is no room for anyone who does not
make room for the Father's claim to deity. This means that the existence of
distinction is the possibility of death. That the Son voluntarily and eternally
subordinates himself to the Father as the *locus*—place—of the Father's monarchy and that this subordination is necessary for unity suggests Pannenberg's inability to think difference as something like side-by-side relation.

The only protection against competition—against the Son perhaps asserting himself as God alongside the Father—is for the shape of the Son's divinity to take the form of stretching himself out to make room for the Father, becoming, as it were (although Pannenberg would not use this language), an empty womb in which the cross may be erected.[52]

Construing self-distinction as constitutive for the shape of trinitarian personhood means that in faithful subordination to the Father, Jesus' identity as Son is carried by his humanly appropriate self-distinction from God. Death and humiliation are written into the relationship between Jesus and the Father as the expression of the relation between the Father and the Son. Death is the mode of being of the Son in the world in obedience to the sending of the Father, yet that mode of being is not something new added on to God. The history of Jesus is, on Pannenberg's interpretation, the history of the consumption of his particular identity in service of his mission of establishing the rule of the Father. The self-emptying (*Selbstentäußerung*[53]) of the Son is contained already within the immanent trinity in his eternal self-distinction from the Father, and that self-emptying is itself the possibility of creaturely existence in difference from God (ST2:320, 377; ST1:325). We are not talking merely, then, of voluntary self-subordination in eternity (nonsensical as such a concept would be) but of the concrete enactment of that self-subordination on the cross. The threat of death is only overcome by voluntary self-identification with the aim of establishing the monarchy of another; that self-identification might equally well be termed disidentification with oneself (since the eternal Son is God). The only possible defense against competitive relations that Pannenberg can conceive, for God as well as humans, is voluntary, ordered submission to one cosmic-paternal monarch. The "positive acceptance" of particularity that makes harmony rather than dissonance among humans possible means accepting the deity of the Father (for which Jesus' obedient death is the model) and submitting to Jesus as "Head and Lord" (ST3:629).[54]

The original problem of humanity was that we "wanted to be like God," but there was no "room" for us "alongside God," so we became subject to death. The death of the Son is how "God gives us room alongside himself even after death" (ST2:434). There is no room alongside God (the Father) for anyone who does not make room for him. In sacrificing his claim to individuality and particularity—the sacrifice that individuates and identifies him as the Son—by being subjected to death in obedience to the will of God the Father, Jesus (as our model) establishes the possibility of appropriate submission to God through acceptance of death for all humans. Jesus' individuation through embrace of death opens up room for others to be included, since Jesus' sacrifice of his particularity makes space for others to take on the shape of his relationship to God.

This logic follows from the seemingly salutary desire to ensure that the events of the cross have meaning for God, that God does not float untouched above the scene of loss in such a way that the drama of history turns into a comedy. The death of Jesus on the cross is the moment that brings together trinitarian and human existence so that the death of Jesus expresses possibilities inherent in trinitarian flows of love. On this basis, ultimately, a series of connections and substitutions appears: death on the cross in obedient submission, self-sacrifice in a moment of ultimate revelatory significance, both leading to the intermediate thesis that *something* in the life of God makes this possible, and that something is the self-emptying way in which the Son distinguishes himself from the Father, modeling and establishing the possibility of any differentiation whatsoever.

Were it not for the Son's free submission, the Father would have no inner-trinitarian monarchy. Were it not for Jesus' preaching and his free, obedient distinction of himself from God, the Father would have no worldly monarchy, and Jesus would not be identified with the eternal Son. Were it not for the Spirit's role in and with the Son in each case, glorifying the Son to the ultimate glory of the Father, the economic trinity would be other than the immanent trinity. But even as Pannenberg's analysis adds a more subtle account of the relation between the content of Jesus' preaching and the nature and shape of the immanent trinitarian distinctions, his account continues to rest primarily on explicit relations between Jesus and the Father in the incarnate Son's road to the cross. The self-emptying of the Son in eternity as he makes himself the locus of the Father's monarchy does not allow for time and sin to make enough of a difference in the way the Son incarnate enacts his eternal relationship to the Father. The Father would not be who and what he is if the Son did not voluntarily subordinate himself to the Father, and the Son is nothing outside his voluntary subordination and deputization by the Father. The Spirit's personhood is the glorification of them both. This is the concrete shape, the "material definition," of love: to exist ecstatically in another person by pointing away from oneself, that is, to deputize, to submit, or to glorify a relationship of submission.

Although Pannenberg effectively distinguishes between the level of constitution and the level of life of the trinity in a way analogous to Moltmann, their differences are telling. Pannenberg ties the different levels of trinitarian unity together through the establishment of the monarchy of the Father throughout the cosmos and in God's own being. Pannenberg does not, therefore, generate inconsistency between relations in the constitution (relations of origin) of the trinitarian persons and in the level of life (mutual self-distinction). Even the unity of the trinity, hidden until the eschaton, will be realized through the same pattern of voluntary submission to the monarchy of the Father that belongs to the entire cosmic-theological drama.

We identified and distinguished between the epistemic and salvific assumptions driving Moltmann's trinitarian theology above and questioned the priority of the epistemic assumption. Pannenberg's salvific assumption is that the possibility of communion requires the sacrifice of all forms of individuality that are nonintegrable into a hierarchically ordered unity.[55] He seeks to preserve the difference between God and creation.[56] Differentiating

God and creation means recognizing the absolute dependence of creation on God. But the difference between God and creation should not apply to differences internal either to God or to creation, precisely because that difference grounds and transcends all other difference (the God who is also the non-other). Pannenberg, however, imports a version of the difference between God and creation into the being of God: differentiating the Father from the Son means that the Son yields to the Father's claim to deity and obediently submits himself to the Father, thus enacting (as an expression of his being as Son) the appropriate form of human submission to God. The dependence of creation on God is brought into the inner life of God. What would happen if neither intra-human nor intra-divine relationships directly imaged the relation between God and creation?

## KATHRYN TANNER'S TRINITARIAN HINGE

We are the ones who gain thereby.[57]

In *Jesus, Humanity and the Trinity* and *Christ the Key*, Kathryn Tanner offers perhaps the strongest attempt in contemporary theology to deal with the traces of subordination in the New Testament and in trinitarian theology more broadly. Rather than denying the subordinationist potential of trinitarian theology, Tanner counters it with the for-us character of incarnation (CK, 147) and the difference that sin makes, emphases that are crucial to the development of an adequate trinitarian theology. Since the trinity is acting in "a human world of sin and death," it has to be admitted that "not everything . . . about the relations among the persons of the trinity in their mission for us also holds for their relations simply among themselves" (CK, 180). So what are those differences?

In Tanner's account of salvation, the incarnation itself—in contrast to, for instance, an inner-trinitarian drama on the cross—takes on a much more prominent role than it does in theologians like Balthasar, Moltmann, or Pannenberg. The incarnation, expanded across the entirety of Jesus' existence (which is the human existence of the Word), saves by uniting humankind as closely as possible to God, and by overcoming whatever aspects of human existence under sin and death that threaten such union. "The point of incarnation is . . . the perfection of humanity," and through incarnation humankind is given the gifts of God's life in a humanly appropriate way.[58] As Tanner points out, "incarnation without attenuation of God's transcendence is no impossibility if one keeps in mind its soteriological, this-worldly point for life in the world—and avoids speculation, unhelpful and unwise, concerning its meaning for God."[59] Tanner therefore turns our attention away from a reconstitution of divinity through the events of the cross, as in Moltmann and Pannenberg.

Jesus' human life is "a trinitarian way of life," which shows "both what the relationships within the trinity are like and what they are to mean for us as new organizing principles of human living" (CK, 140). We discover the correct shape of human life in the history of Jesus. That right and true human life is a trinitarian one in which the human person is adopted as a sibling of Jesus and taken up into the very life of God (CK, 141). Note that although the salvific assumption plays a significant role here—human beings are saved by being given such a relation to Jesus and in him to God—there is also a consequence beyond salvation, namely, the discovery of "new organizing principles" for life. Those new organizing principles are not, however, our direct repetition of inner-trinitarian relationships.

Tanner focuses intensely on the salvific, rather than epistemic, assumption. The transformation of human life into a life shaped by an intimate union with the trinity throughout the course of Jesus' existence just *is* salvation (CK, 145–46). Jesus' trinitarianly shaped life brings human beings into the "household" of God (CK, 146). As the human life of the Word, his life simply is the life of the Word incarnate. It is worth noting how much this argument heightens the for-us aspect of economic trinitarian relations: The priority of the salvific assumption over the epistemic becomes apparent, even as the difference the economy makes *for us* (not God) is emphasized. Knowledge of God's specific, detailed inner-trinitarian constitution is subsumed under inclusion into the life of God and enactment of intra-human relations directed toward the flourishing of all.[60]

In incarnation, the Word assumes humanity, and in assuming it, purifies, elevates, cleanses, and saves it, and unites it with God. The saving effects of this union spread outward into the entirety of human existence. In this process, nothing is overcome until the Word overcomes it in Jesus' actual, historical life. This means that "Jesus does not overcome temptation until he is tempted, does not overcome fear of death until he feels it. . . . Jesus does not heal death until the Word assumes death when Jesus dies; . . . does not conquer sin until he assumes or bears the sin of others by suffering death at their hands" (JHT, 28). The cross "saves because in it sin and death have been assumed by the one, the Word, who cannot be conquered by them" (JHT, 29). The result of this process is "a happy exchange of divine and human powers, a communication of properties, the interpenetration of human and divine, in and through Jesus' acts" (JHT, 30). God, who cannot be overcome by sin, death, and failure, takes all those things upon Godself and frees humankind from them. God also gives humanity a share in God's own life in a humanly appropriate way. Tanner expands on this latter point: in incarnation, "the characteristics of human life become the (alien) properties of the Word, and thereby the properties of the Word (its holiness, its life-enhancing powers) become the (alien) properties of humanity" (CK, 254). The difference beyond difference is always maintained even—especially—in the most intimate union between God and humankind. The disanalogy between God and humankind allows for their intimate union and so for the communication of God's gifts to humankind.

The saving effect of Jesus communicates his divinity (JHT, 18).[61] "Jesus lives out in a fully human form the mode of relationship among Father,

Son and Spirit in the Trinity" (JHT, 19). His particularity is "his relationship to God"; "the shape of his way of life"; and "his effects on others (his saving significance)" (JHT, 20). While these features of his existence set him apart from other humans, they do not do so in a way that threatens his humanity—his full humanity is the way the Word achieves the Word's saving effects. Everything Jesus does is done by the Word (JHT, 26). Jesus' acts "are . . . genuinely two-fold in character, displaying both divinity and humanity as distinct features of the very same acts" (JHT, 49).

In Tanner's theological system, this is made possible by her two foundational principles of radical transcendence and noncompetition. Divinity is radically transcendent without opposition (contrastive relation) to creation; rather, divinity's radical transcendence allows for differentiation without instituting contrastive relationality.[62] This radicalizes both claims of God's transcendence and of God's involvement with the world. As a general rule, it is not appropriate in her system to ask in contrastive fashion whether an act is done by God or by a creature, for all creaturely powers exist in direct dependence upon God, while God can act through or without created powers (or secondary causes) in equally direct ways.[63]

Jesus is the permanent and irreversible climax of God's gift-giving relations with the world, the point at which God gives the creature gifts that (unlike other created gifts) cannot be lost under any conditions. The humanity of Jesus is the Son's "own proper instrument for the distribution of benefits to the world" (JHT, 48). In this distribution of benefits, two levels of gift-giving take place. On one level, those benefits (perfections) that can become features of humanity itself come to belong to humanity (sinlessness, for instance). On a second level, those benefits that cannot come to belong to humanity (immortality) are nonetheless given to humanity through union (although they do not become humanity's *owned* benefits) (JHT, 49–50). Crucially, there is no competitive relation between Jesus' divine will (as Son) and his human will: "from the first [the human will of Jesus] is nothing other than the will of the Son in the very shape or mode that distinguishes the Son from Father and Spirit in their dynamic interactions" (JHT, 50).

The saving effects of Jesus' life extend to all of humanity "because the second Person of the Trinity is the one who assumes [humanity]. The universal range of the incarnation's effects follows from the universal range of all the Son's workings *ad extra*, whereby the Son images the Father outward in the world as a whole, after its own image" (JHT, 54). The Son's imaging of the Father is grounded in the trinity, since "the Father is the source of difference in creative relationship with the non-divine world as a kind of extension outside God of the way the Father is the source of the Son and Spirit within the Trinity" (JHT, 14). This "kind of extension" is Tanner's adaptation of the principle that the missions are the processions extended outward into the created world. God acts as God is in the created world.

Although Tanner uses the language of "making room" on occasion, the room that is made does not pertain to the relations among trinitarian persons but to the way the trinity moves outward (in the missions of the Son and the Spirit into the world) in order to make room for humankind next to the Word: "Room is carved out for us within [the trinity] by [Christ]; we are taken along with him into the space that has opened up for us within it by his side. . . . In Christ humanity is slotted into its place alongside the Word" (CK, 145).[64] The Word does not empty itself, nor does the trinity; rather, the missions are God's actions to place humankind alongside God, in the life of God in the unity of the trinity. The copresence of God and humanity—the way that both can be in the same "place" at the same "time" without one moving away to make room for the other—means that divine fullness need not be sacrificed in order to include human beings within itself.

Tanner's trinitarian theology in JHT exhibits a variety of characteristics that put it in opposition to major trends in contemporary trinitarian theology, especially of the kind we have examined up to this point. She does not emphasize differences among the persons or even the ultimacy of difference in the trinity; their unity is just what allows for their difference (JHT, 38).[65] She argues that the Son and the Spirit have essentially and by nature what they are given by the Father (JHT, 39).[66] This does much to remove any subordinationist implications the relations of origin might otherwise have, and it deemphasizes the notion of trinitarian gift-relations that turn into the Son's gratitude and eucharistic self-offering. She emphasizes that the persons of the trinity are always doing the very same thing, even as each of them works according to its particular constitution (JHT, 40). She does not argue that humans come to imitate inner-trinitarian relationships directly, nor that human community can be modeled directly on trinitarian relationships, because the shape of trinitarian and human relationships are too disanalogous to allow such modeling; her system thus does not display corrective projectionism (JHT, 78–79, 82).[67] Significantly for our purposes, she does not connect the subordination of Jesus to the Father in his historical life closely with his status as Son. What subordination there is pertains to the "historical and conflictual process by which Jesus' humanity is perfected" (JHT, 52).[68]

Each of these themes receives further development in *Christ the Key* where Tanner pays the promissory notes she wrote for herself in the earlier book, and the rest of our discussion focuses on these developments. In the technical trinitarian discussions in *Christ the Key*, Tanner's primary concerns are the relation between the Son and the Spirit (the debate over the *filioque*) and the relation between God's life *ad intra* and *ad extra*. Overall, her motivation is to bring accounts of trinitarian distinctions into a closer relationship with their foundational narratives in gospel form. Ensuring close correspondence between accounts of trinitarian life and their gospel grounding has salvific motivations, first and foremost, although there is an epistemic element as well (i.e., the revelation of inner-trinitarian distinctions).

Tanner assumes economic and immanent distinctions between the persons, equality, and inseparability, so she focuses on solving certain problems rather than developing a trinitarian theology anew (CK, 148). Particularly interesting is the New Testament evidence for "equivalence of power and value" that she adduces. The trinitarian persons are "taken to be perfectly equal in power . . . in virtue of mutually reciprocal relationships that hold among them" (CK, 150). Tanner identifies revealing each other, glorifying each other, and appearing in one another as examples of such reciprocity (CK, 150–51). The action of the story of salvation shows forth inseparability even as each person plays an irreducibly different role in that action (CK, 152). There is full equality among the trinitarian persons "because they are always all actively involved in doing the very same things" (CK, 194).[69]

Tanner narrates the history of Jesus "in trinitarian terms" (CK, 147) in order to excavate the particular patterns of the interactions between the persons. She suggests that her interpretation of their interaction solves the problem of the relation between Son and Spirit while avoiding issues that often plague accounts of the relationship between person-constitution in the trinity and the shape of trinitarian action in the history of salvation, since, in many accounts of trinitarian relations, the persons fall "out of sync" with themselves somewhere along the line, and out of sync with the gospel stories as well (CK, 186–87). Even the Philippians text that grounds the kenotic logic of systems like Balthasar's and Ward's appears on her reading rather as an expression of *our* translation from lowliness to glory: a logic of ascent for us, not descent (followed by ascent) for God (CK, 146–47).[70] Similarly, we "gain access to the Father, enter into the very presence of the Father" directly by the Son (CK, 153) rather than participating in the Son's self-distinction from the Father by giving room to the Father's exclusive claim to deity, as in Pannenberg.

Tanner argues that the New Testament shows unsubstitutable directional (asymmetrical) relations between the persons, which make up the pattern for trinitarian personhood. The pattern reduces to a single, complex movement of Son and Spirit in which either the Son or the Spirit is emphasized, depending on the direction from which it is viewed (CK, 195). With respect to the first problem she seeks to solve, the *filioque*, Tanner accepts that the West's adoption of the clause threatens the full divinity of the Spirit. The underlying argument is that "[i]f the power to generate another is not defining of the Father but part of the one divine nature shared among Father and Son, then the Spirit should share it too" (CK, 188). Yet the advantage of the Western alternative is that it specifies a relation between Son and Spirit at a point where the East simply asserts difference, making the difference between begetting and procession a "mere posit" (CK, 190).[71] Tanner therefore needs to account for the relationship between Son and Spirit in a way irreducible to the origin of one in the other.

In order to do so, she modifies the Thomist principle of relational opposition—only relations of opposition (paternity/filiation, for instance) are sufficient and appropriate to distinguish divine persons—to give each relation a triune shape (CK, 189 n.81). Tanner argues that Son and Spirit contribute to each other's being[72] in different ways. The Spirit contributes power or efficacy to the Son, while the Son gives the Spirit form or shape (CK, 192). The Spirit becomes the Son's reason for being, and vice versa (CK, 193–94). (It is worth noting that the Son and Spirit apparently require reasons for being, while the Father does not.) The Son and Spirit are distinct from one another because they make different contributions to the same action; therefore, their processions from the Father can be distinguished. The Father is unproblematically distinct from the other persons as he is the single origin within the trinity. The Father can never be reached without going through the Son and Spirit, and the Son and Spirit may each be considered adjunct to each other depending on emphasis. "The Father begets the Son so that the Spirit can proceed from him and return: the Spirit is in that way the hinge. Or the Father causes the Spirit to come out of him so that he will have someone—the second person of the trinity—to love and be loved by: the Son is in that way the hinge" (CK, 195). Although Tanner does not give up the language of "second person" for the Son, her emphasis on the singular (complex) movement makes it, strictly speaking, impossible to consider the processions "first" or "second," and as a result, the persons should not be spoken of either as "second" or "third," although the Father can still be spoken of as "first." This trinitarian hinge installs close and constitutive relations between the Son and Spirit, although those relations are not the origin of one in the other.

Tanner's discussion of how this can be the case shows that she is, in fact, modifying both Eastern and Western accounts of trinitarian person-constitution in such significant ways that she could be said to be rejecting both, for she refuses the Western distinction between person-constituting and non-person-constituting relations as well as the Eastern form of person-constitution through incommunicable properties.[73] In the standard Western system, the Father and Son are constituted by oppositional relations of begetting and being begotten (paternity and filiation), while the Spirit is constituted by being breathed (passive spiration), which contrasts with breathing out (active spiration), a relation shared by both Father and Son as it does not stand in opposition to begetting or being begotten. In the East, persons are typically constituted by incommunicable properties like innascibility or unbegottenness (the Father), begetting or generation (the Son), and procession (the Spirit).[74]

Tanner's modifications to both of these systems are substantial. In the case of the Spirit, for instance, Tanner argues that the Son's return of the Spirit to the Father "is at most only part of what makes the Spirit the Spirit. The Spirit is the Spirit in virtue of the whole movement: emerging from the Father, into the Son, and then out again, to return" (CK, 193). The entire structure of trinitarian relationality constitutes each person. If the "whole movement" makes the Spirit who the Spirit is, the Spirit is not reductively constituted as who the Spirit is in virtue of coming forth from the Father; but if the Spirit is such a complex person or better, a simple person constituted by the complex and triune structure of the Spirit's entire movement, then it seems that the Son and Father would have to be so also.[75] (Or else, *mutatis mutandis*, the strength of Tanner's original objection against the *filioque* clause is vitiated from one direction or the other.) The Son seems to be such a simple person constituted by the complex and triune structure of the Son's movement, in his begetting by the Father and reception of power from the Spirit. But what about the Father? He "does receive back from the Son and Spirit, but only the very same things he gave them. . . . The Father's reception is therefore of a different kind from the reception by which Son and Spirit emerge from him" (CK, 192), of a different kind precisely in that the Son and Spirit's exchange is asymmetrical on either side, while the Father's reception is a logically distinguishable, symmetrical correlate of what was given by him.

Tanner's solution to the problems she has identified is extremely creative. Her solution requires modified relations of origin to be constitutive in some fashion for the personhood of the Son and Spirit. It may be that they take "shape" and "power" from one another, but if the singularity of the Father's personhood is to be protected—since the Father gives origin as such—that shape and power cannot in the strongest sense be conditions upon which their origination depends.[76] At a minimum, Tanner is broadening the compass as well as the nature of the constitutive relations, and she provides a pattern for a revisionist trinitarianism that significantly weakens the particular claims made for trinitarian relations of origin. To say that the Spirit gives power to the Son is justified from New Testament patterns of interaction between them, and to infer that the Son gives shape to the Spirit has at least some plausibility based on the relation between the Son and the Spirit in the life of Jesus. As Tanner points out, these are us-ward relations that are undertaken for the sake of human incorporation into the life of God. To make the further claim that these are constitutive relations among trinitarian persons requires an expansion of the notion of constitution in the trinity—it cannot merely be restricted to a matter of origin but must include something like a pattern or a shape, a distinctive personal particularity that is irreducible to an origin but that constitutes the person who is originated. Indeed, it turns out that Tanner's use of "nature" terminology is a way to remove as much meaning as possible from the language of "origin" in the relations between trinitarian persons. For Tanner, the relations of origin only give the persons what is already theirs by nature.

Tanner's addition of shape (form) and power as also constitutive trinitarian relations have the advantage of assuming asymmetrical relations between all trinitarian persons, but unlike in Moltmann's case, her "also constitutive" trinitarian relations do not belong to a different metaphysical level: they are all part of the same, simultaneously complex and simple, movement by which each divine person is distinguished from each other divine person. Only the Spirit receives form (from the Son). Only the Son receives power (from the Spirit). Only the Father receives nothing but the return of what the Father has first given—between conceiving the Father as recipient and as the one to whom return is made, Tanner chooses the latter (CK, 176).[77] On Tanner's account, no single trinitarian relation (to only one other person) constitutes any trinitarian person; all trinitarian persons are simple persons constituted by the entirety of triadic relations in which they stand, although only the Father is constituted by the specific asymmetricity of origination. The desirable result is greater coherence as well as avoidance of the problems we saw in Coakley and, to a degree, Ward's discussions of the need to deflect attention from one trinitarian person to another, or to interrupt potential trinitarian narcissism.

In Tanner's narrative, the trinity does on earth as it does on heaven. Her general pattern, hinging on the Son and Spirit, can be adapted to a wide variety of narrative interactions between the characters of Father, Son, and Spirit without requiring that *every* aspect of their narrative interactions be imported into the immanent being of God. At stake is the question of what it means to say that the trinity does on earth as it does in heaven, and vice versa—and of course this is the question we are facing, the question of the relation between the economic and immanent trinity as well as that of the constitution of the immanent trinity itself.

What difference does it make that the trinity is acting in a finite human world of sin and death? One such difference is that the missions take place in time (CK, 181). More importantly for our purposes, "the appearance of subservience and superiority in relations between the Son and the Father" (CK, 181) is one very significant difference made by finitude and sin. Yet she makes a curious move here, the necessity of which is not immediately apparent. Although at least part of the apparent subservience of Jesus to the Father is a function of Jesus' humanity, she holds on to the idea that "there is something in the relations between Father and Son that corresponds to the suggestion of inferiority in Jesus' relations with the Father." This "*something*" is not subordination, or humanity, but "the fact that the Son is of and from the Father" (CK, 183). Even in her account, coming from another contains within itself the possibility of—indeed, is enacted as—obedience to another, subordination to another. Tanner rightly seeks to avoid inner-trinitarian subordination, but even she does not fully succeed in avoiding the ineluctable temptation the relations of origin present.

For Tanner, Jesus' obedience to the Father implies that "what we ordinarily mean by obedience no longer holds" since he "follows no external mandate" (CK, 184). As the Word, his own nature is to enact the will of the Father: "The will of the Father constitutes him rather than legislates to him from without" so he "knows what to do naturally or intuitively . . . as his own idea, spontaneously" (CK, 185). The relation between Jesus and the Father is one "of perfect friendship or partnership in which the will of one naturally aligns with the other" (CK, 186). But how does the human will of Jesus relate to that of the Word? Presumably, the Word is always aligning the human will of Jesus (freely) with that of the Father.

But the will of the Word is also Jesus' own will, and the Word is constituted by the will of the Father. The free alignment is ultimately conditioned by Jesus' nature as the Word incarnate. Further, the Father's will belongs to the Word as the latter's own because he is *constituted* by it (but does the Father have his will of himself?). That sounds much less like a friendship or partnership agreement. Agreement between friends does not normally mean that it can belong to the essential *nature* of one to be the *reflection* of the will of the other, even if we imagine the single will they share to be fully coincident with the being of each of them—indeed, such an image might seem to vitiate just what friendship language adds here, the implication of the incarnate Word's voluntary and free coincidence with the Father's will. Note that Tanner's account of a noncompetitive relation between God and creation emphasizes that God works in creatures from the inside, such that God can naturally align the will of creatures with God's own without any suggestion of coercion. So the further question is whether the Word is doing anything more or other than what God might do in any particular person should God so choose. The incarnational mechanism (the "own-ness" of Jesus' human will in relation to the Word) does not seem necessary in order to align the will of Jesus with the Father in the way Tanner describes, although it is of course necessary in order to make the alignment salvific for anyone other than Jesus (since the expansive effects of incarnation reflect the Word's universal workings).

As we have seen, Tanner emphasizes that her account allows the pattern of the trinity in heaven and the pattern of the trinity on earth to remain aligned with one another. She uses Hans Urs von Balthasar as a foil for this theme, referring both to his trinitarian inversion and to his insistence that Jesus is directed by the Father in "pitiless" fashion in his earthly life as examples of problems she wishes to avoid. For Balthasar, as we recall, the trinitarian inversion is the subordination of the Son to the Spirit during his earthly ministry. The Spirit mediates the will of the Father to the Son, for on earth the Son must learn obedience through suffering (Heb. 5:8), although in eternity the Son offered himself for this mission. Yet Tanner's position may not be as far removed from Balthasar's as she (and we) might wish. Balthasar's moves parallel Tanner's in several significant respects. For him, too, the obedience of the Son in his human form is an effect of the alignment of will between the Son and Father that follows from the Son's status as the one who has come forth from the Father. Balthasar's language suggests agreement by committee, while Tanner emphasizes the role of "nat-ural" alignment of wills, but the basis in both cases lies in the Word's begetting. Even Balthasar's impulse to generate equality by committee eventually yields to the need for a naturalized alignment of wills based on the order of the processions and the Son's receptivity in relation to the Father. It appears that there is something appropriate about the Son's seeming to obey (a mere seeming, in Tanner's, but not Balthasar's, interpretation; CK, 186) precisely because he is *Son*.

For Tanner, the concept of *nature* does the work of suggesting that it really is the Son's own will that leads him to the cross. In Balthasar, that work is done by the Son's antecedent consent to his own begetting combined, as in Tanner, with his begetting as the full imprint of the Father and the unity of divinity. What Balthasar achieves through consent, Tanner achieves through nature. For Balthasar, the notion of antecedent consent protects against what he sees as the primary problem with Anselm's account of redemption: that it seems that the Son was driven to death rather than going of his own accord. For Tanner, the natural transmission of the Father's will to the Son protects against inequality, giving a "something" in the divine life to which the appearance of subordination in the Son's relations to the Father can correspond. But—and this is the central problem—why must Jesus' humanly appropriate subordination to the Father express something *other* than his humanity, namely that he comes from the Father as Son?

A substantial contribution of Tanner's account is that she traces the appearance of obedience in Jesus' history to our sinful lack of coordination with the will of the Father, in contradistinction to the perfect harmony between the Father and the Son (CK, 186). Yet the value of this move is diminished by the assertion that the appearance of what seems like inferiority in the relation between Jesus and the Father is traceable to the former's status as the begotten. What allows us to be certain that the submission of the Son to the Father is merely apparent if it reflects something of his status as eternal Son? The more closely begottenness and (even apparent) obedience are tied together, the greater the threat to the full divinity of the Son. Further, the connection between receptivity and (apparent) obedience pushes receptivity in the direction of obligatory submission. How can Tanner maintain that submission follows from sin when the pattern of the Son's *behavior* (that looks like submission) is the pattern of his *being*? She asserts that being Son "is a relationship of strict equality" but supports this with a quote from Hilary of Poitiers where Hilary argues that the Father is greater but the Son is not less (CK, 183).[78]

Perhaps the match between the Father's "greater" and the Son's "not less" (which sounds like Balthasar's persisting priority of the male in relation to the female, although the latter is "not less"), the Father's status as origin and the Son's as having-been-begotten, the Father's status as the sender and the Son's as the one sent, the Father's apparent knowledge and command and the Son's apparent obedience, lack of knowledge, and submission, the Father's clearly transcendent divinity and the Son's human submission that nonetheless preserves without shifting the pattern of his divine interaction with the Father—perhaps this series of matches can be destabilized by asserting that the trinitarian persons are necessarily fully equal *nonetheless* (the fundamental "even though" of trinitarian theology, in my idiom). Tanner's use of nature language to emphasize that the Word and Spirit do not receive what they did not have before does as much as possible to render the *nonetheless* efficacious. But even she says that there is something peculiarly fitting about the Son's status as Son that permits him apparently to submit to the Father. The more strongly the connection is made between the patterns of interaction between trinitarian persons in the economy and their essential and eternal relations with one another, the more pressing the problem becomes, because after all, we come to know the patterns of relation and interaction between the persons in the economy. It is unrealistic, even idealistic, to argue that the assertion of the equality of divine persons will trump the never-superseded reality that the Son is the imprint of the Father and comes from the Father—and Tanner's own "something" reflects how irresistible the temptation to ascribe the subordinationist aspects of the economy to something in the immanent life of God is.

Tanner makes a decision about what must be assigned to the humanity of Jesus, what in his history belongs to his status as Word-Son, and what follows from the fact that he is the Word acting in a sinful, alien medium. But I believe that in allowing "something" in God to correspond to the suggestion of inferiority in the relation between Jesus the Son incarnate and the Father, Tanner gives up too many of the advantages otherwise gained in her account. She goes as far as it is possible to go in vitiating the subordinationist aspects of the economy, since she also offers an account of salvation in which the obedience of the Son to the Father plays no role. If her account still maintains a fit between begetting and subordination, however, even in the attenuated fashion she allows, it may be that the strategies for undoing the match between death and trinitarian *taxes* that we have considered so far—rethinking the economy to grant less significance to subordination, rethinking the relations between mission-procession and economic-immanent trinity, and reconstituting the immanent-trinitarian processions in a way that retains a (distant) fit between begetting, sending, and subordination—are themselves inadequate.

## NOTES

1. In ch. 5, I examine Moltmann's and Pannenberg's justifications for use of father-language for God and find that each account sacrifices divine transcendence.
2. Delores Williams, *Sisters in the Wilderness: The Challenge of Womanist God-Talk* (Maryknoll, NY: Orbis, 1993), 164–7.
3. Jürgen Moltmann, *Theology of Hope: On the Ground and the Implications of a Christian Eschatology*, trans. James W. Leitch (Minneapolis, MN: Fortress Press, 1993), 165.
4. Jürgen Moltmann, *The Trinity and the Kingdom: The Doctrine of God*, trans. Margaret Kohl (Minneapolis, MN: Fortress Press, 1993), 184 (hereafter TTK). Note that this requires the logical ordering of the processions as first and second, which renders the Holy Spirit the "third" in an economy where Father and Son are already present.
5. Given that the persons are divine, "existence" does not quite capture the "thereness" of the persons.

6. A technical distinction between hypostasis and person is possible and perhaps even desirable, but Moltmann's distinction tends toward rendering the Son and Spirit composite beings. See also TTK, 183, where Moltmann argues that the "divine existence (*hypostasis*)" but not the "inner-trinitarian form" of the Spirit proceeds solely from the Father.

7. Moltmann says both that the Father "forms the 'monarchial' unity of the Trinity" on the level of constitution (TTK, 177), and that the monarchy of the Father belongs to salvation history as well (TTK, 178), which seems to bring his position closer to Pannenberg's as discussed below. As I argue in chapter 5, it would require an arduous (and I submit, ultimately unsuccessful) process of training to distinguish monarchical-cosmic divine paternity from the divine paternity that belongs only to the Father's relationship to the eternal Son Jesus, the ruler of and model for all creation.

8. The connection between perichoresis and dancing made by many trinitarian theologians rests on a mistranslation (as Moltmann recognizes), but dancing functions as a vivid image of the joyous celebration the trinitarian persons direct toward each other. Moltmann comes to distinguish between different levels of perichoretic interpenetration: trinitarian, christological, and ecclesiological interpenetration that unites human persons with each other. He also develops an odd but intriguing image of temporal perichoresis between present and future. See Moltmann, "God in the World—The World in God: Perichoresis in Trinity and Eschatology," in Richard Bauckham and Carl Mosser, eds., *The Gospel of John and Christian Theology* (Grand Rapids, MI: Eerdmans, 2008), 372–73, 379. This fascinating essay offers Moltmann's most programmatic late statements on the question of perichoresis and "making room."

9. Whether that argument succeeds is dubious. The persons would already have to be distinct in order to interpenetrate each other (see Wolfhart Pannenberg, *Systematic Theology*, vol. 1, trans. Geoffrey W. Bromiley [Grand Rapids, MI: Eerdmans, 1991], 334). Moltmann seems implicitly to grant this, since he suggests that the aesthetic form of the persons is added on to their existence when the level of life is added to the level of constitution of the trinity. But he does not quite recognize the consequences that admission has for the possibility of construing the form ontologically and for giving perichoresis as much significance as origin. Moltmann says explicitly in "God in the World" that "the triadic inter-subjectivity we call perichoresis" is what "constitutes the Unity" of the trinity (374).

10. See TTK, 172: "the Father is defined by his fatherhood to the Son, but this does not constitute his existence; it presupposes it." Christof Theilemann critiques Moltmann's interpretation of Boethius's concept of person on this point in *Die Frage nach Analogie, natürlicher Theologie und Personenbegriff in der Trinitätslehre: Eine vergleichende Untersuchung britischer und deutschsprachiger Trinitätstheologie* (Berlin: Walter de Gruyter, 1995), 203–204, n.3.

11. See, for instance, Aquinas's discussion of why causal language cannot be applied to the trinity (*Summa Theologica* Ia q. 33.1 ad 1).

12. Moltmann connects these levels with creation, reconciliation (level of life), and glorification (see TTK, 178), but it may be important to note that the Spirit's "illumination" of the doxological trinity is a starting point for the experience of salvation (as we live in the time of anticipation of the end, or in the space of expectant hope).

13. See also TTK, 149, where Moltmann connects the unity of the divine persons to the eschaton.

14. "The fact that the Son dies on the cross, delivering himself up to that death, is part of the *eternal obedience* which he renders to the Father in his whole

being through the Spirit, whom he receives from the Father." TTK, 168, my emphasis.

15. Perhaps for this reason, Moltmann has wrongly been accused of tritheism. He is not a tritheist; he is inconsistent. Even if we assume a union of three logically independent beings in a strong social-trinitarian fashion (stronger even than Moltmann intends), the problem is exacerbated rather than ameliorated. Later constitutive relations would do nothing to remove the original constitutive relations, just as I remain the child of my parents forever (even if I later become a parent myself, my relation to my parents specifically remains one of having been generated by them). Joy Ann McDougall recognizes as much when she says that "[a]lthough Moltmann does not render this explicit, it appears that it is this notion of the Father as the source of the Godhead that actually guarantees the common divine essence of the three persons, rather than his notion of fellowship through the three persons' mutual indwelling." McDougall, *Pilgrimage of Love: Moltmann on the Trinity and Christian Life* (Oxford: Oxford University Press, 2005), 98.

16. Although Moltmann insists that no generic terms should be used of the persons (TTK, 188), the distinctions between person and existence and level of life and constitution require some such constitutive aspect of the level of life.

17. A significant disagreement between Moltmann and Pannenberg pertains to the difference between monarchy as a paternal attribute and as a shared trinitarian property. Moltmann seeks the latter. The language of monarchy is confusing, since it seems to indicate straightforward subordination if attached to one divine person, but in its historical use, monarchy (*mon arche*) indicates only the single origin of the trinity. My argument is that single origin turns into subordination, but that translation has to be demonstrated, not presumed.

18. Moltmann, *The Spirit of Life: A Universal Affirmation*, trans. Margaret Kohl (Minneapolis, MN: Fortress Press, 1992 [1991]).

19. Ibid., 290–93.

20. Ibid., 294.

21. Ibid., 295, 297, 298.

22. Ibid., 300.

23. Ibid., 298.

24. Ibid., 299.

25. Ibid., 304.

26. Ibid., 305–306.

27. Moltmann, "God in the World," 374; Moltmann suggests in n.18 that this move could "solve Hans Urs von Balthasar's paradoxes with the kenosis in the Trinity." Similarly, and with a slightly different translation, Moltmann says that the persons should be thought also as "living space" for each other and speak of "the *three trinitarian* spaces in which they mutually exist. Each person actively dwells in the two others and passively cedes space for the two others." Moltmann, *Experiences in Theology: Ways and Forms of Christian Theology*, trans. Margaret Kohl (London: SCM Press, 2000), 318–19. The distinction between activity and passivity is crucial here. In her discussion of this notion in Moltmann, Joy Ann McDougall suggests that, rather than static interpenetration, Moltmann's understanding of perichoresis would be better understood as "'interanimation', that is, a dynamic being and acting together among the divine persons," but this interpretation does not give the resting side of perichoresis enough weight. McDougall, "Room of One's Own? Trinitarian Perichoresis as Analogy for the God-Human Relationship," in Jürgen Moltmann and Carmen Rivuzumwami, eds., *Wo ist Gott? Gottesräume—Lebensräume* (Neukirchen-Vluyn: Neukirchener, 2002), 135.

Moltmann himself explains (although perhaps not extensively enough) the difference of his position from Balthasar's on this point: "Die göttlichen Personen 'entäußern' sich nicht nur aneinander, wie Hans Urs von Balthasar meint, sondern räumen sich auch gegenseitig Leben und Bewegung ein und machen sich füreinander bewohnbar." Moltmann, "Gott und Raum," in *Wo ist Gott?*, 35.

28. McDougall recognizes that Moltmann's application of perichoresis also to the God–world relationship has the danger of collapsing the difference between God and creation ("Room of One's Own?," 139–40), but she assumes too quickly that the bodily limitations of human existence represent a basic limitation on human interpenetration ("Human beings simply cannot mutually indwell in their God given their bodily existence," 140), which fails to take account of the transformed materiality of the resurrected body of Christ. That creatures are distinct *beings*, rather than distinct *bodies*, demonstrates most clearly why trinitarian perichoresis differs so fundamentally from any remote human analogue to it.

29. Moltmann, "God in the World," 372.

30. Ibid., 374.

31. Moltmann, *Spirit of Life*, 291.

32. McDougall identifies this as Moltmann's "eschatological proviso" appended to "all theological statements about the doxological Trinity." Yet Moltmann repeatedly asserts equality and mutuality for relations that belong to the economic trinity, even as those very relations enact subordination and obedience. See McDougall, *Pilgrimage*, 92. See also Miroslav Volf, " 'The Trinity is Our Social Program': The Doctrine of the Trinity and the Shape of Social Engagement." *Modern Theology* 14 (1998): 403–23.

33. Parts of the following discussion of Pannenberg were published in a somewhat different form as " 'The ultimate consequence of his self-distinction from the Father . . .': Difference and Hierarchy in Pannenberg's Trinity," *Neue Zeitschrift für Systematische Theologie und Religionsphilosophie* 51 (2009): 383–99; see the article for a more extensive discussion of the structure of Pannenberg's theological system. Thanks to Walter de Gruyter for permission to reprint.

34. Wolfhart Pannenberg, *Systematic Theology*, vols. 1–3, trans. Geoffrey W. Bromiley (Grand Rapids, MI: Eerdmans, 1991–1998). Hereafter ST1, ST2, and ST3. Here ST3:594.

35. Karl Barth agrees that "God's fatherhood . . . is God's lordship in His revelation." Barth, *Church Dogmatics*, vol. 1, pt. 1: *The Doctrine of the Word of God*, ed. G. W. Bromiley and T. F. Torrance, trans. G. W. Bromiley (London: T&T Clark, 2004), 324.

36. Note that Pannenberg rejects Moltmann's terminology here precisely because the level of life corresponds to the level of constitution in terms of monarchy on the former's account; as Pannenberg says, "the monarchy of the Father . . . cannot be in competition with the life of the Trinity," ST1:325.

37. The German term is "wechselseitige Selbstunterscheidung." See Wolfhart Pannenberg, *Systematische Theologie* Band 1 (Göttingen: Vandenhoek & Ruprecht, 1988), 348.

38. Pannenberg takes for granted that the persons are distinct through relations of origin; he wants to add other, also constitutive, distinctions to the relations of origin. He maintains that "*something*" (*ousia*) is really given in the relations of origin, although Pannenberg redefines *ousia* in relational terms. This retention is seen especially clearly in a comment in Pannenberg's review of Robert Jenson's *Systematic Theology* in *First Things*: "If theology now insists on the

mutuality of these relationships, it must account for the divine unity as being in some way prior to the distinction of the three persons. It will not do to state, as Jenson does, that the three persons are 'prior to the fact that God is.' The Christian affirmation that there is one, and only one, God requires the notion of the one divine *ousia* or essence that the Father imparts to the Son and to the Spirit." Wolfhart Pannenberg, "A Trinitarian Synthesis," *First Things* (May 2000): 50. Pannenberg's second defense against subordinationism is to emphasize that although the Father is the only source of deity, he is so only from the perspective of the Son (ST1:322–23). See also ST1:318–19, where Pannenberg rejects the *filioque* because it reduces relations to those of origin.

39. This is also the basis of the perichoretic unity of the persons.

40. Michael Schulz thinks that Pannenberg assumes that the Father somehow possesses divinity independently "before" he gives it to the Son in the traditional conception. He suspects that Pannenberg is motivated in his reformulation by sympathy with Duns Scotus's briefly considered idea of absolute (not relative) person-constitutors. Schulz is correct in recognizing a certain metaphysical confusion in Pannenberg's attempt to retain the relations of origin while making other relations "also" constitutive for the divine persons. His dismissal of the problem of asymmetry and dependence is too blithe, however. Schulz thinks that what Pannenberg thinks of as dependence "ist vorab als selbst-subsistierende Bezogenheit in Liebe und als Selbstmitteilung und gleichzeitige Selbstbezogenheit zu definieren," but for there to be a reality to the terminology of *Selbstmitteilung* it seems that Pannenberg has a point. Schulz, *Sein und Trinität: Systematische Erörterungen zur Religionsphilosophie G.W.F. Hegels im ontologiegeschichtlichen Rückblick auf J. Duns Scotus und I. Kant und die Hegel-Rezeption in der Seinsauslegung und Trinitätstheologie bei W. Pannenberg, E. Jüngel, K. Rahner und H.U. v. Balthasar* (St. Ottilien: Eos Verlag, 1997), 495. See ST1:94–312.

41. This does not mean that Pannenberg sees the world as necessary to God's self-actualization. The essence of God, the true infinite, already contains love and otherness through the self-distinction of the trinitarian persons. However, once the world comes into existence, God's deity and the monarchy of the Father have to be actualized within it, for it belongs to the concept of God to be lord of any existing world. For Pannenberg, the essence of divinity appears when every moment of its existence is considered together. An individual moment of existence manifests the essence of God but is not identical with it, thus protecting God from utter dependence on history. See ST1:357–58.

42. In ST2:271, Pannenberg admits just how difficult a decision this is, and how decisive an objection may be made against it, since death seems to follow ineluctably from finitude rather than sin.

43. Pannenberg specifies that this is why all that is, is only identical with itself once time has come to an end—only when seen in the totality of connections do essences appear in their full identities (ST3:590). See also ST3:643–44.

44. This point is made especially clearly in Wolfhart Pannenberg, "Eternity, Time and the Trinitarian God," *Dialog* 39, no. 1 (Spring 2000): 13. See also ST2:63, where Pannenberg distinguishes but does not separate the *logos asarkos* from the *logos ensarkos*. The distinction seems clear but is often misunderstood due to confusion over Pannenberg's understanding of the relation between eternity and history. Pannenberg seeks to make history real and meaningful for God. He does so through his understanding of the need to materialize lordship in any existing world. *Had* no world been created, God would have had God's own life in eternal fullness. But once the world *has* been created, God's deity requires actualization in that world—that is, it has to be materialized in

appropriate finite self-distinction from the infinite. It is in this sense that Pannenberg claims that divine lordship stands or falls with the events that take place in the history of Jesus.

45. Note that for Pannenberg, this is a return and decidedly *not* a reception, since the establishment of the Father's monarchy in the world is precisely the aim and goal that ties the immanent and economic trinity together.

46. Emphasis added. *Systematische Theologie* Band 1, 341: "[D]aß Jesus in seiner äußersten Erniedrigung und in der Annahme dieses Sterbens die äußerste Konsequenz einer Selbstunterscheidung vom Vater auf sich nahm und sich gerade darin als der Sohn des Vaters bewährte." See also ST2:375: "Only as he let his earthly existence be consumed in service to his mission could Jesus as a creature be one with God. . . . This obedience [to God] let him into the situation of extreme separation from God and his immortality, into the dereliction of the cross. The remoteness from God on the cross was the climax of his self-distinction from the Father. Rightly, then, we may say that the crucifixion was integral to his earthly existence." This is repeated in ST2:450: "He is thus the Mediator between God and us. He is so by his death, for the acceptance of death was the extreme consequence of the self-distinction of the Son from the Father." In tying sonship and creaturehood so tightly together, the difference sin makes disappears, and "making room" becomes integral to divine personhood.

47. Wolfhart Pannenberg, "God's Love and the Kenosis of the Son: A Response to Masao Abe," in Christopher Ives, ed., *Divine Emptiness and Historical Fullness* (Valley Forge, PA: Trinity Press International, 1995), 249.

48. Moltmann explicitly rejects this designation in favor of a unity grounded in perichoresis ("God in the World," 373–74). But Pannenberg rightly argues that perichoresis cannot serve this role of itself, because perichoresis expresses rather than constitutes unity (ST1:334).

49. These relations and similar ones are described in Pannenberg, ST1:308–25.

50. See also ST2:319: "We must not see [the incarnation], however, as an accidental happening that is external to his eternal essence. It is logically related to his Trinitarian self-distinction from the Father."

51. German: "Schon die ewige Selbstunterscheidung vom Vater enthält das Moment der Selbstentäußerung, und gerade dadurch ist der Sohn Ursprung der Andersheit eines von Gott verschiedenen, geschöpflichen Daseins geworden," Wolfhart Pannenberg, *Systematische Theologie* Band 2 (Göttingen: Vandenhoeck & Ruprecht, 1991), 361.

52. Pannenberg consistently suggests that if the Son ever asserted his equality with the Father, he would no longer be divine.

53. Pannenberg, *Systematische Theologie* Band 2, 361.

54. Pannenberg's distinction of his position from Hegel's on this point is worth noting. He argues that Hegel assigns death to God absolutely rather than seeing that death belongs to Jesus, the *Son* of God, by virtue of his human nature (ST2:434–35). But of course, the Son becomes incarnate precisely as an expression of his eternal, voluntary self-distinction from the Father by yielding to his claim to be the only God.

55. Note that, for Pannenberg, the eschaton means the end of the rule of some over others in human communities but does not envision that possibility for divinity, since its order is free and constitutive (ST3:583–85).

56. See my article "Pannenberg, Particularity, and Eschatology: Shifting the Debate," *International Journal of Systematic Theology* 17, no. 2 (April 2015): 194–211, for a more detailed discussion of the strengths and limitations of Pannenberg's account of the relationship between the infinite and finitude.

57. Kathryn Tanner, *Christ the Key* (Cambridge: Cambridge University Press, 2010), 144 (hereafter CK).

58. Kathryn Tanner, *Jesus, Humanity and the Trinity: A Brief Systematic Theology* (Minneapolis, MN: Fortress Press, 2001), 9 (hereafter JHT).

59. Tanner notes in a footnote that she is disagreeing especially with Moltmann (JHT, 14–15). See the similar, even stronger point in CK: "The incarnation is for the purpose of humanity's entrance into trinitarian relations. In enabling that entrance, the Word's becoming incarnate is for our sake rather than its own. In general, the point of the incarnation is not what happens to the Word but what happens to us" (144).

60. Tanner makes more of this in *Economy of Grace* (Minneapolis, MN: Fortress Press, 2005) and JHT, where she discusses the ways that human beings are to imitate the unconditional nature of divine gift-giving.

61. In CK, Tanner specifies that the salvific works of Christ stand at the center (156).

62. Kathryn Tanner, *God and Creation in Christian Theology: Tyranny or Empowerment* (Minneapolis, MN: Fortress Press, 2005), 42.

63. Ibid., 84–100.

64. Here we find the side-by-side relations that we could find neither in Moltmann's penetrative and room-making/being logic nor in Pannenberg's moving aside to make room for. Note that this is no womb-wound of trinitarian logic either, for the place made for humankind is *by*, not *in*, the Word's side. Similarly, she insists, "The Word is not going somewhere in becoming incarnate with the intent, say, of gaining a new set of experiences to offset its previous ignorance of the sufferings we have brought upon ourselves through sin. What is new in the Word's becoming incarnate is our relation to the Word, our placement, so to speak, with respect to it" (CK, 144).

65. See also Kathryn Tanner, "Absolute Difference," in Chris Boesel and S. Wesley Ariarajah, eds., *Divine Multiplicity: Trinities, Diversities, and the Nature of Relation* (New York: Fordham University Press, 2014), 217–33.

66. She supports this through Hilary of Poitiers, *On the Trinity*, in Philip Schaff and Henry Wace, eds., *Hilary of Poitiers, John of Damascus*, NPNF 2/9 (Peabody, MA: Hendrickson, 2012) 6.27, 108.

67. See also CK, ch. 5, "Politics," for her expanded discussion of this issue. The chapter originally appeared in a different version as "The Trinity," in William Cavanaugh and Peter Scott, eds., *The Blackwell Companion to Political Theology* (Oxford: Blackwell, 2003), 319–32.

68. JHT, 52 n.54 specifies that she is rejecting Karl Barth's account of obedience and subordination precisely because it conforms the immanent trinity too closely to the economic trinity without recognizing the dangers of Arianism that were so vivid to the patristic writers on which Tanner draws. See also JHT, 76–77, for emphasis on the economic and for-us character of the Son's subordination.

69. Note that here, Tanner is referring to the relations in the immanent trinity, not to the economy of salvation. In other words, she is not exclusively grounding divine equality in the economy.

70. "The Word does not appear during its incarnation on earth in the form of God but in the form of a servant—a servant whose very mission requires taking up the position of those burdened by sin and death" (CK, 170). This distances the nature of the Word from submission to sin and death: the Word does not take up a position that in this way is peculiarly expressive of the Word's nature; rather, these aspects are expressive of the Word's aims (i.e., the for-us character of the Word's action).

71. Broadly speaking, where the West identifies the "second" procession as "spiration," the East identifies begetting or generation and procession as two different relations that cannot be subsumed under a generic term (such as procession). Procession therefore names the procession of the Spirit specifically, and not the procession of both Son and Spirit, as in the West.
72. Note that Tanner holds onto divine simplicity and divine persons as subsistent relations, so "being" should not be thought as existence added to the persons, contra Moltmann's distinction between *hypostasis* and *prosopon*.
73. These "Eastern" and "Western" distinctions are, of course, overgeneralizations and oversimplifications, yet express tendencies on either side.
74. Tanner discusses this in CK 189 n.81. Franciscan medieval traditions also use incommunicable properties, conferred by emanation, to distinguish the persons—the Father by "innascibility," the Son by "generation," and the Spirit by "spiration." See Russell L. Friedman, *Medieval Trinitarian Thought from Aquinas to Ockham* (Cambridge: Cambridge University Press, 2010), 17.
75. This may be why Tanner says that "the Father never acts alone in giving rise to either of them" as a way of emphasizing their equality with the Father (CK, 194).
76. Suggesting that the Father's *power* to generate distinguishes him, rather than the Father's *paternity* (or his unbegottenness or innascibility), seems odd, however. The noncommunicable property of the Father is usually taken to be innascibility or unbegottenness (*anarchos*), not the power to generate. See Yves Congar, *I Believe in the Holy Spirit*, vol. 3, trans. David Smith (New York: Geoffrey Chapman, 1983), 58, referring to Photius, for instance (also cited in Tanner, CK, 189 n. 81).
77. She emphasizes that the "correlate" of the Son's performance of his mission in eternity is the "perfect return to the Father of what the Father begets the Son to be" (CK, 176). See also CK, 192.
78. See Hilary of Poitiers, *On the Trinity*, 9.54 and 9.56, 174–75. Again, a surprising resonance with Balthasar appears; Balthasar's "ever-greater" applied inside the divine life is just such a move.

## BIBLIOGRAPHY

Barth, Karl. *Church Dogmatics*. Vol. 1, pt. 1: *The Doctrine of the Word of God*. Ed. G. W. Bromiley and T. F. Torrance. Trans. G. W. Bromiley. London: T&T Clark, 2004.

Congar, Yves. *I Believe in the Holy Spirit*. Vol. 3: *The River of the Water of Life (Rev 22:1) Flows in the East and in the West*. Trans. David Smith. New York: Geoffrey Chapman, 1983.

Friedman, Russell L. *Medieval Trinitarian Thought from Aquinas to Ockham*. Cambridge: Cambridge University Press, 2010.

Hilary of Poitiers. *On the Trinity*. In *Nicene and Post-Nicene Fathers*. Second Series. Vol. 9: *Hilary of Poitiers, John of Damascus*, ed. Philip Schaff and Henry Wace, 40–233. Peabody: Hendrickson, 2012.

McDougall, Joy Ann. *Pilgrimage of Love: Moltmann on the Trinity and Christian Life*. Oxford: Oxford University Press, 2005.

———. "Room of One's Own? Trinitarian Perichoresis as Analogy for the God-Human Relationship." In *Wo ist Gott? Gottesräume—Lebensräume*, ed. Jürgen Moltmann and Carmen Rivuzumwami, 133–41. Neukirchen-Vluyn: Neukirchener, 2002.

Moltmann, Jürgen. *Experiences in Theology: Ways and Forms of Christian Theology.* Trans. Margaret Kohl. London: SCM Press, 2000.

———. "God in the World—The World in God: Perichoresis in Trinity and Eschatology." In *The Gospel of John and Christian Theology*, ed. Richard Bauckham and Carl Mosser, 369–81. Grand Rapids: Eerdmans, 2008.

———. "Gott und Raum." In *Wo ist Gott? Gottesräume—Lebensräume*, ed. Jürgen Moltmann and Carmen Rivuzumwami, 29–41. Neukirchen-Vluyn: Neukirchener, 2002.

———. *The Spirit of Life: A Universal Affirmation.* Trans. Margaret Kohl. Minneapolis: Fortress Press, 1992.

———. *Theology of Hope: On the Ground and the Implications of a Christian Eschatology.* Trans. James W. Leitch. Minneapolis: Fortress Press, 1993.

———. *The Trinity and the Kingdom: The Doctrine of God.* Trans. Margaret Kohl. Minneapolis: Fortress Press, 1993.

Pannenberg, Wolfhart. "Eternity, Time and the Trinitarian God." *Dialog* 39, no. 1 (Spring 2000): 9–14.

———. "God's Love and the Kenosis of the Son: A Response to Masao Abe." In *Divine Emptiness and Historical Fullness: A Buddhist-Jewish-Christian Conversation with Masao Abe*, ed. Christopher Ives, 244–50. Valley Forge, PA: Trinity Press International, 1995.

———. *Systematic Theology.* 3 vols. Trans. Geoffrey W. Bromiley. Grand Rapids: Eerdmans, 1991–1998.

———. *Systematische Theologie* Band 1. Göttingen: Vandenhoek & Ruprecht, 1988.

———. *Systematische Theologie* Band 2. Göttingen: Vandenhoeck & Ruprecht, 1991.

———. "A Trinitarian Synthesis." *First Things* (May 2000): 49–53.

Schulz, Michael. *Sein und Trinität: Systematische Erörterungen zur Religionsphilosophie G. W. F. Hegels im ontologiegeschichtlichen Rückblick auf J. Duns Scotus und I. Kant und die Hegel-Rezeption in der Seinsauslegung und Trinitätstheologie bei W. Pannenberg, E. Jüngel, K. Rahner und H.U. v. Balthasar.* St. Ottilien: Eos Verlag, 1997.

Tanner, Kathryn. "Absolute Difference." In *Divine Multiplicity: Trinities, Diversities, and the Nature of Relation*, ed. Chris Boesel and S. Wesley Ariarajah, 217–33. New York: Fordham University Press, 2014.

———. *Christ the Key.* Cambridge: Cambridge University Press, 2010.

———. *Economy of Grace.* Minneapolis: Fortress Press, 2005.

———. *God and Creation in Christian Theology: Tyranny or Empowerment.* Minneapolis: Fortress Press, 2005.

———. *Jesus, Humanity and the Trinity: A Brief Systematic Theology.* Minneapolis: Fortress Press, 2001.

———. "The Trinity." In *The Blackwell Companion to Political Theology*, ed. Peter Scott and William T. Cavanaugh, 319–32. Malden, MA: Blackwell, 2004.

Theilemann, Christof. *Die Frage nach Analogie, natürlicher Theologie und Personenbegriff in der Trinitätslehre: Eine vergleichende Untersuchung britischer und deutschsprachiger Trinitätstheologie.* Berlin: Walter de Gruyter, 1995.

Tonstad, Linn Marie. "Pannenberg, Particularity, and Eschatology: Shifting the Debate." *International Journal of Systematic Theology* 17, no. 2 (April 2015): 194–211.

———. " 'The Ultimate Consequence of His Self-distinction from the Father . . .': Difference and Hierarchy in Pannenberg's Trinity." *Neue Zeitscrhift für Systematische Theologie und Religionsphilosophie* 51 (2009): 383–99.

Williams, Delores S. *Sisters in the Wilderness: The Challenge of Womanist God-Talk.* Maryknoll: Orbis, 1993.

# Part 3

# 5   A Topography of the Trinitarian Imaginary
## "Through a Critical Mimesis"[1] to God

We believe in one God, the Father All Governing, creator [of all things visible and invisible];

And in one Lord Jesus Christ, the Son of God, begotten of the Father as only begotten, that is, from the essence [reality] of the Father, God from God, Light from Light, true God from true God, begotten not created, of the same essence [reality] as the Father, through whom all things came into being, both in heaven and in earth; Who for us men and for our salvation came down and was incarnate, becoming human. He suffered and the third day he rose, and ascended into the heavens. And he will come to judge both the living and the dead.

And [we believe] in the Holy Spirit.

But, those who say, Once he was not, or he was not before his generation, or he came to be out of nothing, or who assert that he, the Son of God, is of a different *hypostasis* or *ousia*, or that he is a creature, or changeable, or mutable, the Catholic and Apostolic Church anathematizes them.[2]

In this chapter, I examine the ways in which trinitarian theologians contribute to the very gendering of God that they seek to avoid. As the mounting evidence of previous chapters suggests, the perfection of the origin-relationship between Father and Son grounds trinitarian masculinity beyond the maleness of the terms (or personal names) Father and Son. The point of connection between trinitarian and sexual difference lies deeper. We have seen this in earlier chapters, where we have found obedience, subordination, death, self-sacrifice, distance, and humiliation in the eternal trinitarian relationships. In this chapter, we add to our mounting evidence for the translatability of origin into masculinity and for the subordinationist, death-loving aspects of trinitarian theology.

As an experiment in trinitarian theology, this analysis operates in several genres that are not often and not easily brought into conversation with one another. Systematic theology and feminist and queer theory entertain partially conflicting assumptions about the nature of theological language. To the systematician, catachrestic mimesis may seem mocking, unfaithful, or even ridiculous in its apparent inattentiveness to the ways in which Christian canons are authoritatively established—for such canons always contain ways to disavow their apparent consequences. To the feminist and queer theorist, the systematician may appear naïve, or even willfully ignorant, about the extent to which his interpretive categories are contaminated by dependence on heteropatriarchal forms of thought. For systematic theologians who believe (as I do) that transcendence can be good for women and queers,[3] feminist and queer interpretive strategies provide indispensable means for making the case that the Christian God can escape "his" patriarchal determination.

Although feminist and queer theologians have sometimes found the trinity a fruitful ground for the value of difference inside the Christian imaginary, the attempts that have been made hitherto to resubjectify the trinity in feminist or queer terms have mostly avoided serious engagement with the nature and function of technical trinitarian distinctions. Such engagement is necessary, for, as Marcella Althaus-Reid says, "What may worry us theologically is not necessarily what real phalluses may do, but the symbolic ones. . . . It may well be that God has a female sexuality without a clitoris, but with a hymen and a vagina for penetrative reproductive purposes, and this can then make the femininity of God irrelevant for women."[4] The wound-womb in all its forms only extends divine phallicism.

## THE "HERESIOLOGICAL IMPERATIVE" AND THE FOUNDATION OF TRINITARIAN THEOLOGY

Judith Butler's now-classic text *Gender Trouble* attempts to make trouble by identifying what gender makes unthinkable: "Is the breakdown of gender binaries . . . so monstrous, so frightening, that it must be held to be definitionally impossible and heuristically precluded from any effort to think gender?"[5] Making trinitarian trouble with a view to thinking the unthinkable in trinitarian theology will make apparent what the rule-bound affirmations of trinitarian theology entail when put to use but also how those affirmations negate their own ends by the way in which they work. Thinking the unthinkable will allow us to recognize not so much the already queer nature of trinitarian theology, as some theologians[6] have argued, but rather, the ways in which that purportedly queer trinity functions as an ideological support and justification for hierarchies of gender and sexuality inside Christian practice as well as in visions of God's being. Butler writes that an impetus for *Gender Trouble* was noting the "the fear of losing one's place in gender" (GT, xi). Trinitarian theologians, too, demonstrate a fear of unknowing, of losing one's place, if the mysterious threefold repetition of God becomes disordered and messy.

The parodic repetition that may transform gender (GT, 179) does not have that power for trinitarian theology. Repetitions with a critical difference are the abjected Other of trinitarian theology; they are also the very material by which its structuring certainties are maintained. From the beginning, we find it necessary to reformulate over and over what is being forbidden, what is *not* being said, when trinitarian differences are delineated. Claims about scripture, revelation, and authority serve in part to occlude how our own temptations push us toward worship of a Father-God whom we explicitly seek to deny. We make our active participation in his production invisible to ourselves. Our fascination with the infidelities to which trinitarian theology tends (heresies) requires constant discipline. Abjection renders such deformations of trinitarian speech the constitutive other of "orthodox" trinitarian theology, for it is at the moment of abjection that trinitarian speech begins. Language about Father, Son, and Spirit precedes theological determination of how their relationships to each other should be named.[7] But at the moment that *proper* trinitarian theology comes into existence (that is, orthodox and grammatical: in homage to Marcella Althaus-Reid we might term such theology *decent* trinitarian theology), the mode of its positing is in distinction from heretical ideas.[8]

We only discover the work trinitarian theology does as we examine the uses to which it is put, which often contrast with theologians' claims about such work. This is a different way to formulate the experimental nature of the current project. There is a constitutive sense in which the primary locations of the practice of trinitarian theology are worship and praise (glorification); more fundamental even than those is following Christ, the aim such practices subtend. This chapter engages habits of trinitarian speech and histories of reflection on trinitarian doctrine as practices with laws, rules, and regulations that produce trinitarian subjects: persons who accept the rules of trinitarian speech—who are formed by its grammar and speak its language fluently—and subjectivated trinitarian persons. Rule-bound speech does not replace worship and glorification; it is a side effect of the way that reflection accompanies glorification and discipleship.

The first task of a trinitarian theology is usually ruling out mistaken understandings of the trinity. Trinitarian theology claims that the Son is eternally begotten of the Father. The Spirit proceeds from the Father (and perhaps the Son also). The dangers of subordinationism (considering the Son and Spirit less divine than the Father), tritheism (belief in three gods), Arianism (suggesting that the Son has a beginning in time or is created), modalism (viewing the persons of the trinity as masks underneath which an undifferentiated God lurks), and all the other heresies loom large in the imagination of the trinitarian theologian. Steering the trinitarian ship safely through such shoals requires affirmations couched as denials. God is FATHER, but God is not *a* father.

Orthodoxy always finds itself under threat. For example, Karl Barth insists that "God's trinity does not imply any threat to but is rather the basis of the Christian concept of the unity of God," a nicely turned subversion of what triunity appears to mean.[9] Moreover, trinity means neither "plurality of Gods" nor "plurality of individuals or parts" in God.[10] Much earlier, the first letter introducing Gregory of Nyssa's *Against Eunomius* ends on the connective tissue of orthodoxy and heresy; heresy's promulgation cannot go unanswered by orthodoxy.[11] Augustine begins *De Trinitate* by noting that he is writing against "the sophistries of those who scorn the starting-point of faith."[12] They conceive of God in mistaken fashion. He goes on to define essential trinitarian commitments: the unity and equality of Father, Son, and Spirit in one substance, which entails that "there are *not* three gods but one God; *although* indeed the Father has begotten the Son, and therefore he who is the Father is not the Son." Further, "the Holy Spirit is neither the Father nor the Son."[13] It is not the three who lived the life of Jesus, "but the Son alone."[14] Similarly, only the Holy Spirit descended as a dove and at Pentecost. Next, Augustine expresses his concern for those who find these commitments difficult to understand and reconcile. How, they ask, can it be that the trinity works "inseparably" yet some acts belong only to one while being "caused by the three"?[15] Theologians provide gracious assistance to those struggling to make sense of what faith requires one to hold, even as they admit the difficulties and ultimate failure of comprehension.

The various versions of the classical creeds require specification of what is *not* being said in order to say anything—"begotten *not* made." Indeed, the original creed of Nicaea ends with an anathema upon those who might mistake the begetting of the Son.[16] The affirmative form of the credo takes its shape from the dangers of heresy: what *must* be said often follows what must *not* be said. As Virginia Burrus puts it, "The virginal font of orthodox doctrine 'is always conceiving': under the cover of heresiology's negations, the Christian theologian simultaneously staves off sterility and maintains purity."[17] Heretical attacks on the received faith require vigorous (virile?) theological responses. The constant threat of heresy serves to generate the very rules of faith that identify what counts as heresy.

The breakdown of gender binaries is abjected at the moment gender comes to thought. The positive rules of gender depend on refusing its potential undoing. What, then, is abjected when the trinity comes to speech? The defensive move of the trinitarian theologian in relation to this question would be to point to the connection between trinitarian speech and revelation: only the revelation of God in Christ leads to trinitarian speech. This means that theology only "thinks after" God's revelation.[18] God's utterly positive revelation engenders rules for faithful trinitarian speech.[19]

On the level of discourse analysis, however, or within the architectonic structure of the Christian imaginary, the first speech act must be a rejection of the idea that the Father is the father of the Son in any ordinary sense. But as Burrus emphasizes, there is also no point at which the *articulation* of trinitarian difference precedes a connection between trinitarian and sexual difference, even when it denies the inference from one to the other. The connection between divine sonship and the articulation of masculinity suggests an indirect but intimate relation between trinitarian and sexual difference that is irreducible to the sexual and gendered language of paternity and son-ship.[20] Recognizing and analyzing the intertwining of trinitarian and sexual difference requires analysis attentive to such indirect relations, which enact connections denied within the locutionary theological act.

## MIMETIC TRINITARIAN SPEECH, OR HOW "HE" MET "HER"

Let us extend this story to the present and tell it somewhat differently. Despite the gendered and sexed nature of Father-Son language, the degree of malformation in the relationship between the trinity and sexual differ-ence continues to be resisted by a certain type of trinitarian theologian.[21] Such theologians argue that Father-Son language does not install maleness or masculinity in God, and neither does it effect any valorization of human males. "Preserving the traditional names . . . should not automatically be interpreted as endorsing a patriarchal and oppressive vision of Christianity. Indeed, it should do the opposite, provided the significance of the names be properly understood," David Coffey says. One may continue exclusive use of masculine pronouns for all three persons of the trinity because they are "the only appropriate pronominal forms" for Father and Son (perhaps not our primary concern when speaking of a God beyond gender) and because "she" and "her" "explicitly identify God as sexual, which "he" and "his," given their actual background, do not."[22] Presumably this claim follows from the historical elision of men with humankind, which makes masculine pronouns more appropriate to God because they are taken to function as generic personal pronouns.

These theologians hyperbolically insist that correct usage of such lan-guage is the only possibility of faithfulness to God's self-revelation and that revisionist feminist theologians misunderstand the way in which such lan-guage works.[23] "Neither in scripture nor in the history of dogma has God, as Father and Son, been understood to be male—*not even subliminally*."[24] Such feminist theologians install sexual difference in God when they supple-ment or replace masculine language with feminine or nongendered equiv-alents; *they* gender God. They enact idolatry when they refuse humble submission to the revealed name of God.[25] They threaten the unity of church and the stability of society with their "radical and militant" ways of creat-ing "divisiveness between the sexes" in a variation on the "revolutionary fallacy" that "one may remake human relations not by patient rebuilding but by warfare or destruction."[26] The prohibition against replacement (or even supplementation) of Father-Son language is often expressed in terms of the distinction between divine and human begetting. The absence of a female body serves as the differentiating definition of divine reproduc-tion in its utter otherness from crassly biological human "making." What divine fatherhood indicates, one suggests, is "a matter not of maleness but of ontological discontinuity."[27] Or else it points to the "familial intimacy of a particularly intense form" into which we are invited: "we are entitled to call the first person . . . by that proper, private, family name that is the Son's divine prerogative."[28] No projection here!

But this insistence that feminists are idolaters in their identification of divine masculinity lends itself to a different interpretation. Insistence that God has *never* been "male," even subliminally, depends on a disconnection between liturgy, church life, and theology that trinitarian theologians otherwise wish to resist. For trinitarian theology serves more or less directly (at a minimum via Christology) as a justification for the particular roles that only males have been given liturgically. If liturgy and worship serve as the primary locations of trinitarian theology, technical theological assertions must meaningfully overtake such practices in order to become true, for liturgy is not merely a question of what is spoken or recited by the community but of the bodied relationships enacted between congregants and officiants. These relationships are so foundational that we must seek to read the aggressive recalcitrance of these theologians in different terms. We cannot diagnose them merely as hypocrites or special pleaders; we must give a thoroughly theological account of what they do, although our route to that account may appear circuitous at first glance.

Who then is man, the theologian or God? Judith Butler's chapter "The Lesbian Phallus and the Morphological Imaginary" in *Bodies that Matter* begins with an epigraph from Jane Gallop in which Gallop describes the insistence of Lacan's followers that one might "clearly . . . separate *phallus* from *penis* [and] control the meaning of the signifier *phallus*" as a "desire to have the phallus, . . . desire to be at the center of language, at its origin. And their inability to control the meaning of the word *phallus* is evidence of what Lacan calls symbolic castration" (BTM, 57). Butler goes on to discuss Lacan's designation of the empty signifier that stands at the heart of language as the *phallus*. She says, "To claim for the phallus the status of a privileged signifier performatively produces and effects this privilege" even as its "privilege is potentially contested by the very list of alternatives it discounts, and the negation of which constitutes and precipitates that phallus. Indeed, the phallus is *not* a body part (but the whole), is *not* an imaginary effect (but the origin of all imaginary effects). These negations are constitutive; they function as disavowals that precipitate—and are then erased by the idealization of the phallus" (BTM, 83). The structure of the desire to control the signification of the term *phallus* directly parallels theologians' insistence that there is not even a subliminal possibility of patriarchy in the name "Father" for God. The theologian, like the analyst, wishes that language could be subjected to meaning's determination in the same sentence in which the theologian, like the analyst, admits that language's meaning cannot be controlled (for God is "Father" beyond all human knowledge).

The admission of symbolic castration is also the denial of symbolic castration in its determination of the one "thing" (the penis, fatherhood) the contested term does *not* mean, even though it refers to that very "thing."[29]

In Lacanian terms, the production of sexual difference takes place through the threat of castration: women are "always already . . . castrated," while men "look over and see this figure of castration" (BTM, 101) and learn to fear the loss of the phallus.[30] Because "the phallus exceeds every effort to identify with it, . . . this failure to approximate the phallus constitutes the necessary relation of the imaginary to the phallus." Thus the fear of castration is "*the spectre of the recognition that [the phallus] was always already lost*," a fear of "[b]ecoming like her, becoming her" and, as a result, "falling into penis envy" like her (BTM, 101). The lost phallus generates "a fear of the recognition that there can be no final obedience to that symbolic power, and this must be a recognition that, in some already operative way, one already has made" (BTM, 102). Total obedience to the symbolic power of the lawgiver would entail self-identity and phallic plenitude; it would mean full self-possession achieved via submission to, and so authorization by, true authority.

In heightened terms, this coincidence of speech and authorized existence serves as an expression of fallen human desire (yet inability) to attain the identity of *esse* and *essentia*, to have one's foundations in oneself, to determine the conditions of one's own existence. The operative recognition—a spectral haunting not reducible to knowledge—is not that "I" might lose the phallus but that the phallus is "already elsewhere." The masculine fiction of "having" the phallus is an always-failing response to *not* "having" the phallus (BTM, 101). The failure of identification with the phallus generates another form of identification: "a *dis*identification with a position that seems too saturated with injury or aggression, . . . occupiable only through imagining the loss of viable identity altogether"; that is, the loss of the phallus—the very loss that the feminine symbolizes. Protecting oneself against that danger explains why one might sympathetically draw attention to "an injury done to another in order to deflect attention from an injury done to oneself" so that "one feels for oneself *through and as the other*." By demanding the recognition of an injury done to someone else, one might implicitly demand the recognition of an injury done to oneself without "being further steeped in that very abjection and/or launched infelicitously into rage" (BTM, 100). This sequence offers a theological roadmap for analysis of the hyperbolic assignation of idolatry to feminist theologians in their inadequate submission to the rule of faith.

One of the foundational forms of sin is the desire to be like God, knowing good and evil. In the fall narrative, this desire generates disobedience to explicit divine command. Humans arrogate to ourselves knowledge that belongs only to God. Sinful human creatures then find ourselves unable clearly to distinguish between worldly goods and divine things. We make idols for ourselves and of ourselves. We need to learn how to worship the true God instead of sacrificing our sons to Baal (Jer. 19:5), setting up Asherah poles (2 Kings 17:16), or giving the glory that belongs only to the creator to created things (Rom. 1:25).

Revelation tells us who the true God is: Father, Son, and Holy Spirit, one God. The vocation of the theologian is fidelity to that revelation; the temptation of the theologian is misidentification of that God. The theologian recognizes the impossibility of stabilizing reference to God in language.[31] But for the sake of the church's worship, speech, and self-reflection, the fundamental distinction between God and all else must be policed under the sign of submission to revelation. For worship of non-God is idolatry. So the theologian finds himself[32] in a double bind. On the one hand, he, like all people, wishes to be God: he wishes to judge between good and evil, he wishes to be self-sufficient and independent, and he wishes to set the conditions for others' existence.[33] On the other hand, his calling is to point away from himself to God. He must resist the misrecognitions that continually transpose the divine and things of the earth, even as he knows that he has no power of his own that could finally control his own misrecognitions. He knows that he must be taken up and formed into adoptive brotherhood with the Son (who only does what he sees the Father doing) by the Spirit (the only one who searches the deep things of God). And finally all shall be subjected to the Father. The theologian both fears and knows that there can be no final obedience to the symbolic power, the lawgiver, yet that obedience is what is required of him: this is what Butler terms the *"very presupposition"* of the fear of castration (BTM, 101): The phallus is always already elsewhere. It belongs to God, not to him.

He is constituted by a fantasy that he could have had the phallus (he wants to be like God), but obedience to the symbolic power *is* the recognition that the only one whose speech is coincident with himself is God (as the Father speaks his Word). If the classical theological diagnosis of sin is correct, the theologian will constantly transgress this recognition and lie to himself about its transgression. Looking at "woman" (for instance, the feminist theologian),[34] he can be certain that "she" does not have "it," for "it" belongs only to God, whose potent Son-seed is always erect and always coming. But looking at "her" forces the recognition that he does not have it either, a recognition that he can only deflect by an increasingly hysterical insistence that it is *"she"* who does not have it. Policing the boundary then becomes a way of covering over his desire to—like God—be *"man."* But he knows that God is *"man"* (self-identical, *a se*) and he is not. (Otherwise, he does not deserve the name of theologian.) He knows that God has graciously castrated him, and what God requires of him is auto-castration in the imaginary, or feminization. "She" never had the fantasy of the phallus to begin with. "She" then comes to stand in the place that he must, but cannot, inhabit.

The ambivalence of his disidentification with "her" appears as obsessive insistence that it is only "she" who makes the constitutive theological mistake of thinking that God the Father is the only true *"man."*[35] In naming God *"man,"* "she" faces the full inevitability of the constitutive misrecognitions that structure human attempts to speak about God. "She" admits that no safe word will prevent God the Father from turning into father-god. And so "she" provides a figuration far more dangerous than reassuring, for "she" has no difficulty admitting that the phallus is elsewhere. He must then find another claim to bring against "her," and he has no difficulty doing so. *"She"* is the idolater: "she" sets herself up as the judge of divine things, so it is "she" who refuses to submit to castration. Unlike him, he says, *"she"* claims the phallus for herself: *"she"* is an idolater, an avowed opponent of God; *"she"* sexes God—he faithfully worships the (unsexed) Father. She becomes the phallic mother, the most dangerous and threatening form of phallicism.[36]

The phallic mother in this analytic is the imagined feminist theologian. "She" is the "woman" who speaks improperly (without submitting to the rules) of God and who trusts God to make it right rather than insisting on "her" own rightness in the (dis-)avowal of authority through transcendent deferral. "She" appears for him as the one who dares the improper speech that he knows is not permitted him, and "she" accepts the failures of speech that he cannot. His disidentification with "her" requires him to assume the paternal (or divine) symbolic authority that "she" (unlike he) transgresses against. In calling "her" to account for her transgression, by invoking the law according to which "she" is found guilty, he claims the symbolic authority that he explicitly disavows at that moment, and so becomes HIM.[37] His idolatry runs more deeply than "hers." And that is what he cannot forgive "her."[38]

## HE "CALLS [HIM] 'FATHER' IN A SENSE THAT BURSTS ALL ANALOGIES"[39]

> If the phallus *must* negate the penis in order to symbolize and signify in its privileged way, then the phallus is bound to the penis, not through simple identity, but through determinate negation. If the phallus only signifies to the extent that it is *not* the penis, and the penis is qualified as that body part that it must *not be*, then the phallus is fundamentally dependent upon the penis in order to symbolize at all. Indeed, the phallus would be nothing without the penis. And in that sense in which the phallus requires the penis for its own constitution, the identity of the phallus includes the penis, that is, a relation of identity holds between them. And this is, of course, not only a logical point, for we have seen that the phallus not only opposes the penis in a logical sense, but is itself instituted through the repudiation of its partial, decentered, and substitutable character. (BTM, 84)

To avoid idolatry and projection, trinitarian theologians commonly emphasize that God is Father neither in a literal nor in a generic sense but only in relation to the Son.[40] Yet learning that "Father" in God means only "the Father of the Son" still implies that speaking father rightly means remembering that God is not *a* father, but a father of a different sort than any and all others.[41] So although the believer may not know just what it means to call God Father, the believer must learn what it does *not* mean to call God Father—as Gregory of Nazianzus says, "The Father is the begetter and the emitter; *without* passion, of course, and *without* reference to time, and *not* in a corporeal manner."[42] The fundamental relation between divine and human fatherhood is thus one of dissimilarity. Yet a common strategy that theologians employ to describe or emphasize that dissimilarity turns out to generate similarity, and indeed a form of identity, where none such ought to be.

Appeals to the transcendent and analogy-bursting character of God's fatherhood have become an increasingly common defensive strategy among theologians who wish feminist criticism to touch only the edges of the deposit of faith. In William Placher's terms, "What it means that Jesus has a divine Father, and that we are allowed to call this one our 'Father,' transcends every human case of fatherhood."[43] Thomas Torrance insists that

> the concepts of fatherhood and sonship do not derive from any analogy or inherent likeness between the creature and the Creator. They are laid hold of by divine revelation and are made to point back away altogether from their creaturely and human use to their creative source in the transcendent nature of God, who is eternally Father in himself. . . . Since man is created after the image of God, all fatherly relations within humanity derive from and point to the unique, aboriginal, and transcendent Fatherhood of God. Accordingly, human fatherhood may not be used as a standard by which to judge divine Fatherhood, for there is strictly no comparison between human fatherhood and divine Fatherhood. . . . On the contrary, it is according to the uncreated Fatherhood of God that all creaturely fatherhood is to be understood.[44]

Torrance's argument twists agonizingly as he insists that no comparison can be made between human and divine fatherhood, except that the former derives from the latter and ought to be judged by it. He stretches to protect the downward derivation of paternity without introducing a corresponding upward signification—although there is nothing about creaturely fatherhood in general that makes it an appropriate revelatory vessel for the divine, the concept of fatherhood may by the grace of God become an image of the divine. There is no "analogy or inherent likeness" grounding the relation between divine and human fathers, yet the latter image the former and point to it as their ground, origin, and transcendent goal; uncreated fatherhood determines creaturely fatherhood. The concepts of fatherhood and sonship cannot meaningfully point "away altogether" from the creaturely usages to which they are adapted by their divine origin, especially as *concepts*.

Torrance continues, "we must think of the Fatherhood of God and the relation of human fatherhood to it in an altogether *spiritual* and *imageless* way, and thus without ever reading back descriptively into God the creaturely content or finite imagery of human fatherhood."[45] It is difficult to think of the fatherhood of God in an imageless way if all creaturely fatherhood is its image. Perhaps Torrance's difficulties follow from the two irreconcilable New Testament texts he juxtaposes, Matthew 23:9 and Ephesians 3:15.[46] The first enjoins the reservation of the title "father" only to God, while the second extends the name "Father" from God onto "every fatherhood in heaven and on earth." Torrance interprets this to mean that only God is properly Father, while all other fathers are so only in a derivative sense. Yet if the divine signification of fatherhood brought with it other fathers or their attributes, it would be idolatrous rather than proper, as Torrance's rejection of analogy or likeness implies.[47] The signification of divine fatherhood thus depends on a successful distinction between it and the human kind; that distinction is both a positive and a negative connection between them.

In another influential example of this strategy, Jürgen Moltmann distinguishes between patriarchal (or "monotheistic") and trinitarian concepts of fatherhood in God. The first type, "God the Father—the father of the church—the father of his country—the father of the family," establishes a chain of fathers who stand in analogous relationships to each other. Each father gains power from and in relation to the others, while supporting the others in turn. The second, trinitarian, type focuses on the loving relationship between God the Father and God the Son, so that the Father's "fatherhood is defined by the relationship to this Son." An arduous process of training is required to disconnect one from the other, however: "anyone who wants to understand the trinitarian God must forget the ideas behind this patriarchal Father religion—the super-ego, the father of the family, the father of his country, even the 'fatherly providence'. He must gaze solely at the life and message of his brother Jesus: for in fellowship with the only begotten Son he will recognize that the Father of Jesus Christ is his Father too."[48] The Father who is discovered in that gaze is "a father who both begets and bears his son" and so becomes "a motherly father too" (TTK, 164). Moltmann claims that "the doctrine of the Trinity" in this moment "makes a first approach towards overcoming sexist language in the concept of God" (TTK, 165).

Allowing God the Father, who is properly father in the trinity and adoptively father in relation to all other human beings, to transcend his patriarchal limitations by including even maternity within his all-encompassing grasp neither destabilizes divine patriarchy nor serves as an overcoming of sexism. After all, divine males get to be father, son, and mother, thus demonstrating that symbolic divine masculinity includes even maternity in its transcendent perfection. Non-divine females get to be—at best—included in the indeterminate and androgynous spirit and as symbolic adjuncts to the Father's ecstatic maternal self-realization.

Ultimately, Moltmann's training cannot succeed, for it requires a constant reminder—a bind on the self—that *this* use of fatherhood is different from all other forms of the same. This disconnection establishes an irreducible relation between the different kinds of fatherhood as the self directs its attention to one of the forms and reminds itself that *that* one has nothing to do with *this* one. The self must continually submit itself to examination to ensure that it is looking only toward the right forms of fatherhood and disavowing the wrong ones. Such a repudiation effectively generates its own transgression by cementing a constitutive relation between these purportedly different paternal deployments—remember to forget the patriarchal father, as it were. The result is precisely the opposite of what Moltmann intends. Other linguistic usages are able to distinguish the different meanings of the "same" term without such arduous labor. But in this case, the activity of the believer in gazing *only* in the right (and not the wrong) direction, suggests just how closely divine and human fatherhood are tied together. Indeed, the specific term *father* has shown itself as a potent inflammation to Christian practices of gendered hierarchies, especially in combination with the theological significance often given to the maleness of Christ and his disciples. So the disconnection Moltmann requires is from Christianity's own history, and that history is the trinity's history, too.

Wolfhart Pannenberg admits that the use of "father"-language for God derives from patriarchal social organization.[49] Yet "[t]o bring sexual differentiation into the understanding of God would mean polytheism," so the God of Israel has "no female partner" (ST1, 261; although Pannenberg neglects the significance of Israel's symbolic femininity to this point). Interestingly, Pannenberg reads the social, rather than gendered or biological, aspects of the father as decisive. Christ's revelation of God the Father transforms the meaning of divine fatherhood into something like "the duty of a family head to care for the members." Of course, the father is no longer the "head of the family" in many contexts, which might seem to invalidate the analogy. But for Pannenberg, such changes do "not justify the demand for a revision of the concept of God as Father" because revision would imply that theology is no more than projection. Instead, Pannenberg identifies election and covenant as the substantial and material forms that divine fatherhood takes:

> These features can then be taken up into an understanding of God which confronts the changing concept of human fatherhood as a *norm*. In comparison with it all human fatherhood also pales. For this reason it still retains its power even at a time when patriarchal forms decay and the role of the father within the family loses its distinctive contours. Then the fatherhood of God can truly become the epitome of God's comprehensive care—the type of care which human fatherhood can *no longer* offer. (ST1:262)[50]

Divine paternal care confronts failing human paternity (partial, decentered, and substitutable as the latter is) with its own comprehensiveness, exemplary nature, and unsubstitutability. Pannenberg, tellingly, construes this as a defense against rather than a validation of feminist criticisms of the patriarchal nature of the father-god. He continues,

> For all his subjection to the Father, Jesus undoubtedly claimed that God is to be understood only as the heavenly Father whom he declared him to be. . . . Jesus is the Son inasmuch as it is in his message of the nearness of the royal rule of the Father, his subjection to the Father's will, and especially the function of his sending as a revelation of the love of God, that this God may be known as Father. (ST1:264)

Amazingly, the *subjection* of the Son to the Father reveals the nonpatriarchal nature of divine fatherhood. For Pannenberg, the Son's citational practice (obedient submission via invocation or repetition of the law of the Father as the only God) activates and secures his divinity. Jesus' constant insistence that his Other is the lawgiver to whom he submits enacts the truth of the Father's delegation of his authority to the Son. *This* is the mode of Jesus' sonship, revealing the deeper reason why he is *Son* in the theological imaginary. As the eternal locus of the Father's monarchy in this submission, the Son's subjection is a form of kenotic participation in the power of paternity, the form of fatherhood that remains bound to its human instantiation through determinate negation.

Pannenberg's treatment of fatherhood shows that God's fatherhood was initially derived from a patriarchal culture, so it reflected the power of actual fathers. Over time, restrictive quasi-biological fatherhood moved to broader metaphors of care and election—and of course, in the New Testament, the adoption of all humans as Jesus' siblings. As a result, divine and human fatherhood may again be converging rather than diverging. Currently, we live with multitudinous forms of nonbiological fatherhood offering paternal—elective, adoptive, comprehensive—care. Some families have two fathers. In some coparenting arrangements, any number of non-biologically related persons offer paternal care. Some trans* fathers give birth; other fathers parent their children, whatever genetic relation may pertain between them. Indeed, the truest fatherhood may now be the nonbiological sort, since culturally, we see fatherhood as something that must be learned and encouraged—although this learning process plays off sexist assumptions about what men are like, and fathers are like, especially compared to the naturalized care of the mother. Thus it may still not be desirable, even according to such expanded notions of fatherhood, to connect these variations to the divine version.

In her influential essay, "Can a Feminist Call God 'Father'?," Janet Martin Soskice picks up Moltmann's attempt to identify the Father only through the Son's revelation of him, rather than through a general concept of fatherhood.[51] But in the lightly revised version of the essay that appears in her recent *Kindness of God*, Soskice, in a revealing move, begins with the human rather than divine version of the same:

> Fathers, of any sort, get only bad press these days. Fathers—as fathers—seem only to appear in the press if associated with criminal violence of a sexual, physical, or psychological sort (usually all three) towards partners, wives, or children. Or else they appear as absent. Single parent families are overwhelmingly headed by women, while "fathers" cannot, or will not, be found. Yet in the biblical writings, naming God "Father" is an anticipation of great intimacy, new relation, of hope, and of love.[52]

Although her discussion aims to distinguish and even separate divine paternity from the human kind, it starts from human paternity. And not just from human paternity in general, but from the "absence" of fathers in single-parent families, and from the "bad press" that is all fathers get these days. The evidence for such bad press is lacking; Soskice simply leaves the assertion unsupported. The way she contrasts the desirability and uniqueness of theo-biblical paternity with the failures—real and representational—of human paternity serves to cement an already existing relation between them rather than disconnecting one from the other.

Soskice is concerned, however, to block the undesirable consequences of an unchastened divine paternity: "what is objectionable is . . . that the 'divine male' is styled as one who is powerful, dominant, and implacable."[53] Here Soskice mistakenly identifies the almighty and overbearing aspects of divine paternity as the problem with it. She assumes that a gentle, kind, and consent-seeking divine father would be less susceptible to idolatry and less susceptible to deployment in the establishment of gendered human hierarchies, but there is no reason to believe that, nor is any argument offered. Indeed, the trope of the benevolent patriarch or head of the family lies at least as deep in our cultural registers as does that of the "implacable" male, as Pannenberg's discussion shows.[54]

Soskice develops her benevolent father in relation to another programmatic essay, Paul Ricoeur's "Fatherhood: From Phantasm to Symbol,"[55] in which he argues that representations of fatherhood develop and change in the biblical materials, moving toward an ever-greater intimacy grounded in the Son's knowledge of the Father. As Soskice summarizes part of his argument, "The God of Israel is defined, then, over and against father gods, gods who beget the world, and paradoxically, it is this abolition of the biological father God that makes non-idolatrous, metaphorical 'father language' about God possible."[56] Human fatherhood is qualified as the thing that divine fatherhood *must not* be. When Soskice claims that an "incomplete [Father-] figure . . . traverses a number of semantic levels"[57] in order to escape its patriarchal determination, she returns to the above arguments Moltmann developed regarding the motherly Father and the priority of the Son's revelation of the Father.[58]

We have come full circle. These wonderfully nonpatriarchal father-figments of the theological imagination slide back and forth between divine and human fatherhood. Their relations to each other can be measured in units derived from the slippage between the penis and the phallus. One is established by a specific repudiation of the other, ensuring that they are not only bound together, but the divine achieves what the human should have been but never can be. The asserted transcendence of human fatherhood is vitiated in that move. Divine paternity is not like human paternity: it is not fragmented and vulnerable to failure, nor is it in need of intercourse (and therefore an unreliable erection) or a sexually differentiated other. The dream of perfect phallic fatherhood requires just these conditions. What divine paternity is *not* like is human paternity specifically, not, say, human relations of care more generally. Yet in these theologies, divine paternity is the origin of all paternity and all relationality in its generation of the Son, and its perfection further serves to critique the failure of human paternity, the all-embracing care that cannot be offered by a merely human father. Theologians seek to make this perfect inner-trinitarian paternity the only reference point of divine fatherhood.

But can such a shift really succeed (as it has not done in the theologians we have just examined)? Entirely new fathers appear on the scene to replace the old, bad fathers of patriarchal human social organization. These new fathers, or better, this new FATHER, have nothing to do with that old, bad God. Perhaps the shift transforms the constitutive disidentification from one pertaining to a singular relation between human and divine paternity to a relation between different forms of divine paternity. This form, the trinitarian rather than monotheistic form of divine paternity, has *nothing to do* with that other form. It bursts all analogies and transcends every case—and it is that from which "all fatherhood in heaven and earth is named." The use to which these theologians put divine fatherhood establishes, rather than negates, a positive relation between divine and human fatherhood. And this happens just at the point at which that relation is denied. Indeed, this identification is the result of the specific strategies used as defensive measures *against* the suspicion that God the Father may have anything to do with fatherhood more generally.

## *EVEN THOUGH* HE HAS COME FORTH FROM THE FATHER (AND WHERE DID THE SPIRIT GO?)

According to Thomas Aquinas there are five notions: unoriginatedness, paternity, filiation, spiration, and procession.

Four of these are relations of opposition: paternity, filiation, spiration, and procession.

Three relations are person-constituting: the Father is the Father of the Son, the Son is Begotten, and the Spirit is spirated.

There are two processions, being begotten (the Son) and being spirated (the Spirit).

There is only one God, hence only one divine essence.[59]

The technical rules of trinitarian theology become settled in their use through the citational practices of theologians. Such use naturalizes trinitarian grammar: theologians know how to speak rightly. An aspect of speaking rightly is knowing what terms do *not* mean. These denials are especially important when right speech depends on terms with great imaginative resonance, for their power renders them more susceptible to being used in theologically ungrammatical sentences.[60] To be a trinitarian theologian of a certain kind entails the achievement of relative fluency in reciting such distinctions: God is not *a* father, relations of origin are (arguably) not causal relations, and so on. As a result, making the "sexy-gender-y"[61] effects of trinitarian rules of speech visible within and beyond their stipulative limitations requires speaking ungrammatically for a moment. When "she"—the feminist trinitarian theologian or indeed, the human person through any permutation of sex, sexuality, gender, and kinship—speaks of the multiply gendered positions of God Father, Son, and Spirit, *"[t]his is citation, not as enslavement or simple reiteration of the original, but as an insubordination that appears to take place within the very terms of the original, and which calls into question the power of origination that"* the theological tradition *"appears to claim for"* itself. "Her miming has the effect of repeating the origin only to displace that origin *as* an origin" (BTM, 45).[62] Let us examine trinitarian kinship structures using over-literalization, catachresis, and other forms of mimesis.[63]

The trinitarian system of differentiation and distinction works through the appearance of the Father's generative power, which expresses itself in the Word of difference: the Son, who is the perfect image of the Father and the guarantor of his fecundity.[64] The prohibition against subordinating the Son to the Father "even though" he comes forth from the Father grounds trinitarian enculturation. Classifying the relationship between Father and Son as one of paternity and filiation requires an "even though" from the first moment: "*Even though*" he has come forth from the Father, the Son is not less than the Father. This "even though" function of trinitarian language extends into each determination of the trinity and indicates at least one reason why the trinity is so vulnerable to heretical treatments. Such "even thoughs" continually generate the very positions they intend to reject.

Sexual difference in the Christian imaginary is produced by the "procession" (TD3:286) of Eve from Adam. It establishes an asymmetrical reciprocity in which Adam is "first"—not in such a way that Eve is less, but in such a way that his "persisting priority" (TD3:292)[65] cannot be dissolved by her full equality-in-difference from him. Yet her difference from him is no more than a distance, an interval, that allows him to see himself in her as the mirror/image of him: the answer to his question, the place of his becoming.

She is both the reflection of him and the place of human difference—for he is the self-same as the first must always be. Yet she also enacts hom(m)o-sociality by giving birth to a male son, becoming herself the site of another repetition of patriarchal lines of descent.[66]

No wonder the Son is also "supra"-feminine and from a different perspective, "supra"-masculine.[67] The Spirit, too, becomes feminine in its very "placedness" as the relation between the Father and the Son. The typical feminist strategy in response to paternal reproductive determination (Adam/Eve, Father/Son) would be to point to the contrast between masculine reproductive perfection set up against feminized materiality with its instabilities and deformations (the mother's body), which in the trinitarian case is erased by the Father's partho-genesis. And while this strategy has some value, Butler points out that "when and where women are represented within this economy is precisely the site of their erasure. . . . No wonder then that the feminine appears for Irigaray only in *catachresis*, that is, in those figures that function improperly, . . . the use of a proper name to describe that which does not properly belong to it, and that return to haunt and coopt the very language from which the feminine is excluded" (BTM, 37). No wonder then. No wonder? No, wonder! These protean paternities recur on multiple semantic levels and fracture the totality of each other's meaning: the improper sense of paternity that renders the Christian God male; divine, transcendent, accomplished fatherhood from which human paternity takes its name; the human version that divine paternity critiques for its insufficiency in comparison to the masterful, nonbiological divine father's care; and the proper sense of divine paternity that explodes such slippage, yet can be invoked by addressing God with his proper name of "our Father." Divine masculinity never takes a single, determinative, proper form. Can we then figure femininity trinitarianly by speaking improperly of the trinity? That would be a wonder indeed!

The Son is the Word according to whom all of reality is structured and brought into being as an ordered unity; the Son is also the Father's phallus as the symbol and sign of the Father's plenitude. The phallus, symbolically speaking, is the sign of meaning's stabilization and so of the possibility of plenitudinous self-identity.[68] The Father is only himself in the generation of the Son,[69] so the generation of the Son secures the Father's ecstatic self-identity as Father. Moreover, the perfection of the Son's imaging of the Father means that the difference of the Son is only a difference of origin, yet a difference enacted as obedience and gratitude. The Son is also the Father's seed, not just as the *logos spermatikos* but also as the seed that in its death fructifies the womb of Mary-church.[70] The Father's power of self-sharing shows his humility (in his willingness to share himself with another) and just so his supreme, absolute power (for a father who can share himself and all his power fully with another, without being threatened by that other, is greater than a father who cannot[71]). And the fullness of trinitarian distinctiveness shows itself as Father and Son breathe out an Other who is the sign and seal of the perfection—the virginal purity—of their mutual love.[72] Their Other ensures that their otherwise narcissistic focus on each other is always kept open or deflected in new directions.

The Holy Spirit preserves the distinction-in-unity of Father and Son while freeing them from the charge of self-enclosure, for trinitarian theologians like to emphasize that love must always have a third.[73] Mary Daly's famous indictment of the claim that women are "included under the Holy Spirit. He's feminine"[74] expresses a truth about the Western trinitarian imaginary. The Son is the masculine Other of the Father even or perhaps especially when he appears under the guise of "supra"-femininity. His wound-womb, his breasts,[75] and the Father's womb[76] are expressions of their transcendently virile generative powers, which exceed even feminine fecundity. Their feminine Other, the Spirit, is always the not-all. He hovers over the formless and void waters of the world; he teaches the believer to speak "Father" truly in an expansive extension of divine sonship (Rom. 8:15); he babbles on our behalf to God in groans when we cannot speak (Rom. 8:26); he requires authorized interpretation when his speech is directed toward us (1 Cor. 14:5).

The Son points away from himself to the Father, whose sign he is by nature.[77] The trinitarian persons do only what they truly are: the acts and attributes seen in the history of revelation conform meaningfully to who these persons are eternally. These "utterly subjected" subjects "have no choice but to reiterate the law of their genesis" (GT, 135), which is fulfilled when the Son hands the kingdom back to the Father, so that God will be all in all.[78] The distinctions among trinitarian persons are naturalized through the Father, as he is the originary origin, the one in whom all moments of difference find their beginning in his supreme, ultimate act of begetting, in which he shows the power of the divine nature by doing with it what he will.[79] This power of relational self-disposal, identical with the Father's being, generates a trinitarian system of gift exchange through which the Son's reception of his being in gratitude turns into submission and obedience.[80] It makes incarnation and suffering appropriate to him. The world thus remains unnecessary to the enactment of trinitarian distinctions in love: Already within the trinity, infinite distance maps fullness rather than emptiness. That fullness is always already overdetermined in the Father–Son relation because the Son is, in his very being, the full and complete image of the Father, the copy of the origin, the image of the invisible. What role is left for the Spirit in this imagistic perfection? The Spirit naturally and freely enacts the distance and intimacy between the Father and the Son,[81] stretching and yearning toward them both.

Arguably, the most significant difference between "Eastern" and "Western" trinitarianisms is the issue of the *filioque* clause, which in the West stabilizes the distinction between the Son and Spirit by introducing an oppositional relation between them. In the East, the distinction is guaranteed by the name, the law of the Father, who *begets* one and *brings forth* the other.[82] The distinction between the Son and the Spirit is found not in the relation between them, which is nontemporally subsequent to their originary relations to the Father, but in the monarchical act of production or causation. It is not irrelevant that the East has accepted the terminology of "cause" that the West rejects.[83] The East accepts the quasi-subordinationist consequences of this picture, indeed celebrates them, as a manifestation of the all-encompassing monarchy of the Father,[84] who alone is self-grounding existence in the ecstatic mode.

The West, worried about subordination and ontological distinction, subjects even the Father to the rule of trinitarian differentiation by adding the words "and through the Son" in order to secure the difference of the Spirit. In the West, then, paternal monarchy is insufficient to guarantee the distinction between Son and Spirit. Monarchy and productive power are finally nonidentical, for only the productive power of the Father, not his monarchy, is transferred to the Son as the latter participates in breathing out the Spirit, and only the Son receives the name of the Father. Productive power turns out to be transferable (heritable) to an extent. This law of the Son sets him up as a second origin within the trinity. He becomes another "father" (origin) whose fatherhood is simultaneously secured and cancelled out through the name of the "Son," which derives from and extends the name "Father." Reproduction of the name in derived mode, or what we might term the trinitarian structure of kinship, functions to safeguard relation and inheritance. The Spirit is the hidden location of these exchanges of inheritance, monarchy, and the name.[85] The self-identity of Father and Son is secured through the one who escapes representation. The Holy Spirit secures the relation between Father and Son, so the Spirit's absence from the scene of figuration is made evident.[86]

The Spirit's ambiguous escape has a positive and a negative aspect: positively, as the name of the divine being (for God is spirit),[87] and negatively, as the specular other of Father and Son in which they gaze at one another, an infinite mirroring traceable back to the Father's self-imaging in his true Other.[88] Thus the femininity of the Spirit has proven itself the irresistibly subjected condition of trinitarian exogamy as the second difference or as the bond of the mutual love of Father and Son.[89] The invisible Spirit ensures their ineffable visibility, visibility that escapes and transcends limitation; the fullness of their self-having confounds all attempts to grasp it in its excess. Simultaneous insistence on paternal origination, filial obedience, and the effulgence of spiritual motion renders this divine non-family resubjected as each person moves around between the permitted, contrastive positions, reshuffling symbolic hierarchies without undoing them.

If the Son does not participate in the breathing out of the Spirit,[90] yet is subjected to it in her earthly life,[91] then the Father's pregnant womb eternally births a sterile Son. The Son finds herself subjected to the law of her own desire for her counterpart or image, the world,[92] which results in the transformation of the Son's impotence into potent sperm indeed as she impregnates her own maternal Father in their cobirthing of children in her return to the bosom from which she was born. Her potency grants her the production of many female brothers, adopted bride-sons of Christ. The Spirit, "intersex," indeterminable, so unavoidably also feminine, requires proliferations of pronouns and grammars as s/he/it tops Jesus and the disciples, yet submits to their commands according to the fashion of the switch.

Or perhaps the Spirit is the sign and seal of the fecundity of the Father–Son relationship. Then the Father's paternal virility is secured through the generation of the Son, which leaves his womb empty because his *all* (except fatherhood) is given in the begetting (not making) of this Son. The Father's womb renders him auto-erotically penetrable without fragmenting him as he impregnates himself to transcend even parthogenesis through autonomous heterosexual reproduction. His "emptiness" is only symbolic as his Word speaks of love in breathing out the Spirit, showing that he comes over and over again in an endless and excessive procession of ecstatic love. He is no human male whose capacity is exhausted in one final climax. Since he has the phallus (while the Son is the phallus), his permanent climax gushes wetly—the Spirit hovers over the waters—in the transformation of the Son into the Father's seed, a seed that when cast into the ground makes the order of the world.

But is the Son then sterile? If reproduction belongs only to the Father within the trinity, the seed-Son cannot reproduce, and instead suffers castration (or the threat of castration) in order to become the "supra"-feminine space of the Father's self-enactment, for the Son can do only what he sees the Father doing (John 5:19). If the Son also breathes out the Spirit, Father and Son together groan out a sigh of union which enfolds them both. The Son has then been given, not fatherhood, but potency—the ability to reproduce, or just to produce—in so transcendent a fashion that he does not even need to become father. In that case, the law of the Father has been subjected to the law of the Son, who is begotten yet breathes and makes with no hint of his own sexuality. Perhaps the Spirit appears as the only true "man" (generic) in this image, for it is it alone who escapes sexual difference "in the name," and it is not tied to anyone's apron strings as its indeterminacy frees it from full bondage in its originary site as the term of divine dependence.[93]

The Spirit groans rather than speaks and expresses itself in glossolalia—the unintelligibility of the speaking Spirit (subject)—and its nature as the not-all (GT, 147) is thus made visible. Theologically, the Spirit cannot *be* spoken—it blows where it will and speaks on our behalf. The Spirit's subject-position cannot speak itself and cannot be spoken; thus it enacts the unthinkable, the not-all of the trinitarian kinship economy with its desperation-driven desire for paradoxical equality engendered by its continued dependence on dependence. The Spirit is the excess that speaks the truth. Its very non-integrability provides the system with its necessary internal and already ruled excess.

When the Son comes along, trapped in flesh thanks to the Spirit's whispering insinuation, the Spirit makes visible what cannot be seen (filiation):

hovering as a dove, this transcendent non-creature marks Jesus, while a voice speaks from heaven—"this is my beloved Son, in whom I am well pleased" (Matt. 3:17)—showing that the lines of patriarchal inheritance remain intact, and that while the Father may have begotten a Word, he can still chatter. Yet the Spirit offers more. When Jesus proceeds into the arid desert to struggle with temptation, and then along his straight road to the cross, where does the Spirit go?

At a minimum, wherever he will: Jonathan Edwards says that the Spirit is "the principle that as it were reigns over the Godhead and governs his heart and wholly influences both the Father and the Son in all that they do."[94] The Spirit switches between sending and being sent, between topping and whispering, declaring and seducing. The Spirit comes at Pentecost in an unregulated outpouring that shocks the surrounding community and intoxicates the disciples just enough that they declare their allegiance to the Son publicly. This happens just at the moment when the Son seems to be gone for good, not only because he has poured himself out on the cross but because even his ah!-so-penetrable post-resurrection body has gone away in its ascension to a higher heaven in which it sits at the right hand of the Father. The disciples are now "biting and chomping"[95] on Jesus, transformed into bread and wine. Given courage and speech by the Spirit, they are able to speak of these things openly, without secrecy: coming out. In their proclamation, propagated through faithful nonsexual reproduction over the centuries, they come to asymptotically approach the perfection of the Son's relation to the Father under the sign of the Spirit, for they are adopted as "sons" identified by the perfection of their adherence to the form of the Father's originary power (speaking only "begotten, not made").

The Spirit, like the Son, leaves home. But while the Son finds himself utterly subjected—to the Father, to his desire for the world—the Spirit eventually gets to have all the fun. No one can predict (or predicate?) it. Sometimes it whispers—but did it not also storm and light fires? Those who are marked by the Spirit fall into an unregulated frenzy and behave in strange and unpredictable ways: "The Spirit's workings lie beyond control or prediction, but their effects are visible enough. They seize people, transforming them, making leaders of outsiders and reducing kings to comatose nakedness."[96] The enlivening Spirit-dove is tossed out from the Father's hand and enters into the womb—the only member of the trinity who at least brushes against a woman? Or a form of artificial insemination, suggesting that on earth, the Father is not as potent as he is in heaven. Fire licking, hovering above disciples enlivened and transformed, speaking the word anew.[97]

Each of these overliteral readings of moves made in classical trinitarian theology, except the very last, shows how many permutations of sex, gender, and sexuality the persons of the trinity can move around without dissolving their protean masculinity: protean, because it is irreducible to a single story of an ultra-powerful God, or a sacrificial Father–Son relationship, or a motherly Father, or a birth-giving, maternal trinity. Masculinity because, as we have seen, while masculinity can move around, it does not disappear, nor does its relation to femininity, and their ordering in relation to each other cannot be dissolved, for it is the content of what they are when fully abstracted from any particular instantiation. The Law of the Father and its fulfillment in the Word radicalize the always-existing flexibility of Christian sexy-gender-y symbol systems of power. That is the mechanism of their stabilization, not their undoing. Only on that level are they consistent, nonprotean, in their relational differentiation.

Speaking from the Spirit's place denies the priority of inheritance and masculine generativity.[98] The most promising implication of the Spirit's positionality is that in its wildness and unpredictability and most significantly, in that the Spirit has almost never been accused of begetting or generating another divine person, the Spirit's personhood can delineate a model for the theological transformations that Father and Son require. In this way, they, too, may undergo a successful operative transformation (not castration) so as to generate a more adequate trinitarian theology.[99] How, then, shall we start from the Spirit?

## NOTES

1. Judith Butler, *Bodies that Matter: On the Discursive Limits of "Sex"* (New York: Routledge, 1993), 73 (hereafter BTM).
2. The original creed of the council of Nicaea, found in John H. Leith, ed., *Creeds of the Churches: A Reader in Christian Doctrine from the Bible to the Present*, 3rd ed. (Louisville, KY: John Knox, 1982), 30–31 (brackets in original).
3. I owe this formulation to a paper by Larisa Reznik entitled, "Is Transcendence Bad for 'Women'?" which itself refers to Susan Moller Okin's famous question, *Is Multiculturalism Bad for Women?* (Princeton, NJ: Princeton University Press, 1999).
4. Marcella Althaus-Reid, *Indecent Theology: Theological Perversions in Sex, Gender, and Politics* (New York: Routledge, 2000), 73.
5. Judith Butler, *Gender Trouble: Feminism and the Subversion of Identity* (New York: Routledge, 1999 [1990]), viii (hereafter GT).
6. For instance, in Gerard Loughlin's edited volume *Queer Theology: Rethinking the Western Body* (Oxford: Blackwell, 2007), particularly his chapter on Hans Urs von Balthasar and Gavin D'Costa's on "Queer Trinity," as well as in Patrick Cheng's *Radical Love: An Introduction to Queer Theology* (New York: Seabury, 2011).
7. See, for instance, Jesus' baptism, Jesus' assertion that the one who has seen him has seen the Father, his prayer to the Father, his promise to send a helper once he has gone away, the descent of the Spirit at Pentecost, and the baptismal formula.
8. Virginia Burrus, "Radical Orthodoxy and the Heresiological Habit: Engaging Graham Ward's Christology," in Rosemary Radford Ruether and Marion Grau, eds., *Interpreting the Postmodern: Responses to Radical Orthodoxy* (New York: T&T Clark, 2006), 36–37. See also Basil Studer, *Trinity and Incarnation: The Faith of the Early Church* (Edinburgh: T&T Clark, 1993), 242.
9. Karl Barth, *Church Dogmatics I/1: The Doctrine of the Word of God*, ed. T. F. Torrance and G. W. Bromiley, trans. G. W. Bromiley(London: T&T Clark, 2004), 348 (hereafter CD I/1).

10. Ibid., 350.

11. Gregory of Nyssa, *Against Eunomius, Nicene and Post-Nicene Fathers,* Second Series, vol. 5, *Gregory of Nyssa: Dogmatic Treatises, Etc.,* ed. Philip Schaff and Henry Wace (Peabody, MA: Hendrickson, 2012), 33.

12. Augustine, *The Trinity,* ed. John E Rotelle, trans. Edmund Hill (New York: New City Press, 1991), 65.

13. Ibid., 69 (emphasis added).

14. Ibid.

15. Ibid., 70.

16. Perhaps unsurprisingly, many of the trinitarian controversies hang on terms like *ousia* and *hypostasis,* which are here included in the anathema; it later becomes correct trinitarian speech to term the Son a different hypostasis.

17. Virginia Burrus, *"Begotten, Not Made": Conceiving Manhood in Late Antiquity* (Stanford, CA: Stanford University Press, 2000), 99.

18. As Hans Urs von Balthasar, from a somewhat different perspective, puts it in *Theo-Drama: Theological Dramatic Theory,* vol. 2, *Dramatis Personae: Man in God,* trans. Graham Harrison (San Francisco, CA: Ignatius, 1990), 128 (hereafter TD2).

19. Burrus points out that "the temporality of orthodoxy must bend and split in order both to accommodate and to repress the historicity, and thus the inventiveness, of theology. Christian truth is by definition prior, in the terms of the orthodox script: it always already *is*" (*"Begotten, Not Made",* 36).

20. I examine other such forms of inheritance in chapter 7.

21. This insistence is often accompanied or introduced by insistence that there is no patriarchy in resistance to feminist indictments, usually followed by one or all of the following claims: (1) ultimately, God's work in the church is where all such injustice is undone; (2) divine fatherhood and sonship are nonpatriarchal and actually indicate patriarchy's undoing; and (3) any failures the church may have had in this regard are truly unfortunate but warrant no fundamental revision, nor are they other than incidental.

22. David Coffey, *Deus Trinitas: The Doctrine of the Triune God* (New York: Oxford University Press, 1999), 6. One wishes that such theologians would rather not address the issue at all than give such justifications for their usage. Coffey refuses to use "God Godself" because it "seems . . . a linguistic barbarism" (ibid.). He explains that "Jesus' divine Sonship" should become "an asset" rather than a "liability" for feminists (7), on the grounds that Jesus' maleness was nonpatriarchal—a fairly common claim. In its most extreme form, Jesus *had* to have been male, because otherwise the subjugation of the proud would not have been demonstrated in his suffering and sacrifice, since women were already subordinate (see, for instance, Garrett Green, following Susanne Heine, in "The Gender of God and the Theology of Metaphor," in Alvin J. Kimel, ed., *Speaking the Christian God: The Holy Trinity and the Challenge of Feminism* [Grand Rapids, MI: Eerdmans, 1992], 62–63). Contrast David Cunningham, who rightly says that Christian insistence that God is not gendered has been contradicted "where it matters most: in our *practices.*" Cunningham, *These Three Are One: The Practice of Trinitarian Theology* (New York: Wiley, 1998), 46.

23. These theologians often do not agree on how such language works. With equal certainty, they move between justifying the terms as proper names, narrativized identities, metaphors, analogies, tropes, through historical sanctification and continuity with Christ's consciousness, revelation, and so on.

24. One wonders how Paul Molnar knows this. Feminist theologians like Elizabeth Johnson insist, he says, that "God must be emasculated for women to achieve equality"; he is following (rather closely) Roland Frye (see next note). Paul D. Molnar, *Divine Freedom and the Doctrine of the Immanent Trinity:*

212 A Topography of the Trinitarian Imaginary

*In Dialogue with Karl Barth and Contemporary Theology* (Edinburgh: T&T Clark, 2002), 10. Marcella Althaus-Reid refreshingly says that the "ecclesiological hermeneutics" of the church take place "in a closed circuit of signifiers in which the main signifier is a sexual name, the name of the Father" Althaus-Reid, *The Queer God* (London: Routledge, 2003), 30.

25. See several essays from Kimel, ed., *Speaking the Christian God*, especially Elizabeth Achtemeier, "Exchanging God for 'No Gods': A Discussion of Female Language for God," 1–16; Roland M. Frye, "Language for God and Feminist Language: Problems and Principles," 17–43; and Robert Jenson's claim that feminist and womanist theologians who use the term "Father" as a "trope" ought to admit that they are "avowed opponents of the church [rather than] reformers thereof," in " 'The Father, He . . .'," in *Speaking the Christian God*, 105. In contrast, see Luce Irigaray, *Marine Lover of Friedrich Nietzsche*, trans. Gillian C. Gill (New York: Columbia University Press, 1991), 164.

26. Colin Gunton, "Proteus and Procrustes: A Study in the Dialectic of Language in Disagreement with Sallie McFague," in *Speaking the Christian God*, 79. Robert Jenson terms the flourishing of feminist thought an almost unprecedentedly fast-growing "scholasticism" in " 'The Father, He . . .'," 95 n.1.

27. Gunton, "Proteus and Procrustes," 79.

28. J. A. DiNoia, O.P., "Knowing and Naming the Triune God: The Grammar of Trinitarian Confession," in Kimel, ed., *Speaking the Christian God*, 184–85.

29. The Lacanian determination of the phallus as the empty signifier at the heart of the symbolic order follows the death of God—that is, the loss of the one who was once thought to stabilize meaning.

30. As always, these are symbolic positions, not identifiable with individual men and women. To speak is to speak within the symbolic order, thus to take up the "masculine" subject position.

31. *What* theological language refers to is often quite different from *how* it refers, although the how also partly determines the what (e.g., in analogical language). I take it that all reference to the trinity (in itself, not as a concept) is made possible by the grace of the Holy Spirit, who speaks what we cannot.

32. *Man* in what follows moves around with intentional ambiguity between reference to human males, masculine subject-positions, and the self-identity of God who has and is the power that the theologian desires for "himself." The latter option plays off images of the Enlightenment "man of reason" who is constituted by self-determining autonomy. With somewhat different concerns in mind, Shannon Craigo-Snell argues that being a female academic theologian encourages or even requires passing as male, in "Passing as Male in the Academy," in Margaret D. Kamitsuka, ed., *The Embrace of Eros: Bodies, Desires, and Sexuality in Christianity* (Minneapolis, MN: Fortress Press, 2010), 135–50.

33. Or so accounts of sin as pride tell us. There are other sins, and other forms of sin, that are not reducible to these categories, but these forms of sin have pride of place in the historical Christian imaginary.

34. Again, a subject-position or a position of enunciation.

35. Even the manhood of the Son (incarnate and not) is derivative: obedience, submission, and grateful reception constitute his refusal to snatch the manhood of the Father for himself. His perfect disidentification with the Father's manhood entails that it is always given, or at least lent, him (depending on how 1 Cor. 15:28 is read).

36. What's more, " 'having the phallus' is much more destructive as a feminine operation than as a masculine one" (BTM, 103).

37. See BTM, 105–107. Irigaray suggests that it is God who becomes the fictional "he" who stabilizes the masculinity of men (*This Sex Which Is Not One*,

97); I am far more convinced of the phallic masculinity of many theological incarnations of the Christian God than of that of any Christian male. See also Burrus, *"Begotten Not Made"*, 65.

38. Again, this analysis maps on to sexed theological-symbolic subject positions, not directly to actual male and female theologians.

39. Hans Urs von Balthasar, *Theo-Drama: Theological Dramatic Theory*, vol. 3, *Dramatis Personae: Persons in Christ*, trans. Graham Harrison (San Francisco, CA: Ignatius, 1992), 518. Balthasar connects the analogy-bursting character of divine fatherhood to the Father's generous begetting of the Son out of his womb. Balthasar, like Jürgen Moltmann, is a good example of how those who are considered only marginally orthodox are often the best routes into a diagnostic mapping of an imaginary, for marginal orthodoxy indicates a repetition with a terrifying difference—surfacing what orthodoxy most fears is the truth about its own narratives. That said, Balthasar's influence on Roman Catholic theologies of the body, Pope John Paul II, and Jean-Luc Marion suggest that he is rather more central than accusations of unorthodoxy might reflect.

40. The following discussion (through 203) appears in slightly different form in Linn Marie Tonstad, "The Logic of Origin and the Paradoxes of Language: A Theological Experiment," *Modern Theology* 30, no. 3 (July 2014): 57–65.

41. Even to set the comparison up in this way implies just what the comparison intends to deny; namely, that the relevant point of comparison for divine fatherhood is "other" fathers.

42. Gregory of Nazianzus, *The Theological Orations*, in *Christology of the Later Fathers*, ed. Edward R. Hardy (Louisville, KY: Westminster John Knox, 2006), 161 (emphasis added).

43. William Placher, *The Triune God: An Essay in Postliberal Theology* (Louisville, KY: Westminster John Knox, 2007), 80.

44. Thomas F. Torrance, "The Christian Apprehension of God the Father," in Kimel, ed., *Speaking the Christian God*, 129–30. Torrance uses a passage from Barth to support this point: "we do not call God Father because we know what that is; on the contrary, because we know God's Fatherhood we afterwards understand what human fatherhood truly is." Karl Barth, *The Faith of the Church: A Commentary on the Apostles' Creed according to Calvin's Catechism*, trans. Gabriel Vahanian (New York: Meridian Books, 1958), 14, quoted in Torrance, "Christian Apprehension," 130. See also 137, where Torrance again insists that "God alone is truly and ultimately Father—all other fatherhood is a reflection of his."

45. Torrance, "Christian Apprehension," 130 (emphasis in original). See also Thomas F. Torrance, *The Trinitarian Faith: The Evangelical Theology of the Ancient Catholic Church* (Edinburgh: T&T Clark, 1993), 70–72.

46. Torrance, "Christian Apprehension," 131.

47. Robert Jenson comments that "ideological opposition to use of 'Father' and 'Son' and so to the triune name has even led to the manifestly bogus claim that the triune name cannot be a 'proper' name just *because* it has descriptive meaning and so can be translated." Jenson, *Systematic Theology*, vol. 1: *The Triune God* (Oxford: Oxford University Press, 1997), 45 n.28. Jenson is correct to identify such a claim as mistaken. The issue is not whether "Father" has descriptive meaning in addition to being a proper name ("a term of address within a narrative construction that displays a relation internal to the logic of the construction," in Jenson's words). The challenge arises when such descriptive meanings are read into the name in ways that either result in the projection of creaturely characteristics into God or that tie God the Father to creaturely fathers in ways that create indirect identities between them.

48. Jürgen Moltmann, *The Trinity and the Kingdom: The Doctrine of God*, trans. Margaret Kohl (Minneapolis, MN: Fortress Press, 1993), 163 (hereafter TTK).

49. Wolfhart Pannenberg, *Systematic Theology*, vol. 1, trans. Geoffrey W. Bromiley (Grand Rapids, MI: Eerdmans, 1991), 260 (hereafter ST1).

50. Latter emphasis added. Walter Kasper makes an almost identical claim: "the covenantal idea of God as Father can be turned in a prophetic and critical way against the concrete fathers of this world. In all truth the dignity of father belongs to God alone. It is not any earthly father but God, from whom all fatherhood is derived (Eph. 3.15), who defines what true fatherhood is. . . . God's fatherhood, being the source, is also the norm of paternal authority and the critical standard by which it is judged." Kasper, *The God of Jesus Christ*, trans. Matthew J. O'Connell (New York: Crossroad, 1997), 139–40. Kasper claims that sexism is excluded nonetheless since "the Old Testament can also translate the Father's loving mercy into the language of womanliness and motherhood" (140). These claims are sometimes found in other versions in feminist theologians: the nature of Jesus' maleness or the death of patriarchal power on the cross show how different divine masculinity is from any other kind. Such arguments fail for the same reasons.

51. Janet Martin Soskice, "Can a Feminist Call God 'Father'?" in Teresa Elwes, ed., *Women's Voices: Essays in Contemporary Feminist Theology* (London: Marshall Pickering, 1992), 15–29. Also in Kimel, *Speaking the Christian God*, 81–94.

52. Janet Martin Soskice, *The Kindness of God: Metaphor, Gender, and Religious Language* (Oxford: Oxford University Press, 2008), 66.

53. Ibid., 71.

54. Soskice assumes that "*the* feminist objection" (ibid., 72, emphasis added) to father language for God exists, which may be why she holds that the particular form of divine masculinity is the problem. She connects the objection to Sallie McFague's rejection of omnipotence and otherness in descriptions of God. But there is no intrinsic connection between concern about father language for God and rejection of divine omnipotence or transcendence.

55. Paul Ricoeur, "Fatherhood: From Phantasm to Symbol," in *The Conflict of Interpretations: Essays in Hermeneutics*, ed. Don Ihde (Evanston: Northwestern University Press, 1974), 468–97.

56. Soskice, *Kindness*, 76.

57. Soskice does not insist that God ought *only* to be addressed as Father. She follows Susan Brooks Thistlethwaite in admitting that divine father language may carry dangerous associations for women who have been abused by their fathers (*Kindness*, 81–82). But divine father language is not merely, or primarily, risky due to the abusive behavior of some human fathers. When used in the ways examined here, it establishes fatherhood as a particular, especially definitive, reflection of God and conversely, God as a particularly excellent kind of father by which other fathers should be measured: these two moves are unavoidably sexist and idolatrous.

58. When Soskice tells her trinitarian story briefly in the following chapter (*Kindness*, 116), she argues, following Jean-Luc Marion, that God the Father "in some sense" also dies on the cross with the Son, then "'is born'—or better 'becomes father'—with the Son and in the Spirit. This is a vision of a Trinity of complete mutuality" (ibid., 117). It is difficult to sort out the metaphysics of such a claim, especially since Soskice retains a classical account of the processions without quite explaining the different levels of predication with which she operates.

59. From Catherine Mowry LaCugna's list of important terms in her introduction to Karl Rahner's *The Trinity*, trans. Joseph Donceel (New York: Crossroad, 1997), 3.

60. For instance, divine aseity is arguably less vulnerable to such effects than divine power or divine paternity. Aseity is an exclusively technical term in its current usage, and the difference between God and human beings that it names is less susceptible to (mis-) application on the human side. At the same time, terms like aseity may give the theologian the mistaken impression of having achieved some conceptual control over God.

61. Illegitimately adapting Eve Kosovsky Sedgwick's term from "'Gosh, Boy George, You Must Be Awfully Secure in Your Masculinity!'" in Maurice Berger, Brian Wallis, and Simon Watson, eds., *Constructing Masculinity* (New York: Routledge, 1995), 18.

62. Butler is speaking of Irigaray.

63. Parts of the rest of this chapter first appeared in my "Logic of Origin," 65–70. The parts are identified in individual notes below, as the order of the argument in this chapter is somewhat different.

64. This sentence first appeared in my "Logic of Origin," 66.

65. Or see Karl Barth: "Thus man does not enjoy any privilege or advantage over woman, nor is he entitled to any kind of self-glorification, simply because in respect of order he is man, and therefore A, and thus precedes and is superior in relation to woman. . . . For woman does not come short of man in any way nor renounce her right, dignity, and honour, nor make any surrender, when theoretically and practically she recognizes that in order she is woman, and therefore B, and therefore behind and subordinate to man." Karl Barth, *Church Dogmatics* III/4, *The Doctrine of Creation*, ed. G. W. Bromiley and T. F. Torrance, trans. G. W. Bromiley (Edinburgh: T&T Clark, 2004), 170–71.

66. See, for an analogous case, Althaus-Reid's discussion of Rahab's self-betrayal, where she identifies "a woman's tendency to survive by heterosexuality—imperialism, colonisation, and the rule of the mono-loving God" (*Queer God*, 107).

67. Hans Urs von Balthasar, *Theo-Drama: Theological Dramatic Theory*, vol. 5, *The Last Act*, trans. Graham Harrison (San Francisco, CA: Ignatius, 1998), 91 (hereafter TD5).

68. In the trinity, sign and signified coincide in the relation between the Father and his Word. In chapter 6, I consider whether aseity applies only to God as a whole, or whether it belongs to each of the divine persons; in either case, *esse* and *essentia* coincide for each divine person.

69. "For without the Son the Father has neither existence nor name, any more than the Powerful without Power, or the Wise without Wisdom." Gregory of Nyssa, *Against Eunomius*, book II, section 3, 105.

70. Hans Urs von Balthasar, *Theo-Drama: Theological Dramatic Theory*, vol. 4, *The Action*, trans. Graham Harrison (San Francisco, CA: Ignatius, 1994), 351–61, esp. 361: "the Word is empowered to make his whole body into God's seed; thus the Word finally and definitively becomes flesh in the Virgin Mother, Mary-Ecclesia." Althaus-Reid says that "if the Virgin Mary had paws instead of hands and her vagina was in her ear, thus making it easier for the Word of God, the Logos, to 'say its Word' and penetrate her, it would not make any theological difference" (*Indecent Theology*, 39).

71. See, for instance, Richard of St. Victor, "The Trinity," in *Richard of St Victor: The Twelve Patriarchs, The Mystical Ark, Book Three of the Trinity*, trans. Grover A. Zinn (New York: Paulist Press, 1979), bk. 3, ch. IV, 376–77.

72. As, again, Richard of St. Victor suggests, ibid., ch. XV, 388–89; see also Augustine, *Homilies on the Gospel of John*, trans. John Gibb, in Philip Schaff, ed., *Nicene and Post-Nicene Fathers*, vol. VII (Edinburgh: T&T Clark, 1991 [reprint]), tractate 99, sections 4–9, 382–84, as well as Balthasar, TD5:245.

73. Richard of St. Victor, *The Trinity*, bk. 3, ch. XIV, 387–88. The first part of this paragraph first appeared in my "Logic of Origin," 66–67.

74. Mary Daly, *Gyn/Ecology: The Metaethics of Radical Feminism* (Boston: Beacon, 1990), 38.

75. See Caroline Walker Bynum's examples of imagery of the breasts of Jesus in the medieval period in *Jesus as Mother: Studies in the Spirituality of the High Middle Ages* (Berkeley, CA: University of California Press, 1984), 117, 119, and 122–23.

76. An image famously used by the council of Toledo in 675 CE.

77. "[T]he Phallus, though clearly not identified with the penis, nevertheless deploys the penis as its naturalized instrument and sign" (GT, 135).

78. Pannenberg, ST1:312–13, and 1 Corinthians 15:24–28.

79. Or so Balthasar thinks: "God is not only by nature free in his self-possession, in his ability to do what he will with himself; for that very reason, he is also free to do what he will with his own nature. That is, he can surrender himself; as Father, he can share his Godhead with the Son, and, as Father and Son, he can share the same Godhead with the Spirit. Here, too, we are already placed beyond necessity and chance. The fact that the absolute freedom of self-possession can understand itself, according to its absolute nature, as limitless self-giving—this is not the result of anything external to itself; yet it *is* the result of its own nature, so much so that, apart from this self-giving, it would not be itself" (TD2:256).

80. Part of this paragraph first appeared in my "Logic of Origin," 68.

81. The first part of this sentence first appeared in my "Logic of Origin," 69.

82. As Vladimir Lossky puts it, from an Orthodox perspective, there is no need for an oppositional relation between Son and Spirit "because relations of origin in the Trinity—filiation, procession—cannot be considered as the basis for the hypostases, as that which determines their absolute diversity." Lossky, *In the Image and Likeness of God* (Crestwood, NY: St. Vladimir's Seminary Press, 1974), 78.

83. Ibid., 82. Lossky emphasizes that "cause" functions not as a positive statement containing content derivable from ordinary causal sequencing but, rather, as with all trinitarian statements, in apophatic mode meaning something different from but related to its ordinary usage. See also John Zizioulas, *Being as Communion: Studies in Personhood and the Church* (Crestwood, NY: St. Vladimir's Seminary Press, 1997), 40; Gregory of Nyssa, "An Answer to Ablabius: That We Should Not Think of Saying There Are Three Gods," in Edward R. Hardy, ed., *Christology of the Later Fathers* (Louisville: Westminster John Knox, 2006), 266–67; contrast Thomas Aquinas, *Summa Theologica* Ia, q. 27.1 and esp. q. 33.1 (trans. Fathers of the English Dominican Province [Westminster: Christian Classics, 1948]).

84. Lossky says the Father "is thus the cause of their equality with himself" (*Image and Likeness*, 82). Note that "monarchy" in trinitarian theology indicates one origin; it is not referring to kingship.

85. The preceding two paragraphs, starting from "Arguably," first appeared in my "Logic of Origin," 65–66.

86. Amy Hollywood emphasizes that in Irigaray, a mimetic mirroring mirrors back differently. In that sense, the feminist theologian may find herself inhabited by the Holy Spirit, or standing in the place of the Spirit, in the attempt to mirror the mutual gaze of love between Father and Son with a difference. Hollywood, *Sensible Ecstasy: Mysticism, Sexual Difference, and the Demands of History* (Chicago: University of Chicago Press, 2002), 195.

87. See Augustine, *The Trinity*, bk. 5, ch. 3, section 12, 197.

88. This sentence first appeared in my "Logic of Origin," 67.

89. This sentence first appeared in my "Logic of Origin," 66.

90. If the *filioque* is rejected.

91. E.g., as in Balthasar's trinitarian inversion.
92. The Son loves the world; the Son's self-offering enacts that love.
93. This paragraph first appeared, with minor variations, in my "Logic of Origin," 67–68.
94. Jonathan Edwards, "Discourse on the Trinity," in Sang Hyun Lee, ed., *The Works of Jonathan Edwards*, vol. 21, *Writings on the Trinity, Grace, and Faith* (New Haven, CT: Yale University Press, 2002), 147. Quoted in Placher, *Triune God*, 100.
95. Marilyn McCord Adams, *Christ and Horrors* (Cambridge: Cambridge University Press, 2006), 310–11.
96. Placher, *Triune God*, 88. As he also says, "From the start, then, the Spirit can be helpful and life-giving but also unpredictable, uncontrollable, potentially terrifying" (86).
97. The preceding two paragraphs first appeared in my "Logic of Origin," 69–70.
98. This sentence first appeared in my "Logic of Origin," 70.
99. The previous two sentences first appeared, with minor variations, in my "Logic of Origin," 71.

## BIBLIOGRAPHY

Achtemeier, Elizabeth. "Exchanging God for 'No Gods': A Discussion of Female Language for God." In *Speaking the Christian God: The Holy Trinity and the Challenge of Feminism*, ed. Alvin J. Kimel, Jr., 1–16. Grand Rapids: Eerdmans, 1992.
Adams, Marilyn McCord. *Christ and Horrors: The Coherence of Christology*. Cambridge: Cambridge University Press, 2006.
Althaus-Reid, Marcella. *Indecent Theology: Theological Perversions in Sex, Gender, and Politics*. New York: Routledge, 2000.
———. *The Queer God*. London: Routledge, 2003.
Aquinas, Thomas. *Summa Theologica*. Trans. Fathers of the English Dominican Province. Westminster: Christian Classics, 1948.
Augustine. *Homilies on the Gospel of John*. Trans. John Gibb. In *Nicene and Post-Nicene Fathers*. vol. 7: *St. Augustin: Homilies on the Gospel of John. Homilies on the First Epistle of John. Soliloquies*, ed. Philip Schaff, 7–452. Edinburgh: T&T Clark, 1991.
———. *The Trinity*. Ed. John E Rotelle. Trans. Edmund Hill. New York: New City Press, 1991.
Balthasar, Hans Urs von. *Theo-Drama: Theological Dramatic Theory*, vol. 2: *Dramatis Personae: Man in God*. Trans. Graham Harrison. San Francisco: Ignatius, 1990.
———. *Theo-Drama: Theological Dramatic Theory*, vol. 3: *Dramatis Personae: Persons in Christ*. Trans. Graham Harrison. San Francisco: Ignatius, 1992.
———. *Theo-Drama: Theological Dramatic Theory*, vol. 4: *The Action*. Trans. Graham Harrison. San Francisco: Ignatius, 1994.
———. *Theo-Drama: Theological Dramatic Theory*, vol. 5: *The Last Act*. Trans. Graham Harrison. San Francisco: Ignatius, 1998.
Barth, Karl. *Church Dogmatics*, vol. 1, pt. 1, *The Doctrine of the Word of God*. Ed. G.W. Bromiley and T.F. Torrance. Trans. G.W. Bromiley. London: T&T Clark, 2004.
———. *Church Dogmatics*, vol. 3, pt. 4, *The Doctrine of Creation*. Ed. G.W. Bromiley and T.F. Torrance. Trans. G.W. Bromiley. London: T&T Clark, 2004.
Burrus, Virginia. *"Begotten, Not Made": Conceiving Manhood in Late Antiquity*. Stanford: Stanford University Press, 2000.

————. "Radical Orthodoxy and the Heresiological Habit: Engaging Graham Ward's Christology." In *Interpreting the Postmodern: Responses to Radical Orthodoxy*, ed. Rosemary Radford Ruether and Marion Grau, 36–53. New York: T&T Clark, 2006.

Butler, Judith. *Bodies That Matter: On the Discursive Limits of "Sex."* New York: Routledge, 1993.

————. *Gender Trouble: Feminism and the Subversion of Identity*. New York: Routledge, 1999.

Bynum, Caroline Walker. *Jesus as Mother: Studies in the Spirituality of the High Middle Ages*. Berkeley: University of California Press, 1984.

Cheng, Patrick. *Radical Love: An Introduction to Queer Theology*. New York: Seabury, 2011.

Coffey, David. *Deus Trinitas: The Doctrine of the Triune God*. New York: Oxford University Press, 1999.

Craigo-Snell, Shannon. "Passing as Male in the Academy." In *The Embrace of Eros: Bodies, Desires, and Sexuality in Christianity*, ed. Margaret D. Kamitsuka, 135–50. Minneapolis: Fortress Press, 2010.

Cunningham, David. *These Three Are One: The Practice of Trinitarian Theology*. New York: Wiley, 1998.

Daly, Mary. *Gyn/Ecology: The Metaethics of Radical Feminism*. Boston: Beacon Press, 1990.

DiNoia, J. A., OP. "Knowing and Naming the Triune God: The Grammar of Trinitarian Confession." In *Speaking the Christian God: The Holy Trinity and the Challenge of Feminism*, ed. Alvin J. Kimel Jr., 162–87. Grand Rapids: Eerdmans, 1992.

Edwards, Jonathan. "Discourse on the Trinity." In *The Works of Jonathan Edwards*, vol. 21, *Writings on the Trinity, Grace, and Faith*, ed. Sang Hyun Lee, 109–44. New Haven: Yale University Press, 2002.

Frye, Roland M. "Language for God and Feminist Language: Problems and Principles." In *Speaking the Christian God: The Holy Trinity and the Challenge of Feminism*, ed. Alvin J. Kimel Jr., 17–43. Grand Rapids: Eerdmans, 1992.

Green, Garrett. "The Gender of God and the Theology of Metaphor." In *Speaking the Christian God: The Holy Trinity and the Challenge of Feminism*, ed. Alvin J. Kimel Jr., 44–64. Grand Rapids: Eerdmans, 1992.

Gregory of Nazianzus. *The Theological Orations*. In *Christology of the Later Fathers*, ed. Edward R. Hardy, 128–214. Louisville: Westminster John Knox, 2006.

Gregory of Nyssa. *Against Eunomius. Nicene and Post-Nicene Fathers*. Second Series. Vol. 5, *Gregory of Nyssa: Dogmatic Treatises, Etc.*, ed. Philip Schaff and Henry Wace, 33–248. Peabody, MA: Hendrickson, 2012.

————. "An Answer to Ablabius: That We Should Not Think of Saying There Are Three Gods." In *Christology of the Later Fathers*, ed. Edward R. Hardy, 256–67. Louisville: Westminster John Knox, 2006.

Gunton, Colin. "Proteus and Procrustes: A Study in the Dialectic of Language in Disagreement with Sallie McFague." In *Speaking the Christian God: The Holy Trinity and the Challenge of Feminism*, ed. Alvin F. Kimel Jr., 65–80. Grand Rapids: Eerdmans, 1992.

Hollywood, Amy. *Sensible Ecstasy: Mysticism, Sexual Difference, and the Demands of History*. Chicago: University of Chicago Press, 2002.

Jenson, Robert. "The Father, He . . . " In *Speaking the Christian God: The Holy Trinity and the Challenge of Feminism*, ed. Alvin F. Kimel Jr., 95–109. Grand Rapids: Eerdmans, 1992.

————. *Systematic Theology*, vol. 1: *The Triune God*. New York: Oxford University Press, 1997.

Irigaray, Luce. *This Sex Which Is Not One*. Trans. Catherine Porter with Carolyn Burke. Ithaca: Cornell University Press, 1985.

————. *Marine Lover of Friedrich Nietzsche.* Trans. Gillian C. Gill. New York: Columbia University Press, 1991.

Kasper, Walter. *The God of Jesus Christ.* Trans. Matthew J. O'Connell. New York: Crossroad, 1997.

Kimel Jr., Alvin F., ed. *Speaking the Christian God: The Holy Trinity and the Challenge of Feminism.* Grand Rapids: Eerdmans, 1992.

Leith, John H., ed. *Creeds of the Churches: A Reader in Christian Doctrine from the Bible to the Present.* 3rd ed. Louisville: Westminster John Knox, 1982.

Lossky, Vladimir. *In the Image and Likeness of God.* Crestwood: St. Vladimir's Seminary Press, 1974.

Loughlin, Gerard, ed. *Queer Theology: Rethinking the Western Body.* Oxford: Blackwell, 2007.

Molnar, Paul D. *Divine Freedom and the Doctrine of the Immanent Trinity: In Dialogue with Karl Barth and Contemporary Theology.* Edinburgh: T&T Clark, 2002.

Moltmann, Jürgen. *The Trinity and the Kingdom: The Doctrine of God.* Trans. Margaret Kohl. Minneapolis: Fortress Press, 1993.

Okin, Susan Moller. *Is Multiculturalism Bad for Women?* Princeton: Princeton University Press, 1999.

Pannenberg, Wolfhart. *Systematic Theology*, vol. 1. Trans. Geoffrey W. Bromiley. Grand Rapids: Eerdmans, 1991.

Placher, William. *The Triune God: An Essay in Postliberal Theology.* Louisville: Westminster John Knox, 2007.

Rahner, Karl. *The Trinity.* Trans. Joseph Donceel. New York: Crossroad, 1997.

Richard of St. Victor. "The Trinity." In *Richard of St Victor: The Twelve Patriarchs, The Mystical Ark, Book Three of the Trinity*, trans. Grover A. Zinn, 371–397. New York: Paulist, 1979.

Ricoeur, Paul. "Fatherhood: From Phantasm to Symbol." In *The Conflict of Interpretations: Essays in Hermeneutics*, ed. Don Ihde, 468–97. Evanston: Northwestern University Press, 1974.

Sedgwick, Eve Kosofsky. " 'Gosh, Boy George, You Must Be Awfully Secure in Your Masculinity.' " In *Constructing Masculinity*, ed. Maurice Berger, Brian Wallis, and Simon Watson, 11–20. New York: Routledge, 1995.

Soskice, Janet Martin. "Can a Feminist Call God 'Father'?" In *Women's Voices: Essays in Contemporary Feminist Theology*, ed. Teresa Elwes, 15–29. London: Marshall Pickering, 1992.

————. *The Kindness of God: Metaphor, Gender, and Religious Language.* Oxford: Oxford University Press, 2008.

Studer, Basil. *Trinity and Incarnation: The Faith of the Early Church.* Ed. Andrew Louth. Trans. Matthias Westerhoff. Edinburgh: T&T Clark, 1993.

Tonstad, Linn Marie. "The Logic of Origin and the Paradoxes of Language: A Theological Experiment." *Modern Theology* 30, no. 3 (July 2014): 50–73.

Torrance, Thomas F. "The Christian Apprehension of God the Father." In *Speaking the Christian God: The Holy Trinity and the Challenge of Feminism*, ed. Alvin F. Kimel Jr., 120–43. Grand Rapids: Eerdmans, 1992.

————. *The Trinitarian Faith: The Evangelical Theology of the Ancient Catholic Church.* Edinburgh: T&T Clark, 1993.

Zizioulas, John D. *Being as Communion: Studies in Personhood and the Church.* Crestwood, NY: St. Vladimir's Seminary Press, 1997.

# 6  The Lord of Glory

> Within a community of perfect love between persons who share all the divine attributes, a notion of hierarchy and subordination is inconceivable.[1]

Our examination of contemporary trinitarian theology has demonstrated the intimate links between the procession of the Son and Spirit from the Father with hierarchy, subordination, gender and sexuality, and corrective projectionism. All of the authors we have encountered so far intend their trinitarian theologies to avoid subordination in God and in most cases, in humanity as well. This anti-subordinationist focus comports well with the controversies through which the technical distinctions of trinitarian theology develop, in which the need to defend the full divinity of the Son stands paramount. Balthasar exhibits another tendency found in many contemporary trinitarian theologies: a desire to say that eternal, immanent subordination of the Son to the Father does not mean subordinationism.

Colin Gunton, for instance, says that "there is a sense in which the Son is indeed subordinate to the Father. . . . [H]e is Son as he is sent, given, obedient; as he is, in a certain respect, though certainly not in others, passive." Gunton specifies in a footnote that this emphasis "goes some way to obviating those tendencies, especially strong in Western theology, that render the three persons of the Trinity functionally identical":[2] the introduction of something like passivity, obedience, and subordination serves to distinguish the persons, he thinks. On the previous page, Gunton claims that the "parallel" in Philippians 2 between sending and obedience entails "both a divine and a human obedience, whose meanings are inseparable." Contrast, among many examples, Gregory of Nyssa, who parallels the form of God with what the Son is "according to His supreme nature" and the form of a servant with the Son's "becoming other things in His dispensation of love to man."[3] Nyssa expressly equates taking on a human nature for our salvation with the form of a servant. The Son *becomes other* than the Son was—not as change, but as addition. Instead of distinguishing in this manner between what the Son *is* and *becomes*, and instead of respecting the for-us character of the Son's "formation" into a servant, Gunton intensifies the significance of the Son's passivity and subordination. "The point of the notion of Jesus Christ's eternal begottenness is that it enables us to characterize the kind of relationship that subsists between" the Father and the Son and "enables us to do justice to the undoubtedly subordinationist elements of the biblical record . . . : the Son is sent, is given, obeys, and indeed, expresses his eternal sonship in temporal or economic subordination."

Subordination just is the historical expression of sonship. Indeed, in this particular quotation, subordination seems to *generate* a concept of begottenness, despite the common claim that the notion of an eternal begetting serves to *counter* notions of subordination. Even the nature of divine, perichoretic unity means that "[t]hey are one *because* the Son and Spirit are, in a sense, though as God, subordinate in the eternal *taxis* as they are in the economy."[4] His labored syntax reflects the amount of conceptual obfuscation on which the dual concepts of unity through subordination and differentiation through subordination depend. Gunton continues, "in another sense they are not subordinate, for without his Son and Spirit, God would not be God."[5]

Gunton's second statement in no way attenuates the first, for one might equally well say that in another sense, the slave is not subordinate, for without his slave, the master would not be the master. Gunton represents a surprisingly prevalent trend in contemporary trinitarian theology in which valorizing subordination, sacrifice, and obedience becomes the heart of trinitarian reflection rather appearing despite intention, as in most of the thinkers we have canvassed. In certain evangelical circles, the eternal functional subordination of the Son even works explicitly (rather than implicitly) to ground complementarian gender roles through use of the pretense that eternal or indissoluble hierarchies are functional rather than ontological. It is tempting to speculate why this turn to subordination appeared when it did, in the context of what many Christian theologians saw as radical social transformations in gender roles and the social order from the end of the Great War until the upheavals of the late 1960s, including the flashpoint of Vatican II.

There are significant suggestions of subordination in the biblical economy. But it was just those suggestions that motivated much of the development of trinitarian doctrine as the early church struggled to find language for speaking of the presence of God in Christ. They recognized that the salvific grounding of trinitarian doctrine rules out—as Miroslav Volf's chapter-opening statement suggests—any notion of subordination. It is not, then, that theologians concerned about subordination are either importing an abstract idea of the perfect being (as Barth worries[6]) or being unfaithful to the narrative of the biblical economy and seeking a God behind the revealed God. The very rationale for the existence of trinitarian theology is "the potency of what the Son and the Spirit do for us in the economy of salvation. Any argument that seeks to base the subordination of women—whether that is defined in ontological or merely 'functional' terms—misses the point of trinitarian doctrine,"[7] and the point holds even more strongly for the introduction of subordination into the notion of sonship itself. For some, this is obvious. The principle that God reveals Godself as God truly is, as Paul Helm writes, "can be applied with such stringency as to reduce it to absurdity. Thus, in the economy of redemption, the Son is revealed as utterly submissive to his Father's good pleasure. Does it follow that in his eternal relation the Son is utterly submissive to the Father?"[8] Helm thinks this an absurdity, and so it is—yet the structure of trinitarian sense-making permits, rather than rules out, such a conclusion for many theologians.

As I have argued throughout, the language of sonship and begetting, procession, and origin serves as a potent-enough inflammation toward subordination that hierarchies are projected into the being of God with so much vigor that even such apparently straightforward statements become controversial. But a merely critical and diagnostic argument would founder on the need to account in *some* way for the nature of trinitarian relations, differences, and particularities, without begetting, origin, or any other transcendently potent distribution of contrastive powers and activities. It is the task of this chapter to develop a proposal for how the trinity should be understood without relations of origin—a prerequisite, I believe, for avoiding subordination within the trinity. Doing so requires interpreting the biblical economy, examining the relation between the immanent and the economic trinity, and reinterpreting the meaning of sonship and fatherhood to no longer indicate even a crossed-out origin in God.

In Tanner, we finally encountered the possibility of side-by-side relationships between persons, and we moved away from the need for divine persons to "make room" for another that we found in Balthasar, Ward, Moltmann, and Pannenberg. These ways of thinking depend heavily on gendered imagery; they also subordinate the constitution of the trinity to the need to solve social problems through the corrective projectionism we have repeatedly encountered. Balthasar, Ward, Moltmann, Pannenberg, and Coakley install a too-close relationship between divine and human personhood while glorifying sacrifice (or some divinized version of it) for its own sake.

In contrast, Tanner emphasizes that the Word makes space alongside itself for humankind in the incarnation, and the "happening" of incarnation and the history of the Word is a "happening" for humankind, not for the Word. This helps us to see, too, where "making room" language may have limited value: one effect of sin is competition for the same space, for the same goods, and for the same level of recognition that another already enjoys.[9] But only persons with impermeable boundaries or who are constituted by possessive expansiveness (greed) need to be penetrated, or to make room for each other, in order to establish mutually enjoyable, good relationships. The unity of the trinitarian persons, the goodness of God's being, and the sheer gratuity of their love renders any such movements unnecessary for them.

Yet even Tanner's "something" reflected begetting's capacity, despite all protestations to the contrary, to generate subordination, hierarchy, womb-wounds, and the sexuation of God and the God–world relation. Most fundamentally, the difficulty comes from the assumed *reality* of paternity in God: the establishment of divine paternity via origin. I have demonstrated significant linkages between trinitarian discourse and distorted understandings of humanity, gender, and sexuality. But my constructive trinitarian claims are only bolstered by—not grounded in—such linkages. In practice, the relation between a doctrine and its social consequences varies more widely than theologians might wish; distorted trinitarian theologies *need* not (although they generally are) be associated with unjust or mistaken understandings of intra-human relations. The theologians we have examined also believe themselves to have good reasons for interpreting the trinity the way they do, and they are right—just not in the way they think.

The origin of the Son from the Father is the "something" that the (perhaps only apparent) subordination of the Son to the Father reflects. Again, I am not claiming that begetting *necessarily* has the consequences we have encountered. I have made such a connection plausible and experimentally verified it; opponents of the case I have developed would need to show examples of contemporary trinitarian theologies that avoid each and every one of these problems completely.[10] The cases we have examined give us reason to ask whether an adequate trinitarian theology can be developed without relations of origin. If it can, my case against relations of origin and their consequences is greatly strengthened. Even should my proposal fail, it might prompt other proposals that could succeed; if I am right about the seriousness of the theological problems that I have demonstrated, such proposals are desperately needed to avoid undoing central Christian claims about the nature of God and the significance of God's revelation of Godself in Christ.

Before turning to my positive proposals, let's consider an element that serves as a potential confounder to my argument. Just what does procession entail? For most theologians, relations of origin entail that the Father, in begetting the Son and breathing out the Spirit, communicates the divine essence or substance to them; these theologians assume what Brannon Ellis terms "essential communication."[11] In contrast, Tanner insists that what the Son and Spirit receive from the Father is already theirs by nature. In this, she is in consonance with significant strands of patristic traditions, as shown, for instance, by Didymus's assertion that—speaking of the Holy Spirit—he "does not receive what he did not have before."[12] Didymus is describing the nature of intra-trinitarian giving, not merely denying that the Holy Spirit has a beginning in time. Aquinas, too, following Basil of Caesarea, maintains that the Son has "by nature what he receives."[13] Might one avoid my critiques simply by denying essential communication, so that the Son and Spirit are God in and of themselves and not by virtue of their origin in the Father?[14]

As we saw in our examination of Tanner, such a position does much—perhaps as much as possible—to vitiate the subordinationist consequences of relations of origin. Yet it may not do enough. Even Tanner allowed *something* in the immanent trinity to correspond to the apparent subordination of the Son. On the level of constitution, even given their laudable aims, our theologians continually find themselves introducing suffering, subordination, and distance into the being of God and using the relations of origin as justification for such introductions. This does not *entail* that relations of origin necessarily lead to such deleterious consequences, but it does suggest how liable they are to be used and interpreted in that way. My arguments for moving away from relations of origin are not probative but cumulative: They depend on showing, in many ways and from different directions, that these related problems crop up over and over, in despite of theologians' stated intentions. If the meaning of origin is *not* essential communication, the possibility of distinguishing the persons using other strategies becomes easier, since we do not need to account for how the Son and Spirit become divine; they are already divine of themselves. We need merely to account for the distinctions among the persons in some way, other than origin, that is justified by the biblical economy.[15]

The way these problems are intertwined with issues of gender and sexuality also shows that our existence under the regime of sexuality[16] complicates matters materially. The gendered and sexed associations of trinitarian theology cannot be written out by fiat, analogy, or transcendence, even by those who assert that the sexed nature of God-language has nothing to do with human gender and sexuality. As we saw in chapter 5, the very mode of making that argument often strengthens rather than weakens the association. *That* we live under the regime of sexuality is shown perhaps most emphatically by the many church schisms taking place over just such issues. Whatever strategies may have been available in the patristic period for disassociating gender from divinity, such strategies need to be rethought in the contemporary era. The specific attachment of humiliation to the nature of the Son and his procession—indeed, the apparent inevitability of connections between procession, making room or making space, and heterosexualized boundary thinking (penetration, making room for the other within oneself)—show the debt relations between trinitarian theology and sexual difference.

Irigaray's contention that sexual difference would be the salvation of our age if we thought it through is at best a vast overstatement, but her very making of the claim is a clue to the centrality of gender and sexual difference in our cultural moment—and such differences make a difference. For instance, Aquinas's defense of the name "Father" and its correlate paternity for the "first" person of the trinity demonstrates that historical transformations in our understanding of gender and reproduction may make some trinitarian arguments invalid. Paternity is an appropriate specification of generation because paternity is the perfection of generation, he thinks.[17] But the assumptions about human reproduction with which Aquinas operates are false, and that vitiates also the particular argument for the primary applicability of paternity to God that he develops.[18]

The argument of this chapter is not intended as a decisive strategy for countering human tendencies to project our ideas about gender and sexuality onto God. The very demonstrations we have undertaken of how the imagistic register of trinitarian theology overtakes its stipulative assumptions would make such finality implausible and perhaps impossible. My focus in this chapter is instead on trinitarian constitution and the trajectory of the economy of salvation. In consequence, I will have something to say about divine as well as human personhood, but I will not deal much with explicit issues of gender and sexuality until the final chapter. I distinguished in a previous chapter between epistemological and salvific assumptions in contemporary trinitarian theology. One way to describe the project of this book is as an attempt to recover the priority of the salvific assumption. Instead of installing the Father at a remove, hidden behind the Son who comes from him and for whom submission to him is therefore suitable, the salvific assumption invites a very different approach both to "glory" and "humiliation" in God.

## CLEARING THE GROUND AGAIN: THE WORK OF TRINITARIAN THEOLOGY

We start with three questions: What is the nature of technical trinitarian theology? What work does trinitarian doctrine do?[19] By what criteria do we measure adequate trinitarian theologies? The nature of technical trinitarian theology can be approached through Karen Kilby's call for an "apophatic trinitarianism." Trinitarian claims ought to function something like the negations of apophatic theology, even though the claims are couched in positive language.[20] In alluringly tentative terms, Kilby asks, "What if we were to suppose that how the three are one, how to relate divine persons to the divine substance, what the inner relations between the persons are, are all questions which are quite simply beyond us? . . . What answers we may appear to have—answers drawing on notions of processions, relations, *perichoresis*—would be acknowledged as in fact no more than technical ways of articulating our inability to know."[21] Kilby retains processional language but understands it as a way to *confound* rather than *advance* understanding of God, and she finds warrant for such an account in her interpretation of the function of technical trinitarian language in Thomas Aquinas.[22] This process of trinitarian unknowing depends on a genetic and material connection to the origins of trinitarian theology in New Testament narratives. These concrete genetic connections work against a high level of abstraction (or one might say, speculation) in trinitarian theology. Kilby rightly emphasizes the centrality of a high Christology and of commitment to monotheism as driving forces in trinitarian development.[23]

The doctrine of the trinity thus does some positive work: It asserts that "the Son is not the Father . . . which is to say that Sabellianism is wrong," that God really is only one God, although we do not know what that means or how it relates to threeness in God, and "that God does not *need* to be involved in the economy to . . . be who God is."[24] The work of trinitarian theology is, at a minimum, to give us a grammar for stating these fundamental commitments. There are "boundary" conditions for trinitarian theology, as seen in the rejection of Arianism and Sabellianism: the former "distinguishes the Father and Son too strongly," and the latter not enough.[25] All these are salvific[26] concerns, although they interact in the contemporary scene with complicated epistemic assumptions. The nature and work of trinitarian theology give us some criteria for an adequate trinitarian theology.

The most central of these criteria may be described from above or from below. From above, we start from the principle that only God can reveal Godself and its correlative that God is as God shows Godself to be. From below, we start from God's aims *in* revealing Godself to us: "God must love material creation with a love that dual-drives toward *assimilation* and *union*. . . . God's passion for material creation expresses itself in a Divine desire to unite with it . . . and share its nature in a hypostatic union."[27] God wants creation to become as Godlike as possible; God loves creation and seeks intimacy with it—intimacy of the closest kind; God unites Godself with humankind in a way that not only transforms inter-human relations but raises human beings above what they would otherwise be.[28] God's salvific aims and God's nature come together in this central criterion precisely because God shows Godself to us in being the God who unites us with God and raises us up in a transformed community in communion with God.

The aim of revelation is its for-us character. What we learn *about* God from the economy of salvation is, first and foremost, the kind of God that God is: God is the sort of God who does for us what this God does. God is the one who loves us in the way that this God does. God transforms our relations to each other in making us (through union with God) as godlike as it is possible for that which is other than God to be. The nature of that transformation also tells us something about what and who that God is, for that transformation is the outcome and aim of the entirety of God's interaction with the world. The for-us principle of divine interaction with the world in the economy of salvation is the very heart of that to which trinitarian theology must be responsible.

From this central principle, other criteria follow. Since the divinity of God the Father was never in question, the next criterion of an adequate trinitarian theology is whether it maintains the full divinity of the Son and the Spirit. Together, the persons of the trinity work our salvation, and it is for this reason that any notion of subordination is ruled out. "The activity of the Father and the Son and the Holy Spirit is the same. But those who have a single activity also have a single substance. For things of the same substance have the same activities, and things of a different substance have discordant and distinct activities."[29] So we must hold that Father, Son, and Spirit are fully God, that they work inseparably, and that God is Godself in

God's work. The persons need to be distinct enough—but not too distinct. Historically, the formulation of these central criteria happened through argument with those who interpreted biblical texts more straightforwardly to entail subordination of the Son and Spirit to the Father. Trinitarian theology is therefore always a hermeneutical practice, but (thankfully) not one in which we start from scratch. We do not need to prove again that these are the criteria for trinitarian theology; instead, we simply test our proposals according to them.

## STARTING FROM THE SPIRIT

The assumption of many who fulminate about the neglect of the Holy Spirit is that such neglect has not allowed the Holy Spirit to show forth as robust a form of personhood, activity, and individual significance as the Father and Son do. S/he/it needs also to be seen as an actor in her/his/its own right and needs to be brought up to the level of significance that the Son and the Father already enjoy. But this criticism gets the issue wrong, I contend. Instead, the way the Holy Spirit is often treated gives us a model for how the other two should be "neglected" as well.

Theologians have seldom treated the Spirit as an independent center of rational consciousness, in the way that non-social trinitarians fear, for reasons both grammatical and derived from the economy of salvation. Father and Son, too, should be freed from the corrective that emphasizes coinherence and filial submission to paternal command as counters to the distortions of human personhood. Both moves overpersonalize Father and Son in inverted ways that are parasitic on misguided ideas of selfhood. Theologians in both cases discover in the trinity the kinds of selves they suspect, and fear, that humans are not, but that they think humans *ought* to be like. What is often called neglect of the Spirit allows the Spirit to retain a kind of underdetermination that ought to belong to the other two persons as well (albeit in different modes). The Father and Son need less-vigorous personhoods, as it were, rather than giving more vigor to the Spirit—particularly with respect to the practical theological implications of fatherhood, sonship, and origin.

In a certain sense, there is a temptation to let the Spirit castrate Father and Son, freeing them from their insistent masculinity (as many variations on Spirit-centered trinitarian theologies propose), yet doing so would render the Spirit a *vagina dentata*. Better, then, to let the Spirit's breathy caresses give Father and Son a share in the economy of the surface touch represented by the Spirit's translucency rather than by the spatial interpenetration of persons. Said more technically, Pannenberg uses the association between Spirit and field to describe the shape of trinitarian personhood and indeed, the shape of divinity itself.[30] The language of field suggests nonbordered quasi-personhood—not that the divine persons are not "persons," but that the way in which they are persons differs significantly from human personhood. Pannenberg takes for granted that "[a]s a field . . . the Spirit would be impersonal," but that goes too far.[31]

The issue is not primarily whether the trinitarian persons are more or less personal in human terms; even human personhood remains mysterious to us. At the same time, the grounding of trinitarian theology in the gospels and other New Testament texts ensures that, as characters or actors, the narrated relationships between the persons cannot but generate thickly personal impressions. Rather, the primary meaning of trinitarian personhood is incommunicability; "person" is a placeholder (like most trinitarian language) indicating something we must say but do not understand.[32] The value of field language, and of the schemas for person-distinction toward which field language points, is that it takes the discussion beyond penetrable or impenetrable borders of personhood. Better even than field language, however, is the biblical language of light,[33] which indicates the nature of trinitarian copresence to themselves and to us.

Light imagery is especially appropriate because it is so central to the last biblical image of the communion God establishes, in which human beings live together with God and each other in a glorious city situated in a renewed and recreated earth. "The city does not need the sun or the moon to shine on it, for the glory of God gives it light, and the Lamb is its lamp."[34] Augustine uses light imagery to indicate the closeness between Father and Son: "we are image because we are illuminated with light; that one [the Son] is so because it is the light that illuminates . . . it is never by the least hair's breadth separated from [the Father]."[35] Light imagery makes it possible to envision a diffusion of rays without a visible source, the light seemingly coming from everywhere.[36] Light also entails extensibility, since several lights can be present and overlapping in the same place, and the more light there is, the closer we get to loss of sight. If we represent the divine light in the form of the sun, for instance, we can think of God as three suns all shining with the same light—so they are all the source of the good gifts of creation—or we could represent God as a single sun shining with just one light; whether Father, Son, or Spirit, it remains the same light. The images of one and three are not alternatives; they are two inadequate representations that point to the relationship between the one and the three (beyond number or countability) of the trinity.[37]

God is the source of light, and light itself, and the light by which we see. The last is a partly functional designation—were we to look at the divine light directly, we would find darkness and the cloud.[38] If we put light together with dazzling darkness, we find our attempts to start with *any* one person of the trinity baffled. Instead, we encounter something like an ordered circle: an order in which each person has an irreversible relationship to the others but where relationships are not relations of origin but of intensification or gift. Modifying Tanner's triadic relations of origin, we can see them as triune relationships of intensification or gift-circulation. Doing away with the concept of generation allows for something like the exchange of gifts between Spirit and Son on Tanner's account to expand to include the entire trinity, including the Father. Each person gifts something to the others, or better, the persons give the same thing in different modes (for in God there is no-*thing* to give, since the persons are God by nature and identical with the divine essence). These asymmetrical exchanges are triadic intransitive relations. The persons (as persons) are nothing aside from their relations to each other. These relations are circular and reversible in that each person is both a giver and a receiver, but they are irreversible in the mode of giving and receiving in each case. Each returns to the others what it receives from the others; each gives the other the same in a different way. We therefore move beyond any contrast between activity and passivity: the persons are all always "active" and "passive" (although it would be better to avoid that terminology altogether); in relation to each other as to us, they are all always working together in different ways, giving and receiving at the same time.

The Father gives to the Son and the Spirit; the Son gives to the Father and the Spirit; and the Spirit gives to the Father and the Son.[39] These relations are triadic. All give, but in different ways, and those different ways *are* their divine personhood. The designations are determined by the economy, since God is as God reveals Godself to be. Since each person gives differently, the reception (but not the gift) in each case is shareable: the Father and Spirit both receive from the Son, but differently. Since all three do the same thing in different ways, the particularity of the recipient shapes the gift as well. The relations are therefore noninterchangeable and irreducible.

The Son[40] glorifies. A theology of the cross recognizes that the glory of God becomes apparent not in abstract ideas of divinity but in the concrete history of the Son. The Son must then be the glory of God, the light that lights up all creation. The Son is the radiance of God (Heb. 1:3) and the Lord of glory. The hermeneutical key for our discussion is John 14:7–9, where Jesus refuses to point away from himself to the Father in order to make God visible, even *before* his death, resurrection, and ascension.[41] The Father receives glory from the Son who has the power to glorify (power given by the Spirit, as we shall see). So the Son is the glorifier, the one who lights up another. The Father is enabled by the Spirit to glorify the Son (to return to the Son what the Son gives the Father) as seen in Jesus' baptism in the Jordan, in the resurrection (although the Son also comes forth by the life that is in him and by the lure of the power of the Spirit), and eternally. The order of glory moves from the Son outward. We see this in the economy since he is the one who enacts the glorification of God in his history: it is in his face that we see the glory of the Father as well.

The Son thus reveals the Father, but is also revealed by him in turn, when the Father returns the glory that the Son gives him,[42] which is the way we should read "seated at the right hand of the Father." When the Spirit returns glory to the Son, the Spirit lights up the Son so that we are enabled to see him as God-with-us and for-us on the surface and in the depth of the "covering" (envelope) of his humanity.[43] The baptism scene's identification of Jesus makes this relationship especially apparent, and its triadic shape helps clarify what it means to say that the persons of the trinity work together in whatever they do. The identification of the Son with glory also makes sense of the claim that the world is formed according to the Word. The Word lights up all of creation with its glory.[44] Similarly, Jesus' assertion that the Father himself loves those who accept Jesus is an expansive, not a restrictive criterion (John 16:27). Since Jesus simply is God incarnate, this in effect is no more than to say that in loving and accepting the Word, humanity is united with God. This event happens in the Word's own humanity and expresses the economic form of the Word's glorification of the Father, for it is the Word's exposition of the Name of God in the Word's own being that gives us the possibility of participating in the Word's glorification of the Father and the Spirit.

The Spirit gives power to the Father and the Son, although in different ways. The Spirit gives power to the Son to glorify the Father. The Spirit gives power to the Father to name the Son as his own. The Spirit's role as the one who fills us with wisdom and a multitude of gifts reflects that the Spirit is the Lord and Giver of Life. The Spirit's relationship with each of the other persons is thus also shaped by the particularity of that person. The Spirit is the Spirit of power and glory (1 Peter 4:14) and the Spirit of freedom (2 Cor. 3:17). As the Spirit receives glory from the Son, the Spirit also passes that glory on to the world when it shows forth the Son, just as the Son works in the power of the Spirit to shine forth the radiance of what God is. The Father's reception of power from the Spirit makes the giving of the divine Name (which is Love) that is the Father's proper role within the trinity vividly effective. The Spirit plays the same role immanently and economically, and its enlivening power is directed toward the enactment of the others' distinctiveness; it also establishes particularity for human persons as it resurrects them.[45] "[J]ust as objects which lie near brilliant colours are themselves tinted by the brightness which is shed around, so is he who fixes his gaze firmly on the Spirit . . . transfigured into greater splendor, having his heart lighted up."[46]

The Father names the Son. The Father, the namer, allows (given the contingency of creation) the world to be shaped into the image of the Son by being given a name of its own as well. The Father testifies to the Son: because "the working of the Son is the Father's testimony, it follows of necessity that the same nature was operative in Christ, by which the Father testifies of Him."[47] The Spirit, too, receives the name from the Father, as we recognize economically when the Spirit's community (the church) becomes an adopted child of God. The Spirit's return of the name to the Father happens in teaching us to say "Jesus is Lord" to the glory of God the Father and to cry "Abba, Father." The Son returns the name to the Father when he returns to the Father, bringing us up with him as those who are adopted as children in the name the Father gives the Son.

These gift-relationships do not render each person composite; instead, we build on Tanner's identification of each trinitarian person in virtue of the whole movement of its relations to the other two persons. So the Spirit is the Power of God, the Son is the Glory of God, and the Father is the Name of God, which is Love (and its apophatic correlate, "I will be who I will be"). Each person is made what it is by the totality of its relations to the other persons. This permits the unity of the trinity to appear without grounding that unity, intentionally or not, in any one of the persons. The monarchy of the trinity is therefore shared between the persons and realized only in and by them. But the persons should not be seen as static aspects of the one God in such a way that the vitality of the divine life is obscured. It is equally correct to say that the Spirit is Power(-giver),[48] the Son is Glory(-fier), and the Father is Love(r) or Name(r). The latter designations, while awkward on the tongue, hold together the personalness ("quality," improperly said, or the incommunicability and particularity that naming indicates) of each person while retaining a relational component. The particularity of each person is oriented toward the other two. The persons are relations oriented toward each other in the vivid life of God.

As in classical Western accounts, the relations "disappear" into the divine essence, with which they are identified.[49] The persons are only distinguished in relation to each other. Their personal incommunicability is constituted by their differentiated relations to each other, and they work inseparably to do one and the same thing. Interpreting John 5:19, Didymus says that

> when the Son sees the Father working, he is himself also working, yet working not in a second rank after him. After all, the works of the Son would begin to diverge from those of the Father if they were not performed by equals. . . . When the Father and the Son work . . . all the things which they do are the same and not dissimilar, and the Son is unable to do anything on his own accord since he cannot be separated from the Father. Likewise, the Holy Spirit, who is in no way separated from the Son on account of their sharing of will and nature, is not believed to speak on his own accord, but speaks all that he speaks according to the Word and Truth of God.[50]

This interpretation of an apparently subordinationist text points us to the nature of trinitarian unity. That the persons are "in" each other indicates inseparability, not location or some sort of divine spatialization. As Barth says, "We can never have one without the others. Here one is both by the others and in the others, in a *perichoresis* which nothing can restrict or arrest, so that one mode is neither active nor knowable externally without the others."[51] Their unity is shown in their work, as Nyssa says:

> If . . . we understand that the operation of the Father, the Son, and the Holy Spirit is one, differing or varying in nothing, the oneness of their

nature must needs be inferred from the identity of their operation. The Father, the Son, and the Holy Spirit alike give sanctification, and light, and comfort, and all similar graces. . . . So too all the other gifts are wrought in those who are worthy alike by the Father, the Son, and the Holy Spirit: every grace and power, guidance, life, comfort, the change to immortality, the passage to liberty, and every other boon that exists, which descends to us.[52]

The gifts that God gives cannot be given by other than God; every divine person is a gift-giver in union with the others. The drama of salvation is *not* an inner-trinitarian drama: it is a drama in which the God of Glory became incarnate "for us and for our salvation."

## SONS, NOT SLAVES

This bare outline of trinitarian relations leaves a number of issues still unaddressed: the nature of the relation between the immanent and economic trinity, some remaining questions of subordination, and the meaning of sonship and sending language in the New Testament. We need to consider what links the economic and immanent trinity if it is neither processions extended outward as missions, the establishment of the Father's monarchy, nor any of the other options we have encountered.

In practices of communion and table fellowship, the material connection between the form of divine being and the economy of salvation becomes apparent. The link between the immanent and economic trinity is not the establishment of paternal monarchy; it is the establishment of communion. The shape of the kingdom of God is communion: "thy will be done on earth as in heaven." God, who is already communion within Godself, unites Godself intimately with material creation through a hypostatic union that transforms the nature of material limitations without abolishing matter—to the contrary, the transformation intensifies bodied being. The economic trinity is the immanent trinity, but the point of connection is in the "additive" nature of incarnation and incarnation's transformative effects.

As the expression of God's love for material creation, the God who is already love within Godself, the trinity unites Godself with humankind, giving humankind the only good of which there is always more than enough for any need or want. In the process, sin is forgiven, and its distorted relationships are overcome.[53] The establishment of communion with and among human persons is in a limited sense a kind of extension outward of the sort of communion the trinity enjoys. But the type of "communion" (*not* community) that constitutes the joy of the trinity is not identical with the kinds of communion human beings may enjoy with one another. There is a distant analogy, in that communion of this kind does not require self-emptying or making room for the other because of the transformation of materiality that is the condition and end (in both senses: end and aim) of the eucharist. But that analogy does not extend to coinherence in a strict sense. As Didymus emphasizes, only God can be in a human person; when the devil is described as being in a person, "even he did not enter according to substance, but rather according to activity, since entering into another belongs to the uncreated nature which can be participated in by many. The devil is not capable of being participated in, seeing that he is not the Creator but a creature."[54] *Mutatis mutandis*, the same holds for intra-human communion.

In their relation to trinity, humans can be with one another in an unlimited sense, beyond imagery of distance and interior penetration (and penetrability). The unenclosed nature of human personhood—what becomes its rapaciousness under conditions of sin—becomes instead a distant imitation of the infinite capacity for intensification that the trinitarian persons have in relation to each other. Yet human bodiedness continues to symbolize and materialize that human beings do not become absolutely the same in the sense that the trinitarian persons are—the trinity is one (numerically non-multipliable) God, but human beings do not become one human, or one being. But—as we will see in discussing the eucharist and resurrection—the transformation of bodied materiality that the union of finite matter with infinite divinity brings about permits bodied humans to be in the same place at the same time without penetration or shattering.

The nonidentity of divine and human communion, combined with the nature of finite existence, the distortive character of sin, and the transformational aims of divine-human union require that certain distinctions be made between what is said of the Son in regard to his humanity and his divinity. The Rahnerian dictum is often interpreted to imply that such distinctions are illegitimate. But this reticence has not always been the case. As we have continually emphasized, patristic exegetes worked hard to find ways of reading scripture that would not suggest a subordination that would threaten the salvation only God offers. One of their main exegetical strategies was just to make clear what is said of the Son according to his humanity and what is said according to his divinity.

As Nyssa says, the Son became obedient

> when He came in the form of a servant to accomplish the mystery of redemption by the cross, Who had emptied Himself, Who humbled Himself by assuming the likeness and fashion of a man, being found as man in man's lowly nature—then, I say, it was that He became obedient . . . then it was that for our sakes He was made obedient, even as He became 'sin' and 'a curse' by reason of the dispensation on our behalf, *not being so by nature*, but becoming so in His love for man.[55]

Kenosis does not mean loss and self-emptying; it means that the Lord of Glory takes on humanity in all its abasement. Obedience and humility are means, not ends, and they are means oriented toward their own overcoming.[56] Gregory of Nazianzus delights in the paradoxes these distinctions engender in one of the most charming sequences found in any theological text: "He prays, but he hears prayer. He weeps, but he causes tears to cease. He asks where Lazarus was laid, for he was man; but he raises Lazarus, for he was God. . . . He is bruised and wounded, but he heals every disease and every infirmity. He is lifted up and nailed to the tree, but by the tree of life he restores us. . . . He dies, but he gives life, and by his death destroys death."[57] *By his death destroys death*: the axiom that God is as God shows Godself to be is oriented toward the *outcome* of divine engagement with the world. Or as Athanasius puts it,

> we do not deny whatever is said about him that reflects his humanity, for example, that he was hungry, that he was thirsty, . . . and finally, that he accepted death on a cross for our sake. . . . For he became human . . . and being ignorant is proper to human beings, just like being hungry and all the rest[.] . . . [H]e indicated his human ignorance for two reasons: first, so that he could show that he really has a human body; second, since he had human ignorance in his body, *so that he could redeem his humanity from all and cleanse it* and so offer it perfect and holy to the Father. . . . But when he says: *I and the Father are one*, and: *He who sees me sees the Father*, and: *I am in the Father and the Father in me*, he signifies his eternity and that he is the same as the Father in substance.[58]

So overcoming death as the life-giver is a good way to express just who the Son is as God; undergoing death as a human being for our sake is a good way to express just who the Son is as human; and his person is not sundered. The union of God with humankind in Jesus just is the communication of God's gifts to humankind.[59]

The distinction between what is said of Jesus according to humanity or divinity needs to be brought together with two other distinctions: between economic and immanent trinity and between sin and finitude. Sin heavily distorts finitude, rendering it malformed. But sin means that God is not merely revealing Godself in Jesus in a medium that is other than God; God is revealing Godself in a medium that is actively *hostile* to God. Sin makes the difference of finitude even more significant to the form of revelation. When combined with the distinction between economic and immanent trinity, we see how badly we need a distinction between what Miroslav Volf has called love that dances and love that suffers: "The love that dances is the internal love of the Trinity; the love that suffers is that same love turned toward a world suffused with enmity. The first is the perfect love of the world to come; the second is that same love engaged in the transformation of the deeply flawed world that is."[60] When the love that dances engages a world suffused by sin and enmity, the love that dances is translated into love that suffers for the purpose of overcoming sin—not in order to self-immolate but in order to transform the conditions of human existence.[61]

Two things become clear: However much subordination may be said of Jesus according to his humanity or due to the effects of sin that he overcomes, there is simply *nothing* in the immanent life of God that corresponds to even the appearance of subordination. The biblical texts that generate defensiveness—although it would *seem* on this account that the Son is somehow inferior to the Father or that something in the particularity of his being generates that apparent inferiority—become much less pressing when there is just *nothing* in the being of the Son that could correspond to any inferiority. The "suggestion" of subordination simply doesn't arise when epistemic and doxological priority is given to the fullness of God in Christ and the Spirit. But one more element needs to be added. For—contrary to the impression we might be left with in consulting a variety of contemporary theologies—the *aim* of God's work in the world is not just the overcoming of our subjection to sin and our tendencies to subjugate each other by making us humbly and sacrificially obedient to God; the aim of God's work in the world is to transform us from slaves and servants to friends and children of God.

Among the various images of transformed relationships between God and humankind, two in particular stand out in the New Testament: friendship and adoption. Those who participate in Christ are adopted as "sons" and given rooms within the Father's mansion. Sonship language indicates the for-us character of divine action. We cannot become children of God by nature, but we can share in God as adopted children and chosen friends. The "Spirit of adopted sonship" (Rom. 8:15) makes us children of God as we are united with the Son. Sonship is an economic designation, just as fatherhood is. But sonship is not only an indication of the intimacy God offers us. The work such language is doing is to show that being *sons* of God means we are not *servants* of God. The distinction is not between sons and daughters, say (so that we are "sons" but not in a human way, in analogy to the arguments considered in chapter 5), but between sons and *slaves*. As in Galatians 4:6–7, insofar as the Holy Spirit teaches us to cry "Abba," the result is that we are no longer slaves but sons, and *if* a son *then* an heir of God through Christ. Indeed, the reason for the sending of the "Son" is so that we may be transformed into heirs rather than slaves, into friends rather than servants of God. The relevant paradox is not the simultaneity of obedience and freedom or their nonopposition in God, but the simultaneity of "sonship" and friendship: the claim on God we are allowed to make in virtue of our adoption and the side-by-side relations we are given by virtue of friendship with God incarnate. As Didymus says, "*The Spirit himself* adopts us as children and *bears witness* when our spirit possesses the same Spirit by participation *that we are children of God*. In consequence of this, on the one hand, God bestows spiritual gifts upon us like a father bestows a bountiful inheritance, but on the other hand, we are *fellow heirs with Christ*, insofar as we are called his brothers through his grace and kindness."[62] The Spirit of freedom sets us free and gives us full access to the banquet that God has prepared for God's people.

The emphasis on father-son language in the early trinitarian debates reflects not only its presence in the New Testament and in the baptismal formula—after all, the language always coexisted with many other images.[63] The Son is Radiance, Word, Wisdom, Character, River, and the Lord of Glory, for instance. The Spirit is the Spirit of Power and Glory, the Bestower and Creator of sanctification who consoles, seals, and confirms, the Spirit of joy and peace. But father-son language proved especially alluring to those named heretics, since that language and imagery seemed so obviously to entail that the Son *was* less than the Father. The language of father and son had to be kept front and center and had to be twisted over and over in order to show that it did *not* entail undesirable, subordinationist consequences.[64]

So much for sonship; now to sending. The sending of the Son and Spirit is a spatial way of describing our relation to God as God unites Godself more closely with the world. We run away from God; therefore, the Father sends the Son and Spirit, and the Son and Spirit bring the Father with them as they come. They do not leave the Father behind in some transcendently distant heaven: the Father is right here, naming the Son as his own, returning glory to the Son, revealing the Son to the world as the truth of God. The imagery used by Gregory of Nyssa in which "he who lays hold on one end of [a] chain pulls the other to him, so he who 'draws the Spirit' . . . by His means draws to him at the same time both the Son and the Father,"[65] indicates just this inseparable closeness of the persons of the trinity to each other. These spatialized relations reflect that our false attempts to go away from God are overcome by God, who brings God to us so that we may be brought to God. These paradoxical relations of distance and closeness reflect the closeness between the trinitarian persons, the "distance" between God and us, and the overcoming of that distance through relations of adoption and friendship established between us and God. As Barth says,

> the absoluteness of God strictly understood . . . means that God has the freedom to be present with that which is not God, to communicate Himself and unite Himself with the other and the other with Himself. . . . No created being can be inwardly present to another, entering and remaining in communion with him in the depths of its inner life. . . . The essence of every other being is to be finite, and therefore to have frontiers against the personality of others and to have to guard those frontiers jealously.[66]

It is just these barrier functions that are overcome in God's transformation of human community. Human tendencies to maintain frontiers against each other are not overcome by being conformed to trinitarian personhood in its essentially relational and perichoretic nature, nor by some exaggerated valorization of supposed humility and suffering subordination.

In the life we now live, to be internal to another person would be our death and that of the other. In God's unitive transformation of humankind, we still do not become internal to each other in the way trinitarian persons are. But we do become able to be in the same place at the same time—as it were—without shattering, breaking, emptying, or penetrating, through the transformation of materiality that comes from God's unitive and assimilative love of mattered creation. Because the finite is taken into the infinite, the form of finitude itself shifts in order to allow for properly finite relations that nonetheless do not involve even the possibility of hierarchy, competition, and death. If the object that is given to the finite to enjoy in creation is the world, then the "object" that is given to the finite when taken up into the infinite is first the infinite itself, in such a way that the finite is not superseded but transformed. We are even permitted to participate in some of the essential activities of the trinitarian persons who reveal and glorify each other as we glorify them and are conformed into the image of Christ, God incarnate. Again, Barth: "As the living God is the source of light, and light in Himself, He also has and is the radiance of light. Standing in contrast to all other beings, He is the radiance of light that reaches all other beings and permeates them. He is not separated from them by any distance, but changes such distance into proximity."[67] As distance becomes closeness, and difference becomes intensified copresence, the light of God lights up the world with its glory.

Before turning to a more detailed examination of matter's transformation and the significance of the eucharist, let us return to the criteria for trinitarian theologies developed earlier. My account of trinitarian relations emphasizes the reality of God's revelation and presence in the economy of salvation, but it does not mislead us into thinking that, in considering trinitarian constitution, we have *understood* God or the nature of relation in God. Just as the tradition has twisted language of begetting, proceeding, and causation to render it as unrecognizable as possible, I have done the same with language of gift or intensification. In providing an account of the trinity in which the divinity of the Son and Spirit is not derivative, but as original as the Father's, I remain faithful to the original aims of trinitarian theology and, more importantly, to the salvific axiom. God reveals Godself to us and creates a place—a house with many rooms, a place where we may live as adopted children of God—by conforming us to God the "Son," the Lord of Glory who unites God with us in the most intimate manner possible.

We have emphasized the for-us character of the economy of salvation throughout. We need now to consider the nature of the relationships God establishes among human beings and with human beings. Those relationships, too, are revelatory of who God is, although in a somewhat different way: God is as God does. What God does is establish communion, giving us God's friendship, making us God's children and God's siblings, and doing so in a way that demonstrates the very nature of God's power. The power of God is alluring, beautiful; as Balthasar puts it, "the Beautiful never overwhelms those who resist it but, by its grace, makes prisoners of those who are freely convinced."[68] Barth expounds:

> To say that God is beautiful is to say how He enlightens and convinces and persuades us. It is to describe not merely the naked fact of His revelation or its power, but the shape and form in which it is a fact and is power. It is to say that God has this superior force, this power of attraction . . . in the fact that He is beautiful, divinely beautiful, beautiful in His own way . . . He acts as the One who gives pleasure, creates desire and rewards with enjoyment. And He does it because He is pleasant, desirable, full of enjoyment . . . God loves us as the One who is worthy of love as God.[69]

This way of approaching God's revelation of Godself moves away from explicit consideration of the trinitarian persons and their constitution. Instead, it turns us to the nature of the unrestricted community that God establishes among humans when God establishes communion with humans.

## BANQUETS WITHOUT BORDERS

The aim of the trinity's action in the world is to give human beings a share in the life of God. What such a share in the life of God looks like is best seen in New Testament passages dealing with food and banqueting practices. Salvation entails "fellowship with God and the related life, which also embraces a renewal of fellowship with others."[70] What is promised in the life and ministry of Jesus is a reality in which death no longer has power, in which "obedience" to the "law" of love is the only "law," and that will one day culminate in God's making God's home among human beings. Jesus preaches the kingdom of God—a kingdom without masters and servants, one that manifests the logic of friendship without flattening or cancelling the difference between humans and God (John 15:15). The transformation of human existence is not its translation into a world other than this one. It is, rather, the promise and reality of God's coming close in love, so that the love of God for humans is made directly available in their sibling relation to Jesus, through which God comes to live among humans as an adoptive parent for the sake of new creation. God comes close in love to transform human difference from its seemingly inevitable, sinful tendency to turn into competition necessitating self-sacrifice into the possibility of table fellowship in friendship with each other and Jesus, as adoptive children of God all seated around the banquet table enjoying the overflow that characterizes the life given by God.

Food practices serve as both the symbolization and theo-logic of God's "unnatural," affiliative relationships with humankind. The beginning of Jesus' ministry is a feast at which Jesus transforms scarcity into abundance for the purpose of celebrating and enjoying new relationships among people previously unrelated to one another. The end of Jesus' ministry is another banquet at which he will once more drink of the vine that he refuses to sip in anticipation of that day, a banquet of reunion, restoration, and new beginnings. Central events of Jesus' life and ministry involve setting the table for a casual, outdoor banquet (feeding the five thousand men and unnumbered women, children, and others), telling stories of banquets—planning them, declining or accepting invitations to them, attending them and socializing at them, eating and talking at them, behaving in scandalizing and indecent ways at banquets, and so on. The shape of Christian existence is celebration of the presence of Christ at a banquet. The promise of Christian existence is that banquets without borders express the victorious truth of human existence. Equally, the shape of Christian conflict is over who gets to participate in that celebration and under what conditions.

In the banquet that God provides, Jesus has made room for us by his side in the house of God. The transformation of materiality signalized in the eucharist, and extending behind the cross in Jesus' statement, "This *is* my body," signals that multitudes may be present in the same space. The transformation of the body here works with the body's limits to make visible relation without spatialized wound-wombs or penetration. The body's limits do not disappear, but spatial location becomes coinhabitable, and the colocality of different bodies—presence in the same place at the same time—transforms the nature of relationality and community beyond their deformation. One need not move aside to make room for the other, for there is enough space for all.[71] Connecting trinitarian relationality to materiality and the body, we discover the possibility of bodies that do not crowd each other out, make room for each other, or penetrate each other in order to be in relation and to be in the same place at the same time. To be in the same place at the same time does not necessitate the establishment of a relation; but some ways of being in the same place at the same time do mean the establishment of a relation. Yet the category "relation" is in itself neutral; the *nature* of that relation needs to be specified. The aim of God's action is the establishment and recreation of *good* relationships, relationships in which persons are in the same "place" at the same "time," enjoying each other. This reformation of both materiality and spatiality allows for relational intensification as persons come closer to each other. This kind of intensification is, as we have seen, a way in which human beings become distant images of the inner-trinitarian relations (in the sense of intensified copresence), but much more importantly, this kind of intensification takes place between human beings and God as God establishes God's city-home with human beings.

Certain understandings of the eucharist make sense of all this, but stories about Jesus' post-resurrection meals with disciples are important as well. The eucharist is conditioned by matter's transformation: God can be bread, a single body can be omnipresent and potentially infinitely multipliable, and so on. For my purposes, a eucharistic theory of impanation has significant advantages over a doctrine of transubstantiation since it expands on a basic Christological category, the Word's assumption of a human nature. Nothing about that assumption precludes the assumption of multiple and nonhuman natures as well.[72] In the eucharist, the Word assumes a bread nature in addition to a human nature rather than, as in transubstantiation, transmuting the substance (but not the accidents) of the bread into Christ's body. Unlike transubstantiation, impanation is an "external" or additive relation that permits the copresence of two particular bodies in the same place, rather than requiring the substantial nature of one to yield to the other.

It seems that "two bodies cannot be extended in the same place at once" due to the quantitative density of the body, and in part for this reason Aquinas opts to advance a theory of transubstantiation.[73] But impanation dramatizes an alternative possibility that need not be exclusively relegated to post-resurrection existence even in our experience, since it takes place every time the eucharist is performed: Two bodies *can* be in the same place at the same time without crowding each other out and without breaking or shattering each other into pieces. Impanation may take place through the Word's assumption of a second body, so that the bread has the same kind of relationship to the Word that the humanity of Christ has. For instance, the bread body might be individuated by the Word in a relationship of dependence—individuated by its very belonging to the Word. Or it could be the *body* of the Word that assumes a second (bread) body; the bread body is then proximately supposited by the humanity of Christ and remotely by the Word.[74] Impanation heightens the drama of the copresence of Christ's divinity, his humanity, and his breaded being as believers digest the "breaded Christ."[75] As Carolyn Walker Bynum says, "Food was filth; it was also God."[76] This is incarnation without reserve, but neither the degradation nor the shattering of the transformed and now plenitudinous body of Christ. In analogy to creation *ex nihilo*, God gratuitously multiplies the breaded Christs. In disanalogy to creation *ex nihilo*, our cooperation assists in bringing the bread-Christ, for we bake the bread with the material gifts God has given us. Our baking of the bread is an invitation and a hope: Come, Lord Jesus.

Yet the image of baking bread risks obscuring the complex nature of the relations bread materializes on the altar. As the product of human hands, the bread brings with it all our relations to each other—our financial, material, gendered, and raced relations. Sometimes the only way women participate in performing the eucharist is to bake the bread. Bread and wine must be paid for with labor and money that, when used for this purpose, cannot be used for other purposes, dramatizing the way scarcity currently characterizes our choices and gifts. Yet the eucharist cannot be reduced to scarcity alone. As in the feeding of the five thousand plus, what is scarce is expanded so that others may ever be brought into its orbit—the finitely shareable is still shareable. In contemporary Western culture, eating of any kind brings anxieties about unbounded, undisciplined—fat—bodies. The multiplicative capacity of Christ's body is also expansive and undisciplined. His remains a body, thus finite and located, but its multiplication also entails the transformation and elevation (not cancellation) of finitude into something that looks much like the ever-expanding body of cultural anxiety. This real-symbolic transformation is, however, the penultimate chapter in a longer story.

The first chapters of that story tell of creation and fall. The most significant difference between finitude considered from the perspective of the goodness of creation and finitude marred by sin is the way limits enter into finitude marred by sin. In unfallen finitude, each "thisness" has its particularity, but that "thisness" does not appear against an abyss of nothingness. Created finitude is not suspended above non-being, which would be a substantialization of the *nihilo* "out of which" creation comes. Created finitude can be affirmed for what it is. What becomes limit when finitude is marred by sin is, from the perspective of creation, simple "thisness" that can be enjoyed for what it is. It is not subjected to the question, "Why this and not that?" Human possibility, from the perspective of creation, is just its ability to become and be in relation to particular, actual existents. Desire is not rapacious here; it responds directly to whatever good presents itself. Desire's motility is not a danger, for that motility reflects the multitude of particular, finite goods in existence. Desire's object is not this *rather than* that; it is *this*. Even death appears not as threat (of non-being) but as the completion of what each particular "thisness" is. But once finitude is marred by sin, sin introduces the self-consciousness of "this-or-that" and even "this-and-that." Rather than responding to whatever particularity presents itself, sin-marred finitude invents a neutral and apparently blank background against which particularities may be measured and evaluated—against each other and against nothing(ness).

Under sin, the will finds itself without an object; it finds itself an empty canvas—not in the positive sense of being transformable by whatever it encounters (to find desirable whatever it encounters in its particularity), but in the negative sense of being unable to recognize particularity as anything other than a limit carved out of plenitude (so that plenitude becomes its contrast, rather than seeing each particularity for itself) and suspended over nothingness. This desire may become both nihilistic and rapacious, and this desire is what the theologians we have examined seek to counter in their corrective projectionism and in their valuation of shattering and sacrifice. Such disorder does indeed exist in fallen desire, although it mars rather than destroys the nature of desire's orientation toward the particular other. But commanding a total orientation to the other *rather than* the self, or self-limitation for the sake of leaving "enough" for the other (enough space for the other to come to be), extends the logic of (self-) possession into the goodness of the created order itself: It makes self-possession the fundamental human state that has to be overcome. Actually existing finitude always participates in both logics, suspended between the goodness of its creation as particularity and the expansion of that particularity promised in consummation, and its sin-marred existence in which desire for the other can become a desire of nothing and a desire without limit. Under sin, particularity becomes limit and so a threat. But the eucharist does not just perform some sort of sacrifice of rapaciousness for the sake of affirmation of the tragic and limited character of human existence, for the eucharist points forward to consummation, apocalypse, and second coming even more than it anamnestically summons the sacrificial aspect of Christ's for-us. The bringing of the bread and wine in hope is not primarily (though it is also) hope of forgiveness; it is hope for reunification and consummation.

From the perspective of consummation, the eucharist symbolizes the nature of the life to come and the reconfiguration of the conditions of materiality that the life to come brings. Why does Jesus promise not to eat or drink of the vine until he is reunited with his community in heaven? The promise reflects the end of just this logic of having to be taken in by or to take someone in in order to have a relationship with someone. It is the final end of (violent or consensual) penetrative logic, an end that in the always-not-yet logic of Christianity has been overcome for us even as it remains an invitation. The multiplication of the breaded Christs means enough Christ for all; our participation in (taking part in) Christ brings us together in face-to-face relations that show us to each other more clearly—or that at least have the potential to do so, for better and worse. The sufficiency of the eucharist, and the intensified relationships among humans that it symbolizes and makes possible, suggests reconfiguration of the conditions of bodied, material existence themselves. As in unfallen creation, particularity will no longer entail the duality of rapacious unlimitedness and threatened limitation. But the fullness of this transformation remains in some sense a future hope, for the last enemy to be overcome is death. While death in creation means completion, death under sin means loss, devastation, and meaninglessness. Particularity and specificity, marked by death, become lack and competitive scarcity. Thus death becomes an enemy, and in the cross and resurrection, God takes up and overcomes death in a dual movement of healing and new creation. Limit as threat of scarcity, and limitation rather than particularity, is healed and returned to its original nature, because death has encountered a God in whom and for whom *no* particularity threatens to turn into limit and sacrifice. As Christ awaits our arrival at his banquet table, new creation does not undo the conditions of creation as it was, for the incarnation is irreversible and the intimacy between God and creation that it entails means that we walk in a city where God is its light, rather than in the twilight of the garden. This awaiting protects against Christianity being nothing but a magical counternarrative constituted by a denial of the world as it is. Scarcity does not simply disappear, and finitude is not straightforwardly overcome. We do not yet know what we shall be; we see through a glass darkly; we live in the time of the already-not-yet. Then we shall see as we are seen and know as we are known.

The end toward which the trinity works is overcoming and transforming the kind of relations generated by the not-enough conditions of human existence. One spatial way to represent the character of this transformation is to imagine the heavenly banquet table around which we gather as simultaneously huge and tiny—everyone crowds in next to each other, yet somehow, the closer everyone gets, there is always room for all. Relations between persons get intensified—side-by-side relations can represent this, but an economy of surface touch works as well. Those intensified relationships can be symbolized through the very type of materiality that we see in the risen Christ—here's where his ability to walk through walls matters (one way of reading Jesus' unexpected appearances in the upper room). His body no longer competes with other bodies for the same space. His body and the wall or door can be in the same place at the same time without crashing into each other or shattering each other, yet his body has not become ethereal or vaporous—he eats and drinks, he can be touched. This transformation and intensification of materiality shows itself in other actions that Jesus performs after the resurrection. Jesus can walk through walls because his body has become most real: body without limit as threat, body as presence and particularity. Jesus' most intense encounters before and after the resurrection involve neither penetration nor internalization—when Mary rubs expensive ointment into his feet, that, too, is a surface touch rather than an invading touch. (Both *noli me tangere* and Thomas's desire to invade Christ's body are presented as a form of unbelief, not as the maximizing of the truth of the resurrected body.)

The same logic of material intensification is represented in the quantities of fish that the disciples catch on the shore of Lake Galilee and cook and eat together with the risen Lord. Matter itself becomes a site of intensification—a *more than* rather than a condition of scarcity (yet still particular), and the extensibility of relationship that we can experience in passionate relations and forms of (non-)biological kinship becomes the very form of human existence in togetherness with each other and God. This, too, is present already in Jesus' relations with his disciples, when he points out that he calls them friends rather than servants. Events in Jesus' ministry also move along the trajectory from materiality as a logic of exclusion to materiality as a site of intensified relationality without loss.[77] Aspects of this reversal are indicated in some of the banqueting stories Jesus tells. In one of these banquets, from Luke 12:35–39, the normal order of things is upended: in gratitude, finding the servants alert, the master waits on them instead. In another, the party-thrower, finding distracted guests busy with property and marital concerns, brings in those who are excluded from participation in the "normal" order of society (Luke 14:16–24). Such upending should not be read as the enactment of *ressentiment* that delights in the imagination of the mighty brought low, the charge that Nietzsche and others have correctly brought against aspects of the Christian imaginary. Rather, what is upended is the logic of hierarchy and scarcity among people, and beyond even that once the banquet is given by God. If God sits down in fellowship with humans at the banquet God provides, jockeying for position no longer has any meaning because *whatever* stratagem one employs to gain a high place avails for nothing; the order of things is upended, turned inside out, for God is all in all. These enactments of multiplication exemplify the nature of divine celebrations; seemingly stable lines of separation and division no longer capture and hold in the new order. This is a true transvaluation of value. No longer does self-sacrifice occupy the highest space of loving existence.

Jesus' multiplication of food at the feeding of the five thousand plus and his transformation (at a wedding banquet) of "mere" water into "rich" wine are also significant. In the feeding of the five thousand plus, the leftover baskets—utterly concrete—indicate the more-than-enough character of divine giving (and divine concern that no one go away hungry). At the wedding banquet, relational and material intensification are implied by the transformation of water into heady wine and its correlative implications for the conviviality of the occasion. But there's also a move beyond the logic of "sober" assessment and toward rejoicing in the more-than-enough.

When we see the Spirit descending in medieval paintings as rays of light, that is something like the noncompetitive materiality that the trinity gives in the transformation of conditions of the body. (This is related to, although not identical with, Karl Rahner's unthematic presence of God that lights up everything in the world in its own character.[78]) When the Spirit is present, other bodies and things need not move out of the way to make room for the Spirit; instead, the Spirit's presence serves to intensify those things just in their own characters. In a sense, the Spirit doesn't shine from inside the person because it's the person that we see in the power of the Spirit. Light remains on the surface even as it intensifies enjoyment that pervades one's entire being. Light—that by which we see—shows otherness on the surface, without the need to penetrate to being's depth.

The Son's road to the cross cannot be straight: It cannot be reduced to (self-)sacrifice or expiation. He has too many tasks to do on the way: friends to make, disciples to call, wine to drink, people to heal, demons to drive out. The resurrection symbolizes the outcome of his entire ministry: the final transformation of human persons through their rematerialization. Their bodies relate without logics of penetrative shattering either consensual or not (the womb-wound). Their reunion takes place around a banquet table covered with fish piled high and freely flowing wine.

Despite these images of abundance, we should not treat the eucharist as a talisman or a theopolitical act that in mysterious fashion makes all this true of the lives we now live. We need to recognize the degree of brokenness that forms human existence, the truth of our existence between creation, fall, and consummation. To assert future or symbolic superabundance as a response to the world's need is a spiritualizing ideology that renders Christianity vulnerable to Karl Marx's classic designation of religion as the opiate of the people and the sigh of a heartless world—it risks what I term a dematerialized utopian idealism. Angel Méndez-Montoya's creative eucharistic study, *The Theology of Food*, is marred by just such assumptions. Since the eucharist reflects a prior "desire and fulfillment among intimately related persons" in the "community" that is the trinity[79] and "imitates a prior gastroerotic performance within the intra-Trinitarian alimentation,"[80] Méndez-Montoya posits plenitude across the entire Christian narrative, including the lives we now live. His "theopolitics of superabundance"[81] requires self-dispossession that imitates God's intra- and extra-trinitarian self-giving, which holds nothing back in its move through death to life.[82] The superabundant logic of the eucharist may even solve world hunger.[83] In his conclusion, Méndez-Montoya laments "how far we are from the vision I have outlined in this book,"[84] but that distance seems to have little theological significance. He does not pay sufficient attention to the differences between divine and human giving, for God gives without loss, while we are not always able to do so.

We do not yet live fully under the sign of the resurrection. The eucharist is Christ's body *once-for-all broken* for the world (it need not be broken again) and transformed into an inexhaustible source of reconciliation and community formation in the power of God, for the glory of God, and in and through the love of God. The eucharist represents Christ's participation in the brokenness of the world just because such brokenness is part of the human condition. Christ's brokenness is an expression of the *unreserved* union between the Glory of God and humankind. But the eucharist, like baptism, represents the possibility of life *nonetheless*—without forgetting or abandoning the loss that shapes human existence. The eucharist is an intensified materialization of the goodness of creation itself, in its own identity, both in its beginning and its end. The beginning is a shared celebratory meal, for the eucharist begins not at the last supper but at the wedding feast of Cana; its earliest antecedents are the food without labor found in the garden of Eden, the feast under the trees at Mamre, and the liberation symbolized by Passover, and it culminates in Jesus' earthly history in the sharing of grilled fish by the side of Lake Tiberias. Its end is a banquet beyond all distance, sacrifice, and loss (symbolized by our reunion with him with him and with each other), yet retaining the particularity that creation *ex nihilo* grants us. When we then eat the bread and drink of the vine, we will be doing so *as* the body of God rather than imbibing and incorporating the body of God into ourselves. The nature of the eucharist is only locally, in its anamnestic qualities, that of a narrative fulcrum representing the undoing of the world's self-enclosure by the cross. As thanksgiving, or (better) holy communion, the banqueting practices of God move from the establishment of creation's goodness in its finite materiality to the end of particularity and difference as separation and border-crossing. The eucharist reminds us of the cost of our salvation, but much more, it makes us look forward to our reunion with the one who was dead but now lives.

Eschatological fulfillment takes place through the enactment of God's transformative aims with respect to creation. While creation is itself good in its finitude, particularity, and diversity, the entrance of sin demonstrates the vulnerability of the goodness of material creation to distortion when the diversity of aims and goods in human existence turns into a source of threat. The logic of the broken body of Christ is one in which the only good of which there is always more than enough, God Godself, becomes instantiated and available in the specific character of bodied existence. But the broken body of Christ is the middle, not the end, of our stories with God. The resurrected body of Christ, and the ascended body of Christ with its ondrawing of hope, move beyond the broken body of Christ. Kallistos Ware tells of a saying some early Christians ascribed to Christ: "Lift the stone and you will find me; cut the wood in two and there am I."[85] Christ's body moves past even sexual difference and joins itself to the materiality of the entire world. The body of God is also bread, and stone, and tree—a tree the leaves of which are for the healing of nations.

Jesus came to invite human persons to a feast at which God sets the table and is the food. Resurrection, not cross, is the site of whatever epistemic certainty his mission provides. But resurrection is, oddly, a far more ambiguous site of epistemic certainty. (If Christ is not raised, our hope is nothing.) The risen Christ remains unrecognizable to his disciples until a word is spoken. Jesus himself promises not to eat again until he does so in the coming kingdom, with us. What will the grape of the vine symbolize then? What memory of blood and bone will be enacted?

## NOTES

1. Miroslav Volf, *After Our Likeness: The Church as the Image of the Trinity* (Grand Rapids, MI: Eerdmans, 1998), 217.
2. Colin Gunton, *Father, Son and Holy Spirit: Essays Toward a Fully Trinitarian Theology* (London: T&T Clark, 2003), 67.
3. Gregory of Nyssa, *Against Eunomius*, in *Nicene and Post-Nicene Fathers*, second series, vol. 5, *Gregory of Nyssa: Dogmatic Treatises, Etc.*, ed. Philip Schaff and Henry Wace (Peabody, MA: Hendrickson, 2012), 158.
4. Gunton, *Father, Son and Holy Spirit*, 73, my emphasis. Gunton's use provides a much-needed check on tendencies to say that perichoresis necessarily prevents subordination.
5. Ibid.
6. Karl Barth, *Church Dogmatics* II/1, *The Doctrine of God: The Knowledge of God, the Reality of God* (Edinburgh: T&T Clark, 1957), 333–34 (hereafter CD).
7. Lois Malcolm, "On Not Three Male Gods: Retrieving Wisdom in Trinitarian Discourse," *Dialog* 49, no. 3 (2010): 45.
8. Paul Helm, "Of God, and of the Holy Trinity: A Response to Dr. Beckwith," *Churchman* 155 (2001), 354.
9. Some finite goods are only partly shareable: this apple, that plot of land; I still assign competition (rather than limited sharing) to sin rather than finitude as such. I return to the distinction between sin and finitude later in the chapter.

10. Even if patristic theologians were more successful than those we have examined in ruling out such implications (which I would contest), the correlation (not causation) between great trinitarian theologies and ecclesiastical misogyny across history is frequent enough to require our opponents to do far more than has yet been done to prove the invulnerability of patristic theologies to such critique.

11. Brannon Ellis, *Calvin, Classical Trinitarianism, and the Aseity of the Son* (Oxford: Oxford University Press, 2012), 12–15.

12. Didymus the Blind, "On the Holy Spirit," in John Behr, ed., *Works on the Spirit: Athanasius and Didymus*, trans. Mark DelCogliano, Andrew Radde-Gallwitz, and Lewis Ayres (Crestwood, NY: St. Vladimir's Seminary Press, 2011), par. 163, 194.

13. Aquinas, *Summa Theologica*, trans. Fathers of the English Dominican Province (Westminster: Christian Classics, 1948), Ia, q.33.3 ad 2. Aquinas may simply be referring to how the Son holds what he receives.

14. Some hold that the Father is the origin of the Son and Spirit in a personal sense, rather than in an ontologically communicative sense. Yet on such accounts, origin is still associated with the problems I have demonstrated in theologians who *do* hold to ontological communication, so the distinction is conceptually interesting but not practically determinative.

15. It is important to emphasize that the issue here is not that we are abandoning the regulative character of the biblical economy and projecting "another" trinity. It took a long time and a great deal of struggle for trinitarian theologians in the patristic period to develop strategies that they thought satisfactorily addressed and interpreted the apparently subordinationist passages of the New Testament. But they were not straightforwardly operating with assumptions about deity that they imported from elsewhere. Instead, they thought—as do we—that subordination is incompatible with intrinsic elements of the biblical economy of salvation and so sought arguments to counter subordination, degrees of divinity, and Arianism.

16. See the discussion of Mark Jordan in chapter 2.

17. Thomas Aquinas, *Summa Theologica* Ia, q.33.2 ad 2, ad 4.

18. This is only one of his strategies, of course, but it illustrates just one way in which shifts in understandings of gender and sexuality affect the validity of trinitarian arguments.

19. In this case, primarily in its stipulative sense, for that is where we discover its *aims* (although its achievement of those aims cannot only be measured by examining the stipulations for plausibility, coherence, and explanatory value, as we have seen).

20. The structure of trinitarian thought, as we analyzed it in chapter 5, problematizes this assumption while indirectly strengthening the relationship between apophatic and trinitarian language. Karen Kilby, "Is an Apophatic Trinitarianism Possible?" *International Journal of Systematic Theology* 12, no. 1 (January 2010), 67.

21. Ibid., 68. Note that even if an apophatic trinitarianism (only Father and Son know what begetting means and so on) is combined with a denial of essential communication, the explicit assertion has to be matched on the implicit level of use. One cannot then make much of paternity and the gratitude of filiation and call it an apophatic trinitarianism. Kilby herself does not quite succeed in limiting the application of paternity and sonship in this way, since an apophatic trinitarianism is directed toward "acknowledg[ing] infinite depths that exceed our grasp in the Father who is contemplated through the Son" (72). Kilby succumbs to the ondrawing lure of the absent Father, which requires a strange distance from the centrality of the Christ-event that prompts the development of the trinitarian theology that she wants to defend, since "the

fundamental structure of Christian contemplation" is that "[t]he Spirit allows
us to contemplate the Father in the Son." Although we might "add" that
the Son and Spirit "are themselves fully divine," the object of contemplation remains the Father rather than "three-in-oneness" or, by implication, the
(divinity of) the Son and Spirit themselves (72). So the Son is central to this
process only because he points away from himself to the one he reveals, the
one to whom contemplation is really directed, and suddenly we are back in the
standard picture but with the further complication that the high Christology
of Nicene orthodoxy turns out to be only indirectly significant.

22. She argues that "[i]n God we precisely *cannot* think of difference between that
which proceeds and that from which it proceeds: divine simplicity requires the
denial of this. . . . We do not, from the created analogue, get a glimpse into the
nature of God: rather, we so modify the language drawn from this analogue
that when we arrive at a language to talk about God, it is a language we quite
clearly *cannot* understand. What is a procession which does not occur in time,
nor involve change, nor allow of any diversity between the one who processes
and the one from whom the procession takes place? I have no reason to affirm
that there is no such thing, but also no way of grasping or imagining what it
might be." Karen Kilby, "Aquinas, the Trinity and the Limits of Understanding," *International Journal of Systematic Theology* 7, no. 4 (2005), 420.
23. Kilby, "Apophatic Trinitarianism," 69–70.
24. Ibid., 71.
25. As John T. Slotemaker puts it in "Calvin's Trinitarian Theology in the 1536
*Institutes*: The Distinction of Persons as a Key to His Theological Sources," in
Kent Emery, Jr., Russel L. Friedman, and Andreas Speer, eds., *Philosophy and
Theology in the Long Middle Ages* (Leiden: Brill, 2011), 804.
26. I use "salvific" as a more general term than it really is, for simplicity's sake. As a
supralapsarian, I assume that God's unitive aims with respect to creation—see
the following quotation from McCord Adams—ground the incarnation, and
that redemption from sin is a side effect of those unitive aims.
27. Marilyn McCord Adams, *Christ and Horrors: The Coherence of Christology*
(Cambridge: Cambridge University Press, 2006), 39.
28. Kathryn Tanner, "In the Image of the Invisible," in Chris Boesel and Catherine
Keller, eds., *Apophatic Bodies: Negative Theology, Incarnation, and Relationality* (New York: Fordham University Press, 2010), 127–34.
29. Didymus, *Holy Spirit*, par. 81, 168.
30. Wolfhart Pannenberg, *Systematic Theology*, vol, 1, trans. Geoffrey W. Bromiley (Grand Rapids: Eerdmans, 1991), 382–84 (hereater ST1). For Pannenberg,
field means both the totality of the divine essence and the Spirit's personhood
specifically. I wish to expand a version of the idea of field, thought as light, to
include the personhood of the other two as well.
31. Ibid., 383.
32. Karl Barth rightly argues that "[t]he more the distinction of persons is
regarded as taking place in and grounded in the divine essence itself, the more
inconceivable in fact becomes the inconceivability of this distinction . . . neither *persona* nor any other term can perform of making this distinction really
conceivable," CD I/1, 356.
33. Among the many biblical texts that could be cited, Psalm 36:9, the *locus clas-
sicus* in John 1:4–9; 2 Corinthians 4:6 (which refers to the revelation of "the
glory of God in the face of Jesus Christ"); 1 John 1:5 and its correlate interrelating the light of God and the love of other in 2:9; and Revelation 21:22–25
and 22:5 are especially important in guiding this discussion.
34. Revelation 21:23, New International Version.
35. Augustine, *The Trinity*, book 7, ed. John E. Rotelle, trans. Edmund Hill (New
York: New City Press, 1991), 223. Augustine continues in the same vein to say

that "the Father is light, the Son is light, the Holy Spirit is light; but together they are not three lights but one light" (224). God, as uncreated light, is the proper referent for light, as Edmund Hill notes in a footnote. The patristic influences on my constructive project are not a return to origin of the kind critiqued in the prelude; rather, they represent alternatives that can be twisted in ways the authors themselves would only partly approve.

36. My favorite representation of this is Giovanni Bellini's painting *St. Francis in Ecstasy* (Frick Museum, New York), where the whole landscape is lit up by a light that is not localizable inside the space of the picture even as it makes visible the concrete materiality of the landscape in which Francis stands transformed.

37. As Denys Turner enjoys reminding me, it matters greatly that the trinity is neither two nor four. But that assertion takes place on a different level than the negation of the countability of trinitarian persons does. The number that they are not is three, as it were. Saying that God is one negates a plurality of gods as well as division; it does not imply that God is countable by the number one.

38. See also Martin Luther's utterly charming image of faith's relation to Christ: "faith is a kind of knowledge or darkness that nothing can see. Yet the Christ of whom faith takes hold is sitting in this darkness as God sat in the midst of darkness on Sinai." *Lectures on Galatians 1535: Chapters 1–4, Luther's Works*, vol. 26, ed. and trans. Jaroslav Pelikan (St. Louis, MO: Concordia, 1963), 130.

39. This reflects the differentiated taxes found in the New Testament; see, e.g., Jürgen Moltmann's tracing of different variations in *The Trinity and the Kingdom: The Doctrine of God*, trans. Margaret Kohl (Minneapolis, MN: Fortress Press, 1993 [1980/1981]), esp. 65–96.

40. In the following discussion, I use the names Father, Son/Word, and Spirit for the sake of clarity in reference. Naming the persons as first, second, and third is no less (and in some ways more) risky than using the traditional names in this way. Gregory of Nazianzus lists names for the Son, including "The Way, the Truth, the Life, the Light," "Wisdom," "Power," "Effulgence, the Impress, the Image, the Seal," "Lord," and "King," "Third Theological Oration," in *Christology of the Later Fathers*, ed. Edward R. Hardy (Louisville, KY: Westminster John Knox, 2006), 172. Basil of Caesarea lists some other terms, including "Shepherd, . . . Physician, Bridegroom, . . . Door, Fountain, Bread, Axe, and Rock," *On the Spirit*, in *Nicene and Post-Nicene Fathers*, second series, vol. 8, *Basil: Letters and Select Works*, ed. Philip Schaff and Henry Wace (Peabody, MA: Hendrickson, 2012), ch. 8, 11. The Spirit is "royal, Spirit of truth, and Spirit of wisdom," *On the Spirit*, ch. 19, 30.

41. Augustine reads this as indicating that "neither can be shown without the other" (*The Trinity*, book 1, 77) but I think it justifies a stronger reading. Gregory of Nyssa rightly emphasizes that the point is "the complete absence of divergence in the likeness, as compared with him whose likeness he is." *Against Eunomius*, NPNF 2/5, 201.

42. An alternative reading of John 17:5. Although John 17:22 and 24 refer explicitly to glory given to the Son by the Father, two biblical and theological considerations weigh strongly in favor of reading that particular gift as an economic *return* of glory to the Son from the Father. The cross is also the glory of God, and the Lamb *is* our salvation. The Lamb is the only one found worthy to open the scroll in Revelation 5, and just that is the glory of God (vv. 12–13).

43. Martin Luther, *Lectures on Genesis 1–5, Luther's Works*, vol. 1, ed. Jaroslav Pelikan and Helmut T. Lehman, trans. George V. Schick (St. Louis, MO: Concordia, 1958), 14–15.

44. See also the related discussion of the materialization of glory by Mayra Rivera, "Glory: The First Passion of Theology?" in Catherine Keller and Laurel C.

Schneider, eds., *Polydoxy: Theology of Multiplicity and Relation* (London: Routledge, 2011), 167–85.

45. See Günter Thomas, "Resurrection to New Life," in Ted Peters, Robert John Russell, and Michael Welker, eds., *Resurrection: Theological and Scientific Assessments* (Grand Rapids, MI: Eerdmans, 2002), 262, for a brief summary of biblical and scholarly evidence of the Spirit's role in resurrection.

46. Basil, *On the Spirit*, NPNF 2/8, ch. 21, 34.

47. Hilary of Poitiers, "On the Trinity, in Nicene and Post-Nicene Fathers," second series, vol. 9, *Hilary of Poitiers, John of Damascus*, ed. Philip Schaff and Henry Wace (Peabody, MA: Hendrickson, 2012), 20, 161.

48. "Empowerer" would be a better name in some ways, but my distaste for empowerment language in contemporary discourse prevents my using it. "Spirit of power" also has potential, especially in the visions and dreams that the Spirit promises.

49. See for instance Anselm, *On the Procession of the Spirit*, trans. Richard Regan, in *Anselm of Canterbury: The Major Works* (Oxford: Oxford University Press, 1998), 392–96. Karl Barth discusses this in CD I/1, 365–66.

50. Didymus, *Holy Spirit*, par. 161–63, 193.

51. Barth, CD II/1, 660.

52. Gregory of Nyssa, *On the Holy Trinity*, NPNF 2/5, 328.

53. Since this is not a systematic theology (brief or otherwise), I leave the details of how this takes place aside for the moment, but I assume an incarnational soteriology.

54. Didymus, *Holy Spirit*, par. 264, 224.

55. Nyssa, *Against Eunomius*, NPNF 2/5, book II, 121, emphasis added.

56. This remains true irrespective of whether obedience is itself salvific. The kind of obedience entailed in becoming a follower of Christ is different from any other obedience, and it comes to an end in any case. A good example of such obedience in intra-human relations may be something like this: A person, afflicted by the limitations imposed by structural and personal sin (internalized self-doubt and defensiveness in response to previous experiences of derogation), encounters someone above her in a functional hierarchy—a teacher, perhaps—who tells her, "You can do this—I believe in you." The student may not believe the teacher, but may nonetheless seek to make true what the teacher sees in her, for love of the teacher. (There are clear disanalogies as well—I am certainly *not* suggesting that humans overcome sin by their own power, simply through the invitation of Christ. To the contrary, he does for us all that we cannot do for ourselves.)

57. Nazianzus, "Third Theological Oration," in *Christology of the Later Fathers*, ed. Edward R. Hardy (Louisville, KY: Westminster John Knox, 2006 [1954]), 174–75.

58. Athanasius, *Letters to Serapion on the Holy Spirit*, in *Works on the Spirit*, 114–15, first emphasis added.

59. Kathryn Tanner, *Jesus, Humanity and the Trinity: A Brief Systematic Theology* (Minneapolis, MN: Fortress Press, 2001), 9.

60. Volf, " 'The Trinity is Our Social Program'," 413.

61. Ibid., 415.

62. Didymus, *Holy Spirit*, par. 196, 203.

63. Kathryn Tanner emphasizes this in "Gender," in *The Oxford Handbook on Anglican Studies*, ed. Mark Chapman, Ian Douglas, Martyn Percy, and Sathi Clarke (Oxford: Oxford University Press, forthcoming).

64. That is not to say that patristic authors saw this as the only function of Father-Son language; clearly, it was authorized by its presence in the history of the Son as well as by gender hierarchies.

65. Gregory of Nyssa, "Letter 38," previously attributed to Basil of Caesarea, in Philip Schaff, ed., *Basil: Letters and Select Works*, in *Nicene and Post-Nicene Fathers*, second series, vol. 8, (Peabody, MA: Hendrickson, 2012), 139. Coakley considers the image clear evidence of hierarchal trinitarian order (*God, Sexuality and the Self: An Essay 'On the Trinity'* [Cambridge: Cambridge University Press, 2013], 138–39), but I differ from her interpretation.
66. Barth, CD II/1, 313. I do not fully agree with Barth's characterization of essential finite existence in the last lines, but arguably, sinful human beings do sometimes seek to erect impassable barriers against each other.
67. Barth, CD II/1, 646.
68. Hans Urs von Balthasar, *Theo-Drama: Theological Dramatic Theory*, vol. 1: *Prologomena*, trans. Graham Harrison (San Francisco, CA: Ignatius, 1988), 35.
69. Barth, II/1, 650–51.
70. Wolfhart Pannenberg, *Systematic Theology*, vol. 2, trans. Geoffrey W. Bromiley (Grand Rapids, MI: Eerdmans, 1992), 398.
71. See also Miroslav Volf, "Enter into Joy! Sin, Death and the Life of the World to Come," in John Polkinghorne and Michael Welker, eds., *The End of the World and the Ends of God: Science and Theology on Eschatology* (Harrisburg, PA: Trinity Press International, 2000), 270–78, where he argues that justification or sanctification of the "lived life" is insufficient; what is needed is something like awakening to new life in a transformed time and a transformed space.
72. Marilyn McCord Adams, *Some Later Medieval Theories of the Eucharist: Thomas Aquinas, Giles of Rome, Duns Scotus, and William Ockham* (Oxford: Oxford University Press, 2010), 264.
73. Ibid., 86–87.
74. See Adams, *Christ and Horrors*, 306–07.
75. As Adams puts it, this is how Franciscus Mayronis "could almost mock impanation for having the vices of its virtues" since the implication is that "Christ's Body was still [in its bread nature] corruptible after the resurrection." *Later Medieval Theories*, 265.
76. Caroline Walker Bynum, *Fragmentation and Redemption: Essays on Gender and the Human Body in Medieval Religion* (New York: Zone Books, 1991), 142.
77. The latter is sealed in the resurrection but is a feature of Jesus' trajectory throughout his concrete encounters with others.
78. On a similar note, see Pannenberg, ST1, 359: "Materially, however, the specific form of the existence of God as Father, Son, and Spirit is identical with the unlimited field of God's nonthematic presence in his creation."
79. Ángel F. Méndez-Montoya, OP, *The Theology of Food: Eating and the Eucharist* (Malden, MA: Wiley-Blackwell, 2012 [2009]), 68. See his "Eucharistic Imagination: A Queer Body-Politics," *Modern Theology* 30, no. 2 (April 2014): 326–39, for an expansion of the argument in the direction of a queer eucharistic body.
80. Méndez-Montoya, *Theology of Food*, 72.
81. Ibid., 113.
82. Ibid., 145–47.
83. Ibid., 151.
84. Ibid., 160.
85. Kallistos Ware, *The Orthodox Way*, rev. ed. (Crestwood, NY: St. Vladimir's Seminary Press, 1995), 23. The saying is actually from the Gospel of Thomas (unattributed by Ware); Ware uses it to indicate the theophanous nature of the world.

# BIBLIOGRAPHY

Adams, Marilyn McCord. *Christ and Horrors: The Coherence of Christology*. Cambridge: Cambridge University Press, 2006.

———. *Some Later Medieval Theories of the Eucharist: Thomas Aquinas, Giles of Rome, Duns Scotus, and William Ockham*. Oxford: Oxford University Press, 2010.

Anselm. "On the Procession of the Spirit." Trans. Richard Regan. In *Anselm of Canterbury: The Major Works*, ed. Brian Davies and G. R. Evans, 390–434. Oxford: Oxford University Press, 1998.

Aquinas, Thomas. *Summa Theologica*. Trans. Fathers of the English Dominican Province. Westminster: Christian Classics, 1948.

Athanasius., "Letters to Serapion on the Holy Spirit." In *Works on the Spirit: Athanasius and Didymus*, ed. John Behr, trans. Mark DelCogliano, Andrew Radde-Gallwitz, and Lewis Ayres, 51–137. Crestwood, NY: St. Vladimir's Seminary Press, 2011.

Augustine, *The Trinity*. Ed. John E Rotelle. Trans. Edmund Hill. New York: New City Press, 1991.

Balthasar, Hans Urs von. *Theo-Drama: Theological Dramatic Theory*, vol. 1: *Prolegomena*. Trans. Graham Harrison. San Francisco: Ignatius, 1988.

Barth, Karl. *Church Dogmatics*. Vol. 1, pt. 1, *The Doctrine of the Word of God*. Ed. G. W. Bromiley and T. F. Torrance. Trans. G. W. Bromiley. London: T&T Clark, 2004.

———. *Church Dogmatics*. Vol. 2, pt. 1, *The Doctrine of the Word of God*. Ed. G. W. Bromiley and T. F. Torrance. Trans. G. W. Bromiley. London: T&T Clark, 2004.

Basil of Caesarea. "On the Spirit." In *Nicene and Post-Nicene Fathers*. Second Series. Vol. 8, *Basil: Letters and Select Works*, ed. Philip Schaff and Henry Wace, 1–50. Peabody, MA: Hendrickson, 2012.

Bynum, Caroline Walker. *Fragmentation and Redemption: Essays on Gender and the Human Body in Medieval Religion*. New York: Zone Books, 1991.

Coakley, Sarah. *God, Sexuality and the Self: An Essay 'On the Trinity.'* Cambridge: Cambridge University Press, 2013.

Didymus the Blind. *On the Holy Spirit*. In *Works on the Spirit: Athanasius and Didymus*, ed. John Behr, trans. Mark DelCogliano, Andrew Radde-Gallwitz, and Lewis Ayres, 143–227. Crestwood, NY: St. Vladimir's Seminary Press, 2011.

Ellis, Brannon. *Calvin, Classical Trinitarianism, and the Aseity of the Son*. Oxford: Oxford University Press, 2012.

Gunton, Colin. *Father, Son and Holy Spirit: Essays Toward a Fully Trinitarian Theology*. London: T&T Clark, 2003.

Gregory of Nazianzus. *The Theological Orations*. In *Christology of the Later Fathers*, ed. Edward R. Hardy, 128–214. Louisville: Westminster John Knox, 2006.

Gregory of Nyssa. *Against Eunomius*. In *Nicene and Post-Nicene Fathers*. Second Series. Vol. 5, *Gregory of Nyssa: Dogmatic Treatises, Etc.*, ed. Philip Schaff and Henry Wace, 33–248. Peabody, MA: Hendrickson, 2012.

———. "Letter 38." Previously attributed to Basil of Caesarea. In *Nicene and Post-Nicene Fathers*. Second Series. Vol. 8, *Basil: Letters and Select Works*, ed. Philip Schaff and Henry Wace, 137–41. Peabody, MA: Hendrickson, 2012.

———. "On the Holy Trinity, and of the Godhead of the Holy Spirit." In *Nicene and Post-Nicene Fathers*. Second Series. Vol. 5, *Gregory of Nyssa: Dogmatic Treatises, Etc.*, ed. Philip Schaff and Henry Wace, 326–30. Peabody, MA: Hendrickson, 2012c.

Helm, Paul. "Of God, and of the Holy Trinity: A Response to Dr. Beckwith." *Churchman* (2004): 350–57.

Hilary of Poitiers. "On the Trinity." In *Nicene and Post-Nicene Fathers*. Second Series. Vol. 9, *Hilary of Poitiers, John of Damascus*, ed.Philip Schaff and Henry Wace, 40–233. Peabody, MA: Hendrickson, 2012.

Hofstadter, Douglas, and Emmanuel Sander. *Surfaces and Essences: Analogy as the Fuel and Fire of Thinking*. New York: Basic Books, 2013.

Kilby, Karen. "Aquinas, the Trinity and the Limits of Understanding." *International Journal of Systematic Theology* 7, no. 4 (2005): 414–27.

———. "Is an Apophatic Trinitarianism Possible?" *International Journal of Systematic Theology* 12, no. 1 (January 2010): 65–77.

Luther, Martin. *Lectures on Genesis 1–5. Luther's Works*, vol. 1, ed. Jaroslav Pelikan and Helmut T. Lehmann, trans. George V. Schick (St. Louis: Concordia, 1958).

———. *Lectures on Galatians 1535: Chapters 1–4. Luther's Works*, vol. 26, ed. and trans. Jaroslav Pelikan. St. Louis: Concordia, 1963.

Malcolm, Lois. "On Not Three Male Gods: Retrieving Wisdom in Trinitarian Discourse." *Dialog* 49, no. 3 (September 2010): 238–47.

Méndez-Montoya, Angel F. "Eucharistic Imagination: A Queer Body-Politics." *Modern Theology* 30, no. 2 (April 2014): 326–39.

———. *The Theology of Food: Eating and the Eucharist*. Malden, MA: Wiley-Blackwell, 2012.

Moltmann, Jürgen. *The Trinity and the Kingdom: The Doctrine of God*. Trans. Margaret Kohl. Minneapolis: Fortress Press, 1993.

Pannenberg, Wolfhart. *Systematic Theology*, vol. 1. Trans. Geoffrey W. Bromiley. Grand Rapids: Eerdmans, 1991.

———. *Systematic Theology*, vol. 2. Trans. Geoffrey W. Bromiley. Grand Rapids: Eerdmans, 1992.

Rivera, Mayra. "Glory: The First Passion of Theology?" In *Polydoxy: Theology of Multiplicity and Relation*, ed. Catherine Keller and Laurel C. Schneider, 167–85. London: Routledge, 2011.

Slotemaker, John T. "Calvin's Trinitarian Theology in the 1536 *Institutes*: The Distinction of Persons as a Key to His Theological Sources." In *Philosophy and Theology in the Long Middle Ages: A Tribute to Stephen F. Brown*, ed. Kent Emery Jr., Russel L. Friedman, and Andreas Speer, 781–808. Leiden: Brill, 2011.

Tanner, Kathryn. "Gender." In *The Oxford Handbook on Anglican Studies*, ed. Mark Chapman, Ian Douglas, Martyn Percy, and Sathi Clarke. Oxford: Oxford University Press, forthcoming.

———. "In the Image of the Invisible." In *Apophatic Bodies: Negative Theology, Incarnation, and Relationality*, ed. Chris Boesel and Catherine Keller, 127–34. New York: Fordham University Press, 2010.

———. *Jesus, Humanity and the Trinity: A Brief Systematic Theology*. Minneapolis: Fortress Press, 2001.

Thomas, Günter. "Resurrection to New Life." In *Resurrection: Theological and Scientific Assessments*, ed. Ted Peters, Robert John Russell, and Michael Welker, 255–76. Grand Rapids: Eerdmans, 2002.

Volf, Miroslav. *After Our Likeness: The Church as the Image of the Trinity*. Grand Rapids: Eerdmans, 1998.

———. "Enter into Joy! Sin, Death, and the Life of the World to Come." In *The End of the World and the Ends of God: Science and Theology on Eschatology*, ed. John Polkinghorne and Michael Welker, 256–78. Harrisburg: Trinity Press International, 2000.

———. " 'The Trinity is Our Social Program': The Doctrine of the Trinity and the Shape of Social Engagement." *Modern Theology* 14 (1998): 403–423.

Ware, Kallistos. *The Orthodox Way*. Rev. ed. Crestwood, NY: St. Vladimir's Seminary Press, 1995.

# 7    Apocalyptic Ecclesiology
## Temporality, Futurity, and the Reproduction of God's Body

Bisexuality disconfirms in the future what the present verifies.[1]

In honor of Mother's Day, 2011, the organization *Believe Out Loud*—slogan: "a million Christians for LGBT equality"—released an ad showing a white-appearing female couple with a blond-haired, blue-eyed child entering a church, hesitant about their welcome. As they walk down the aisle toward the front of the church, the camera lingers on the wide-eyed child as he registers the surprise, whispers, and pointing that ensue. The majority of the congregation appears white; the camera moves past one black-appearing male and what looks to be an Asian woman placing her hymnal next to her to prevent the family from taking a seat. When they get to the front of the church, however, they are met by a robed, older white male pastor saying in an authoritative voice, "Welcome, *everyone.*"[2] In response, a woman (apparently the same Asian woman) shifts to the side so that the family may sit.

The future suggested for lesbian and by implication, gay, bisexual, and transgendered Christians in this ad is the opening up, without significant transformation and via authoritative discourse, of an already constituted church space so as to include them.[3] Notwithstanding the initially unsettled reactions of the "normal" people in the pews, God's message of love reaches out even to nuclear families in which parents are of the same sex! Self-satisfied smugness regarding this congregation's distinctiveness from other Christian churches pervades the ad as it focuses first on the tentative entrance of the lesbian couple and then on their surprise and joy when met with welcome rather than hostility. Parenthood, or more specifically motherhood, can be included, and the camera's repeated lingering on the blond, white, male child triggers the cultural imperative to view an innocent white child sympathetically. The church constitutes itself as a site of welcome through the speech of its authorized representative, who—by way of their child—recognizes the humanity, the intelligibility, of a lesbian couple.

This ad campaign dramatizes the characteristic shape of mainline Christian discourses around homosexuality, while also touching on issues now at the forefront of queer political struggles around what Jasbir Puar terms "homonationalism,"[4] as expressed currently in the ascendency of marriage equality as the political focus for gay and lesbian activism in the United States. Perhaps most visibly in relation to marriage equality, but also in much-discussed quasi-political acts like Dan Savage's *It Gets Better* campaign, queer theory, like queer politics, finds itself riven between seemingly incompatible visions of political and social futures. On the one hand, the mainstreaming and bourgeoisification of many gay, lesbian, and bisexual lives,[5] along with the sociopolitical effectiveness of rights-based arguments in the United States, have made marriage equality seem a significant and achievable political goal: rights-based arguments are ready to hand; the issue at stake is solvable by relatively simple legal means, as the recent victory on DOMA suggests; and increasing support among young people for marriage equality implies ongoing triumph. Supporting marriage equality has, for these reasons, become a low-cost way of being on the right side of history's arc toward justice, in Martin Luther King Jr.'s famous words.

On the other hand, many other challenges affecting queer persons and queer communities—particularly in their intersection with poverty, race, immigration, gender identity, the legal system, and disability—seem much less tractable.[6] Dan Savage's *It Gets Better* campaign, launched in response to a purported epidemic of suicides due to homophobic bullying, mostly avoids attention to structural and political changes to better the lives of queer people.[7] Time—construed as the future promise of adulthood, in which one might move perhaps to some queer urban utopia—seems almost by itself to make things better. "It gets better" is a passive construction basing hope on little more than the neutrality of time passing and the expected arrival of the future. The present inability to envision a livable life can be survived, endured, via the imaginary projection of oneself into a promised future where suffering will cease and one will be integrated into a community and granted recognition.[8]

In response, many queer theorists wonder whether the critical and radical edges of queer theory and queer activism haven't been blunted here by a neoliberal focus on individual choice and self-realization, one that makes large-scale responses to social challenges seem inconceivable or even undesirable and opts instead for the expansion of market logics into all areas of life. The histories of failure and loss that once structured queer lives in the age of AIDS and before can be left behind now that the promise of a viable life has been extended to queers.[9] Critics of these developments ask how a radical or utopian edge is to be maintained in a world that both demands transformation yet seems to exclude meaningful change (whether because of political constraints, or the impossibility of recognition, and therefore integration, of all persons in their in-any-case always-shifting differences from one another). Must hope for a better future mean that all persons will live in keeping with their positive identities within an integrated social whole? Or does an ethical relation to the future mean, instead, acceptance of limitation, fragility, loss, and death, and along with it, valuation of a symbolic order that admits fragmentation, incoherence, and negativity? Queer politics have transformed from ACT-UP to the end of DADT and DOMA, and the Supreme Court ruling on marriage equality. Yet these gains on the fronts of marriage and death simply shift the burden of being nonintegrated to racial, national, and religious others, the poor, and those indecent queers who seek neither reproduction nor integration.[10]

Similar disagreements structure theological debates over the status of same-sex relations. Mainline churches' response to homosexuality usually focuses on issues of inclusion of the other, a logic that extends rather than challenges normative distributions of power and recognition: the justice of sanctioning marriage and ordination for gays and lesbians. Theologically, this dominant discourse of inclusion is often based in sloganeering about God's love for everyone, where an implicit theology of creation (the Christian version of "born this way") grounds positive affirmation of the identity of gay, lesbian, bisexual, and transgender persons. Willed extension to others of a privilege already enjoyed oneself leaves ethics in the hands of the powerful. When validation of the family in religious (as in "secular") contexts combines with a focus on committed and monogamous same-sex relationships and refusal of radically alternative social imaginaries, Christian approaches to same-sex relations are nothing more than an expansion of what already exists to include gays and lesbians, who turn out to be no different from anyone else. This approach denies a real reconfiguration of structures of power and exclusion. The New Testament suggests, to the contrary, not that the last will have what the first have once the first decide to include them but that the *mighty will be cast down from their thrones* and *the rich will go away empty*. The logic of the kingdom in many of Jesus' parables, and in early church debates over Gentile inclusion, is less about who I (the presumptive insider) get to include than about the dangers I run in seeking to weed out others (Gentiles, those of lesser faith, the tares, the least of these) from "my" righteous, holy community, thereby using my own presumed piety as a weapon against them.

The previous chapter ended with a question. After criticizing the way distortive models of relationship (and their gendered implications) are imported into the trinity, I developed an alternative reading of the biblical economy that justified a different constitution of the trinity. We saw that the trinity acts in the world to reconfigure human community and so transform, without abolishing, human finitude. This reconfiguration corrects distortions introduced into finitude by sin, in which finitude's particularity becomes threatening or rapacious because it is viewed as a "this-or-that" against an empty horizon. Such a reconfiguration also transforms particularity as enjoyment of a specific other into copresence and intensification. A priority of resurrection over cross resulted from my emphasis on the for-us character of divine action, and from my stress on the ultimate end of the friendship God extends to us: enjoyment of God and each other.

The optimism of all this required me to end on a note of ambiguity and uncertainty. Too many theologies of the eucharist suggest a liturgical magic that history emphatically contradicts: perform eucharist rightly and community will be right, too. Such an unlimited positive trajectory toward community stands in tension with our experience of the world. We look around and see neither God nor unrestricted community, except in the sort of imaginative representation of the *Believe Out Loud* ad—a community that simply expands the normative order without shifting its registers of value. Taking these tensions between reality and hope seriously requires us to think about the implications of the ascension of Christ with more care, for the kingdom has not yet been realized in its fullness.

In order to do that, I develop in this chapter two ideal ecclesial types and set them against each other. Contrary to the tendency in recent ecclesiological discussion to focus on the church as God's living body and a sign-symbol of fidelity to God's order, I interpret the church as a sign of judgment, transformation, and the nonpossessible body of God. An ecclesiology of nonreproduction emerges out my conversation with queer critiques of imagined wholeness, temporal extensibility, and the reproduction of the self-same. Along the way, I face the obvious criticism that the optimistic orientation of the previous chapter ought to engender: that prioritizing resurrection and material transformation is world-denying. In answer, I seek apocalyptic transformation rather than eschatological fulfillment.

> Eschatology would then be the science of postponement, because in theology, the filial always looks at the past in search of traditions of authority. However, there is no eschatology, no possible reflection on the alternative project of the Kingdom of God, unless the capitalist dictum 'there is no alternative' is also overthrown. That, however, would also require a process of disaffected investment in what we have grown to believe without questioning. . . . Can a second coming of theology, this time a Queer one, the most unfilial of all theologies, facilitate the final coming out of God?[11]

## ECCLESIOLOGY, REPRODUCTION, AND CHRIST'S PRESENT BODY

The ascension entails the disappearance of Christ's resurrected body from sight, the loss of its presence.[12] That lost body is transmuted into community at Pentecost when the Spirit arrives; but without the resurrection appearances before the ascension, there would have been no gathering at which the Spirit could arrive and constitute the church. The Spirit returns Christ's disappeared body to the church as the one by whose power the eucharist becomes, not just the sign but the *res* of his body and blood. After the formation of the church (theologically, not historically, speaking), there are two ultimate sites of investment and identification in relation to Christ's disappeared body: the church itself and the eucharist as the body of Christ. Being or having the body of Christ, and eating it, are thus the relations to the body of Christ that found ecclesiological investigation. Both are made possible by the Spirit, who mediates Christ's presence and is the authoritative guide for interpretation of his authoritative word.

The first form of ecclesiological response to the loss of Christ's body insists that his body is handed over to the church, which both becomes and mediates that body to its members. This body includes myriad bodies that are in some way like the body that ascended into heaven but have not yet been in the grave, except in baptism. These forms of the Christic body are *presences* of this body under signs of its *absence*.[13] The presence of the body is invoked, identified, and claimed under and in its absence—indeed, such invocation and naming is made possible by that absence—yet that absence is denied as absence.[14] This mode of response refuses to consider the ascended body lost; instead, it opts for a heightened assertion of presence through the Spirit's orientation to Christ. Thus the content of the Spirit's action in the world is the identification and mediation of Christ's presence in and to his authorized representatives. This presence is predicated of the church and of its distribution and eating of the bread.

In the eucharist, the mediation of Christ's body takes place through word-signs uttered by Christ's authorized representatives (priests or pastors), those who have received and inherited the deposit of faith legitimately and who are thus enabled to speak the authoritative word: "*This* is my body." The fidelity of these authorized representatives is characteristically figured as submission to a logic of faith that they themselves can do nothing to change or affect; they receive it unaltered. The content of faith and its authoritative lineage, expressed in terms of fidelity to the creeds and traditions of the fathers and their authorized interpreters, is handed down from ecclesial father to ecclesial son through faithful nonsexual reproduction.[15] To become an ecclesial son means to submit to an ecclesial father, and to the fathers of the church, and to become adapted and adopted into a proper posture of faith.[16] This is reproduction's repetition through orders of authoritative inheritance.[17] In sexed reproduction, change, distance, and interval are always present. But these forms of adoptive reproduction achieve the perfection of repetition of the self-same as the condition of fidelity. As a condition of inclusion, baptized, catechized members affirm both their own reproductive sonship and that of faith's legitimate, paternal authorities.[18]

This emphasis on authority and inheritance also requires that the faithfulness of the church make itself visible in two distinct but interrelated modes of reproduction. This first type of nonbiological reproduction, representing the church's status as Christ's present, visible body, is the preservation and maintenance of the hedges that enclose the virginity of the church and its doctrines, in analogy to medieval representations of the *hortus conclusus*, Mary sitting in or near a walled-off garden.[19] Said otherwise, nonbiological reproduction means propagation of the logic of faith, which must be handed on unchanged from generation to generation—think here of Gregory of Nyssa's insistence in *On Virginity* that virginity serves as the only protection against the corruption that characterizes marital and parental relations, which, if all goes well, end in loss and the death of the beloved other.[20] So only a virginal, nonbiological form of reproduction can be used to propagate the church across time.

The second mode of reproduction emphasizes the church's responsibility to *be* the body of Christ and to order its own life so as to *distribute* the body of Christ to and in the lives of its members. Here, a relation between the proper reproduction of faith and its forms, the propriety of the distribution of Christ's body, and the propriety of the lives of Christians becomes apparent. Against the disorder of the world around, and against indecency, idolatry, and depravity, the order of the church orders reproduction.[21] To gain access to the body of Christ, those who intend to eat it must order their own lives and abjure the impropriety and disorder of alternative, ecclesially unsanctioned forms of reproduction. In so ordering their lives, the members of the body of Christ indicate their separation from those outside that body; infidelity to these reproductive orders is punished by excommunication from the community of the faithful. The right ruling of marriage is the first and foremost form of this ordering, since it symbolizes the faithfulness that Christ shows to his only bride, the church, through the exclusivity of nuptial love between man and woman. (This basic theological logic shifts only slightly when marriage is expanded to include a relation between man and man.) Second, the order and decency of Christic bodied reproduction appears in the fidelity that the celibate priest shows to the body of Christ, for the priest gains access to it, becomes identical with it, and is penetrated by it precisely as he refuses to touch or penetrate other bodies. Both these modes of reproduction imply a relation to time.

The temporal logic of both these forms moves unchanged from past to future as the church makes itself or finds itself made into the body of Christ. These reproductions are perfect and exclude difference; an imperfect reproduction would mean infidelity and loss of the body whose presence is *known* because it is not submitted to the question of its presence. To ask about real presence, or to suggest that the body of Christ is elsewhere, means losing access to the *res* of Christ's body. Instead, the decency of one's bodied relations of touching—or not—expresses the spiritual virginity that makes the personal body an appropriate vessel for the reception of Christ's body. The potential instability across time introduced by sexual reproduction is warded off by the regulation of reproductive propriety, while the potential instability across time introduced by the unsubstitutability and unrepeatability of the founding events of Christianity is warded off by the establishment of authoritative lines of inheritance that ensure that faith's logic is handed on unchanged through participation in the once-for-all handing over of Christ's authority to his authorized *Stellvertreter*. Improper bodied relations skew the reproductions across time that are the sites of time's ascent into eternity. Failure to identify authoritative lines of inheritance, given the motility of history's transformations, leave the body of Christ without the security of its own future. Thus the presence of the body happens under the sign of other absences, and in denial of absence itself through repudiation of the question of presence. This makes up an ecclesiology of reproduction.

## RESURRECTION'S MEMORY

Ecclesiologies of reproduction depend on resurrection to ground two forms of continuity: the continuity of the risen Christ with the Jesus the disciples knew and the continuity of the church and its authority across history's vicissitudes. These forms of continuity repeat, homologously, the forms of reproduction of the self-same that structure reproduction ecclesially. The continuity of the church, grounded in resurrection, expands the logic of resurrection's continuity across death to the church's self-identity across change and transformation. The continuity of the risen Christ with Jesus founds his deputizing of Peter, while the Spirit's retrospective confirmation at Pentecost ensures the communicability and expansiveness of Peter's participation in the power of the Lord. The first form of continuity might also be expressed by Jesus' pure obedience to his mission received from the Father, whatever the cost (Balthasar), for instance, or in the Father's vindication of Jesus' claims to his authority in the resurrection (Pannenberg). In the resurrection, the vindication or affirmation of the crucified expresses his victory over the forces of sin, evil, and death that threatened him. This affirmative vindication is then transmuted into the body of the church, which receives its authority through the reliability of witnesses (personal testimony, the Spirit's moving, conciliar authority, and so on) whose authority depends on the referral to (and so participation in, by deferral) an authority not their own. Again: Jesus' authority is established by his deferral to the authority of the Father, which constitutes his participation in the authority of the Father; the church's authority is established by its deferral to (and so participation in) the authority of the witnesses; the witnesses' authority is established by their deferral to (and so participation in) the authority of Jesus, and so on. Ultimately, deferral (yielding, obedience, fidelity) is the only way to receive a full share in the authority of God.[22] The church participates in the power of the resurrection (by deferring to it) across history's dangers and deaths, and in so doing it remains faithful both to the vindicated power that establishes it and to its own status as the mediator of this vindicated power to the world: the city beautiful and terrible as an army with banners. The bountiful plenitude of Christ's body distributed by the church grants participation in Christ's death to every faithful Christian, and the distributional availability of that body is conditioned on and by resurrection's continuities.

In part for these reasons, Marcella Althaus-Reid argues that the Christian imaginary of resurrection can serve as a "repetition or vicious circle of sexual ideologies." This form of resurrection is an "idealist" event that "reif[ies] an order of things by which being 'risen' is made exemplary." Resurrection thus "fix[es] geographical and biological spaces of destiny" so that "people respond to the call to purity by abnormally resurrecting the parody of heterosexualism."[23] So the 144,000 untouched (by women) male virgins of Revelation 14 sing a triumphant, secret new song, while the wicked fornicators of the earth receive no respite from the torment that enfolds but does not consume them. The purity of the church is materialized in decent Christian subjects who are promised eventual victory over all that threatens them in this life.

Althaus-Reid offers a counter thought-experiment in which women, writing theology "in a patriarchal fashion" while "objectifying men's bodies," might have developed a theology of the body "from the single question about Jesus' elusive penis, that sexual promise never (narratively) fulfilled."[24] Instead, the Gospel writers "wrote from the perspective of purity and resurrection," which leaves "a gigantic communal quasi-memory of Jesus' malehood . . . built upon a trace, a footprint or outline which has the characteristic of being present in the text only by denoting an absence or otherness."[25] The transcendental phallus promises "direct translation of certain relationships between men, God and women in the New Testament in our lives,"[26] for its idealism ignores material particularity and nonidentity.[27] Having rethought the trinity beyond sonship and sexual difference, we may nonetheless find phallicism in resurrection's promise of authority through disavowal.

In his wonderful book *Ecce Homo*, Kent Brintnall mounts a powerful assault on Christian narratives of resurrection, arguing that the resurrection instantiates a masculine plenitude that underwrites the illusion that there are subjects not subjected to death, subjects who are whole and whose projects are not subjected to the futility endemic to all human endeavor. Brintnall's critique of Christian conceptions of resurrection belongs in part to the tradition of ideology critique, an inheritance from the masters of suspicion that has generated much salutary (self-) critique of Christian strategies for claiming authority. Brintnall develops a psychoanalytic account of Christianity's strategies of deferral in relation to the resurrection of Jesus, the (male and masculine) redeemer who (masochistically?) subjects himself to the Father, apparently "losing" himself briefly in a form of quasi-sacrifice that never touches his divinity, only to be reinstalled at the right hand of the Father as the judge of all creation (a few hours of agony, a couple days of death, for a reward of that size?).[28] In relation to the Son of the Father, all subjects are judged inadequate—they are neither as triumphantly divine nor as self-sacrificially abased as he was.

Like many psychoanalytically-inflected projects, Brintnall's work takes the slippage among Father and fathers, Son, man and men, for granted.[29]

This follows in part from an appropriately strong sense of the theological maleness of Jesus in Christianity. Brintnall does not, however, investigate the possibility of speaking otherwise about God than about humans, assuming (in line with much of Christian history) that certain ways of speaking about God in practice stabilize distinctions among human persons.[30] For Brintnall, any attribution to God of plenitude, transcendence as well as immanence, or difference neither equivocal nor univocal stabilizes (masculine) plenitude as the ideal for human persons. The result is that human beings are sorted into categories, determined by how close they (appear to) approach that ideal, thereby denying human solidarity based on shared vulnerability. In other words, the hope of identity's wholeness refuses solidarity between differently subjected subjects, even as this hope generates inequitable distribution of access to fantasmatic power since representations of wholeness connect plenitude to invulnerable masculinity.[31] Brintnall also emphasizes the trinitarian form of this plenitudinous power realized by deferral: "What is resurrection if not a promise that the losses of this life will someday be recompensed? And who, in the Christian imaginary, offers such a promise? The Father, through the Son."[32]

As an alternative, Brintnall promotes an ethic based on fragmentation, laceration, and the vulnerability of all persons to death and loss. Brintnall argues that recognition of shared vulnerability can redistribute the sociopolitical field away from contestations over who has access to privilege, in which the contrast between subjects who have fantasmatic access to self-identity and invulnerability and those who embody the deferred denial of vulnerability and fragmentation supports the illusion of self-possession by the former. Rather than extending humanization to new subjects, which denies the failure and incompleteness of all human lives and social orders, we must accept the loss and (self-)shattering that permits solidarity across difference. Christian representations of crucifixion play a crucial role here because they show the "male-body-in-pain," male vulnerability, thus (potentially) refusing phallic power and its display. Christian representations of resurrection, on the other hand, play an equally significant role in the logic Brintnall's project seeks to overcome, since they leave behind the male-body-in-pain and exalt the whole (albeit eternally wounded), unbroken, and triumphant body of the resurrected Christ.[33]

The "resurrected" action hero that Brintnall discusses comes back continuous with who he was, but better than ever and free from self-doubt. The action hero is still engaged in the same project(s) as before "death," which appears as a mere interruption, an apparent defeat easily overcome by triumphal self-assertion.[34] The "resurrected" one is an improved version of the same, and the hero's strength and inability to give up are rewarded with a transformed return. Brintnall follows Georges Bataille's understanding of salvation as a project of work, which projects the subject into the future and stabilizes it.[35] Work's productive requirements depend on continuity between present and future, a continuity that institutes anxiety because "the future is uncertain."[36] Resurrection as a project and function of salvation allows subjects to identify with their "future" selves in a way that denies the reality of loss and lack in human existence.[37] Brintnall argues that resurrection thus secures the ideal(ization) of the invulnerable, plenitudinous subject, the fantasmatic masculine subject, whose identification with the phallus may be achieved either triumphantly or masochistically.[38] Brintnall's critique of the redemptive logic of Christianity provides a bracing challenge for Christian theologies of the resurrection.

But a different understanding of resurrection, entailing representational discontinuity and apophasis, ambiguity, and epistemic frangibility, can, I suggest, recenter Christianity around a spectral vision of redemption that denies neither fragmentation nor futility, while recognizing the surprising goods of existence amid fragility and loss. By considering only the crucifixion as inexplicable, meaning-shattering, and necessarily multifarious, Brintnall locks resurrection down as a fixed site of meaning rather than allowing it its own complexity.[39] He assumes thereby that the resurrection can function *only* as a representation of hoped-for and unambiguous wholeness. But resurrection is not such an uncomplicated site of representation, and the identity of the resurrected one can be understood as an intensification without the overly defined boundaries that install plenitudinous self-identity.[40]

The ambiguity of resurrection is especially apparent in the distance between two truths of ecclesial existence: On the one hand, church is constituted by a chain of memory and proclamation going back to the first witnesses of the empty tomb. On the other hand, the church has no direct access to Christ's body, for Christ is not only resurrected; he is also ascended. Resurrection then *disallows* the simple extrapolation of the whole-healed subject and its projects into the future. Resurrection's representational register requires apophasis and disidentification rather than identification. Resurrection need not then *necessarily* serve as a site of maintenance of Christian phallic power. Brintnall's critique applies primarily to what I would consider inadequate representations of the resurrection, representations that depend too heavily on continuity with pre-resurrection existence, self-subsistence (if contrasted with dependence), and the maintenance of identity across death's shattering. But resurrection installs two different kinds of boundary markers: one in relation to the risen Christ and the experience of the absence of his ascended body from the world; the other in the self's hope of resurrection as it is appropriated for and by the "I." Resurrection hope is hope for the return of Christ's absent body, not the securitization of the self and its projects.[41]

This is the effect of *apokalypsis* on identity and representation. The revelation of John, one scholar says, "signifies the end of signification; he symbolizes the end of his own symbols" based on "the piercing gaze of religious criticism cast upon its own work."[42] Numerous traces in the New Testament suggest Jesus, and indeed much of the early church, anticipated an imminent end of the world (although the anticipation of the end should not be confused with living within the time of the end). Paul's injunction "as if not" is very much a program for living toward the apocalypse in both its registers—as the end of history and as the final unveiling of who God is: the lamb that was slain, the one not tempted by violence's apparent power and the concomitant desire for self-assertion either through having or through sacrificing all the power there is or ever could be. "The time is short, so that from now on even those who have wives should be as though they had none, those who weep as though they did not weep, those who rejoice as though they did not rejoice, those who buy as though they did not possess, and those who use this world as though not misusing it. For the form of this world is passing away" (1 Cor. 7:29–31). The ambiguity of these verses destabilizes expectation's relation to time. Expectation cannot be wholly indexed to the world as it is. If the form of *this* world is passing away, resurrection time is not continuous with the order of the now, and future expectation cannot be for either the continuance of the self or the social integration of whole-healed subjects.

## APOCALYPTIC FUTURITY

Developing the potential of apocalyptic in relation to resurrection and sub-jectivation requires rethinking not only the church's relation to the body of Christ but also its relation to time. A (presumably unwilling) ally in this refiguration will be Lee Edelman's influential polemic *No Future: Queer Theory and the Death Drive*,[43] in which he refuses the priority of the future over the present as the horizon for political and ethical action. Instead, he develops a vision of the future of "queer" as ethical inhabitation of society's death drive in the form of the figure of the *sinthom*osexual, who refuses hope for intelligibility, inclusion, and the coincidence of identity and rec-ognition in the social. To come into the social means to give up what can-not be integrated within the social, what cannot be reproduced inside the order of the normal. Such hopes, Edelman suggests, reproduce the self-same across time. Instead, the *sinthom*osexual "looks back, not ahead," in imita-tion of Walter Benjamin's famous angel of history, at the "constant calam-ity," expressed in "the antagonism at the core of the social that reflects the calamity of its self-constitution through the positing of an identity that occasions the storm of history."[44] This is the nonidentity that belongs to any "subject." Identity's positing denies the "void, . . . the particularity of the stubbornly non-identical." Identity's posturing mocks the refusal of its others, the nonidentical, to submit to the responsible requirements of the sociopolitical order's need for its own reproduction.[45]

Edelman argues that queers should take the "side of those *not* 'fighting for the children' " (NF, 3). The structure of political action, which he terms "reproductive futurism," is dominated by the "fantasy" of the figure of the Child to come, the one who is the "fantasmatic beneficiary of every political intervention" (NF, 3). Succumbing to the logic of the Child determines the horizon of political action and political possibility.[46] We act politically for the sake of the/our children, or so we tell ourselves. The Child is invoked as the beneficiary of any political action, and as such the Child institutes a false universality that stands in antagonistic relation to particularity both on social and individual levels:

> the figure of the Child, whatever political program it may serve, whatever particularity of race or sex or ethnicity it may bear, *performs a universalization at the expense of particularity*—at the expense, above all, of the particularity of access to the jouissance that makes all subjects, even those committed to disciplinary norms, sinthomosexuals despite themselves. Female, Asian, Hispanic, Black, disabled, impoverished, or protoqueer, the image of the Child polices the horizon of social potentiality by maintaining the iron-clad equivalence of sociality, futurity, and reproduction.[47]

Edelman coins the term *sinthom*osexual, combining the Lacanian *sinthome* (symptom) with "homosexual" into a term of refusal: refusal of meaning and of the fantasy of self-presence and recognition (NF, 34–35). The *sinthom*osexual stands against the Child, against reproduction, and against the future, and it bears the cost of that refusal in its exclusion from the orbits of meaning that structure the social. The *sinthom*osexual figures the threat of death in an active antagonism that sets itself outside, and against, meaning's stiflingly settled orbit.

Invoking the Child for whom sacrifices must be made, the Child who must be protected and whose well-being must be the central concern of political action, serves as a trump card inside political debate. It seems unthinkable, impossible, to be against the Child, but this unthinkability is itself the force of the determination of the political by a constrained set of requirements and figurations: "If not this, what?" names the rhetorical posture of the invocation of the interests of the Child, and its implication is that to refuse this formulation is to be "inhumane" (NF, 4).[48] To be against the Child is to be against the human; it is to position oneself as the nonhuman, the inhuman. Politics, under these constraints, can only be for the sake of the Child of the future. Inside the political, contestations may take place over which particular intervention is better suited to ensuring the health and happiness of the Child, but the condition of intelligibility is acceding to the Child's figural status as the one for whom all must be made better. For example, in response to conservative claims that same-sex relationships threaten society or Western civilization as a whole, the standard neo-leftist response has been, "Oh no, we gays are parents too, just like you," or, "We only seek the rights that everyone else already enjoys," or even more effectively, "Oh no, I am the child of gay parents, and I have become a responsible and upstanding member of society. Therefore I wish for the recognition of the union that fostered me (the straight and decent child)."[49]

Edelman argues that the needs of the Child trump the needs of existing humans both in the social imaginary and the sociopolitical order. As a result, freedom's possibilities as projected for the figure of the Child constrain, or even negate, the possibilities of freedom for existing persons. Edelman does not make as much as he might have about the issues involved in the distinction between the "image of the Child" and the "lived experiences of any historical children" (NF, 11)—the way such historical children are sacrificed for the benefit of the Child that is to come—but he recognizes that these children must be treated as strictly dissimilar, and his argument pertains to the former. In crude terms, Edelman is not arguing that the needs of adults are sacrificed in order to meet the needs of children; instead, *all* persons—white and black, gay and straight, adults and children—are damaged by the figural invocation of the Child who is to come, the Child who is the figuration of constraint within the sociopolitical order.

In opposition to this logic, which allows queers to gain social recognition at the cost of acceding to what Marcella Althaus-Reid terms a process of "decenting," Edelman argues that queers[50] should knowingly and intentionally inhabit the position of negativity, the threat to the social order represented by the "homosexual's" refusal of reproduction while clinging to pleasure for its own sake. Queers should stand in the place of death and refusal, not for the sake of some social good to be achieved thereby—access to social recognition for those previously refused it, for instance—but rather, as a "radical challenge to the very value of the social itself" (NF, 6). For if the decent queer is able to enter the social order as a productive member of society, that entry is made possible "only by shifting the figural burden of queerness to someone else" (NF, 27).

To accept the terms of the debate—that queer persons should have access to the same rights as all other decent and productive members of society, that queer families need legal protection as families in order to have rights, that the state's power of recognition and regulation is central to sexuality's redemption, and that these are the political imperatives for which we ought to fight as members of or allies to queer communities—is to accede to the "politics of reproduction. For the liberal's view of society, which seems to accord the queer a place, endorses no more than the conservative right's the queerness of resistance to futurism and thus the queerness of the queer" (NF, 27). Two arguments, then: First, if queers, *qua* queer, become decent and receive identitarian recognition, that only shifts the burden of figuring society's death drive onto someone else. Second, to become a decent queer means to accede to a politics of reproduction in which the future takes priority, and in which that future can be nothing other than the self-same. This latter part of Edelman's argument is crucial and requires further consideration.

Edelman wishes to resist "the fantasy . . . of form as such, of an order, an organization, that assures the stability of our identities as subjects and the coherence of the Imaginary totalizations through which those identities appear to us in recognizable form" (NF, 7). In theological terms, this is a fantasy of the church as a site of access to the truth of one's identity in its positive, achieved form in Christ, an identity that provides a stable site for action and recognition and can be decisively distinguished from other, non-Christian identities. In making this move, theologians transform faith into an identity that does just what it apparently refuses: they place the logic of faith on the same level as other identities. Importantly, the position of judgment (distinguishing between the Christian and the other) is then arrogated to the Christian herself, rather than left to the judge to whom she claims faithfulness. Politically, much Christian organization around the figure of the Child (the fetus, in this case) protects the Child over children and over the indecent poor, as well as using the threat queers, predatory gays, and man-less lesbians pose to the Child's innocence as a mobilizing cry for political action. As the vignette that opens this chapter suggests, it is no less dangerous, however, for the Christian to put herself in the position of the one who can recognize the other as other in order to welcome the other to what she already has for herself.

The social maintains the structuring fantasy of nostalgia for a lost plenitude, the fullness and joy to which the subject imagines it once had access or the fullness the forward-projected Child (a fantasmatic image of the self without its histories of doubt and disappointment, its constitutive incompletion) might one day enjoy, when "the subject's alienation would vanish into the seamlessness of identity at the endpoint of the endless chain of signifiers lived as history" (NF, 8).[51] The eschaton (not, of course, Edelman's term) is the point toward which history tends and at which it ends. The end retroactively fulfills and stabilizes all history's incompletions, guaranteeing all its promises and redeeming all its failures.

The essential insight that Edelman offers is that nostalgia and futurity seek and believe in the *same* past-future, the missing component that would stabilize the subject's position in the social through the fantasy of the Child (with whom one identifies), the end aim toward which the subject works in purportedly disinterested fashion. Nostalgia and hope for the future coalesce into a noxious, disavowed narcissism in which I dream of my own goodness via my purported orientation toward the good of the Child. As "I" include and become included into the social order that now expands to allow me, the queer, inside, someone else (other than the now-integrated "queer") will have to serve as the symbolic site of what cannot be integrated, what stands in opposition to the social (or in my reading, the ecclesial). Edelman's argument is thus ethically motivated.

In theological terms, the fantasy is also of the collapse of signifier and signified: the space undergirding the structure of culture's possibilities of thinking the whole and redeeming what appears fragmented[52] (once occupied by the divine, in the wake of whose death Nietzsche recognized that new horizons of becoming would be needed) in the place, or rather, time, "where being and meaning are joined as One" (NF, 10).[53] The Child is "the

prop of the secular theology" that structures collective belonging and interpretation so that redemption in the future is guaranteed by the figure of the
Child (NF, 12–13).[54] Edelman identifies the death drive (symbolized by the
queer, by the heretic, by the impure, and so on) with "the negativity opposed
to every form of social viability" (NF, 9). The destructive principle is not the
death drive itself but "the conservative force that defends the entrenched
positivity of the 'extant.'" A second transformation is needed; the death
drive must range itself *against* this conservative force in the latter's attempt
to "preserv[e] the extant social reality."[55]

Given the penchant of many contemporary theologians to characterize as
nihilists those who do not fall into line with reproductive ecclesiologies or
orthodoxies of various denominations, Edelman's injunction to defend what
such projects reject amounts to a theological provocation. Edelman diagnoses the "secular theology" that promises identity's fullness in order to preserve the social (the church, the world) as it is. Christianity claims a relation
(established in baptism) to the Son of the Father, the identical repetition of
the self-same (the dream of phallicized reproduction and identity's achievement via deferral). Resurrection and eucharist coconstitute the presence
of identity. Subsequently, Christian identity establishes itself in the same
way by faithful repetition of the identitarian designations that demarcate a
proper relation to Christian faith (through affirmation of the divine Father's
specificity of reproduction [origin] in trinitarian logic, or yet more dangerously, efforts to weed out the unfaithful prior to the day of judgment).

Edelman's manifesto rejects the hope of inhabiting our elliptically constituted identities successfully: "we do not intend a new politics, a better
society, a brighter tomorrow, since all of these fantasies reproduce the past,
through displacement, in the form of the future. We choose, instead . . . to
insist that the future stop here" (NF, 31). Unless the future is brought to a
full stop, identity's fantasies of its own (fore)closure and fulfillment extend
outward and forward and ensure that the world remains as it is.

## ECCLESIOLOGY, ABORTION, AND CHRIST'S LOST BODY

If ecclesial reproduction is repetition without a critical difference, refusal of
reproduction can be figured only where reproduction is a possibility. That
which is refused becomes apparent from the perspective of what might otherwise have been brought to birth. Althaus-Reid argues that the Christian
"Holy Family" is predicated on the abortion of women. The Holy Family
is "the primal site of women's disappearance and abortion in Christianity," but it is by no means the only site of such sex-selective abortion.[56]
Throughout the Bible, and in systematic and T-Theology, "theology as a
text is a deathbed where the woman author has never existed, and has been
aborted."[57] "Her" abortion, the fact that "she" "has never existed, and
has been aborted," means not only that the figure of "her" is an idealist

construction, nonrepresentational, and nonexistent in relation to actual women. It also involves the material exclusion of real women from biblical texts and of historical women from positions of symbolic authority in the church. The abortions, "spiritual" in some cases, violent in others, and deadly, too, to which women have been subjected by way of the idealist and idealized figure of the "decent" woman, must be brought to account. The "decent" woman loves and acts inside the rules. She is the site of social reproduction and its stability, and she is the space in which the name is exchanged. *She* has been disappeared (in becoming a place) and has never existed (in her idealist form). Under the banner of sexual difference, "she" is denied, disappeared, and forced into the stifling confines of sexual identity. The nonreproductive value of her difference is denied.

When Edelman suggests that queerness "may well take the form of figuring [social] reality's abortion" (NF, 7), his ethical and apophatic injunction may be connected with the history of female infanticide that Althaus-Reid ascribes to systematic-theological practice in order to delineate a new/old task for Christianity: the abortion of the church, or aspiring to be a church that chooses abortion over reproduction. For the church signifies its own end: There is neither church nor temple in the new Jerusalem, and the Lamb's presence is its light.

None of the transformations of Christ's body we encountered in previous chapters took the apocalyptic orientation of Christianity with any seriousness. Christ not only ascended into heaven; he also promised he would come again. The second coming, with its promise of redemption, transformation, and judgment, changes the church's relation to time. The church must refuse both its own and society's (this is an analytic, not a material, distinction) reproductive urges, for the church properly symbolizes the negation of the stability and viability of the symbolic order.[58] As Christianity reproduces itself, it denies its own constitutive, founding logic: the *imminent* expectation of the advent.[59] To name the founding logic of Christianity in this way moves beyond crucifixion, and even resurrection and ascension, to hope for the return of the lost body in the transformation of the entire cosmos, for creation, too, groans awaiting its redemption.

To live between resurrection and *apokalypsis* has consequences for theological epistemology. Resurrection interrupts the order of death, understood as being's fixity and the inescapability of the subject's subjection. Resurrection does not stand over against death as its alternative or negation (there is no disjunction between identity and shattering), for resurrection contains multitudes and entails the translation of the self and its identity into newly unstable cases and places. These multiplicities of witness and representation challenge theological or epistemological continuity in predication, imagination, and forward projection of the self.[60] Ward rightly emphasizes that Jesus' body has multiple yet interwoven modalities of presence and absence. Such multiplicity of representation is internal to confessional Christology and cannot be driven out without denying the resurrection itself. Resurrection means that death and negativity are figured alongside, yet not in competition with, futurity and flourishing. Yet resurrection also transforms the very nature of such futurity and flourishing.

The challenge to theological epistemology entailed by the difference between what now is and what is to come means that our postures in relation to both our dogmatic work and our understandings of ourselves as churched Christians should be the search for a faithfulness that does not assume transparency with respect to our own motivations, and therefore a faithfulness does not presume its own purity of achievement.[61] We must accept that rather than being transparent to us, our faithfulness escapes our control and so is not even ours; it depends on a relationship to a Jesus whom we fail to recognize. The analysis required to admit as much is better learned from the masters of suspicion than from reproductive forms of Christianity; the various deferrals of one's own temporal authority onto God that we discussed in previous chapters fit only too well with reproductive ecclesiology's filiations and with sin's temptation to pious self-securitization.[62] Reproductive ecclesiologies show exaggerated optimism about the church's ability to monitor its own adherence to the form of God's promised kingdom. Contra the regnant consensus in some theological (or post-secular) circles, the forgetting of the theological origins of secularity does not render the secular nihilistic. Rather, the goodness of the secular has to be seen in limited opposition to the claim of the church on the whole existence of humankind as a result of the church's overreaching with respect to secular power as well as a reflection of Christ's assertion that he has children not of this flock.

In ecclesial relations, and in our celebration of ourselves, typified by the vignette with which this chapter opens, we seek to be left as the good in our (own) goodness,[63] as those mediating the goods we already enjoy to those we identify as others in extending our own ecclesio-social spaces to them. Imagining ourselves as the good, (generously) distributing recognition to those who do not have it, we claim recognition, distribution of grace, election, for ourselves. Protestantism's best impulses, seldom enacted—refusal of one's own goodness and insistence on total depravity—deny just such self-securitization via deferral (in which one insists one's total submission to God entitles one to weed out the wicked from among the good for the sake of faith's purity). Such self-securitization also assumes self-transparency and motivational purity that are illegitimate on theological as well as theoretical grounds. Worse yet, assertion of our own goodness in contradistinction from the unfaithful other may align us with the one who masquerades as an angel of light.[64]

The Bible associates the temptation to identify Christ—to say, he is here, he is there, I know where he is—with infidelity in the last days.[65] In Matthew 13, as we remember from the prelude, Jesus' parable about the wheat and the tares insists that the distinction between the saved and the damned is a matter of God's judgment. In distinguishing between them, one takes up the place of God. The audience for this parable is the faithful disciples themselves, who seek to weed out the unfaithful *within* their own community.

The New Testament identifies the only unforgivable sin with sin against the Holy Spirit, the one who speaks *on our behalf* rather than giving us our own safeWord. The most dangerous position, then, is to assume final determination of fidelity itself. When church bodies split over identitarian designations, they place themselves under judgment and risk everything. To risk everything is to risk refusal of the other in Christ, the one we do not recognize.

The failure, rather than the success, of the church is the means of its symbolic pointing toward the body of Christ that lies outside its walls in whomever the church understands as its others—Matthew 25's story of the least of these and the debates over religious insider and outsider in the early church support this. The church hopes to be given the body, to become it, to be recognized by Christ on the day of judgment, but as Matthew 25's description of the Christ who identifies himself with the least of these implies, Christ's body lies elsewhere in those the church does not know ("Queer holiness . . . is always the holiness of the Other"[66]). The body remains unrecognizable to the church, for even the righteous—the sheep Christ the shepherd recognizes as his own—do not know they served Christ when they served the least of these. This also suggests the failure of theological speech in its identifying function ("not all who call me, 'Lord, Lord'") and even of theological epistemology itself. Not only is one's relation to Christ determined by response to a Christ whom one does not recognize when encountering him, but one does not *know* what one's relation to Christ is until judgment day arrives.[67] Even on that day, recognition of Christ entails memory of one's own failure with respect to him.[68] The truth of theological statements lies, too, in the hope of confirmation or verification by God's judgment.[69] In Matthew 25, Christ says that he himself is the other, the other whom one *identifies* as the other or in whom one does not recognize Christ. Christ becomes the one from whose contamination one attempts to protect oneself in the fervent and death-driven clutching of one's own virginal state in refusing to touch or be touched by the other. In so doing, we put ourselves in opposition to Christ's own indiscriminate distribution of his body. Christ distributed his own body, and his presence and attention during his life, to and for those who did not recognize him and denied him (Judas, the woman at the well), those whose status as religious outsiders excluded them from the justice of the just (the Samaritan woman, who knew he did not come for her and hers), the indecent, the unclean; Christ thereby set himself in direct opposition to the logic of concern for one's own religious purity.

It can hardly be emphasized enough that one's *claimed* relation to Christ has nothing to do with whether Christ will recognize one on the day of judgment.[70] The sacramentality of the church is first and foremost a negative sacramentality, figuring the uncontrollability (and free gift-giving) of the other Christ not by abjuring positive claims for itself (which is the constant danger of an inverted kenotic Messianism or self-securitization through self-denigration) but in its free distribution of the sign of what it neither is nor has: the body of Christ, and by extension, the goods that body symbolizes and grants. The wholeness of a subject with full self-possession lies on *neither* side of resurrection. Nor is the subject required to pour itself out ecstatically unto death, "for I have overcome the world"; the one who poured himself out accomplished for us, as Luther says of faith in the form of Christ, quickly and easily what would otherwise amount to the burden of an infinite demand, the demand of a master or tyrant.[71] The latter is the kenotic demand.

The early Barth is right in claiming that God's first no is to religion with its constant idolatrous temptation to rest on its own laurels, even as God's universal no is in the service of God's universal yes, said in Christ. The church of a reproductive ecclesiology is the place of those who believe themselves (ourselves) to be religious insiders; we find ourselves constantly reminded that such is not the case. The church's idolatries point, in the failure they enact, toward the relation of nonidentity between the world as it is and the kingdom of God.

The church sees itself as a word of judgment to the world; but this church was founded on Christ's crucified, resurrected, ascended body. We do not yet know what we shall be, nor do we know what we now are. Such epistemological apophasis has consequences for how we understand the resurrected body of Christ. Resurrection should not be the reinstatement of phallic plenitude. It inaugurates a different logic. The words of institution in 1 Corinthians 11:26 say: "For as often as you eat this bread and drink this cup, you proclaim the Lord's death until he comes." To proclaim death in the double negation of Christian speech means hope for a life different from what now is, without promising the redemption of what we know now *in the form that we know it*. But the words of institution also invite the question: Will the Lord's death still be proclaimed after he comes?

The crucified one is also, now and forever, the resurrected one, who ascended into heaven and disappeared from view except under other signs. Yet resurrection means not, primarily, that identity is interrupted (except as it is subjected to sin); resurrection brings a *more than*, an intensified intimacy that no longer depends on shattering supposedly stable boundaries that separate people. The colocality of Jesus' resurrected body with other bodies, and its expansion of itself to include bread and wine, indicate the more-than of resurrection. But the disappearance of the resurrected body from view also indicates the epistemic fractures that forbid rendering resurrection a forward projection of the self and maintains instead the ambiguity of the current order's relationship to the realm of resurrection.

The expectation that the lost body of Christ will return from heaven requires the church to take a dual stance of expectation and refusal inside this current order. Christ's body went away; it never belonged to the church in the first place. The church lost the body of Christ or never had it for itself; and the church exists in anticipation of a redirection of its own action as its primary mode of being.[72] The church continues to anticipate the return of the body of Christ that went elsewhere. In that anticipation the church symbolizes the end of history, the inadequacy of reproduction in an order of the self-same; it anticipates the arrival of a word that it cannot straightforwardly speak to itself. This is a church of sinners, not saints.

Instead of having and being the body, the sign-symbolism of a nonreproductive ecclesiology points to the lost and ascended body of Christ, holding absence and expectation together as forms of relationship to the nonidentical body. This second fundamental form of response to the loss of Christ's body, the theological value and justifications for which stand in danger of being eclipsed to the detriment of contemporary ecclesiology, recognizes the loss of the body of Christ *as loss* and admits the consequences for theological epistemology. Instead of asserting that the body of Christ has been handed over to the church, it recognizes that the body of Christ, elsewhere and outside itself, is its only hope.

This form of response refuses the promise of the future as reproduction of the self-same in favor of a radically apocalyptic stance in relation to the world, which stands under judgment.[73] But it also, and more importantly, knows itself as a community that also stands under judgment and that may even be subject to a higher standard of judgment than the "world."[74] Resurrection means that the community established by a relation to Christ "identifies and understands itself as forgiven"[75] rather than as pure; to know oneself forgiven means knowing and admitting oneself a sinner, the nontransparency of self to self, and the weakness of one's good intentions. The church is formed by the hope of a relation to the body of Christ that is elsewhere and unrecognizable, absent and ascended, but that hope also entails the death of its identification with its own goodness. Apocalyptic as I use it here[76] emphasizes judgment and the end of history's reproduction of sameness, of the order of identity's distinctions that claim goodness and finality for themselves and that set about to exclude those thought to threaten the stability of such an order of goodness.[77] The world is coming to an end and will be (and has been) submitted to judgment; ordinary time no longer makes up the matrix of existence. The world no longer promises the repetition of the self-same, for its form is passing away, and its time has come to an end.[78]

Said more provocatively, this form of ecclesiology figures forth the abortion of the current order of continuity and repetition, and ultimately the abortion of the church. Abortion here indicates a fundamental refusal of the logic of reproduction in both its biological and socio-symbolic senses.[79] This is Christianity's death drive, the excess accessed only by refusing identity's positivity and representation's stability. Jesus went away, but in a strange logic of multiplication, there is always more at the Lord's table. (Remember that the drive abides by a logic of excess and surplus rather of lack.) The relation of the church to time then becomes one of nonreproduction, in which only the difference of the future from the past can save the present.

To be an indiscriminate church that inhabits the space of abortion in relation to time is then the form of fidelity to the absent or unrecognizable body of Christ that was and is to come. The church does not represent the judge of the world in its purity, in its potential for successful sociopolitical totalization amounting to an alternative political order, or through a purportedly alternative economy of mutual submission according to the oft-invoked horror that is the late capitalist fiction of servant leadership. At best, the church may symbolize the hope that, since its own failures are the most radical of all, the judge of all the world will perhaps give his body's touch even to the church that refuses him—as he did to the disciple who betrayed him. Christ's transformed materiality becomes available beyond incorporation or self-shattering. In these bodied relations, bodies do not need to be made penetrable; instead, bodies are made capable of passionate intensity through ever-increasing proximity without penetration or shattering. These "non-limitative horizontal relations" establish a "possible social relation which is not vertical but horizontal."[80]

The church figures the refusal of symbolic orders of reproduction, as in Jesus' denial of the importance of biological family ties and in the Pauline "as if not," which introduces a fold[81] in the subject's ties to itself and its identities. The apocalyptic injunction robs the apocalyptic subject of any fixed identitarian position. Paul's rebuke of Cephas/Peter in Galatians 2 for the latter's hypocrisy in eating with the Gentiles only until believers in circumcision arrived to judge him reflects the falsity of Cephas's attempt to remain what he once was. Hypocrisy's suturing of identity's folds reclaims identity's sundered futural extensibility. Death to the "law" of identity sets free; reestablishing the law of distinction around the table returns the community's members to the reproduction of ordinary time where nothing but the world can be the case. As an ecclesiological test case, the stakes in this story are not about the relationship between Jews and Gentiles in a historical sense, nor even about whether Gentiles who will eventually become Christians ought to be circumcised as well. The positional clash must be read from the perspective of the New Testament's function as scripture in a community that believes itself Pauline in this sense but is in fact Petrine (Cephasite?).

The church longs to become the body of Christ, but the condition of the church's transformation is that it distributes the body's sign indiscriminately. It might seem that the investment that reproductive ecclesiologies have in what we now term the "real presence" of Christ in the eucharist ought to be paralleled in abortive ecclesiologies by its rejection. But the logic of indiscriminate rather than limited distribution and the cancellation of Christianity's identitarian impulse mean that abortive ecclesiologies are compatible with any account of eucharistic presence (or lack thereof)—the crucial site of distinction is not a particular eucharistic theory but the form of distribution of the body of Christ, symbolic or real. Permitting laypeople to say the words of institution, open communion, and similar practices are all forms of recognition that the body of Christ does not belong to the church. Thus it is not the contrast between the indecency of the world and the decency of the church that maintains the church's sign-status; instead, the church knows it does not possess the body of Christ and so distributes its sign freely, for the church stands in need of that body as much if not more than others do, those who at least are not tempted to believe they have it.[82] The primacy of the church's need for forgiveness is the only condition under which the words of institution ought to be spoken; recognizing the primacy of that need is to recognize what Jesus' deliverance to judgment as the one excluded from the presence of God means for the church.

Ecclesiologies of reproduction dominate recent theological discussion. In this theological climate, ecclesiologies of abortion might be accused of accommodating cultural change; fear of the "Enlightenment's corrosive effect on Christian identity"[83] requires protecting the full plenitude of Christian identity, some argue. Such protectiveness (attack as defense) diagnoses accommodation's failures and offers an idealized, even mythical, description of Christianity's truth. The need for a positive plenitude of faithfulness makes ecclesiologies of reproduction seem more powerful than ecclesiologies of abortion; the former set up a purportedly clear and distinctive alternative to the "world's" failures and injustices. To claim that the church is a positive (albeit imperfect) sign of the arrival of the kingdom allows the church to claim an ideal rather than actual identity. In so doing, it pretends to recognize Jesus and control the distribution of his body, and it risks encountering a Christ who does not recognize the church. Instead, the futurity of the church may be no future at all—at least in the ordinary sense of the forward projection of ordinary time.


## THE SEX OF RESURRECTION

God gives alien gifts to humankind.[84] One such alien gift is the fulfillment of gender in its overcoming. There is no reason to figure the resurrected Christ as masculine or male.[85] The end of gender means also the end of marriage. The redemption of sexual difference must then be its end in the form that we know it.[86] The transformation of space and materiality developed in chapter 6 entails the end of both wound-womb and phallic logic. Resurrection does not mean the fulfillment of sexual difference, unless we reduce fulfillment to the end of the interplay of plenitude, sacrifice, and lack, active and passive penetration, theology done only in the missionary position. Clitoral pleasure becomes a sign of resurrection. This is not because the clitoris is more phallic than even the phallus in its potential for multiple orgasms; many comings never approach eternity or infinity. Nor is it because the mystery of *jouissance*, in the exclusion of women from representation, allows women to remain the dark continent of becoming. The figure of the clitoris represents the nonbounded self that resurrection promises to transform without destroying, for the clitoris can be assigned neither to the "inside" nor the "outside" of a body. The uselessness of the clitoris in reproduction (and even its history of being represented as a miniature or inverted penis) signals—in and through female morphology, not coincidentally—the possibility of nonreproductive sexuality beyond the pleasures of submission, penetration, and (self-)shattering. The clitoris symbolizes the economy of surface touch in which intensification and copresence permit ever-greater intimacy between those who remain different in their particularity.

In the vignette with which this chapter begins, we encountered the expansion of an already constituted church space via authoritative speech to include those identified as other. In examining the theological logic of such an approach to the borders of church, we discovered yet another place in which sexuality and gender appear in unexpected form: in imaginaries of a pure reproduction and extension of a virginal church, and in the contrasting reclamation of abortion as a figure of Second Coming hope. Instead of arguing for inclusion as an alternative to exclusion, we found ourselves at risk of being excluded—not just from the church, but from the kingdom of God and the communion God seeks to establish with us. Even if taking a stand for inclusion of the identitarian other is necessitated by the exclusion of that other, discourses of inclusion are thereby forced into accepting the basic premises of exclusion, indeed into advancing them in self-congratulation over their own inclusiveness. Inclusive ecclesiology is as reproductive as exclusionary ecclesiology when it emphasizes identity's goods and holds out the fantasy of recognition inside a symbolic order of affirmation.

The ecclesiology developed here has little to do with inclusion and nothing to do with reproduction. To stand with God "outside the gates" means more than to distance oneself from projects subject to judgment. That God stands with the excluded demands more than agitating for the inclusion of the formerly marginalized. Christ's crucifixion outside the camp means that no one is cut off from the presence of God.[87] But if resurrection is a site of nonidentity, relation to the future cannot be one of forward-projected hope for the imaginary self. In odd inversion of psychoanalytic tropes, resurrection places the subject's nonidentity with itself at the exit from language (into death through the symbolism of baptism) rather than at its point of entry into language (through symbolic death). To speak theologically from outside intelligibility does not mean the cessation of theological speech; it means that such speech stands under the sign of judgment and cannot pretend to ultimacy or finality. From the implications for the church of the loss of Christ's body, I developed a theology of a church that cannot close its borders for fear of shutting Christ out. Instead of accepting the current terms of the debate—should we or should we not include "practicing"[88] gays, lesbians, and bisexuals in church—we start from resurrection hope, ascension's difference, and Christ's promise that he will come again, and that we will be reunited with him in the eucharistic feast-beyond-sacrifice in the kingdom. The otherness of God's life, particularly the life of the resurrected, almost spectral Jesus, draws our lives into themselves in ways similarly unsettling. The Holy Ghost's sensuality is perhaps best represented by the wind, since its light caress reaches the surface that the divine phallus can only shatter, yet this light touch drives people wild.

If Christ is not raised, our hope is nothing; our hope is not nothing. We cry out, "How long, oh Lord, how long," since the Lord seems slow in fulfilling God's promise. We thereby forget our hope with the apparent continuation of ordinary time. But the Pauline fold of "as if not" calls us away from weeding out the tares within our borders (whether porous or not) and toward expectation of the soon-coming end. In the interim, if we hope to be recognized by Christ on judgment day, we know what we are to do.[89]

## NOTES

1. Marcella Althaus-Reid, *The Queer God* (London: Routledge, 2003), 22.
2. Emphasis in original inflection. See http://www.believeoutloud.com/latest/got-moms-ad-about-church-welcome, May 6, 2011 (accessed July 12, 2011).
3. The racial logic suggested is one in which white liberal patriarchy overcomes nonwhite homophobia.
4. Jasbir Puar, *Terrorist Assemblages: Homonationalism in Queer Times* (Durham, NC: Duke University Press, 2007). Puar defines homonationalism as "a form of sexual exceptionalism—the emergence of national homosexuality . . . — that corresponds with the coming out of the exceptionalism of American empire . . . this brand of homosexuality operates as a regulatory script not only of normative gayness . . . but also of the racial and national norms that reinforce these sexual subjects. . . . The fleeting sanctioning of a national homosexual subject is possible . . . through the simultaneous engendering and disavowal of *populations* of sexual-racial others who need not apply" (2). For a similar set of concerns about the racial logic of homonormativity, see Roderick Ferguson, "Race-ing Homonormativity: Citizenship, Sociology, and Gay Identity," in E. Patrick Johnson and Mae G. Henderson, eds., *Black Queer Studies: A Critical Anthology* (Durham: Duke University Press, 2005), 61.
5. The story is very different for trans* people, especially trans* women of color.
6. Cathy Cohen offers a severe critique of queer politics for just such reasons in "Punks, Bulldaggers, and Welfare Queens: The Radical Potential of Queer Politics?," in Johnson and Henderson, eds., *Black Queer Studies* (Durham: Duke University Press, 2005), 21–51. Arguably, we live in a time where radical social imaginaries are excluded from viability by our political discourse. As Peter Sloterdijk puts it, it seems that "nothing but the world may be the case." Peter Sloterdijk, *Weltfremdheit* (Frankfurt: Suhrkamp, 1993), 106, quoted in Miroslav Volf, "Johannine Dualism and Contemporary Pluralism," in Richard Bauckham and Carl Moser, eds., *The Gospel of John and Christian Theology* (Grand Rapids: Eerdmans, 2008), 19.
7. It also ignores the complicated challenges raised by the racial politics that shaped the interpretation of at least one of the cause célèbres of *It Gets Better*, the suicide of Rutgers student Tyler Clementi. See Jasbir Puar, "In the wake of It Gets Better," *The Guardian*, November 16, 2010, http://www.guardian.co.uk/commentisfree/cifamerica/2010/nov/16/wake-it-gets-better-campaign; and idem, "Ecologies of Sex, Sensation, and Slow Death," *Periscope*, November 22, 2010, http://socialtextjournal.org/periscope_article/ecologies_of_sex_sensation_and_slow_death/, for concise discussions of some of these challenges (both accessed April 24, 2014).
8. The envisioned life outcomes of the bullied queer high school students who consider suicide in this *It Gets Better* music video by the band Rise Against

are: male congressman, male artist, and a lesbian wedding. See http://www. youtube.com/watch?v=XP4clbHc4Xg.

9. The latter assumption is ably and beautifully critiqued in Heather Love, *Feeling Backwards: Loss and the Politics of Queer History* (Cambridge, MA: Harvard University Press, 2007).

10. Puar, *Terrorist Assemblages*, 118, 128.

11. Althaus-Reid, *Queer God*, 45.

12. Compare Oliver Davies, who admits that the ascension entailed "a removal of the body from view," but interprets the resurrection to mean that "Jesus must still in some sense have 'local' existence and thus be in continuity with our own space-time reality today." Davies, "The Interrupted Body," in Oliver Davies, Paul D. Janz, and Clemens Sedmak, eds., *Transformation Theology: Church in the World* (London: T&T Clark, 2007), 50, 39. Davies goes on to argue that, since reference to heaven is no longer real (indicating the actual place where Jesus now is) but has become metaphorical, "Spirit and Church have surely become for us substitutes for [Christ's] body, rather than its mediations" (44). Davies insists it is the *material reality* of the ascended body of Christ that grounds a real relation to him inside space-time; indeed, the entire spatio-temporal order is reconfigured following the ascension (48). So although the ascended body is no longer visible, and although it retains a "local" character in the truth of Jesus' full humanity, Christ now also has a "world-body" so that we may be "in" him in quite a material sense (50), albeit as a "dynamic relation" (rather than in a merely physical sense) that is only apparent to us by grace (53).

13. Douglas Farrow, *Ascension Theology* (London: T&T Clark, 2001), 62, 65–66.

14. After admitting that, "viewed from below," the ascension implies "the incomprehensible absence of Christ," Farrow develops a view from above in which the church's authority becomes a new form of Christ's presence. "The eucharist, . . . through the equally incomprehensible presence *in* the absence . . . provides that the present age should not be altogether without Christ and so without hope or experience of the age to come. . . . The appearance of the church brings to light . . . the plan to unite all things under one head. . . . If indeed Christ is present in his absence . . . he is present . . . in his freedom to create by the Spirit a community of ascension and oblation, which is what the church is" (ibid., 65–66). Farrow goes on to argue that denial of transubstantiation "wittingly or unwittingly denies the reality of the church on earth," and turns whatever the believer offers to God " 'unholy fire' upon the altar of God" (ibid., 80–81). In his brilliant discussion of the diversity of eucharistic theories in medieval theology, in contrast, Gary Macy says that "[f]or most medieval theologians . . . a mere recognition of the Real Presence in the ritual of the Eucharist did not itself offer any aid in salvation. The Real Presence alone, in fact, had no spiritual effect." Macy, *Treasures from the Storeroom: Medieval Religion and the Eucharist* (Collegeville, MN: Liturgical /Pueblo, 1999), 179.

15. See Nancy Jay, *Throughout Your Generations Forever: Sacrifice, Religion, and Paternity* (Chicago: University of Chicago Press, 1992), 113, 116, 123, 126–27, and *passim*. Jay focuses on the sacrificial character of the eucharist. Guy Hocquenghem notes that since "heterosexual reproduction" happens through "hierarchical succession," those who are lower in the hierarchy know that one day they will occupy the higher rungs of the ladder: this is another way to gain authority through deferral. Hocquenghem, *Homosexual Desire*, trans. Daniella Dangoor (Durham, NC: Duke University Press, 1993), 109.

16. For this reason, Gerard Loughlin's question in the introduction to *Queer Theology*—"Why is this refusal of fecundity—the celibate lifestyle—not also

a threat to family and society?"(5)—fails to recognize the interrelation and mutual reinforcement of orthodox Christian reproductive practices.

17. As, for instance, Christopher Beeley assumes when discussing Irenaeus and Eusebius of Caesarea: "A crucial part of opposing heresy is the task of identifying the true succession of Christian teachers and the history of the passing down of orthodox doctrine." Beeley, *The Unity of Christ: Continuity and Conflict in Patristic Tradition* (New Haven, CT: Yale University Press, 2012), 59. The problem is that so many of those true Christian teachers disagree with one another.

18. Robyn Wiegman (in summarizing an argument from Judith Roof) says, "Generational models . . . always reinscribe the hegemony of the family and its heterosexist regime of reproduction," "Feminism's Apocalyptic Futures," *New Literary History* 31, no. 4 (2000), 812.

19. It is not incidental that Douglas Farrow insists on a "proper Mariology" (*Ascension Theology* 83; see also 86) in his *plaidoyer* asserting the inadmissibility of Protestant ecclesiologies.

20. Gregory of Nyssa, *On Virginity*, in *Nicene and Post-Nicene Fathers*, second series, vol. 5, *Gregory of Nyssa: Dogmatic Treatises, Etc.*, ed. Philip Schaff and Henry Wace (Peabody, MA: Hendrickson, 2012), ch. 3.

21. See Farrow's fulminations against those who do not accept the "gender complementarity or procreative purposes" of marriage; *Ascension Theology*, 108.

22. The section "When he met her" in chapter 5, above, describes a similar dynamic among theologians.

23. Marcella Althaus-Reid, *Indecent Theology: Theological Perversions in Sex, Gender, and Politics* (New York: Routledge, 2000), 103. The "quest for transcendence" is one of Althaus-Reid's targets here; I disagree with her reading of transcendence to the extent that it is definitional, rather than empirically descriptive of many accounts of transcendence.

24. Ibid., 104.

25. Ibid., 104–05.

26. Ibid., 105.

27. Direct translation and the transcendental phallus are different instantiations of the notion of total, stable, self-identity (the coincidence of essence and existence).

28. Kent Brintnall rightly notes that "[i]f one takes up one's cross, one will gain life, not lose it." Brintnall, *Ecce Homo: The Male-Body-in-Pain as Redemptive Figure* (Chicago: University of Chicago Press, 2011), 89.

29. Too much so, I would argue—the concrete mechanisms of these relations need to be explored, as I have attempted to do in earlier chapters, although he is certainly right to find such mechanisms.

30. See Kathryn Tanner's *Politics of God: Christian Theologies and Social Justice* (Minneapolis, MN: Fortress Press, 1992), chapter 3, for an argument that transcendence can support self-critical cultures within Christianity.

31. These logics are also racial, as Brintnall indicates in his discussion of Robert Mapplethorpe's photographs, but Brintnall's focus throughout is specifically masculinity and maleness. His argument thus develops problems in the moments near the end of the book where he turns his attention to Bataille's representations of femininity as also desiring and plenitudinous, and suggests that these representations redeem femininity as well.

32. Brintnall, *Ecce Homo*, 97.

33. Brintnall emphasizes that while resurrection is a problem, the solution is not necessarily crucifixion: "Injury . . ., wounds . . ., death: each can be . . . presented as proof that the hero is a stoic and valiant warrior. . . . Although a narrative without a recuperative moment will not necessarily signify limitation,

vulnerability, and mortality, a narrative with a triumphant conclusion precludes such signification." Ibid., 60, emphasis added; that part of the argument is contestable.

34. Brintnall argues that Christianity remains responsible for the way action movies reflect its historical influence: "The action genre's tropes and themes . . . are a decoder ring for the gendered logic of crucifixion and resurrection." Ibid., 56. This overstates the case, and assumes a structural, transhistorical notion of resurrection. Similarly, "The triumph of life over death in the previously brutalized, but eternally male, body of God funds a particular fantasy of masculine plenitude. . . . [I]t may very well be that the doctrine of the resurrection—with its quiet, subterranean, structural influence—has played the *largest role* in maintaining the illusion of masculinity necessary for the patriarchal denigration of women and womanish men." Ibid., 62, emphasis added. Again, more work would need to be done to make so strong an argument persuasive.

35. Ibid., 22.

36. Ibid., 11.

37. "Fantasies of resurrection . . . are kin to fantasies of masculine power and plenitude, told in more palatable, seemingly gender-neutral terms. The fantasy . . . is understandably seductive, but it nourishes problematic conceptions of what it means to be a subject. . . . It is difficult to face our limitations, to admit our vulnerability, and to acknowledge the certainty of our death. But our unwillingness to do so prevents us from genuinely encountering the other." Ibid., 63.

38. Even if the Son's triumph is deferred onto his processional submission to the Father who, as the source of life and divinity, raises him back to the glory that once belonged to him, Son and Father are not sufficiently distinct for this relation to undo stabilization of the Son's identity. Neither does the Son's masochism provide a resource, since the submissive directs the action in a scene, and the Son's pleasure in his little death is followed by, depending on how the text is read, either his signing of a permanent contract (in which he hands over the kingdom to the Father) or the end of his temporary switch-hitting as he takes back control of the Spirit.

39. Ibid., 167–68.

40. Selves that are not assumed, even in the imaginary, to have fixed boundaries avoid some of the Manichaean and monist aspects of Leo Bersani's condemnation of the social order (not as contradictory as they seem, in this case) that Jeff Nunokawa identifies. These critiques extend also to Lee Edelman and, in his valoration of self-shattering as the *only* way to achieve the social ends he seeks, to Brintnall as well. See Nunokawa, "Queer Theory: Postmortem," *South Atlantic Quarterly* 106, no. 2 (2007), 558. Conversely, I suggest that Bersani, Edelman, Brintnall, and a significant subset of theologians overestimate the dominance of images of plenitudinous or bounded selves at all levels of the social order—except, importantly, in economic theory.

41. Nor should any theological significance attach to the assumed masculinity of Christ's body, especially in its resurrected form. Under our current conceptual regimes of sexual difference, despite valiant attempts to queer and undo male–female binaries, representing sexual difference still takes place inside such orders. The only theological significance the assumed masculinity or maleness of Christ's body ought to have, is as a "generic" marker of human particularity and specificity. Given the transformational capacities of resurrection, while Jesus' resurrected body may (or may not) be gendered, it is decidedly not male in a sense continuous with our current referential registers of maleness.

42. Steven J. Friesen, *Imperial Cults and the Apocalypse of John: Reading Revelation in the Ruins* (Oxford: Oxford University Press, 2001), 157.

43. Lee Edelman, *No Future: Queer Theory and the Death Drive* (Durham, NC: Duke University Press, 2004); hereafter NF.

44. Edelman, "Ever After: History, Negativity, and the Social," *South Atlantic Quarterly* 106, no. 3 (2007), 476.

45. Ibid., 475–76.

46. In the aftermath of the US recession, political debate has shifted from the need for jobs to the debt ceiling and the national deficit. So we must attack the national debt for the sake of the/our children. That requires austerity and denial for those now living. We must reform Social Security for the sake of the/our children. We must protect marriage either by extending it to same-sex couples or by denying it to them for the sake of the/our children. And so on.

47. Ibid., 473–74, my emphasis.

48. Here again we find the insistence that there is no alternative.

49. During the debate over same-sex unions in the state of Iowa, Zach Wahls's testimony in the Iowa House of Representatives along these lines went viral (February 2011); eventually, it resulted in a book deal for his autobiography and his participation at the 2012 Democratic presidential nominating convention. Wahls's argument focused on his own indistinguishability from the children of straight parents, and on his success in school and life. The text of his testimony and a link to a video of it appear at http://www.zachwahls.com/?page_id=273; note especially the lines, "I'm not so different from any of your children. My family really isn't so different from yours."

50. Queers are, for Edelman, not identical with persons who are not heterosexual, since nonstraight persons can also identify with the symbolic order and its demands—by, for instance, seeking recognition of marriage for the sake of the Child. Conversely, as the quote above from "Ever After" makes clear, even "subjects committed to disciplinary norms" are "sinthomosexuals despite themselves."

51. Nostalgia for a lost plenitude imagined as the self without damages and fissures is, in this formulation, a Lacanian idea, but this part of Edelman's argument (and my use of it) does not depend on accepting Lacanian psychoanalytic categories. A theological case for a Christian future is not necessarily subject to the conditions of possibility provided by a Lacanian account of subject formation. A looser way of describing the same kind of problem can be described as a narcissistic dream of total recognition, in which that recognition includes only my best parts, or the most delusionally optimistic vision I might have of my own generosity, goodness, and kindness, which I would express if only life's challenges and other people didn't keep getting in the way. In the fantasy, that best self is my true, authentic self, and I can credit its good impulses to myself although I cannot always realize them (as in the fundamental attribution error identified by social psychologists).

52. See Friedrich Nietzsche's insistence that redemption means "to compose and collect into unity what is fragment and riddle and fearful chance," a position developed in direct connection with Zarathustra's encounter with a group of "cripples and beggars." Nietzsche, *Thus Spake Zarathustra*, trans. Thomas Common (New York: Random House), 153.

53. In classical Christian terms, this is the position of the Word (Logos).

54. Edelman indirectly invokes redemption in quoting from the Lutheran pastor and writer Walter Wangerin Jr.'s review of *Children of Men* in the *New York Times*.

55. Edelman, "Ever After," 474. The reference is to Theodor Adorno, *Negative Dialectics*, trans. E. B. Ashton (New York: Continuum, 1994), 320.

56. Althaus-Reid, *Indecent Theology*, 100.

57. Ibid., 101.

58. Edelman, "Ever After," 470. Friesen says about the Revelation of John that "[i]t is not evident that such an inherently unstable cosmology can support the life of a community, but success and longevity do not appear to have been major concerns for John." Friesen, *Imperial Cults*, 166.
59. The attentive reader will recognize that my argument that dominant ecclesiologies miss the significance of this point reflect the very distant sense in which this chapter reconfigures Seventh-day Adventist ecclesiology. Although the top-heavy institutional structure of the Seventh-day Adventist church does not conform to this, a church founded on the expectation of the *immediacy* of the Advent—quite possibly today or tomorrow—*cannot* or better, *must not* reproduce itself or seek to secure its own future.
60. Nancey Murphy, "The Resurrection Body and Personal Identity," in Ted Peters, Robert John Russell, and Michael Welker, eds., *Resurrection: Theological and Scientific Assessments* (Grand Rapids, MI: Eerdmans, 2002), 204–05.
61. Karl Barth, *The Epistle to the Romans*, trans. Edwyn C. Hoskyns (New York: Oxford University Press, 1968), 35–38.
62. "Our relation to God is *ungodly*. We suppose that we know what we are saying when we say 'God'. We assign to Him the highest place in our world: and in so doing we place Him fundamentally on one line with ourselves and with things" (ibid., 44). See also John Calvin, *Institutes of the Christian Religion*, volume 1, ed. John T. McNeill. *Library of Christian Classics* vol. XX (Philadelphia: Westminster Press, 1960), bk. 3, 12.8, 762: "[I]f we would give ear to Christ's call, away with all arrogance and complacency! Arrogance arises from a foolish persuasion of own righteousness, when man thinks that he has something meritorious to commend him before God. . . . [W]e are ready to seize and grasp God's grace when we have utterly cast out confidence in ourselves and rely only on the assurance of his goodness."
63. Edelman, "Ever After," 475.
64. A dramatic contrast may be drawn with Douglass Farrow's identification of the Antichrist with Islam, communism, fascism, anti-Zionism, democracy, those who do not support gender complementarity, human rights commissions, and so on. See Farrow, *Ascension Theology*, 99–111.
65. Matthew 24:23–26.
66. Althaus-Reid, *Queer God*, 134.
67. This does not undercut assurance of salvation; it is directed against we who claim to possess Christ by exerting control over his body, its distribution, and its boundaries. Paul uses God's judgment to resist intra-community competition and judgment of the other (see Wayne Meeks, "Apocalyptic Discourse and Strategies of Goodness," *Journal of Religion* 80, no. 3 [2000]: 473–74).
68. Rowan Williams, *Resurrection: Interpreting the Easter Gospel*, rev. ed. (Cleveland, OH: Pilgrim Press, 2002), 28.
69. As Pannenberg argues.
70. Here I differ from Williams's assertion that "assurance of future grace is implied in our connectedness with Jesus: as we consciously and deliberately articulate our commitment to 'being with Jesus'" (ibid., 37), as well as from Coakley's assumption that development of the spiritual senses makes it easier to know where Christ is to be found.
71. Martin Luther, *Lectures on Galatians 1535: Chapters 1–4, Luther's Works*, vol. 26, ed. and trans. Jaroslav Pelikan (St. Louis, MO: Concordia, 1963), 128.
72. See especially Karl Barth's discussion of Jacob and Esau in the *Epistle to the Romans*.
73. Were apocalyptic (as in Wiegman, "Feminism's Apocalyptic Futures," 813) to suggest only a "desire for prediction" that allows a "subjective formation"

to be reclaimed through "ground[ing] its own narrative of ruin in a positive and productive origin," apocalypsis would fall victim to the lure of filiation. Apocalyptic must include the dimension of hope, which Meeks expresses in ethical terms: "Apocalyptic language is used (1) to redress an asymmetrical relationship of power, (2) to make way for innovation, (3) to revitalize or transform traditional norms, and (4) to relativize human judgments." Meeks, "Apocalyptic Discourse," 463.

74. Although Williams does not develop his position in this direction, he rightly starts from the acknowledgment that "the Church is *never* the object of its own faith: it is necessarily under the judgement of what it points to. So, of course, is its theology." Williams, *Resurrection* xiv–xv.

75. Ibid., xii.

76. A somewhat idiosyncratic usage, admittedly. Many feminist theologians critique the logic of apocalyptic for its violence and claim to finality. See, for instance, Catherine Keller, *Apocalypse Now and Then: A Feminist Guide to the End of the World* (Boston: Beacon, 1996), Tina Pippin, "Eros and the End: Reading for Gender in the Apocalypse of John," *Semeia* 59 (1992), 193–210. According to Wiegman, apocalyptic longs for a past that promised a "whole and transformed future" and issues dire warnings of a future destroyed by the present's malformations. As a result, "[t]he violence that all forms of apocalypse express becomes . . . a violence towards the nonidentical" ("Feminism's Apocalyptic Futures," 813). Wiegman's description applies to the feminist generational wars that she describes, but because the future of feminism is to be realized through the efforts of feminists themselves, the apocalyptic she describes is precisely a judgment imposed on the other, and so diametrically opposed to the apocalypticism I develop here, and arguably to that of the apocalypse of John itself, in which "apocalyptic personhood includes the renunciation of force. . . . [H]uman victory was redefined as nonaggression" (Friesen, *Imperial Cults*, 189). Contrast also Anathea E. Portier-Young, who suggests that "[a]pocalyptic language, symbol, and vision gave readers tools and frameworks for thinking beyond hegemonic constructions of reality. Theologies affirming God's power and providence as Creator . . . and guarantor of justice counteracted the coercive rule of Antiochus IV and its totalitarian claims over the bodies of his Judean subjects." Portier-Young, *Apocalypse Against Empire: Theologies of Resistance in Early Judaism* (Grand Rapids, MI: Eerdmans, 2011), 383–84.

77. As Friesen frames it, the apocalypse of John has contributed to real problems, but "it is also a text from within the western tradition that challenges the very foundations of modernity. Religious criticism (of the academic variety) of the modern world becomes possible" as a result. Friesen, *Imperial Cults*, 215.

78. Meeks admits that apocalypticism's destabilization of the order of the world as it stands may be a strategy for claiming the power of which one is wrongfully deprived now ("Apocalyptic Discourse," 465). Crucial for my argument is the fact that the *first* target of apocalyptic discourse is the church itself, or the speaker of apocalypse, rather than some other power and principality. The church passes away first, then the world (in its malformation)—but then the world is made new, and the church no longer exists within it.

79. As Meeks suggests, the parodic language of *apokalypsis* is an "assault on the common language" and so "an assault on the world that language represents. It is an assault on common sense" ("Apocalyptic Discourse," 469). Meeks describes the dangers that may ensue as apocalyptic communities seek to live into the new world that they proclaim. In my understanding of apocalyptic, the apocalypse as end, as judgment, as recreation, and as fulfillment

is entirely in God's hands, and any attempt to become the faithful remnant speaking the word of judgment to the other falls victim to self-securitization and idolatry.

80. Hocquenghem, *Homosexual Desire*, 109.

81. Adapting Catherine Keller's Deleuzian term from "The Apophasis of Gender: A Fourfold Unsaying of Feminist Theology," *Journal of the American Academy of Religion* 76, no. 4 (December 2008), 908.

82. This is why Rowan Williams's insistence on the self-critical nature of the church is inadequate to protect against the church's sense that it has Christ and embodies the right to speak in his name (*Resurrection*, 46–47). Perhaps this is due to his vivid sense that the church embodies the *possibility* rather than the *inevitability* of failure (ibid., 49).

83. Cyril O'Regan, *Theology and the Spaces of Apocalyptic* (Milwaukee, WI: Marquette University Press, 2009), 26.

84. Kathryn Tanner, *Christ the Key* (Cambridge: Cambridge University Press, 2010), esp. ch. 3.

85. The overcoming of phallicism by its Christic adoption, as suggested obliquely by Brintnall (*Ecce Homo*, 63) and directly by Tina Beattie ("Sexuality and the Resurrection of the Body: Reflections in a Hall of Mirrors," in Gavin D'Costa, ed., *Resurrection Reconsidered* [London: Oneworld, 1996], esp. 142–43), reinstantiates rather than overcomes it.

86. Utopian strands in feminism and Christianity converge on this point; as Kathi Weeks frames an aspect of the Left backlash against feminist utopianisms in the 1980s, "the aspiration to move beyond gender as we know it was supplanted by efforts to secure the recognition and equal treatment of a wider variety of the genders we now inhabit." Weeks, *The Problem with Work: Feminism, Marxism, Antiwork Politics, and Postwork Imaginaries* (Durham, NC: Duke University Press, 2011), 184.

87. See Marilyn McCord Adams, *Christ and Horrors: The Coherence of Christology* (Cambridge: Cambridge University Press, 2006), 254–55.

88. The specification of "practicing" seems odd in light of Jesus' pronouncements about lust in the heart.

89. Martin Luther, "Preface to the Letter to the Romans," in *The Works of Martin Luther*, vol. 6 (Philadelphia, PA: Muhlenberg Press, 1932), 447–62.

## BIBLIOGRAPHY

Adams, Marilyn McCord. *Christ and Horrors: The Coherence of Christology*. Cambridge: Cambridge University Press, 2006.

Althaus-Reid, Marcella. *Indecent Theology: Theological Perversions in Sex, Gender, and Politics*. New York: Routledge, 2000.

———. *The Queer God*. London: Routledge, 2003.

Barth, Karl. *The Epistle to the Romans*. 6th ed. Trans. Edwyn C. Hoskins. London: Oxford University Press, 1968.

Beattie, Tina. "Sexuality and the Resurrection of the Body: Reflections in a Hall of Mirrors." In *Resurrection Reconsidered*, ed. Gavin D'Costa, 135–49. London: OneWorld Publications, 1996.

Beeley, Christopher. *The Unity of Christ: Continuity and Conflict in Patristic Tradition*. New Haven: Yale University Press, 2012.

Brintnall, Kent. *Ecce Homo: The Male-Body-in-Pain as Redemptive Figure*. Chicago: University of Chicago Press, 2011.

Calvin, John. *Institutes of the Christian Religion*, 2 vols., ed. John T. McNeill. *Library of Christian Classics* vols. XX and XXI. Philadelphia: Westminster Press, 1960.

Cohen, Cathy. "Punks, Bulldaggers, and Welfare Queens: The Radical Potential of Queer Politics?" In *Black Queer Studies: A Critical Anthology*, ed. E. Patrick Johnson and Mae G. Henderson, 21–51. Durham: Duke University Press, 2005.

Davies, Oliver. "The Interrupted Body." In *Transformation Theology: Church in the World*, ed. Oliver Davies, Paul D. Janz, and Clemens Sedmak, 37–59. London: T&T Clark, 2007.

Edelman, Lee. "Ever After: History, Negativity, and the Social." *South Atlantic Quarterly* 106, no. 3 (2007): 469–76.

———. *No Future: Queer Theory and the Death Drive*. Durham: Duke University Press, 2004.

Farrow, Douglas. *Ascension Theology*. London: T&T Clark, 2001.

Ferguson, Roderick. "Race-ing Homonormativity: Citizenship, Sociology, and Gay Identity." In *Black Queer Studies: A Critical Anthology*, ed. E. Patrick Johnson and Mae G. Henderson, 52–67. Durham: Duke University Press, 2005.

Friesen, Steven J. *Imperial Cults and the Apocalypse of John: Reading Revelation in the Ruins*. Oxford: Oxford University Press, 2001.

"Got Moms? An Ad About Church Welcome." *Believe Out Loud*. May 6, 2011. http://www.believeoutloud.com/latest/got-moms-ad-about-church-welcome. Accessed July 12, 2011.

Gregory of Nyssa. "On Virginity." In *Nicene and Post-Nicene Fathers*. Second Series. Vol. 5, *Gregory of Nyssa: Dogmatic Treatises, Etc.* ed. Philip Schaff and Henry Wace, 343–71. Peabody, MA: Hendrickson, 2012.

Hocquenghem, Guy. *Homosexual Desire*. Trans. Daniella Dangoor. Durham: Duke University Press, 1993.

Jay, Nancy. *Throughout Your Generations Forever: Sacrifice, Religion, and Paternity*. Chicago: University of Chicago Press, 1992.

Keller, Catherine. *Apocalypse Now and Then: A Feminist Guide to the End of the World*. Boston: Beacon, 1996.

———. "The Apophasis of Gender: A Fourfold Unsaying of Feminist Theology." *Journal of the American Academy of Religion* 76, no. 4 (December 2008): 905–33.

Loughlin, Gerard, ed. *Queer Theology: Rethinking the Western Body*. Oxford: Blackwell, 2007.

Love, Heather. *Feeling Backwards: Loss and the Politics of Queer History*. Cambridge, MA: Harvard University Press, 2007.

Luther, Martin. *Lectures on Galatians 1535: Chapters 1–4. Luther's Works*, vol. 26, ed. and trans. Jaroslav Pelikan. St. Louis: Concordia, 1963.

———. "Preface to the Letter to the Romans." In *The Works of Martin Luther*, vol. 6, 447–62. Philadelphia: Muhlenberg Press, 1932.

Macy, Gary. *Treasures from the Storeroom: Medieval Religion and the Eucharist*. Collegeville, MN: Liturgical, 1999.

Meeks, Wayne. "Apocalyptic Discourse and Strategies of Goodness." *Journal of Religion* 80, no. 3 (July 2000): 461–75.

Murphy, Nancey. "The Resurrection Body and Personal Identity." In *Resurrection: Theological and Scientific Assessments*, ed. Ted Peters, Robert John Russell, and Michael Welker, 202–18. Grand Rapids: Eerdmans, 2002.

Nietzsche, Friedrich. *Thus Spake Zarathustra*. Trans. Thomas Common. New York: Random House, n.d.

Nunokawa, Jeff. "Queer Theory: Postmortem." *South Atlantic Quarterly* 106, no. 2 (2007): 553–63.

O'Regan, Cyril. *Theology and the Spaces of Apocalyptic.* Milwaukee: Marquette University Press, 2009.
Portier-Young, Anathea E. *Apocalypse against Empire: Theologies of Resistance in Early Judaism.* Grand Rapids: Eerdmans, 2011.
Puar, Jasbir. "Ecologies of Sex, Sensation, and Slow Death." *Periscope.* November 22, 2010. http://socialtextjournal.org/periscope_article/ecologies_of_sex_sensation_and_slow_death/.
———. "In the Wake of It Gets Better." *The Guardian.* November 16, 2010. http://www.guardian.co.uk/commentisfree/cifamerica/2010/nov/16/wake-it-gets-better-campaign/.
———. *Terrorist Assemblages: Homonationalism in Queer Times.* Durham: Duke University Press, 2007.
Rise Against, "Make It Stop (September's Children)." *YouTube.* Last modified June 21, 2011. http://www.youtube.com/watch?v=XP4clbHc4Xg.
Tanner, Kathryn. *Christ the Key.* Cambridge: Cambridge University Press, 2010.
———. *The Politics of God: Christian Theologies and Social Justice.* Minneapolis: Fortress Press, 1992.
Volf, Miroslav. "Johannine Dualism and Contemporary Pluralism." In *The Gospel of John and Christian Theology*, ed. Richard Bauckham and Carl Moser, 19–50. Grand Rapids: Eerdmans, 2008.
Wahls, Zach. "The Testimony." 2011. http://web.archive.org/web/20130423175512/http://www.zachwahls.com/?page_id=273.
———. "Zach Wahls Speaks about Family." *YouTube.* February 1, 2011. https://www.youtube.com/watch?v=FSQQK2Vuf9Q.
Weeks, Kathi. *The Problem with Work: Feminism, Marxism, Antiwork Politics, and Postwork Imaginaries.* Durham: Duke University Press, 2011.
Wiegman, Robyn. "Feminism's Apocalyptic Futures." *New Literary History* 31, no. 4 (October 2000): 805–25.
Williams, Rowan. *Resurrection: Interpreting the Easter Gospel.* Rev. ed. Cleveland: Pilgrim Press, 2002.

# Postlude

It is the Queer at the margins who is entering into a dialogical healing of the Trinity.[1]

Over the past seven chapters, I have argued that the trinity should do much less theological work; we should avoid importing relations of origin into God; the trinity should not be interpreted in terms of sexual difference; we should avoid corrective projectionism; and we should not collapse the different forms of difference by reading the God–world relation into sexual difference, or by reading trinitarian or human difference into the God–world relation. Instead, I have focused on the transformative work of God in the world. Along the way, I have critiqued the transformation of the trinity into an increasingly demanding shibboleth for orthodoxy and theological seriousness while seeking to demonstrate the value of interrelating different theological methodologies and genres.

One of the significant, albeit subterranean, influences on this project has made only occasional appearances: Friedrich Schleiermacher, who is a target for most contemporary trinitarian theologians despite his successful attempt to secure the centrality of Christ for Christianity without a speculative trinitarian doctrine, and who—beyond almost any other theologian—considers humanity and creation intrinsically relational—intrinsically related to God, to each other, and to the world around—with no kenosis or fracturing needed.[2] For Schleiermacher, such relatedness simply is the shape of the human person.[3] Where trinitarian theology often says that we can only have relationship and difference through right trinitarianism (in the form of egalitarianism, equality, hierarchy, obedience, or submission without subordination), our primary modern antagonist in this regard—the theologian we are told to fulminate against for his attempt to speak very loudly of "man" as a way to speak of God—sidelines the very element on which everything supposedly depends, namely, detailed knowledge of immanent trinitarian distinctions. Simultaneously, Schleiermacher offers a better way to think about human relationality and of the relationship between the different forms of difference, for he preserves as few modern theologians have done the difference beyond difference.

Schleiermacher's trinitarianism was long relegated, following Barth and Claude Welch,[4] to a postlude offering no "constitutive significance"[5] for his doctrine as a whole. It may show the persistence of the epistemological assumption that this judgment has mostly been taken for granted in the revival of trinitarian theology. Since Schleiermacher's trinitarianism departs in suggestive respects from classical assumptions, his own description of trinitarian doctrine as a "*Schlußstein*" (coping-stone)[6] of Christian doctrine has, until recently, been neglected or dismissed.[7] This neglect of Schleiermacher's trinitarianism is not merely the result of slavish adherence to Barth. One may trace it to a relative decline in engagement with liberal theology in circles for which matters of revelation and cross determine orthodoxy (and thus participation in the same conversation) or heresy (and thus irrelevance). For theologians on the more liberal side of the spectrum, Schleiermacher's extreme disinterest in trinitarian mythopoetics makes him less interesting, since his trinity is not very useful. A recovery of Schleiermacher on the trinity could take place in two ways. One could demonstrate the significance of the doctrine to his system, showing that a robust Schleiermacherian trinitarianism is compatible with quite different assumptions about the nature of the God–world relation and the nature and shape of revelation than the regnant consensus permits. Alternatively, one could develop Schleiermacher's own *plaidoyer* for a robust reformulation of the doctrine, a task left unfinished in the Reformation, he says. The current project is not exactly an attempt to do either of these—a mild flirtation with the latter, perhaps. However, one of Schleiermacher's most significant critiques of regnant trinitarian distinctions has played a significant role behind the scenes.

Schleiermacher opens the door to a historical development and reformulation of doctrine in relation to the needs and dangers of a particular context—in a modern context, once the danger of heathenism is past, the strictures attached to theological "skewing" of pagan concepts might generate rather than protect against theological misunderstandings.[8] Schleiermacher puts it beautifully: "Cautions could not but be attached to the use of such descriptions [of such plurality] . . . but even so it is seldom that such cautions do not approximate to one extreme in seeking to guard against the other. Also they must lose their value once the danger of misunderstanding to which they relate has disappeared, and in that case the sinister suggestion they contain of the opposite error will come out all the more emphatically."[9] This is a fantastic description of how a constitutive negation installs a constitutive relation and of how theological moves developed to counter misunderstanding in one context may well produce that very misunderstanding in another. The development Schleiermacher describes may be a central trinitarian problem. Immanent divine paternity and filiation first developed to counter categorical subordinationism. Now that such subordinationism has been vanquished in theory, paternity and filiation may advance subordination rather than counter it, or so I have argued. This is one of the many sites where trinitarian theologians need to be schooled by radical feminist, womanist, and queer thinkers. These discourses have taught us the futility of dislodging subordination and hierarchy by striking through the greater than sign and replacing it with the equals sign when the very relationship between the terms is constitutive inequality.

Schleiermacher offers another significant critique, this time of Christology. He points out that the hypostatic union, when brought into contact with trinitarian doctrine, requires equivocal use of nature language—nature language that does not apply in the same, or even similar, ways to God and creation.[10] Following Schleiermacher's intimations, another use of the language of nature, or rather, un-nature, might unite the revelatory work of Jesus across God's aims in creation, reconciliation, and consummation, for God's work in humankind is *un*natural in three senses. In the first sense, the difference beyond difference between God and creation means that there is no ontological continuum between humans and God, any more than there is an ontological binary or a gap between them. They simply are not on the same plane of existence; the relationship between them is not one of nature or natural affinity. Schleiermacher construes the relationship as the absolute dependence of all that exists on God (and this does not vitiate finite power but establishes it, in Schleiermacher's reading). The relationship establishes nature, itself a contested term, yet the relationship itself cannot be internal to nature.

In the second sense, sin rips away much of what, in human beings, is God-like. Built to be creatures who, like God, share their lives and goods with those to whom they are not related (by biology or natural[ized] affinity), creatures instead sinfully curl themselves up in their natural relationships. Created to turn outward, and to establish bonds of communion where there were none before, creatures instead give gifts on the basis of affinity and preference (self-love, as Kierkegaard so aptly says). The "natural" bonds of human creatures, while not intrinsically evil, nonetheless turn evil, offering access to material goods from which others are fundamentally excluded. This may take place at the level of family structure, wealth, nation, or race, where different groupings enjoy to greater or lesser extent the benefits of unnatural forms of kinship that in their naturalization enact evil.

In the third sense, God's action on and for humankind gives humankind a destiny beyond what is given in creation—an unnatural end. Consummation depends on creation but is logically independent thereof—that is, there is no guarantee of consummation built into creation.[11] The aim of God's action in Jesus is the incorporation of human persons into the life of God, the establishment of a more intimate, unnatural kinship where previously, there was only nature (creation). We can distinguish between the natural and unnatural aspects of the order of creation. Considered externally, as an act of pure gift, creation itself entails an unnatural relationship between creation and God. "Unnatural" operates in this sense as an imaginary of gratuity, superfluity, voluntary affiliation, and dissimilarity. Considered internally, from within the existence of the world, creation names what is.

"Natural" operates in this sense with an imaginary of necessity, (af)filiation, and emanation. If we map the imaginary constituted by this distinction, we must shift our understanding of the relationship between the natural and the unnatural. Ordinarily, we think of the natural as the order of things, and the unnatural as that which is against the order of things, the exception to the rule, the constitutive outside against which that which is right and proper (decent) stands out in its fitting shape. We might consider it natural, right and proper, that the pattern of God's filiative shape repeats itself in the ordering of creation and in the patterns of salvation history. But the wild destiny of the God-breathed world suggests instead that the natural only operates as a delimited space inside the priority of the unnatural.

The first two kinds of unnature reflect different kinds of discontinuity between God in Godself and where God reveals Godself to us (the discontinuities do not, of course, lie on the God side). The first discontinuity between them should be strictly understood according to the dictum of Barth's dead dog: Since nothing points to God by its own power, nothing can*not* serve as a pointer to God. The second discontinuity—between our created and our sinful selves—affects the medium in which the Word acts as sinful humanity is taken up and cleansed by the Word. The third kind of unnature reflects the style of divine action. The different levels and kinds of God's engagement with humanity do not follow from each other—God always finds new ways to love and engage the world.

The work the doctrine of the trinity is being asked to do in contemporary theology is work that the doctrine simply cannot do. This is not only because the "trinitarian form of relationship" is analogous to the quest for the historical Jesus—the theologian only finds what she was hoping to find in the first place. The trinity becomes about sex, sexuality, or other differences when it fails to be about the for-us character of divine action and the *vere deo* that is Christ. My refusal to put the trinity to work is not an effect of hostility to materiality, to the body, to the erotic, or to many of the (often admirable and desirable) ends that theologians seek in their trinitarian labors.

The logic of transformed materiality, the end toward which God works in God's engagement with humanity, is colocality: persons present in the same "place" at the same "time," enjoying each other in a "passionate communion."[12] But a significant portion of my argument has been for a disanalogy between divine and human personhood and for a divine personhood that does not find itself subjected to the theological necessity of correcting in its metaphysical constitution whatever problems or fears theologians find in human personhood. Human personhood, too, is mysterious, however: our lives are "hid with Christ in God" (Col. 3:3) and "we do not yet know what we shall be" (John 3:2) for to be "personed" is to be in movement, never quite settled or self-identical. The very shape of the human being, then, is one in which the human is expansive—not in the sense of taking the other into itself but in the way the God relationship in its different forms of intimacy is a stable and intensifying substrate even as the self takes on whatever particularities it has in its own finitude. Kierkegaard's temporal and eternal poles of the self ultimately mean something like this, that the self is freed to be shaped and reshaped across time because at every moment of time it stands in relation to God as the source of its possibilities.

Passionate communion, with its subnarrative of reconciliation, the making-good of what goes wrong with sin, takes place through the enactment of God's unitive aims with respect to creation. Our dance through the gardens of trinitarian metaphysics has partnered us with a variety of bodies, some spectral, others transcendent, some wounded and pierced, others preemptively made into rooms so they do not invite such deflationary tactics. Let us end, then, with the glory of God in the body. The glory of God takes up residence not just in the world as a whole, not just in the sanctuary's holy place, and not just in exile with God's people, but in a specific, historical human being who is the living out in human form of the life of God. The power of God resides in and on and comes out of the glory of God in the world, and the glory of God is the glory whose name is love, the love that walks bodily in the world in the union of the trinity.

## NOTES

1. Marcella Althaus-Reid, *The Queer God* (London: Routledge, 2003), 69.
2. Schleiermacher's critique of the inequality and dependence introduced by the relations of origin, and the inconsistencies introduced thereby, were a significant spur to my thinking on this issue, as was his thesis that God cannot be placed "under those conditions and antitheses which have arisen in and through the world" (§40); see Friedrich Schleiermacher, *The Christian Faith*, ed. H. R. Mackintosh and J. S. Stewart (Edinburgh: T&T Clark, 1999), §171, §172.3, hereafter CF with paragraph and section number.
3. See Schleiermacher, CF §§46–49; §4.
4. Claude Welch's "endlessly repeated" claim of Schleiermacher's "relegation of the dogma to an appendix" has structured much discussion of Schleiermacher's trinitarianism (Welch, *In This Name* [New York: Scribner's, 1952], 4), as Paul DeHart says in his excellent *"Ter mundus accipit infinitum*: The Dogmatic Coordinates of Schleiermacher's Trinitarian Treatise," *Neue Zeitschrift für Systematische Theologie und Religionsphilosophie* 52 (2010): 17.
5. Karl Barth, *Church Dogmatics*, vol. 1, pt. 1: *The Doctrine of the Word of God*, ed. G. W. Bromiley and T. F. Torrance, trans. G. W. Bromiley (London: T&T Clark, 2004), 303.
6. Schleiermacher, CF §170.1.
7. The situation is not helped by Barth's anxiety-of-influence relationship to Schleiermacher, in which he praises the latter for his achievements while suggesting that Schleiermacher has missed everything essential. Barth's relationship to Schleiermacher was characterized by the former's devotion to the Nietzschean principle of keeping the enemy closer than the friend.
8. See Tanner's discussion of a similar problem in a different context in chapter 3 of *God and Creation in Christian Theology: Tyranny or Empowerment* (Minneapolis, MN: Fortress Press, 2005 [Oxford: Blackwell, 1988]), 152–60. Her solution also requires finding the right balance of theological assertions to respond to the particular tasks and dangers of a certain historical time (160–62).

9. Schleiermacher, CF §172.1.
10. Schleiermacher, CF §96.1–2.
11. David Kelsey, *Eccentric Existence: A Theological Anthropology* (Louisville, KY: Westminster John Knox, 2009), 442.
12. I owe this terminology to Luke Moorhead.

## BIBLIOGRAPHY

Althaus-Reid, Marcella. *The Queer God.* London: Routledge, 2003.
Barth, Karl. *Church Dogmatics.* Vol. 1, pt. 1, *The Doctrine of the Word of God.* Ed. G. W. Bromiley and T. F. Torrance. Trans. G. W. Bromiley. London: T&T Clark, 2004.
DeHart, Paul J. "*Ter mundus accipit infinitum*: The Dogmatic Coordinates of Schleiermacher's Trinitarian Treatise." *Neue Zeitschrift für Systematische Theologie und Religionsphilosophie* 52, no. 1 (2010): 17–39.
Kelsey, David H. *Eccentric Existence: A Theological Anthropology.* Louisville: Westminster John Knox, 2009.
Schleiermacher, Friedrich. *The Christian Faith.* Ed. H. R. MacKintosh and J. S. Stewart. Edinburgh: T&T Clark, 1999.
Tanner, Kathryn. *God and Creation in Christian Theology: Tyranny or Empowerment.* Minneapolis: Fortress Press, 2005.

# Index

191–2, 196; stipulative 2–3, 6,
10, 21n25, 29, 49n9, 107, 204,
225, 247n19; trope 11, 59, 64,
69, 77–8, 90n42, 129n101, 202,
212n25, 276, 280n34; univocity
50n14, 58, 61, 88n14, 262
repetition 30, 39, 46, 139, 148, 155,
159, 169, 190, 201, 205, 213,
258, 261, 268, 273
resurrection 83–5, 117, 138, 240, 245,
246, 264, 269, 272, 275–7; *see
also* Jesus Christ, resurrection of
Reznik, Larisa 210n3
Richard of St. Victor 22
Ricoeur, Paul 202
Rivera, Mayra 249n44
Rogers, Eugene F., Jr. 15
Ruether, Rosemary Radford 90n42

sacramentality 271
sacrifice 1, 14, 133, 136, 140, 147,
149, 221–2, 241–2, 261,
265–6; in Graham Ward 72,
78, 79–82, 84–86, 89n24; end
of 158, 244–5, 276; in Hans
Urs von Balthasar 30, 34, 35,
38, 39–40, 42–3, 47, 52n42; in
Sarah Coakley 108–10, 112–18,
128n93; in Wolfhart Pannenberg
164, 166–7; *see also* self-sacrifice
Sain, Barbara K. 54nn50, 66
Savage, Dan 255
scarcity 78, 81, 115, 118, 238, 240,
242–3; *see also* debt
Schleiermacher, Friedrich 10, 19, 80,
287–9, 291nn2, 4, 7
Schneider, Laurel 21n23
Schulz, Michael 182n40
Sedgwick, Eve Kosofsky 215n61
self-sacrifice 38, 71, 85–6, 114–18,
128n90, 133, 136, 189, 238
servant(s)/servanthood 79, 184n70,
220, 233, 235, 238, 243
sexism 18, 49n3, 58, 75, 91n53, 199,
214; heterosexism 3, 4, 18, 58,
70, 90n42, 91n53, 105
sexual difference 1, 21n34, 22n42,
47, 49n3, 86, 89n36, 92n69,
93nn89, 90; 99, 133, 140, 195,
204, 246, 269, 275, 280n41,
287; theological form of 4,
10, 13, 15–8, 21n35, 27–30,
33, 39–40, 42–4, 48, 51n22,

53nn45, 47; 54n50, 55n79,
58–9, 63–6, 67–71, 76–80,
89n34, 91n50, 93n51, 99,
105–6, 136, 147, 189, 192–3,
208, 224, 261
sexuality 1, 3–4, 13, 15–17, 21n34,
39–40, 43–44, 49n6, 55n74,
58, 64–6, 70, 72, 75–77, 90n40,
98, 100–1, 104–5, 123n23,
128n101, 133, 135, 137–8,
190, 204, 208–9, 220, 223–5,
247n18, 266, 276, 290
shattering 55n74, 233, 237, 240–1,
243–4, 262–3, 269, 272, 274,
276, 280n40
sin 38, 40 52n42, 81–2, 84, 94n109,
108–11, 117–18, 125n50,
133–4, 148, 160, 164, 167–9,
177, 183n46, 184nn64, 70;
195–6, 212n33, 222, 232–3,
235, 242, 246, 248n26, 250n56,
260, 271–2, 289, 291; effects on
finitude 9, 14, 17–18, 21n31,
74–5, 82–83, 86, 99, 115, 117,
149, 162, 175, 182n42, 233–4,
241, 246n9, 256
skin 22n45, 85, 136
Slotemaker, John T. 248n25
Sloterdijk, Peter 277n6
social trinitarianism 12, 21nn25, 26;
83, 104, 107, 157, 180, 227
Söngen, Gottlieb 53n47
sonship 14, 35–6, 48, 49n9, 73,
82–3, 107, 109, 111, 114, 133,
148–9, 152, 158, 162–3, 165,
183n46, 192–3, 198, 201, 206,
211nn21–2; 227, 232, 235–6,
247n21, 258, 261; adoptive 77,
112–13, 235; as cruciformity 5,
101, 111; as eucharistic 34–6,
55n69, 81–2, 88, 133, 171; as
obedience 2, 10–11, 35–8, 41,
44, 46–7, 51n33, 60, 79, 125,
135, 147, 152, 154–5, 164–6,
175–8, 179n14, 201, 205–7,
212; as responsive gratitude
32–6, 38, 51–2, 133, 136, 171,
205–6, 247; as sacrifice 34–5,
81–2, 84–5, 111, 137, 139, 147,
164, 166, 244; as subordination,
1–2, 10, 21n35, 22n39, 44,
47, 135, 148–9, 153–4, 164,
167, 171, 175–8, 184n68, 191,